Immortal Light

BOOKS BY SWAMI AMAR JYOTI:

Retreat Into Eternity
Spirit of Himalaya: The Story of a Truth Seeker
Dawning: Eternal Wisdom Heritage for Today
In Light of Wisdom

Immortal Light

THE BLISSFUL LIFE AND WISDOM OF SWAMI AMAR JYOTI

A BIOGRAPHY IN HIS OWN WORDS

Edited and Compiled by Sita Stuhlmiller

TRUTH CONSCIOUSNESS / SACRED MOUNTAIN ASHRAM
BOULDER, COLORADO

Copyright © 2004 Truth Consciousness
Distributed by Desert Ashram
3403 West Sweetwater Drive
Tucson, Arizona 85745-9301 U.S.A.
Ph: 520.743.8821
truthconsciousness.org

Library of Congress Catalog Card Number: 2004100653

Simultaneously printed in three editions:
ISBN 0-933572-76-x (cloth)
ISBN 0-933572-77-8 (cloth/slipcase)
ISBN 0-933572-78-6 (soft cover)

Printed in Hong Kong

*Truth Consciousness was founded in 1974 by
Swami Amar Jyoti. For further information about the books and
audio Satsangs of Swami Amar Jyoti and the ashrams founded
by Him, please see page 433.*

This biography is offered at the Lotus Feet of my beloved Gurudeva, Swami Amar Jyoti, without Whose grace and blessings it would not have come to be. May He grant us the openness and insight to behold its wisdom and truth.

Contents

Foreword   *ix*

Preface   *xi*

Notes on the Editing   *xvii*

Introduction   *xix*

Acknowledgments   *xxvii*

1 THE DAZZLING PLAY OF THE LORD   1
    Night of Realization   27

2 IN HIS OWN HAND   33
    School Days   57
    College in Karachi   83

3 RENOUNCING HOME, EARLY GLIMPSES   87
    Refugee Camp of Bengal and Calcutta Experiences   93
    A Tiny Form of the World Mother   109

4 KUTASTHA: THE GREAT SILENCE   117
    Realization   138
    Initiation   140
    Planned by God   143

5 THE PROPHETS: PURE SPIRIT EMBODIED   147

6 THE GRACE OF SRI KRISHNA   167

7 LORD BUDDHA: THE EMBODIMENT OF PEACE   197

8 JESUS AND THE QUIET REVOLUTION   215

9 SRI RAMA: THE UPHOLDER OF DHARMA   233

10 GOD THE MOTHER   255

11 A FRIEND OF THE BIRDS   275

12 DIVINE COMPASSION OF THE GURU   287

13 GOD'S PRESENCE ON OUR PATH   307

14 GIVING GOD'S SECRETS   327
     The Matrikas   337

15 REPAYING THE GURU   339

16 KALKI AVATAR: PROPHET OF THIS AGE   357

17 DEVOTEES' REMEMBRANCES FROM BHARAT   379

18 DEVOTEES' REMEMBRANCES FROM AMERICA   401

Bibliography: Sources by Chapter   427

Foreword

WHO AM I?

WHY AM I HERE?

WHAT IS MY TRUE STATE OR IDENTITY?

*B*lessed few have such questions. Eternally blessed are those who have a Satguru to guide them. Our Beloved Gurudeva, after attaining full Realization and Consciousness in the Himalayas, wanted to leave His physical body, as He found no use for it anyway. As He was lying down on the sacred turf of the Himalayas in a state of pure bliss, getting ready to leave His body, Divine Mother appeared before Him and told Him to go back to the people and help them also to reach their True State. He accepted Mother's wishes and came down to help and guide us.

Everybody who has had the opportunity to spend a moment with Him is blessed. Blessed is mankind, for our Beloved Guruji was an Incarnation of Wisdom and Love. He has left us with His treasure of teachings, His Love and His Divine Grace. He used to say that in each of His Satsangs there is enough wisdom to help one realize God. He also used to say that He would be able to guide us better from the astral world, without the limitations of the physical body.

All of His disciples and so many more have benefited by His Grace and healings. As an old Native American healer said, it is time for us to pay back—pay back by way of sadhana and meditation, pay back by way of taking His teachings to the rest of the world, to those who have not been as fortunate as we have been, pay back by realizing God, which is our True State of Bliss that He wants us to reach. Let us all together make a promise to our Beloved Gurudeva, Who is watching over us, that we will follow the path that He showed us, that we will live His teachings and strive to attain Liberation in this very birth.

Blessed by His Light,

narendra

Preface

While plodding our weary way on this planet, it is indeed a providential grace for us to come across an enlightened soul, whose very life, words and deeds, become an open book for us, the spiritual aspirants, a pole star that can guide us to reach the yonder shore of Existence. From time to time this morning star appears on the horizon guiding the seekers and novices where and how to find this Light of lights, this Life of lives, as once the magi "from the East" were guided by a star to proceed to Bethlehem and there adored baby Jesus in a manger.

All Prophets are equally great in their own sphere and mission. There is a galaxy of enlightened souls who, after attaining Liberation through enlightenment, went around the globe sharing their experiences with those who were seeking the path of conscious immortality even while breathing in a mortal body. Of the so many names that rush into memory, some outstanding souls are there who shine as the signposts and hallmarks of perennial spirituality. They are the epoch-making prophets like Krishna, Buddha, Jesus, Zoroaster and others who stand out as a beacon light for the whole human race.

In each century the spiritual Masters wear their distinctive keynote features that perfectly correspond to the needs of the spiritual aspirants. When the disciple is ready, then the Master appears on the scene. Spiritual wisdom cannot be learned from the university halls, from books and lectures. Spiritual wisdom and sanctity can be learned only from the example of a living sage, or by listening to the silent whispering of the Cosmic Intelligence, that Logos, "the true Light that enlightens every man who comes to this world." (John I.9)

Those who are Enlightened directly by God are called Theodacti, and such enlightened ones are few, very few. But most people need a human teacher, a spiritual Master who has undergone the needed discipline and attained spiritual Perfection. "Be you perfect, as your Heavenly Father is perfect," is the injunction of Christ to all of us. The present writer had the fortune to sit at the feet of Mahatma Gandhi in the year 1946 and thus experience the magnetic power that a highly evolved soul exercises on aspirants. As spiritual experience is transpersonal—transcending the frontiers of nations, religions, races and sex—it has an international mission to fulfill.

During this earthly pilgrimage, to meet and be guided by a Self-Realized Master is indeed God's grace. Extremely rare are those who persevere in this quest for Self-Realization and reach the topmost height of Perfection, as evinced in the words of Sri Krishna who said: "Out of thousands of men, only a few strive towards Perfection. From among those who strive to reach Me, perhaps one may truly know Me." (Bhagavad Gita VII.3)

Meditative reflection on our daily experiences will teach us that our spiritual warfare within is an unceasing tug-of-war between the extrovert senses on the one side, and Consciousness on the other. The short interval between the cradle and the grave is granted to us only to learn from our own experience that our mission on this planet earth is to gain such self-knowledge that can lead us to Self-Realization, the dewdrop falling into the shining sea, the rivulet getting lost in the limitless ocean. As Swami Amar Jyoti puts it: "This body-mind is a shell. In this cocoon is a spiritual entity—call it Christ Consciousness, Krishna Consciousness, or Consciousness Itself. *That* wants to be delivered, to be emancipated, to manifest." (p. 228)

When one receives a human body, there comes the possibility of manifestation of God immanent in us. As Swami Vivekananda says: "Religion is the manifestation of the Divinity already in man, even as education is the manifestation of the perfection already in man." In this Kali Yuga or "Dark Age," we have to employ science, psychology, technology and all other available means to awaken our lethargic, somnolent and sensorial minds to our divine potentialities and celestial heritage. Time has come for us to affect a convergence between the scientific technology of the West and the spiritual heights of the East, thereby heralding the advent of the Cosmic Man, rising beyond the dichotomy of East and West.

It is for this great task of bridging the scientific West with the spiritual East that great souls from India—Swami Vivekananda, Rabindranath Tagore, Sri Aurobindo, Mahatma Gandhi, Swami Rama Tirtha, Swami Amar Jyoti and other kindred souls—came forward, linking both East and West in that Perennial Philosophy (Sanatana Dharma), which is valid here, there, everywhere, now, then and always. The Third Millennium after Christ is well poised for the formulation, understanding and acceptance of this cosmic ecumenical gospel of God-attainment or Self-Realization through knowledge, devotional love and selfless performance of our duties, known as jnana (gyana) yoga, bhakti yoga and karma yoga.

Great spiritual Masters, who by dispelling darkness engender knowledge and wisdom, are the real Gurus. In the words of Swami Amar Jyoti, the Guru is "the dispeller of darkness or ignorance, the One who awakens you or shows you the path. Therefore, if he is a real Guru, a *Satguru*, he never sees that you are ignorant, that you are dark, that you are any antonym of the Awakened One. He sees: 'You and I are the same, One.' From that premise they work. And it may be one year's work, ten years' work, a whole lifetime or lifetimes. They work from that premise because you and I are the same Consciousness, Light, Truth, God. Therefore until you are Awakened, until you come to your Consciousness, until you get Enlightened, compassion is needed." (pp. 291-292)

God in His inscrutable providence sends His emissaries to guide genuine seekers to reach the divine Perfection immanent in them. While the overwhelming majority of humankind is deaf and blind to the gospel of salvation, that esoteric wisdom which enables human beings to be reborn of God, there is a microscopic minority who are in right earnest to see God face to face. We all need a second birth, which is our passport allowing us to enter the kingdom of God. With our first birth through a man and woman, we are only mammals. Our second birth is from God and God alone.

Our Gurudeva, Swami Amar Jyoti, after a long training at home, school, university, in the solitary mountain peaks and in pilgrimage spots of the holy Himalayas, attained God-Realization, rebirth in Divine Consciousness. Then he traveled the length and breadth of the Indian subcontinent and afterward throughout the United States and other countries, proclaiming the message of Liberation and Enlightenment to those famished souls groping in darkness, athirst for quenching water, hungry for that bread of life, which wholly satisfies our souls. Swami Amar Jyoti graciously came to visit the present writer at his Sat-Chit-Ananda and Yoga Meditation Centre in Assisi, Italy where, some seven centuries ago, Saint Francis lived and worked as a bhakti yogin, living out the quintessence of all religions in Self-knowledge, Self-purification and Self-Realization. I lift up my heart to our Heavenly Father-Mother for having allowed my path to cross the path of such spiritual Masters who have confirmed and strengthened my own vocational path.

Considering the precariousness, brevity and uncertainties of life, it is well worth to utilize every minute of our earthly pilgrimage to know God, love God with the whole heart, mind and soul and serve God in His creation. Today we are heirs to a world culture and we have to vindicate our world citizenship in a globalized world. Time is long overdue for us to embrace the entire planet as our homeland. We cannot any longer live in a compartmentalized world with religions, nations and races fighting against each other. Beyond the European Union we must work for a United States of Humanity where we all can work for the real Kingdom of God on this earth. As birds fly from one country to another without a passport, so should human beings be free to go anywhere without hindrance to drink deep waters of divine wisdom and thus heralding the advent of the Kingdom of Heaven, that Rama Rajya (Divine Life) for which enlightened Masters like Swami Amar Jyoti and others lived and worked.

But in order to achieve this utopia we need to educate people all over the world. A new heaven and a new earth will only come when we can see and sense everywhere and in everything only God shining as Consciousness, whose Name-and-Form expression is the phenomenal universe. From a practical point of view, the life and example of so many seers, sages and Prophets should urge us to undertake this man-making and God-realizing education. The role of a genuine Guru is that all-round education that enables us to "render unto Caesar what belongs to Caesar and unto God what belongs to God." Speaking of the characteristics of a genuine Guru, Swami Amar Jyoti says: "The Guru is your father and mother and friend and brother and son, your Lord and consort. He assumes practically all the roles, otherwise karmas would not exhaust. All this needs compassion." (p. 294-295)

The advent of so many sages and Prophets should serve as an eye-opener to all the thoughtful few: human beings can lift themselves to their divine inheritance by following the teachings and example of the great ones. In this Kali Yuga, when spiritual darkness and vices run rampant, God himself comes to our rescue, assuming human forms. Says Sri Krishna: "Whenever ethical and spiritual values (dharma) decline and unrighteousness gains the upper hand, then I come, incarnating in a body for the protection of the righteous and for punishing of the evildoers." (Bhagavad Gita IV. 7-8)

Swami Amar Jyoti is a remarkable example of catholicity in religion, walking in the footsteps of Sri Ramakrishna, for whom God was both Father and Mother, more a Mother than Father. We are all fragments of the Divine Consciousness. We have a body but we are not body—body being a temporary residence for the soul. The automobile is changed from time to time but the driver remains the self-same. This process of births and deaths of bodies continues until all the karmic effects are exhausted and our individual life joins the mainstream of that Universal Life, becoming one with Existence-Consciousness-Bliss—*Sat-Chit-Ananda.*

Dearly beloved Gurudeva, now that you are freed of the mortal coils, you are freer to instruct and teach us much better than in the past, your silent look and whisperings reaching our soul-depths. We thank our heavenly Father-Mother for the grace showered upon us by bringing Swami Amar Jyoti to us, teaching us the gospel of Enlightenment and Liberation. We assure you and all the Gurudevas who came to this earth to show us the royal highway to God that we will walk in your footsteps without faltering until we reach our destination, full Realization, and compassionate service to our human family and all sentient beings. AUM

Father Anthony Elenjimittam (Bhikshu Ishabhodananda)
Assisi, Italy, 9th December 2003

Notes on the Editing

Normally Gurudeva was very particular that His English, although very lyrical and sweet to hear and imbibe, be corrected grammatically and linguistically for publishing in print. In this volume of His handwritten words and Satsangs, taken from various gatherings over four decades, a very light touch has been kept in editing so that His voice, with all its beauty, wit, power and charm comes through to the reader. A bibliography of the chapter sources is given at the end.

In Hindi there is no capitalization of pronouns such as "I" within a sentence. Gurudeva sometimes pointed out to American disciples that capitalizing "I" and not "you" or "he" or "she" is a Western "me first" attitude, which is not found in most other languages. For this reason, some of Gurudeva's American disciples use "i" in writing. When a few Americans read this manuscript and found that the "i" they had written or spoken had been capitalized in their remembrances, they requested that the original "i" be replaced. Also, most of Chapter Seventeen was shared orally by Indian devotees who are the essence of humility and simplicity, and many of whom do not speak English nor have an awareness of English grammar. To accede to the American devotees' wishes and the sensitivity of the remembrances gathered from Indian devotees, the pronoun "i" has been given in lower case throughout Chapters Seventeen and Eighteen, except where originally capitalized.

And lastly, many of Gurudeva's English-speaking disciples use the capitalized pronoun when writing of Him. This is in keeping with the respectful pronouns used for Gurudeva and other Holy Persons in Indian languages. So, throughout Chapters Seventeen, Eighteen, and in the Introduction, notes and footnotes of this editor, these pronouns have been retained except where given otherwise.

Introduction

*I*n the desert southwest of the United States there is a flower that blossoms only one night a year. The Night-Blooming Cereus bursts into bloom with an intoxicating fragrance that transforms the hot summer air into a celestial garden. More than twenty years ago, one early morning just before the light of dawn, my beloved Gurudeva called me to "come quickly," as He slipped out of His door at Desert Ashram. i followed Him silently down the gravel driveway where He turned onto a smaller drive and then into the desert itself. An extremely heady fragrance filled the night air but there was no time to imagine its source. A devotee met us at the road's edge and led us to the place where the fragrance exuded. There we saw with astonishment a radiant white lily-like blossom rising delicately from a thin cactus stalk hardly waist high. The heavenly upturned petals were already beginning to wilt as the intense desert sun lit up the horizon. Within a few hours this miraculous flower would melt into itself and remain hidden for another year until it would repeat its mysterious unfolding.

In the Orient, especially in India, the lotus is revered as the symbol of perfection and purity, which is why it is always associated with the Deities. Among nature's wonders in this part of the world, the Cereus seems to most perfectly capture the essence of those rare Souls—Prophets, saints and Realized Masters—Who come to this world for a brief time and divine purpose, illuminating the darkness of our ignorance with Their celestial splendor before melting back into the Source from which They came.

This biography is the story of one such rare Soul, a story that began eons ago and reaches inestimably into the future. It is a story that is still alive, the original Hero's Journey, and it beckons us to undertake our ultimate journey as well. Each of us will find in these pages a different and unique meaning as it unfolds within us. The key to this story resides in the heart, and the passage it unlocks is that of the soul.

Biography and hagiography are limited at best for understanding the life of a Prophet, Satguru or Realized Soul. In previous eras such exalted lives were retold through epics and scriptures, oral or written, a wealth of which is found in every faith and culture on earth. In our modern Western culture, the majority do not find relevance in the old epics, so new ones are being created all the time and communicated in nearly every art form—written, pictorial, oral and cinematic—whereas older civilizations mostly draw inspiration and meaning in life from scriptures and epics of Divine Beings.

The story that follows—the life of my beloved Gurudeva, Swami Amar Jyoti—is only a tiny glimpse of His radiant Personality. What it cannot begin to describe is the depth of His wisdom and love, His gentleness, sweetness, compassion, brilliance and grace. No one who ever met Him was unchanged. Hearts and minds opened effortlessly in His presence to the infinite capacity of the Spirit that He evoked. He loved to move among the common people of America and abroad as much as among seekers. His heart encompassed the whole of humanity and His vision the whole of eternity. These are not just words but the reality He lived every day.

Unusually beautiful and brilliant as a child, Gurudeva grew up in an orthodox Hindu family, middle son among twelve siblings. His father was a hardworking, simple and humble man who raised his children to be righteous and cultured citizens. His mother and father both were revered in the community and sought after for their wisdom and foresight. As a child in pre-independence India, Gurudeva was a staunch follower of Mahatma Gandhiji and devoted much of His time to studies, in which He excelled. Prior to His teens, He showed no particular interest in religion or spirituality until, as He describes in Chapter Two, one day a cousin brought Him a book by an itinerant holy man, Swami Rama Tirtha.

By the time Pujya Swamiji reached college, the partition of India was imminent and inner stirrings were beginning to open in Him to find His own path. He longed to "read the book of life." In His final year at the university, He "dropped out," as He liked to say, equating Himself humorously with the many Americans who had dropped out during the late 1960s and early 1970s. He left the family home in Mumbai and went to His sister's home in Rajasthan for some months where His mother stayed with Him, hoping to convince Him to remain "in the world." His inner calling was deep and from that town He departed one day by train for an unknown destination and broke all family ties. As the most promising son of a prominent business family, His renunciation was a tremendous blow, especially to His widowed mother who never gave up on finding Him one day.

Twelve years He spent in wanderings and in spiritual practices. His first experience away from home was in Calcutta where He worked in a record store and then for an aviation company during the Second World War. His next calling was to the border of Bengal, helping the refugees flooding into India from what is now Bangladesh during the painful partition following India's Independence. Later, after nearly dying of jaundice while in Calcutta, He traveled northwest, eventually reaching Haridwar, Rishikesh, Uttarkashi and other Himalayan pilgrimage centers of ancient renown. In a quiet ashram on a canal of the Ganga River outside of Rishikesh, He did sadhana (yogic spiritual practices) and meditation and kept silence—*maun*—for years. At other times He stayed in a simple hut in an ashram in Uttarkashi, and in between spent the passable seasons in Gangotri at 10,500 feet elevation, the place where the goddess Ganga is believed to have first touched the earth and one of the most revered pilgrimages for Hindus.

Years of meditation in a cave at Gangotri culminated in His full Realization, which He reveals in sublime and vivid detail in Chapter One of this volume. From that night onward, the purpose of His life was entirely taken over by the Divine, Whom He worshiped most of all in the form of *Maa*—Divine Mother. Having no wish to continue this life after achieving His Goal, He was instructed instead by Her to descend from the Himalayas and bring to humanity the eternal message that potentially everyone is Divine. At Badrinath, in the presence of several sadhus, He took the rare initiation of *vidyut sannyas*—"lightning sannyas"—and accepted the name of Swami Amar Jyoti—Swami: "Knower of the Self," Amar Jyoti, "Immortal Light." Thereafter He traveled the length and breadth of the Indian subcontinent, staying at temples and pilgrimages, wandering without any means of support, blessing all silently wherever He went. Some of His experiences were incorporated later into the spiritual novel He wrote in 1976, *Spirit of Himalaya: The Story of a Truth Seeker,* though He admitted that His own experiences were woven with those of other holy men in such a way that the real story will never be known.

Around 1959, He was walking one day on a road outside of Madras when a car stopped to give Him a ride. The gentleman, without further comment, drove Him to a conference at a college where many eminent speakers had gathered, including the teenage Dalai Lama, newly arrived in India from Tibet. Although Gurudeva had learned English in school, He had not mastered it comfortably as a spoken language, so He was quite surprised when His host seated Him among the speakers and then summoned Him to give a discourse in English, which He did, amazing even Himself!

He visited Calcutta around that time and there met and initiated His first disciple, a young boy of ten or twelve years who eventually became an ashramite along with his father. Gurudeva's wanderings finally brought Him to Mumbai where He confided to the man who had given Him a lift into the city that His brothers' business was in the vicinity where they had arrived. When the elder brother received a call from the one who had brought Him to the city, he ran outside without shoes to the office, afraid to let the auspicious moment slip away. That day, in a joyful procession many vehicles long, Gurudeva was brought home and reunited with the entire family. He described to us how, some months later, He got up one midnight at the family residence and saw something in the dark over the threshold of His room. A relative sleeping nearby woke and whispered that it was His mother who had slept every night in that manner after He had returned, desperate not to lose Him again.

Seeing His mother's deep suffering and wanting to comfort her for the years she had waited for Him, Gurudeva offered to do anything she wished except give up the renunciate life. She requested Him to cut His matted hair and shave His beard, to wear white clothes instead of the ochre customarily worn by sadhus in India, and to settle somewhere nearby so that she could visit Him whenever she wished. When a devotee brought Gurudeva to see Pune, on the Deccan Plateau some hours east of Mumbai, He decided to found a small ashram there. The first rented house eventually opened the way to the few acres of land and a house on which Jyoti Ashram was originally founded and registered as a Public Trust in February 1961.

Gurudeva was soon afterward invited to come to America by a devotee whose son lived and taught in Appleton, Wisconsin. Sent first class on the Queen Mary by His family, Gurudeva arrived in New York City and from there traveled to the Midwest. After some time He left His hosts and embarked without any particular destination on a Greyhound bus that happened to be bound for Albuquerque, New Mexico. It was in Albuquerque that He was discovered by a small group of seekers who sought Him out to impart the timeless wisdom of the East to their thirsty souls.

From 1962 until 1973, Gurudeva remained in India, working with disciples who would find Him either through dreams or by word of mouth, and regular Satsangs* were held at Jyoti Ashram. Over the years He had received pleas from seekers who had met Him in America to come again to this country. In 1973 He returned for nine months and traveled in a whirlwind tour arranged by His former hosts, giving Satsang and informal talks in innumerable homes, churches and colleges. Often He stayed at each place for only a day or two and then was driven to the next destination, giving spiritual nourishment and guidance to countless souls everywhere He went.

His first ashram in America was founded in a rented home in Ranchos de Taos, New Mexico, where He had held a small retreat in 1974. When several of the newly initiated disciples begged Him to

---

* *Satsang*: lit: "communion with Truth" (Sanskrit), a spiritual discourse.

found an ashram, He blessed them and told them to remain where they were, and to continue their meditations and sadhana together. From this small beginning, Sacred Mountain Ashram was born, and later moved to a canyon outside of Boulder, Colorado. In 1975 it was finally located in Gold Hill, at 9000 feet elevation in the Rocky Mountains, half an hour's drive northwest of Boulder. Gurudeva called this ashram "Kailash"—the abode of Shiva, the Mahayogi— and often spoke of the Rockies as the American Himalayas. A year later, a home and ten acres of land were donated by a devotee for the establishment of Desert Ashram on the outskirts of Tucson, Arizona.

From 1961 until 2001, Gurudeva divided His time and physical Presence between ashrams in India and America and traveling around the world. For a decade He maintained Rishi Ashram on a mountainside above Manali in the Kullu Valley, India, where He spent months at a time in His beloved Himalayas. In one of these early stays, He began writing *Spirit of Himalaya*. During these four decades He gave ceaselessly in Satsang, retreats and guiding seekers and disciples in America, India and other countries. His message is the timeless wisdom of the Himalayan sages in a language understandable to a modern world, regardless of East or West. He did not espouse any one path but taught that all paths lead to the One God and that we are all potentially Children of Light:

> *On the path of love and devotion, God and His creatures are the Totality. The way of reaching is what differs. We choose our path according to our tendencies and temperaments. I do not consider one way inferior to the others. It is simply what suits you and you feel comfortable with. Also the impact or quality of the age partly determines the paths—in which times we live, in which country we live, what kind of associations we have, our home and the family in which we live. . . .*

Gurudeva, whom American devotees also call *Prabhushri*, "Radiant Lord," seldom spoke about His personal life or sadhana. What little He revealed in Satsang, He had erased from recordings directly afterward. Only rarely when He was alone with a disciple or two, or in small, intimate gatherings did He speak of some of His experiences and details of His life and, extremely rarely, give reference to other lives as well. Some of the chapters in this biography are from Satsang recordings that He had preserved unknown to all but one or two disciples, discovered after His *Mahasamadhi** on June 13, 2001. He did not place great importance upon this one life and made it clear that most of His life would never be known to anyone. In July 2000, during His last illness and nearly a year before His Mahasamadhi, He began writing by hand a description of His childhood and early life, which He left off in a few months and never finished. These pages comprise Chapter Two of this volume.

When the idea of writing Gurudeva's biography was suggested to me, i knew that the perspective any disciple might have would be sorely inadequate and inaccurate to capture the essence of His Being. His life on earth was most of all His teachings and His teachings are His Being. Gradually it became clear that the only authentic biography—the term He had used instead of autobiography when writing the pages that appear in Chapter Two—could come from His own words. From that opening, the story that you are about to read began to unfold. i pray that this small offering is a worthy introduction to the life of my Divine Guru, Whose compassion, wisdom and love have guided my soul and innumerable others in countless births. As a devotee commented after reading the manuscript, this story is an epic that transcends time, space and all dimensions in its magnitude and power. It is a glimpse of the divine mystery as has seldom been given to humanity. It is His gift to us— His children—and our divine inheritance, which He wants us to receive. It is our past and present and future, and the key to our Immortality lies within its depths.

Sita Stuhlmiller
December 2003

---

* *Mahasamadhi*: conscious departure from the mortal body by a Realized or Liberated Soul. In Buddhism this transition is called *Mahaparinirvana*.

Acknowledgments

*T*o the disciples in India, America and abroad who have shared their inspiring remembrances of Gurudeva, my deepest gratitude. Each one is a treasure. Only a few of these experiences have been included in this biography, but there will be other volumes; this is only the beginning.

This biography has been an offering of love and a gift of Divine Presence. To those who entrusted this blessed work to me and allowed me to follow my heart and soul in whatever form it would take, i offer my sincere pranams. To the ashramites and devotees in the United States and India who helped with transcribing, proofing, translating the Sanskrit and Hindi terms and invaluable suggestions throughout the manuscript, we are all one in this endeavor. May God's will be done.

1

The Dazzling Play of the Lord

How should I reveal my life story—as Divine play or as a human play reaching the Divine? I have thought I will leave it up to disciples to make a mess of my biography after I am gone. Unless I tell someone, nobody will ever know my life story beyond a portion—never. And even those who might know a little more of it— whatever it is—their angle will be such they probably cannot see the deeper view unless I grant that understanding.

I know I have been very sparing in talking about myself. Not that I haven't talked—but totally I cannot avoid either. Living here on earth with disciples, how could I not say anything? Whatever I have said, I used to get erased from the recordings. Not that talking about myself is a secret, only that I am reluctant. If I were to impartially analyze myself as a person, I would explain it this way: I am talking about "him." Partly my reluctance is, for want of better word, not to leave my attitude of humility by talking about myself. When I am talking with those who are very communicative, intimate and near me, those with whom I could share as my own, then I would be all right. I do not want to waste my words on those who may not have that much faith and intimacy, who are not that open to me or have that much acceptance. This has been my attitude since years. This has made me reluctant to tell about my life. And if some who are listening do not find what I say acceptable or totally believable or understandable, why to waste words? That is the second reason.

There is a third reason also, which to me is actually the most important. There are two ways of looking at the life of this One. The first is, as you describe historically: I was born on such and such date under such and such planets, father, mother, brothers, sisters, society, acquaintances at school, grew up, left home, et cetera. As a kind of story it is very interesting, even to me. That is one way to see. Now since we are talking a little more intimately than usual, it occurred to me—*but that's not the truth.* Another way to see this life is by looking from "there," as a Divine Being who has come here. Here is the dilemma: If I were to describe in the latter way or tell how I see it or know, then it will be sensational news. And this has been my dilemma, because telling that way would be the truth.

Sometimes the thought has come that when God allows me to know my last years, when my public work is over, I may retire to a cave or forest cabin or ashram and write an epic, a story, as a biography in a fictional garb, but the real story, and put a note on that: "Open this after my body is gone." I would let them do whatever with it, not that it is a decision.

Whenever I say something about me, I have given hardly twenty to thirty percent of the story's *real* picture. Even when I wrote *Spirit of Himalaya*, which was spontaneous, I mingled so much truth, fiction, imagination and the experiences of others so that no one can ever sort out which is from my life and which is not. Even if you pinpoint, "This is probably your story," I have mixed it so much that nowhere will you find my life story exclusively, not even in one paragraph, although many of the things written there could apply to my life story. This is one way of saying that I did not want to come out openly to say things. Now another point, which is very valuable to me, is that some people know this episode of my life, some know some details from birth onward as well as my wanderings in India and elsewhere. There are a *million* details, though it may not look like that. You would not believe what an adventurous story my life has been. *No one on this earth up till now* knows more than a little bit of my life's episodes. Nobody knows the whole story—that is impossible—but even the major portion of my life no one knows.

Some may have known me in one place, but beyond that, they never knew the next day, the next place or village, what I did and what occurred. Alone if I were to write a fictional account impartially as a writer, it would be marvelous. I am saying this as if about myself, but that is what it is! I could not then say: Should I reveal in a divine play way, or a human play way reaching the Divine? I have thought I will leave it up to disciples to make a mess of my biography after I am gone. Unless I tell someone, nobody will *ever* know my life story beyond a portion—never. And even those who might know a little more of it—whatever it is—their angle will be such they probably cannot see the deeper view unless I grant that understanding.

These are the reasons I have mostly kept mum about my life. There is nothing to hide. I could tell you the whole Srimad Bhagavatam* about myself—how I did *tapasya*,† whether it was Buddha's way or not. Unless I reveal the real truth, I do not think I can do justice to my life story. By this I do not mean as a biography or journalism. It is quite different than that, and I do not think it can finish telling in one Satsang anyway. If I sit with you for thirty days and you go on writing, it will not finish, it is such an adventurous, bigger than life story. You will never know unless I tell it. And nobody, even up until now, has seen more than a little of it, so they cannot do justice to me either. So I wait for Lord Ganesha‡ to instigate me to tell it. I am not eager otherwise, but it is a very colorful story, alone from the story point of view, apart from the ups and downs, and pains and pleasures that any human being has. How much I could reveal?

Offhand I can give a synopsis, like a movie trailer. It is a really, really colorful and adventurous story, even leaving aside the Divine aspect. It is easy to say I am self-made, but that does not explain well. If it is descriptive only—which year I was born, where I was born,

---

* The Srimad Bhagavatam (Bhagavata Purana) was written by the Enlightened Sage, Veda Vyas (Vyasa Krishna Dwaipayana) after he compiled the Vedas, the Puranas and authored the Mahabharata. Veda Vyas, who lived c. 3100-3500 B.C. was said to be the twenty-eighth of the Vyasas or compilers of Vedic knowledge. He was somewhat older than the Avatar Krishna and his work continued after Krishna's Incarnation. An encyclopedic history and philosophy of India, the Srimad Bhagavatam tells the glories of the Ten Avatars (Das Avatar) of Vishnu, including the full life story of Sri Krishna, the Eighth Avatar.

† *Tapasya,* from the Sanskrit root *tapas:* "to burn," refers to austerities or purifications undertaken to burn or remove impurities of body and mind.

‡ Lord Ganesha is the elephant-headed son of Shiva and Parvati and one of the most popular deities of Hinduism. Ganesha is propitiated at the beginning of each new undertaking, as He is the remover of obstacles. He is also the embodiment of dharma (see footnote on page 23) and the symbol OM. Known for His immense wisdom, Ganesha was the scribe of Veda Vyas when he wrote the epic, Mahabharata.

how I grew, which school I went to, when did I leave home—these are just the outer description, the outer story. It has nothing to do with anything. If there were fewer people present here, it would probably encourage me. I would talk nonstop the whole night. I will still give you unconditionally the story as fully as I can, and you take it. Talking about "me" is not a human life story. It may sound like boastfulness, such as some holy people who reveal some things—"the greatest incarnation . . . the greatest of this or that." That is not my interest. On the contrary, I deliberately put Divine Mother in front— not that I'm putting Her; She's too great for that—so that I could hide behind Her. I could call Divine Mother my consort, but I accepted the Divine Mother role, not to oblige Her. She could have been my consort, too, but I said, "I'll hide behind Your apron." I have tried to do that. I could have been very popular in America, from east to west coast. That I renounced even, in earlier years, in order to get settled somewhere. But that is again a very tiny issue.

I can give an example of my "boastfulness": practically all— Krishna, Rama, Buddha, Divine Mother, Chaitanya, and others have revealed in me. So who am I? This is where my problem is, whether to reveal the truth. I was supposed to leave my body in the 1980s and come again for the major mission on earth. But then I would have been a small boy and so we decided to continue in the same body, keeping it healthy and younger, that's all. I have tried to keep my body younger or at least healthy for that reason, to do the main job that is still due. So I did not leave the body and come back. The next body would have been a young age of at least sixteen, if not eighteen, years old. To save that, I continued in the same body.

I was doing already too intense sadhana—*too much*—in the caves of Gangotri.* I had given up coming down to earth *at all*. I was totally resigned there. There was a sage where I did meditation and sadhana

* Gangotri is a temple and pilgrimage center just below the source of the Ganga (Ganges) River, the place where it emerges as a visible river, tumbling through a water-hewn rock gorge at 10,500 feet elevation in the Garhwal Himalayas, India. The Gangotri temple is the site at which the celestial River Goddess is believed to have first touched the earth.

in Gangotri, who later died at the age of 148 years. He used to live naked, which we called *digambara.** At that time, I was going to accept him as my Guru. When I went to this sage who gave me the ultimate Vedantic Realization, he was a great man, of course. He was called Ramanand Avadhut—tall, matted hair, dark and rough-skinned like a water buffalo. He lived all twelve months in Gangotri in a small wooden cabin. He was a worshiper of Rama. When I first went to him, I did not know what his realization was but I believed that he was Enlightened. Surprisingly, when I first bowed down to him— this was in 1956 or 1957 or earlier—my idea at that time was, not as you might call an ego trip, but I was seeing the way was inside me. Many things had revealed by themselves in me, including yogic powers, such that I knew I did not have to go to anyone, that it would unfold as I wanted. Before that, I had done many sadhanas in many places: Amarnath, Rishikesh, the Himalayas, Bengal. Each practice I was taking up was revealing thoroughly, but at one point in Gangotri, I was attracted to this Sage Ramanand.

He was over one hundred years old at that time, as per the story. I went just to see or check with him, in a way. I remembered that Buddha had two teachers in the first two years, and then in the last five years before Enlightenment, he went on his own. Such great ones are self-made and Self Realized. But I did go to Ramanand Avadhut. He, of course, knew everything. He smiled and understood why I had come. He had heard about me. He lived on the opposite bank of the Ganges and I was on the other side of the Ganges in a cave. His cabin was not luxurious; it was very austere. And he lived there all the twelve months, in the snow even, ten or fifteen feet of snow, totally naked, with no clothes or blankets, only the fire he burned inside the cabin whenever he could manage firewood. He is gone now.

I came inside his cabin and sat down. I said I had a question to ask him. He smiled, a simple, matter-of-fact smile, as if it was child's

---

* *Digambara,* from *dig:* "direction or space," and *ambara*: "clothes," lit: "sky clad" or "clothed in space," signifying those sadhus who are completely emancipated from physical and social constraints.

play or something, which I liked—that such a great sage was so
matter-of-fact. Each day he would sit in the sun, when it was sunny,
and read the Ramayana.* Often the question came to me—*why is
such a great sage in the Himalayas, living one hundred years or so, all
naked and in these extremely austere conditions, reading the
Ramayana?* Not that the Ramayana is low or anything, but when you
are a Vedantist, as were most of the sages, the Ramayana, which is
an epic, is considered to be for family people in cities, towns and
villages. So I thought that he is probably not very high on the path
of knowledge or Vedanta.†

Most of the sages and serious practitioners in the Himalayas and
forests or on the Ganges banks would be more deeply into wisdom
and knowledge than epics, which are written for the common man.
The epics give the same truth, but because the common folk do not
have that kind of capacity to go into serious theses, the epics, the
Ramayana or Mahabharata‡ were given. This was my notion about
this Ramanand Avadhut—*avadhut,* meaning: "crazy one," those fools
of God. So with that understanding or intention, I went to him still
because I was attracted. He was very sweet and nice. Sometimes I would
go to him and he would feed me molasses or ghee or *chappatis.*§ I went

---

* India's great epic, Ramayana, written by Sage Valmiki, is the story of Sri Rama,
the Seventh Avatar of Vishnu, an Incarnation of God, born on earth approximately
7500 years ago.

† Vedanta is one of the world's oldest religious philosophies. It affirms the Oneness
of God pervading all existence and the Divinity of the soul. Based upon the Vedas,
the most ancient scriptures known to man, Vedanta means literally, "the end of
all knowledge." Vedanta is the nondualist search for God or Self Knowledge.

‡ The Mahabharata, written by Veda Vyas, is India's second great epic and
contemporary with the life of Sri Krishna. The Bhagavad Gita, the "Song of God,"
the Bible of Hindus everywhere, forms a part of the Mahabharata. This revered
treatise by Krishna was given on the battlefield to his disciple, Arjuna, at the outset
of the Kurukshetra War.

§ *Chappatis:* unleavened flatbread similar to whole wheat tortillas, the staple bread
of northern and central India.

to him because he was the one I liked the most at that time in Gangotri. During that period of the mid-1950s there were nine sages in that Gangotri area.

I went to him one night and sat down inside his cabin. He looked at me and smiled. Without my questioning, though I did say something but not exactly this question, he said—I still remember— "You don't need a Guru. You are your own Guru. I'll only guide you to the point so that your Guru opens. Then you are going to teach many." I wasn't at that time planning to teach at all. I never wanted to teach others. It is just not in my nature, though I seem to teach you. But I suppose that sometimes I feel—since this body is there, what have I to do? I will not open a grocery shop or rent a shop in a mall . . . Naturally, I have to do something! So I "babble." He said, "You'll teach many. You are your Guru." And he added one thing: "We'll all listen to you." He said, "I will simply give you a little guidance for one year. Then you are on your own." I am not sure whether he said one year or not, but I presume he said or I gathered it. And that was the first time that I really went to someone.

This was the acme period of my sadhana in pure Vedanta and transcendentalism. I used to live in a cave. It got very cold. I had just one blanket and no shoes, socks—nothing, just matted hair and, by God's grace, a young body at that time. I had no disease, no medicines or vitamins. Two and a half hours daily I would do hatha yoga. I would sit in the sun and do concentration on the sun, not in the daytime but early mornings and sunset time. Do not do that! Your eyes will go blind! If you ever saw a little shining in my eyes, it is due to those practices.

This was the third or fourth phase and last phase of my sadhana. I was not only concentrating on Vedanta but also upon the sun, the galaxies, and so on. How I learned, how it came to me, it would take one year of telling you stories, and even then I am a little shy. One evening, it was dark; there was no electricity in Gangotri that time. There were no roads or transport coming there. We used to walk about seventy miles with a backpack of some sort with a blanket to go there. And one evening, partly because it was cold and rainy, and partly

because I thought—*all these sadhus do these dhunis,** *so let me try it.*
I was very much a novice in that. I built a fire in my cave but there
was no ventilation. It got all smoky and I started coughing. In just five
minutes, I had to extinguish it. That was it. I sat in meditation as usual.

The majority of my hours were in meditation. I used to get up at
2:00 or 2:30 A.M. and took a very little nap in the afternoon. Once a
day I had a meal. Most of the time when I went to the town I wore
something; otherwise I used to be naked under the sun. If the sun
was not out, I would be inside the cave. There was one blanket on
the bed, which was built out of wooden *sleepers*.† The bed was hardly
two feet across—a half-cut log as a pillow, which the blanket
overlapped, and the blanket over me, that was all. When I went out,
I just threw the blanket around me to sit down. I had only one brass
vessel, used for water or for bringing *dal*‡ when I used to beg food.
There were no fruits, ghee, milk, et cetera. Tea, fortunately, I had and
molasses. So one evening, I got frustrated over the fire. I thought—
nothing doing; it's not my job. I extinguished it and sat again in
meditation. At that time I was in the climax of Vedantic Realization,
especially of those four *Mahavakyas*,§ the great truths: *Aham Brahma
Asmi, Tat Twam Asi*, et cetera. Now theoretically or philosophically
these Mahavakyas were clear to me—that was no problem. I had no
doubts. But that evening, though not desperate, I got so much
longing—not impatience—I could not take it just on understanding.
I wanted the Realization of the highest Truth—Vedantic Realization.
I had meditated, meditated, meditated, but it was as if the answer
would not come to me. I asked myself: *what is preventing me, actually?
What is keeping me from achieving this Realization?* Theoretically

---

* *Dhunis:* wood fires that sadhus often maintain to keep warm.

† *Sleepers* in Hindi are wooden railway ties.

‡ *Dal* is a curried split lentil soup; in this case a thin, watered-down version.

§ *Mahavakya*, lit: "a great statement." A Mahavakya is an aphoristic support of a
philosophic viewpoint. Shankaracharya's famous Mahavakyas that support the
Vedantic philosophy are: *Aham Brahma Asmi, Prajñana Brahma, Sarvam
Khalvidam Brahma*, and *Tat Twam Asi*.

everything was clear, so why was I not opening into Oneness? As much as I tried, I could see no block. Love of people, love of country, serving others, scriptures, getting occult powers, love of the body—there was nothing there. There was no memory of any relative or friend. Earlier dreams and heavenly visions—even these were not there, yet I could not reach that Realization.

We did not have clocks in Gangotri; we just lived by sunset and sunrise. The only thought that came to me was—*let me go to Ramanand Avadhut.* At that time it was dark. It could have been eight, nine or ten o'clock, God knows. In that area, nobody went anywhere in the dark. The Ganga is roaring—you hear the sound. There is no electricity, only some lamps in certain quarters. There was no village there. Ramanand Avadhut's cottage was on other side of the Ganges. At that place, the Ganga is not in one flow but divided into streams and rivulets all flowing through those Ganges stones, those round *Shiva Linga** kind of stones. The only bridges were makeshift wooden ones made by villagers, but only in daytime can you see them.

I would not say I was mad—I was quite silent—and I made it to the other side of the river to his cabin. I could see a very thin sliver of an oil lamp through the cracks of the door and Ramanand inside. These sages do not lock their doors. A small fire was burning inside. The Ganges sound is so roaring in that place that if you knock on a door, the person inside may not hear it. So I just opened the door. The sage was sitting against the wall, tending his fire as if he was expecting me, or God knows what. He saw me and said, "So-and-so"—my name was different that time—"come in, come in." So I closed the door and sat opposite him with the fire in between. Now, I must say how he helped me. Previously he had said he would guide me. On this night, I was sad but not as you think of sadness. It was a spiritual sadness— we call it dispassion and detachment. I closed my eyes and leaned against the wall. He, of course, understood. He said, "What's troubling

---

* *Shiva Linga:* the primary Form in which Shiva is worshiped. The Shiva Linga stones He refers to are generally ovoid in shape and taken from one of several rivers in Bharat (the ancient name for India).

you, So-and-so?" I said, "Not troubling. I've tried and tried and tried to get these doors open to the Vedantic Mahavakyas—*Aham Brahma Asmi*—and I'm not reaching it. I know what it is—it's there and I don't see barriers even. There is nothing clinging or any temptation or anything pulling me back or pulling me down. Nothing." That was why I was so baffled. Why is it not happening? Why am I not making a breakthrough, blasting through to this, which I want? And I could see that it could happen, but it was not happening.

He smiled again; his nature was like that. He had a large forehead with the beautiful wrinkles of a sage and big eyes. He was matter-of-fact, like an elder talking to a child and understanding that this is a kid's affair. I thought—*here I am waiting for the fire to burn and he's smiling as if nothing is happening.* I did not get angry but I wanted him to take it as seriously as I was. He wasn't. So I thought—*either he is only a devotee of the Ramayana and perhaps doesn't know anything more than that, or he's just not understanding me, or he thinks I am not ready, or God knows what!* I knew I was ready, but it was not happening—that was true. Well, here lies the whole magic: there and then, while he was tending the fire, he looked at me with big eyes open wide—not angrily, but I could see his shining eyes for the first time. "You can't understand?" he rebuked me, but it was a divine rebuke. "You can't understand this easy matter?" I was certainly ready at the threshold, but I wasn't able to do it. I kept quiet and he looked at me and I looked at him. "This is this, this is this"—he said a few lines only, and I will not reveal everything, but I got pinned against the wall. I lost all outer consciousness. I got Conscious, actually. He did not touch me; he just spoke two or three lines with a little divine rebuke. "You can't understand this?"

By that time, all my hunger for the scriptures, for knowledge and learning was over. Many things had revealed in me that I did not much care to pursue, but they were there. This was my last Realization. And I do not know how long I stayed there—one hour, two hours, three hours. He had patience and was sitting there although I was not aware of him. I remember that after a long time, when I opened my eyes, my heart felt very warm. Tears were rolling down and I could see his figure in a very divine halo. And believe me—this is not a made-up story, but my belief—I saw Ramanand then quite in a different light. The reason why he read the Ramayana epic, I came to know later on, was his camouflage for people not to know who he was. It was all quiet. We did not talk anymore. Whatever time it was—midnight or three o'clock—I slowly got up and walked over the Ganges, back to my cave.

When I first got realizations or visions, they were unasked for, unpracticed, unheard of and not taught by anyone. That was when this body was hardly nineteen or twenty. I was in the suburbs of Calcutta. I had not gone to the Himalayas yet. That was the first and the experience with Ramanand was the last. In between many things were revealed. I am still telling in a story form. In Calcutta, at that time I was going to a part-time job to earn my bread and butter. I had not become a mendicant yet. I used to go every week to Belur Math on the Ganges to the Ramakrishna Mission Headquarters. By this time I had learned Bengali. I used to learn sitar. Going to a job a few hours was more or less philanthropic, to help poorer people, educate them, and so on. I had a roommate who was a Bengali. He used to go to his office, a British jute mill, I think. No one taught me yoga or meditation, nor was I seeking. A few scriptures I was reading, that is all. But daily, though not exactly as a routine, when I used to come back in the evening after work, my habit before eating was to do a few minutes of prayer to *Maa Kali* (Divine Mother). Her temple, Dakshineswar, was not too far, a mile or two away, and I had seen Her there. So I would just sit, not even meditate, on a mat on the cement floor and pray.

We had no furniture, only mats to sleep on. My dress was Bengali* but ragged and poor. I did not have a beard or long hair at that time. My name was different. My roommate and I used to take turns cooking the meal. One evening before dinner—it was only two things: dal and chappatis—my roommate was cooking outside on the verandah on

---

* This dress normally consisted of a *kurta* (men's shirt) and *dhoti*, a simple cloth secured around the waist and flowing to the knees or ankles. Sometimes a *chaddar* or shawl-like cloth is also wrapped around the shoulders, such as was worn by Swami Vivekananda.

a coal burner and I was inside. Fortunately the door was closed, though not locked. Sometimes I would practice my sitar during that time, but that evening I was sitting in prayer, though I had no particular posture of sitting. I knew no *pranayama** at that time—nothing, and there was no prescribed prayer. I had no desire to fulfill or wish to ask of Divine Mother—*give me this, this, this, this.* Renunciation was a part of my nature from childhood, but I did not know this at the time. So I did not think to ask Mother to give me anything, from any angle, neither health nor money nor peace—nothing of that sort. Peace I had, so there was no problem. The only thing I remember is that I just innocently said: "Mother, make me good so I do not hurt anyone and I do good to others. Make me purified. May I remain truthful . . ." A few things I spoke like that, not a made-up prayer. I asked Her to make me truthful and purified so I would not harm anyone and I would do good to others. I did not tell Her then, "Let people leave me alone." That was much later! And daily, probably, I spoke about the same prayer, just that kind of small talk to the Mother.

The landlady lived downstairs. It was a small house with very noisy, dirty surroundings, but I did not notice that. We kept our room clean with a broom but it was a degraded locality, actually. It was a simple room of bricks, not even mortared, with a cement floor. It was damp and only a mat to lie down on. I did not even have a pillow; a few clothes I used to put under my head and that was it. On that particular evening, when my friend was cooking outside, I prayed to Mother and my eyes were closed, and all of a sudden something lifted in me, raising my inner, what you may call, Consciousness or energy. The vibrations began to lift up inside me and gradually this body became lighter, joyful, and somewhere inside my head, a solid but astral form, the embodiment, the figure of Divine Mother was descending, full with Light. It was a golden bluish light, but the formation was Divine Mother's. And I did not ask for Her to appear. I was just praying, "Make me good and harmless and truthful and

---

* *Pranayama* is the science of yogic breathing, including exercises for purification and breath retention.

loving"—and She came Herself! Boy! This all happened in seconds or a few minutes, I cannot even describe. Inside I was feeling my whole body and head lifting up somewhere. At first there was a little awareness that my friend was cooking outside, but that also got transcended. I was not asking for these things, you know; Mother just gave. And Her full figure descended actually—all joy, Light, this, this, this. It all happened in a few minutes.

This was my first spiritual experience in this present life. I did not know what to do. At one point, my nature of shyness came up. What if somebody sees me? That thought came and then She began to, not exactly evaporate, but at least ascend. The light was off; I did that at prayer time. I opened my eyes and I could see the whole walls and everything—Light shimmering. Everywhere, Light was shining. Then a slight fear came—*what if he comes in? . . . He will see it!* My sadhanas and tapasyas, even in later years, have remained personal, never told to anyone. I did not want anybody to know what is going on in me; this was inside me all the time. And when I got up, my body was so light and Light-full both. I thought—*how am I to live now? . . . Everybody will see it*—which I did not want.

We lived in a very congested area. Much later on I knew that just in the next block was actually the prostitute quarters. I did not know then that we were in a bad locality. We had searched for a very low rent room because we did not have money, so for five rupees or ten rupees we found this room. We did not bother to see who is who, whether it was on trams, buses, donkeys or cows. It was just a noisy place. But in this kind of dirty swamp, a lotus was being born, in a sense.* To make an escape so that my friend would not see me or the landlady would not see me downstairs—because when we went down, somehow they stood there to look at us—I went out, God knows why, with bare feet and dhoti, the Bengali type, ragged. Supposedly we were to sit down, eat dinner and talk together or

---

* The lotus flower blooms in muddy or unclean ponds, in which it stands above the water, unstained and unaffected. Thus in Bharat, the lotus is considered to be the symbol of purity and perfection.

perhaps read a book. I made an excuse, which was not false either. Someone had written to me that he wanted the Bengali *Geet Govinda*, and I had heard that at the end of the road there was a bookseller. I thought—*I'll go and buy it for a few rupees*. My friend asked, "Where are you going?" I said, such and such book, I want to buy. I went down with bare feet, alone. The roads were not clean; there was cowdung, sputum and other things—hygienically very bad, especially Calcutta, though this was a suburb. Even then, it was very bad. It was evening time when markets and vegetable markets are full, plus cows, bullock carts, trams, and everything was there. When I began walking, there were crowds on the roads, because everyone was coming from work. There were no cars, as you may understand.

I began to walk to the other end of road and, all of a sudden, while walking within this crowd, I am not seeing it is dirty. I'm feeling myself the purest possible ever one could imagine, and I did not know any philosophy at that time either, nor did I read books of that kind. So, what was going on? I was not surprised but I was witnessing something that certainly was my heritage opening up. As I was walking—untouched by noise, filth—I felt like a pure lotus rising up from the swamp. And all of a sudden, I felt my feet were not touching the ground! Again I got shy—*what if people will see . . . I'm flying . . . or what?* But up to that time, occultism, flying, none of these had I ever read. And it was happening. Somehow the way my body felt that time, uplifted, light, I managed to turn my gaze down toward my feet and I saw, yeah, it is up! Boy, and people would see it! Somehow, I said, "Please, Mother, make the feet touch the ground." That's it. And my feet thumped down! I regretted this later on, because I should have flown up and that would have been the end of the story! But, thank God, I did not do that because there were electric tram wires on the street and I would have hit them! Whatever it was, I just got shy.

Then I walked as usual and was feeling all joy, lightness, whatever you call it; I was not able to philosophize at that time because I did not know much about spiritual things. I came to the bookstore. It was small, not like the big bookstores you see here, and it was not modern either—very rugged, very few books, lower middle class.

There was a step up to the bookstore and underneath that step was open drainage. I stepped up to the counter and there were two people, one elderly man at the back and one middle-aged man wearing handspun* clothes at the counter. He looked at me. I just said, "Have you such and such book?" and he said, "Yes, I have." He went to the shelves and came back. "No, it is sold. I can order for you if you want." I said, "Okay. When will it come here?" "Tomorrow." I asked, "How much money should I give, deposit or pay?" "Don't worry," he said, "don't give. Come tomorrow, take the book and give the money." He was very kind, a nice, middle-aged, simple man. This all happened in few minutes. I retreated back over the step with bare feet, but somehow, instead of going back the same way, the thought came to me to go to the end of the road, then return. Partly I was walking because I was avoiding to go home to that room with my friend, feeling—*if he discovers something, I'm in trouble.* Trouble, meaning: I was shy not to reveal anything.

The next day, when I came from my work, I was supposed to cook and I was such a reluctant cook; I always knew he would come. But when he came I said, "Look I'm not going to that bookstore." Somehow it occurred to me I would not go there—I do not know why—but I asked him, "Can you go?" He said, "If you want." He used to wear pants, coat and all that. I had that dhoti-type of traditional Bengali dress. I said, "You go and I will cook," though I did not cook until he came back, actually. In the meantime I thought—*let me practice my sitar.* So I went inside the room. I knew what had happened the previous day. My whole body—pores and everything—was still in joy, Light, but I was not saying anything. I was not searching spiritually, in a sense; it all just happened.

In that room we did not wear shoes or any kind of sandals, so I was practicing the sitar on the mat. After some time my friend came and walked right into the room with his black shoes on—he used to polish his shoes like a mirror; he wanted to live like an Englishman;

---

* *Khadi* is a handspun and handloomed cloth, the cottage industry of which Mahatma Gandhi promoted by spinning and wearing the finished fabric.

that was his craze. I had told him, "That's up to you, but I want to live like *Bapuji*."* Anyway, we were brothers and friends, as you might understand. He came right inside the room with shoes on and sat in front of me next to the mat while I was sitar playing. He was smiling, crazy-like, looking at my face. I stopped my practice and said, "So-and-so, what's the matter?" He said, "You know. You know everything." I said, "What are you talking about?"

"What did you do to that man?" I said, "Which man?" "In that shop, the bookstore." I said, "I didn't do anything. I just went and asked for the book. He said, come tomorrow, I'll order for you." My friend said, "No, you're telling a lie." I said, "You know I don't tell lies." "Right. Then what did you do to him?" I said, "I did nothing to him." I said, "What's the matter?" He said, "He didn't give me the book. He wants you to come." I said, "Why?" He said, "When I went to his store, he was weeping and sobbing. When I asked for the *Geet Govinda* book that my brother came and ordered, he said, 'Where is he who came yesterday?'" My friend said, "Well, he may be at home. I'll give you the money and you give me the book." The shopkeeper said, "No, *please!*" And he got up sobbing, weeping, touching my friend's feet in the store, as he told me. My friend said, "He wants you to come." I said, "What's the matter?" Now at that point it was dawning on me that yesterday these things had happened, so there may be something. I was quiet, mum, and didn't want to reveal anything. This small story is taking one hour, you understand; there are *hundreds*. Therefore I do not say these things, because some may take it as boasting. And I am saying with the least revelation to you. If I would really reveal, you would perceive the Light, actually.

Anyway, my friend told me, "He was sobbing and weeping. He said that when you got down from the shop to go, he saw you, according to him, as *Shyamasundara*†—Krishna with a crown, yellow dhoti and

---

* *Bapuji* is the endearing name by which Mahatma Gandhi was called.

† *Shyama* is one of the names of Krishna, lit: "dark one," because his complexion was supposedly dark; *sundara,* lit: "beautiful." Thus *Shyamasundara* means "beautiful Lord."

everything." Of course, I might have been a Krishna devotee—that's different—but this is what he said. I had rugged clothes on at that time and I was thin. I used to keep a sword-type of mustache, no beard. My hair was cut like this, et cetera, and he saw Shyamasundara! And this man said, "I had *Darshan** and I ran after him," meaning me, but I'd gone to the other side of the road, not deliberately; somehow I felt it. And he ran after me in the crowds, he said, but didn't find me. Thank God, because when I returned on the road I knew, I took the other side. He must have searched me whichever way, and I looked different than others in the sense of how I was dressed, but he didn't find me.

My friend said, "He's waiting for you to come and he asked me take him to where we live. He wants to come here." Now somehow my friend and brother knew that I was shy of people, that I was avoiding people. He knew that if ever he had brought that man to me, I would not have seen his face in this lifetime. He died, actually, after one year. But on this occasion, he did not bring him. He had told the man in the bookstore: "First I'll take his permission, then I will take you to him." My friend requested me, "Please go to him." This was the first extraordinary thing that happened to me. Of course, there are many more, but how many I can tell you?

One year Chaitanya Mahaprabhu† appeared, but if I say this, I will be a sensation monger. That same year I was staying at Rishikesh on other side of the Ganges, which is certainly *Vedantic-Bhumi*, the land of Vedanta. I had only one book at that time, Gosh's life story of Chaitanya, the original Bengali book. There was a small picture of Chaitanya's ecstasy on the wall, not framed even, and no other picture in my room. I had just torn it from a book and put it up. That

---

* *Darshan*: "vision of God." This term is used both in the sense of seeing God's Image in a temple or a holy person, as well as for an actual interior *vision* of God.

† Sri Chaitanya Mahaprabhu was born in the holy place of Navadvipa in West Bengal in 1486. He was one of the greatest devotees of Sri Krishna and is considered by Vaishnavas (devotees of Lord Vishnu) to be the Incarnation of Sri Krishna and Sri Radha combined.

year I read the life of Chaitanya and I would sit and weep and sob. Nobody has seen me in these *leelas,** weeping and sobbing, nor did I want that. I was living in an octagonal room that someone gave me to live in, back in the fields in Rishikesh. I would go for number one and two outside in the jungle. Nobody ever visited, nor did I want visitors. The whole day I would be Chaitanya Mahaprabhu. This was in 1955, I think; I am not good at dates.

For some months I was soaked into Jesus Christ. How did that come to me? I was trying to learn English, so somehow I bought a book, a paperback, about Thomas Jefferson; I don't know why. Maybe it was to my liking. I still remember the author: Saul Paddores, I think. I bought a dictionary and a notebook to look up each word I didn't understand, but there were so many words on each page that I got fed up. So, I was reading that biography of Thomas Jefferson. That was in Rishikesh. During that time, Jesus Christ must have been mentioned somewhere in the book, or perhaps some kind of Christian church. I got fascinated and thought—*I know him somehow.* And so I got into him. Then I bought other books about Jesus Christ. I was not thinking of Christianity—nothing to do with that. I thought he was well known to me—*I'm familiar with him.* And for a few months, we were One.

There are so many stories and I am so sad I am telling these things. Once I was drowning in the Ganges in the suburbs of Calcutta. It was daytime; nobody was there. The Ganga is one or one and a half miles in width at that spot. I was not a swimmer even, but I tried to swim to the other bank. I didn't even reach the mid-stream, but it was sufficiently deep that I would drown. I lost all my strength; couldn't swim more. I wanted to come to the bank but couldn't. In a way, I gave up. I was going down. Water came up to here. This was the fifth death experience in my life. The last one was, of course, in the Himalayas, which I brought in *Spirit of Himalaya.* You may believe or not, but I said, "Mother, I've heard so many stories and things about me in horoscopes and so many things I've seen. And this is the way

---

* *Leela:* divine play of an Incarnation of God or great Soul.

it's going to end?" I just said that and She pulled me out. It was ten o'clock in the morning. Her temple was hardly a quarter mile away—Maa Kali's Temple, Dakshineswar. She pulled me out and I was coughing and coughing.

Ultimately I did not want to come down from the Himalayas—that is another story. I was in the same cave from where I had gone to Ramanand, but this occurred before the experience of the Mahavakya aphorism. At the backside of my cave was another cave where a Nepali sadhu used to live, Gangadhar by name. He was a young man. He wore an ochre robe; I wore white. At that time my name was different. I assumed the ochre robe later on. This sadhu used to admire me. Many times he saw me in the cave in the morning when I would forget what time is and that we were supposed to go for begging. There was a community kitchen for beggars or holy people—practitioners. It would open at a certain time—10:00 or 11:00 A.M.—and close at 11:30 or so. They gave us chappatis and dal—thin soup actually. The door to my cave was only this much. I would crawl in and come out from that. Inside, the cave was about three by seven feet. I could not stand even. The cave was about a foot or so over my head when I sat down. The only thing I had in the cave was water. So when I closed the door, there was no ventilation or light. I would not know it was ten, eleven or twelve o'clock. I would be meditating, and this sadhu would not disturb me. But at certain times he saw I did not go for food at the community kitchen, which was only once a day. When I would get up and come out, the kitchen would already be closed. He felt pity for me because, possibly, one of his weaknesses was that he was very food-minded. He could eat three people's food. But that meal was the only time he ate. So he felt pity that I was not eating. He told me, "Why don't you go at the right time?" I said, "One thing, I don't know what is the right time. Second, when I'm in meditation, I really don't remember food." He said, "If you don't mind, I'll bring for you."

Now in the Himalayas, this is not a very common practice, unless you are very old or infirm. For a young person like me, normally others would not bring food. Anyway, I said, "I feel bad if you bring for me," but he started bringing. Sometimes my door would be closed and he would keep the food outside. The only tragedy was by the time I came out, the chappati and dal were so cold, at 10,000 feet elevation! But I didn't complain, nor I would. I would eat it somehow. The thing was—which I didn't know at the time but came to know later—that among the other sadhus or holy people, some were prejudiced, jealous or whatever. Each one has weaknesses. Some of these sadhus would taunt him: "You're serving your Guruji now." As a matter of fact, from seniority point of view, he was senior to me, with ochre robes, and he was a swami; I wasn't yet. Naturally, his serving me was kind of a bloodshot for the other holy people. "You're serving your Guruji"—and he was a shy person. He really minded it, but still didn't stop bringing food for me.

However, he used to go to a certain sadhu on the Gomukh side, higher than Gangotri, on the way to the Ganges source. There was another big cave where one holy man lived who was a great astrologer too. And this Gangadhar was friendly with or used to go to him— whatever connection was there. I had never met him nor seen him. One day Gangadhar told me, "So-and-so wants to see you." I said, "Who is he?" and he described him. I said, "Why would he see me?" At that time I didn't talk much, actually. He said, "Oh, I talk about you to him, that you're doing meditation, this, this, this." Gangadhar didn't know what my experiences and meditations were, that I had reached heaven even, and some of you I saw there, actually; some of the girls are not here now. But that is a separate story. Gangadhar said, "Would you like to come? He would like to see you." I didn't tell him, why doesn't *he* come, because this other holy man had been there for some years and had a temple-cave for meditation, his own food and everything. He was a little more moneyed in a sense; he used to get money orders. But that was not the problem.

So one day I went with Gangadhar in the afternoon, and this holy man gave us tea. His was a big cave—not as big as this hall, maybe half of it, actually. It was a natural cave. He had his own cooking things, bedding and everything. It was real comfortable compared to others there. We sat and he talked with love, sympathy and respect. I was much younger than him, bodily, and he was very reverential. He said, "I've heard so much about you from Gangadhar. Please sit down." I didn't have any horoscope, nor were these things at all in my brain at that time. He saw my hand, eyes and eyebrows, and brought in some other things, testing, you know. That was why he called me, actually. Whatever his science was, or yoga knowledge, he began to tell me whole revelations of the future, about the six shaktis,* which I read later on in the Srimad Bhagavatam, and other things. He said *so many* things that time. I wasn't even thinking of going down from the Himalayas and he was telling me so many things—that I would go down from the Himalayas and these things would happen. Quite a number of those came true, as a matter of fact. He said: "Gangadhar told certain things about you, so I was curious. I was suspecting this would be the case, but I wanted to be sure that this is you," and so on. Quite a number of things have come true afterwards, except one, which yet has to come—probably some years in the future. He said so many praiseworthy things—not only praiseworthy as holiness, but revelations—that I could not believe it. I didn't know why I had to be that One. I just was not interested and still I am not.

Well, I have told you already more than enough. That is why the combination of love and dharma,† wisdom, yoga—if you could ever measure the extent—you will understand that all have combined in

---

* The term *shakti* is used by Gurudeva primarily in two ways throughout this manuscript. He describes shakti as divine energy or power, which according to Vedic belief is an emanation of the feminine or active aspect of God. But often He uses shakti as a proper name for the Goddess Herself in Her manifold Forms. The six shaktis referred to here are the six primary aspects of the Divine Mother described further in Chapter Nine.

† *Dharma*, from the Sanskrit root: *dhri*, "to hold," translates as "that which holds together." In Gurudeva's Satsangs and in normal usage, dharma has multiple meanings, which include: righteousness, religion, divine law, truth, and doing one's duty in life. Dharma in Pali is *dhamma*: the truth about the way things are, and will always be, in the universe and nature, as preached by the Buddha.

this body, leave aside Ramakrishna, Vivekananda, and others. But everything has happened in such a way that nobody else knows. In that very cave, Gangadhar did not even know; I did not tell him.

I would get up at one or two in the early morning, go number two outside, make my tea in a broken aluminum pot, on a wood fire, and then sit in meditation. And one morning, long before the Vedantic, Mahavakya Realization, all of a sudden, my body lifted—not physically; astrally, of course. I didn't know even where I was going. I was in the astral plane, as if, and seeing all the stars and skies and things like that. My body was in the cave; I wasn't practicing these things, it just happened. I didn't know where I was going but energy was rising up. It wasn't that early experience in Calcutta; that was different. This was in Gangotri. All of a sudden I'm knowing through which stars I'm going, and the Indian word came to me: *swarga*, which means heaven. I was going to heaven. I reached there. I wasn't wishing that; it happened. And whatever things I saw—heavenly, celestial. And when I reached there, some of you I saw, actually. Some are not here anymore. I would not name them. In the heavens where I reached, I still remember the landscape or whatever design, whatever things were. To say it was very exquisite is an underestimate.

Then I entered a chamber and there—I wouldn't say who she is— one lady said, "Stay with us." I was climbing those heavenly, flowery, celestial gardens. And this all happened while I was meditating, not asleep. I was walking, smilingly and very joyfully. I liked the place. And there was some celestial music, an instrument something like a harp that they had, but they were talking in Sanskrit. I am not a scholar of Sanskrit—I don't know much—but in that kind of vision, I was understanding and speaking Sanskrit as much as God's language in heaven would be. And some of these people were singing and speaking in Sanskrit but I saw that they were making a few mistakes. A few of them were what I would now call Americans. And while smiling and climbing up, I was joyfully saying, "Oh, you made this mistake, you made that mistake." And one of them said, "Why don't you stay with us and teach us?" I said, "No, I won't."

So I came back to that chamber, which I won't describe how

heavenly it was—very heavenly, not only architecturally. It was very beautiful, very celestial, with *gandharvas** and God's language, Sanskrit. And they were giving me a very high post to be there. And that goddess said, "Why don't you stay with us?" I said, "No, I have to go . . . I'm *Nachiketa.*† I won't stay here." Not that I disliked it. I just thought—*what shall I do here? It's a place of pleasure, that's all.* Then they allowed me to go. And I still remember, I descended through the same stars, the same way back to the cave, and lodged in my physical body and opened my eyes. I was sitting in meditation, back to the body. I got up, had a second cup of tea. There were many more experiences like that . . .

I have not spoken about my practices. Nobody has ever seen them. They are only known to me. One *sadhubaba*‡ in Rishikesh tried to disturb my sadhana. In the place where I was staying, there were many sadhus. I had my room, a cottage on the Ganges outside of Rishikesh— two miles away. That place was managed by one holy man, though it didn't belong to him; it belonged to an organization. But this man was the organizer. He was not a Guru. There were many sadhus or holy people staying there. This man had an air about him—self-image—that he was *somebody* there. In those days I was in *maun*, meaning silence. I did not talk to him, and everybody else respected him, whether young or old. I had my routine. In the afternoon I would bring a scripture outside and sit in the sun and quietly read. After that I would have tea, go for a walk in the fields, and come back. One time a day there was a meal, and I did my meditation night and day.

This man had a self-image problem. I was much junior to him, agewise. I did not know him and he did not know me. We just lived

---

* *Gandharvas:* celestial musicians.

† In the Katha Upanishad, Nachiketa journeyed to the underworld to seek forgiveness for his father, a holy man who had been cursed by Brahmins for gifting to them old cows. Yamaraj, the Lord of Death, granted the pure-souled Nachiketa three boons, including the secret of immortality. In the audio Satsang, *Three Boons from the Lord of Death,* Gurudeva reveals further on this exemplary dialogue of Nachiketa with Yamaraj.

‡ *Sadhubaba*: respectful term for a holy man or monk.

freely as holy men. But his idea was that whenever he came, I should get up and bow down to him. That was no problem, but I used to be so immersed in meditation, deep solidly within me, that if I was sitting here or there or lying down, I did not pay attention to what else was going on. There was no arrogance; I just could not disturb my solidity to make a ritual of bowing down, which otherwise was fine. And he made it a point that I should get up and bow down to him. He would come and stand near my mat, though he was not rude or anything. So during that time he used to disturb me. He would smile benignly, as if he was being polite, and I could not tell him, "You're disturbing me"—I wasn't talking. Therefore, sometimes I did not get up.

I did not mean to be rude or disrespectful to him, but you know, when you're in deep contemplation, meditation, you cannot just get up and bow down to someone. And he was not my Guru either. So this man went and told the organization that this young novice, he's quite this or that. And what would the organization people know about these things? Fortunately there was one sadhu in that same area who not only respected me but also admired my seriousness about sadhana. He went and told them this humbug person had a problem with self-image, and that was the problem. And then it was forgotten.

This all happened in a place on the Ganges bank in Rishikesh. I used to have my routine: one meal a day, a little *chywanprash** and a little honey, because at that time I was getting a small money order. There was a raised bed, wooden, one blanket only. I made my tea, cut my wood and brought it. We had an outhouse. The room was not bad. Apart from one time begging food, the rest of the time I was to myself. Daily in the afternoon, I would walk two miles about, back and forth, to visit Lord Shiva's Temple called *Virbhadra*.† I was practicing *raja yoga*‡ at that time. This was before Vedanta. I was doing

---

* *Chywanprash*, a common Ayurvedic tonic in India, is jam-like mixture of amla fruit, herbs, ghee and raw sugar.

† *Virbhadra* is an Image of Shiva. Powerful vibrations still emanated from the *Murti* when Gurudeva took a few disciples for Darshan in 1985.

‡ *Raja yoga*, lit: "the Royal Path." Patanjali formulated this ancient yogic science

pranayama and hatha yoga—*mudras, bandhas,* all those *Hatha Yoga Pradeepika,* Goraknath's* practices all the time. I was having deep meditations. My body at that time was not fat or anything; it was strong and muscular. I used to cook one chappati weighing half a pound! Some people saw it. And I did not have a sense that inside it was all unbaked. I used to just eat it. Another sadhu saw this one day and said, "You'll get crazy! What are you doing? How do you digest this?" My principle in hatha yoga at that time was to be able to digest even stones. So one night—this was even earlier than the Vedantic Realization—it was the dark of night and I was lying down straight on my spine. There was hardly a pillow. There used to be only one piece of wood to put under my head . . .†

Night of Realization

I angered my mother, displeased her, angered my brothers and sisters, my friends, my father and the principals in college. I displeased everyone . . . I didn't do what they wanted me to do. You see how "bad" I am.‡ I forsook all duties toward my parents, my brothers, sisters, friends, countrymen, my college studies, everything. I became unsocial. I became inhuman, inconsiderate, ungrateful, unthankful. I didn't keep up my promises . . . I was ready to go to hell and then it dawned upon me that there is one place where I can escape from

_____

into a definite system under the name, *Raja Yoga Sutras: the Eightfold Path to Enlightenment.* Raja yoga is primarily concerned with the mind, its modifications and control. Through a progression of seven levels of purification and preparation for meditation, the eighth level, raja yoga leads the aspirant to Enlightenment.

* *Hatha Yoga Pradeepika* is an ancient hatha yoga treatise by Svatmarama. Goraknath was one of the nine *nathas,* (ancient sages), known for his great achievements in practicing hatha yoga.

† Unfortunately the recording of this Satsang ended abruptly at this point.

‡ Much of what Gurudeva is saying in the beginning of this section is told "tongue in cheek" for effect to Americans who, at that time (1974), were not familiar with the concept of renunciation, particularly not as it was practiced in India. Even His dialogue with God here seems most likely told in irony, since none of the ashramites ever heard Him speak of God's "punishments" in the decades afterward.

both these duties and hell. I told God, "If You are in the hell, I will go. If You're not there, I won't go." Well, He said, "First I'll punish you for having been ungrateful and unthankful to all those who did good to you: the parents who bore you, fed you, educated you, the friends who loved you." I had spent so much money and didn't give back to my parents—not loans; I was free from loans.

He said, "First you'll be punished for a few years. Meditate. Pray. Eat once a day. Remain in a vow of silence. Sleep a few hours in the night, not in the daytime. Don't talk to anyone. Don't write to anyone. Don't keep money in the pocket. Don't ask anything from anyone unless it comes to you unasked. Don't live here; don't live there; don't stay in one place more than this and that . . ." So many rules He made. "Read these scriptures. Don't read novels. Don't go to movies. Don't see magazines. Wear simple, ragged clothes. Don't think what is not there. Don't think of milk, fruit, vegetables, sweets, cakes, puddings or ice cream. Forget about all that. Just the bare necessities: water, air, ether and sunshine. And nobody should know what you need and not need in the mind also, because I will know that."

So all these "punishments" He gave, and after a few years, I was all alone, penniless—neither here nor there. And I said, "God, what next? You have punished me, now what else?" He said, "Well, this was it. What else do you want?" I said, "But I have not received what I wanted." "What do you want? You have never asked Me." I said, "Yes, I've forgotten all these years to ask from You what I wanted. I was busy with paying the debts back." Now the debts were over, the obligations and duties were over. The punishments were over. So what next? God said, "You never told Me." I said, "Yeah, I told you in the beginning that I want to know my Self." He said, "Okay, start knowing your Self now." That is how it started. After hell it became heaven. Angels came. Fairies came. Beautiful celestial music they would sing for me on instruments. Celestial flowers they would bring with flights in the air and sky, heavenly things with twinkling lights and many, many beautiful colors not of this earth.

Then God said: "Now you are in heaven." I said, "Yes, true, but that's not what I want." He said, "But you seem to enjoy it." I said,

"Well, You gave me punishments and I accepted it. Now You have given me enjoyments and I'm accepting it. What else? Am I lost?" Then He said, "No. What do you want?" I said, "I have told You." He said, "Why didn't you reject it when I gave you heaven?" I said, "I didn't reject it because You gave it to me." He said, "Yes, true, but you were enjoying it. Now you are putting it on My head that I gave it to you. You seemed to be quite happy with those things."

I said, "Well, I was happy, but that doesn't mean I was wanting these things. I don't want this celestial music and dancing and beauty and space and multitudes of colors and all these different planets." God said, "What do you want then?" I said, "I want to know my Self." He said, "Okay, now hell is over; heaven is over. See if you want anything else." You know how the judge asks the murderer for his last wish before he is to be executed? God asked me that way. He said, "Hell is gone; heaven is gone. Any last wish you have?" I searched my mind for my father, my mother, brothers, sisters, countrymen, friends and my Guru, who was also gone. I had displeased him also— not displeased in the sense. My Guru had told me, "Go ahead, you're over me now. You are your own Master."

When I looked back, I realized—*oh my God! What a height I have gone, beyond hell and heaven.* I didn't realize I had traveled so far. I thought I was just playing here all the time. During my meditation, yoga and other things, I always thought I was playing. But when my Guru told me, "No, you have gone too far . . ." I looked down from the mountain peak and, my God! Then God asked me, "What do you want now? Hell is done; heaven is done." I said, "I want to be One with You." What a great demand! God said, "You're very clever." I had said, "I want to be One with You." I didn't say, "I want to be a slave or at Your Feet." Not out of arrogance. I thought—*there's no joy in just remaining at Your Feet . . . I want to be One with You.* And God replied, "Not yet." When He said that, I thought—*what deficiency is there still?* He said, "Find out."

In the meantime, another three or four months passed away. I was in the Himalayas then. There was no electricity, no roads, just wooden bridges on the streams and the Ganges River. And nobody goes out in the night because it can be dangerous sometimes—animals, cold, et cetera. Well, one night I took a bold step. I came out of the cave. I went to that great sage, Ramanand, my last Guru. Four months I had tried to find out what was preventing me that God had said, "Not yet." I had searched and searched within me. Fairies and celestial beings came and failed. They were ringing music round my ears. I said, "Go on, I don't mind. You share the background orchestra, I'll play." Kingship or lordship and many other things were offered to me—not that I disliked them; I didn't need them—that was all. They were not for me. My role was different.

I was not able to find the answer, by God's grace. I again called God, "God, tell me what is it?" He didn't come even—that's God. He didn't come even to tell me! I did ask Him, "At least tell me why is it that You are not making me One with You?" He came just once and said, "Not yet. Find out." So after three or four months, one night I went to that Himalayan sage who is now dead. He was 142 or 148 years old then. I used to be in much touch with him; he was a great sage. At that time, he had lived since forty or fifty years or perhaps more years in the Himalayas. He used to stay there year-round in the snow. Not snow as you get here with all the snowplows and cars and heater. I'm talking about the Himalayas—no facilities, no roads, no electricity, no food, no shops. There if you live, you accumulate things in a little cell. He lived in a small cabin with no carpet or furniture. And in the night, when nobody travels, I went to him.

He was waiting, sitting near the fire inside the cabin. He said, "What's the problem?" I didn't tell him what God had told me. I said, "I'm suffocating. What to do? Something is yet in me that is obstructing me from becoming One with God, and without that, I have no satisfaction." I told him, "I have wept; I have laughed; I have meditated. I have forgotten everything; I don't need anything. The earth is gone; the veil is gone; good and bad are gone; sin and virtue are gone; hatred, prejudice, attraction and repulsion are all gone. I do not find what is remaining, but God says, 'Not yet.'"

He looked at my face. He was a Realized Soul. Really big eyes he had—a tall figure, six feet. He had very dark skin, rough like a buffalo;

he lived naked in the Himalayas year-round. I had scanty clothes also; now these [indicating His robe] are better. A fire was burning; a candle was there, no electricity. Ramanand was sitting on the other side of the cabin with the fire in between us. He looked at me with those big eyes and said: "What's difficult about it to understand?" I told him, "Well, I've searched and searched. All my desires, all my belongings, all my sense of possession, none is there, and even God told me so. I find no desire in me anymore, not even to help my countrymen. I had a love for the people, to serve them; even that is gone. Heaven I've traveled to and seen. Hell I saw in the punishments He gave, though those were not punishments but simply austerities and penances." I told him, "My heart does not crave for anything except I want to be One with Him. I feel joy. I've got beauty. I've got powers . . ." Occultism was in my hands at that time, though I didn't use it, ever. I didn't need it. I've never used occult powers; they did not attract me.

Ramanand looked at me for a long while. Then he said, "Don't you understand this simple factor?" I said, "For four months I've been trying to . . ." He said, "It's very simple. Try to find out why God told you, 'Not yet.'" It was a tortuous sensation. The sage was smiling and I knew it was simple, but I was not catching it. Then he looked at me, his eyes like fire. He was very loving to me. I was a small kid next to him. I was looking at him with tender eyes and he was not fierce but very stern, and light was projecting through his eyes to me. I thought he was doing something to me but it wasn't that. He said, "Do you know what is separating you from God? Don't you understand this? How can God tell you this? You want to be One with Him while wanting to retain yourself! You don't want to merge that. You don't want to be lost in God. Had you wished that, He would have, there and then, blessed you! You said, 'I want to be One with You,' but you didn't wish that you should not exist and only God exist! The two cannot exist. You have to be lost in Him," and he just penetrated his eyes through me.

I was lost. I became unconscious. I was there how much time, I don't know. I got Realization in his cabin, actually. That was the only thing that was separating me and God would not tell me. He does not tell you your ego is in the way. We have to merge in Him. And when we merge, our existence is gone, like the traffic merges when it comes into a freeway. It loses its existence. That was the simple factor I was not understanding, and even God would not tell me. "I want to be One with You," meaning: there cannot be two. It's simple logic, like two plus two is four. The sage said, "You want to exist and be One with God. How can that be possible? Both cannot exist simultaneously. You have to perfectly merge and be an instrument of God, simply be gone." That was the whole enigma in the end.

2

In His Own Hand

Do you have any of these human weaknesses
that we have?
I do not find any weakness.
No ill feelings towards anyone?
I do not find anyone else but my Self.

*G*urudeva's Introduction: I never kept a record or diary like a journalist or an author would do. I had no need of dates/years or even some names of persons or places connected with episodes. Didn't even dream about one day writing all this! Thus it's all on memory. Whenever some years are mentioned, though mostly they are correct, it could be flawed sometimes. In any case, they are not deliberate. I hope the reader can understand it. Some names of persons/places may have been deliberately kept anonymous on different occasions for unavoidable reasons. According to municipal records, the birth date was mentioned as 6 May, 1928, although the birth registration was done on 7th since the office was closed for 6th that evening.* Somehow in those days they were not particular about birth time, and there is no way now to vouchsafe for it anyway. Among the elders of our family, only the eldest sister is living as an old lady, at present.† She remembers very well, as she says, that the baby was born within about half an hour before sunset on the 6th. Sun was still up. After cleaning and washing the baby, some ladies of the house took him to our family temple where a Brahmin priest anointed the baby. My elder sister was one of those ladies. They didn't stay much there, and when they returned home, it was dark. Years later, a few astrologers, judging from the past episodes of the child as well as family history, determined a certain time accordingly to match the time. In all respects, the eldest sister's version seems correct. But still, I would not swear to its one hundred percent accuracy, nor probably there is a need to be serious about it at this moment.

---

* He was born on a Sunday.

† Paribai, the eldest sister, passed away in November 2002, in her late eighties.

I was born in a Hindu family. As was and is common in India, a Brahmin priest, based on the scriptures and considering the day and astrological *nakshatra*,* et cetera, chooses a baby's name according to calculations. The alphabet stipulated for my name was "R"—thus the family decided to name the baby Ram. We lived in a small district town of Larkana in Sindh Province of then India. That was a time when British ruled most of India except many small and large kingdom states and feudal lords. Town had no electricity and all roads were dusty. Larkana mostly had two seasons: cold winter and intense summer. If ever rain came or only a few drops, cloudy even, schools and offices would close in joy.

There was no running water or flush toilets worth any name. Outhouses and open drainage were common, and people lived naturally with it since they had seen nothing better than that, except a few who had connections with the outside world. Rarely, if rain showers came, roads would be extra muddy and would remain so for days until the sun dried them or from pedestrian usage. Technically Larkana, then, would be called a desert, but had neem trees—a blessing—and mango and some other trees. The British had dug some canals, large and small, from the Indus River for irrigation for agriculture of rice and other grains and vegetables, which gave lushness to the town and surrounding areas.

Sindh is derived from the word "Sindhu" (Sanskrit), which means "ocean." It is understood that when Alexander invaded from west and crossed the Khyber Pass, he reached the Indus, which runs through Sindh Province from the north, coming from the Himalayas of Ladakh and flowing toward the delta in the Arabian Sea. Alexander, seeing so wide an expanse of water, took it to be the ocean. As the Greeks could not pronounce the word "Sindhu" except as "Hindu," he called the water the Indus. Later this name became "India," as pronounced by the British. During Alexander's day, there was a great Indus civilization on the river's banks.

---

* In Vedic astrology (Jyotish), *nakshatras* are the twenty-seven phases of the moon, each ruled by a different deity.

Being a district town, Larkana had an English Collector (District Magistrate) and a government high school. Some years later, D/C* electricity did come four hours every evening. The generator for electricity, which often failed, worked on wood fire. Other than this, hurricane and oil lamps worked for the rest of the needs. There were no radios in the town in those days. No one even knew about TV. Later on, due to four hours of electricity, a small cinema house was started by someone where silent films were played (no "talkies" yet), which were brought from Bombay. Often in the middle of the film it would be interrupted by the shut-off of rickety electricity—but who cared? People would wait, since it would start again anyway.

In addition to ayurvedic doctors and a few homeopath doctors, there was a small, basic allopathic dispensary or hospital with a few beds run by the British Government where minor surgeries could be performed.

Larkana had a small railway station on the outskirts of the town. Trains ran on coal, putting out a lot of coal smoke. These were narrow gauge lines. The town was connected with several other villages and towns right up to the port city of Karachi on the Arabian Sea and the Indus Delta. There were horse carriages for transportation in Larkana, but people mostly walked, and later when bicycles were introduced, some owned them. Cars and buses were nearly nil.

I don't know why but it was a common hearsay in a local rhyme that if you have money, then tour Larkana! The town was known throughout the province of Sindh as a place of poets and singers, in addition to some commerce and agriculture. It was a peaceful place and people—both Hindus and Muslims lived in harmony. As it was, Sindhis were and are known for their mild and peaceful nature. Thus riots and major quarrels were almost unheard of. Both communities lived side by side, and in many cases mixed in the same locality. Often they exchanged pleasantries on their respective religious festivals and visited each other during those times. The Hindus were mostly

---

* D/C (direct current) electricity was a precursor of the A/C (alternating current) we are accustomed to today.

businessmen and the Muslims, though some were in business, had jobs and other vocations.

In Sindh, especially in Larkana, the main caste* was that of Vaishya, the merchant class, though there were a few Brahmins and Kshatriyas. The fourth caste, that of Shudras, mostly came from the neighboring states of Gujarat, Rajasthan and other places. They came to Sindh mainly to earn their livelihood, as there were no Shudras among Sindhis. As far as I understood, there was not much caste prejudice or strong delineation between castes in Larkana. Things in these respects went on peacefully.

Hollaram, my father, and Totibai, my mother, had already seven children before me, though the first two died in childhood. I was the eighth one. They were all born boy then girl, in that sequence. Total born were twelve. There was no family planning or birth control in those days, nor heard of. People wouldn't even think about it.

As I had heard subsequently, father as a small boy was a minor employee on a very paltry wage, just to subsist, at a local grocery shop for packaging the products for customers. His family was poor by today's standards but that was not uncommon in those days. If they got employed, that was enough—an obligation. There were no government rules regarding salaries or minimum wages. It was purely between the proprietor and the servants or employees. Father grew from there bit by bit, earning a little more and more until eventually he came on his own, all self-made. Later he grew to be one of the best and richest merchants in the district.

In course of time, he married. Since he was born on Holi—Krishna's Festival of Colors—he was named Holo or Hola, and in his adulthood, a respectful suffix was added and thus he was called Hollaram. Toti (meaning female parrot) was a daughter of a sweetmeat shop owner, a relatively respectable family in the town. Both my parents were totally illiterate and their signatures, when

---

* The four Hindu castes from ancient times are: Brahmin (priests, scholars, doctors), Kshatriya (kings, rulers, military), Vaishya (businessmen, farmers) and Shudra (laborers, servants).

required, were done by their thumbs. [Ironically nowadays, most authentic signatures are by fingerprint, even though a host of cards, papers and documents are possessed!]

When I was born, father was already an established businessman, and considered a very respectable and imposing personality, a moralist to the core, very socially conscious and mostly a quiet person. He talked very little when necessary. Although he was always generous with family, for building construction, clothes, food, education for children and medical expenses, for himself he seldom spent. He was always very simply attired in a dhoti just below the knees and collarless shirt, never with full sleeves, and wore ordinary sandals. He seldom carried even a penny in his pockets. Some considered him a miser but at home he was definitely not. He never wore shoes except once or twice a year when he went to attend a businessmen's conference in Karachi. He had only one dress for such occasions through his entire life: a long coat with collar and full sleeves, a dhoti of a better quality up to the ankles and a certain cap. Otherwise he kept shaven head. He never wore a coat or sweater in winter, just a woolen shawl.

To the question of being a "miser," we had heard father say once or twice that he was not a miser; he knew he could spend on himself but he didn't need anything more than he had at the shop or at home. Mostly, he said, being socially conscious, he did not want people to point a finger at him and say, "Here goes a rich man who is now showing off." He didn't want to forget the humble origins from where he grew. He wished to remain true to his small town, rural background of dress and upbringing. He was happy seeing his children having good food, clothes, housing and education. He always walked between his shop or office and home, though he could have easily traveled by horse carriage, though distances in the town were not far either.

Father's business mainly was Commission Agencies wholesale, mostly connected with English companies. English officers often would respect him more favorably than many others of his line in Sindh. Since he only knew and spoke Sindhi, his mother tongue, he would have an interpreter when conversing with the officers. He never went to a movie throughout his life nor ate in a hotel, now called restaurants. All his life he spent his days either at his shop (later office-cum shop) or at home. He seldom went on outings except for swimming in the canals in summer. He was known to be a great swimmer and practically taught all the family members to swim, including those of his two brothers and their families.

Not far from our home was a large forest of date palm trees that stretched up to the river Indus, which was about two miles from Larkana. This area was called a caravanserai, where often traders stayed who came from neighboring places. They came mostly on camels, sometimes on a few horses, to trade with Larkana. Sometimes they came from as far away as Baluchistan, the Northwest Province, even up to the Khyber Pass from Afghanistan, et cetera. They pitched their tents for days. They wore various exotic and colorful costumes native to their land and were often seen on the roads and streets of the town doing business with shops. They were quite friendly and honest people, true to their native ethos. They had learned a little of the Sindhi language and mixed it with their native dialect, which was quite amusing—in Pushti, Baluchi, et cetera.

Through this caravanserai flowed the Rice Canal, the widest, from the Indus, gradually distributing into a network of small and smaller canals around the town and flowing in other surrounding rural agricultural areas. In addition to irrigation, nearby dwellers used the canals for various purposes—the washerman for laundry, for washing kitchen utensils, bathing, swimming, children's play, and filling pots for domestic use. These canals were not deep except perhaps the Rice Canal. Later two parks were developed for the town people on the banks of the canal by the municipality and with private funds.

Father was fond of shopping for vegetables and mutton and fish for the family, which was not vegetarian. He was quite good at it. He always would eat lunch and dinner with the children—ladies, in those days ate later. If, for any reasons he would be late, we would wait. Not that it was a "rule," but more that he and we wished that way. Being very hot summers specially, and in winter too, it was a common practice that people would have a siesta after lunch. It was almost compulsory to do so, more so for children. Father would say he didn't want the children to go out in the hot sun and loiter and catch sunstroke. He himself could have easily rested at home, and many times the ladies of the home and others would entreat him to do so, but he almost never rested at home during daytime. He would walk to the shop and rest there where he had a small bed at the back of the office, saying that if he stayed at home, the ladies would lose their freedom to be themselves.

Again, it was not a rule, but whenever he would enter, everyone would be more sober and behave. Some might say that it was out of fear of his personality and presence. Part of this was true, but the fear was neither imposed nor invoked. It was done out of respect and love for him, and would be as religiously welcomed as "fear of God." We children addressed him as Baba—Father. He respected us and expected us to be respectful also, particularly toward the ladies of the family, and women in general. He would not tolerate us boys to "order" our sisters to bring something, even if this was quite natural in a combined family in India. He would give a mild rebuke if we did this: "Why don't you get up and do it yourself?" But certainly in his absence we brothers would teasingly order younger sisters to bring a glass of water, and they would jokingly refuse saying: "Why don't you get up and do it yourself? I'll tell father . . ." though they would bring the water anyway.

Father seldom fell sick. Even in minor sickness, he still would go to the shop and rest there, et cetera. Rarely, when he would fall more sick, he would stay home and others would serve him most willingly and with utmost regards, though he would be eager to get well and get back to work. He was regularly an early riser, before dawn, and would be the first to open his shop, so he could do some cleaning before the servants or employees would come, who could easily do all this. Then he would have a glass of tea* sent for from the nearby teashop and set his hookah, which he quietly smoked and mused. I don't know if he especially read any religious book, but sometimes we had marked that he would take a small booklet out from his

---

* In India, tea (*chai*) is often drunk from a glass rather than from a teacup.

personal little wooden box, kept nearby him, and read or write a little bit in it—not regular Sindhi, which he did not know how to write, only his ancient native script, probably used in Mohenjodaro! This script had neither grammar nor prepositions. Only he and his other such colleagues could read or understand it.

Mohenjodaro was located in the same Larkana district, about twenty-seven miles from our home. Father, though I have no exact proof, seemed Aryan. His features were eloquently so, though he himself never said so, at least not among us children. I don't think he even knew what Aryan is. I suppose he had no historical knowledge even, but who knows what he talked about among adults and his friends, being so intelligent and sharp to grasp and ahead in knowledge among his peers, many of whom were educated. He was well respected in society and often sought after for advice, counseling and settling disputes and quarrels among business people and families, often averting court cases because of that. He never charged for arbitrations and it all remained strictly among those involved. He never spoke about it anywhere to anyone.

He had a good friend, well educated, who was a *vakil* or attorney of the town. The pair seemed so incongruent and one would wonder that theirs was such a bosom friendship and intimate—father being totally illiterate and hardly in touch with the "modern" world, and the vakil, so educated, modern, et cetera. We all respected this vakil and bowed to him whenever he came. He would daily come to the shop after business hours and sit in front of father and read a Sindhi newspaper to him. He would read the article titles, and if father did not make any gesture, he would shift to another title. If father nodded, the vakil would read the details to him. Sometimes they discussed a topic. We who happened to be there sometimes would keep quiet and listen, even though we did not understand what they were discussing. Not that father was politically minded or had great interest in such things, but probably he kept abreast with what was going on.

Father often would wake someone up, mostly me (when I grew to be a boy) to accompany him to his shop in the early mornings. Not that we would necessarily like it, but we went anyway, to assist his early work before going to school. He had sometimes told me: "This will keep you humble." Sometimes when I would grumble before my mother, "Why me mostly?" she would say that my father had expressed, "Because you listen to him more than others and are intelligent to grasp his 'commands.'" As he was very simple himself, he didn't encourage pride.

In hot summers, it was a common practice and we children were expected to wear shorts or knickers above the knees, although a full *pyjama** or pantaloons were allowed in winter for obvious cold. At one time or so, I wore a pyjama to look better and came to the shop. He looked at me—he had a very sharp intellect—and he said, "Don't be proud. One day later in life, when you grow up, pride won't be useful to you." Whether he knew my future or this simply was his usual way of training us in those formative years, I would never know.

Whenever father would pass by on the street of shops, between his shop and home or elsewhere, most people who saw him would stand up or at least salute him respectfully. Of course he would return the salute to each one and even sometimes exchange a word or two. A few with whom he was close, while passing by on the way to his shop in early mornings, when it was still dark, he would call a man's name little louder outside their house, "Awake. It's getting morning." Of course, nobody minded it or was even grateful. Whether they got up or not, who can say?

Father was particular about cleanliness and organizing, in his own way, according to his cultural background and upbringing, whether at shop or home. One wouldn't say that there was anything "modern" about it, just in the scope of his known surroundings and things. Practically every day when he would come home for lunch, he would start to clean and organize the things around him, with the help of whosoever was available, and place things in proper places. Ours being a huge house and courtyard, even though cleanliness would not be bad with so many family members, there were always things to do,

---

* *Pyjama* (singular): the wide, loose drawstring trousers worn as daytime wear by men and boys in Bharat (India) and neighboring countries.

at least according to his standards of cleanliness. Unless all was done, he would not stop.

As was the custom, he and we took a bath at noontime before lunch, with the exception of some children who would bathe before going to school in the morning. It was also a common practice and one that he insisted upon that his children have a light massage on the body with mustard oil before taking a bath. Due to the very dry climate of that region, this was done to maintain health. He would do the same and then bathe outside in the sun from buckets filled in at the hand pump nearby. Then we would have lunch together, brothers and sisters with father.

Our house was big and almost surrounded by many rooms. Though "primitive" by today's standards and almost looking like a small fortress, it was built on four sides with a courtyard in the center that had sufficient privacy from the outside road and streets. This he had consciously done to give "freedom" to the family members to be themselves. He didn't much like for us to loiter outside in the streets. Being a "Hindu United Family," we and our two uncles and their families—children and grandchildren—lived in each of the four corners of this fortress, having separate kitchens. The courtyard was common. At one point in later years there were about thirty members of our combined family living there.

Daytimes were very busy and noisy with children running around, except when father was at home. I don't know why but there was only one hand pump for all to use. This was used to fill buckets for bathing, for laundry, cooking, washing utensils (dishes), et cetera. This was so, throughout the years—nobody complained. It was as if what was supposed to be. Maybe again, it was due to father's upbringing from humble origins. But outhouses were many—ten at one point—all located in the four corners of the large, rooftop terrace so that the smell would evaporate. There were three floors on all four sides and four staircases located in the four corners. One outhouse was later built on the ground floor for those who fell sick and couldn't climb upstairs. Otherwise it remained locked so that, out of laziness, as father called it, others didn't use it. Daily scavengers came and cleaned all the outhouses, on a monthly payment basis, with occasional gifts and extra payments and other needs.

In the summer it was impossible to sleep downstairs. We slept on the terrace under the open sky. In the winter we slept on *coir* beds* with light bedding downstairs in a large dormitory, like a small meeting hall—all together, parents and all children. Our parents had two beds in one corner and almost all twelve children were procreated there. We children didn't know anything about it! We would be fast asleep anyway. Afterwards when some elders married, the girls went to their husbands' homes and the boys got private rooms upstairs on the second floor, enclosed from part of the terrace.

Father was very particular about the friends that we boys chose. Although he was mostly at his shop, still his careful and protective eye would catch what we were doing eventually. Mother would know more of our friends. Perhaps this body was about ten years old when father returned home in the evening one day, as usual. It was summer and all our beds were on the terrace, mine being about five feet or more to the right of his bed and mother's on his left. It was an intense day for me as I had heard indirectly that some accusation had gone to father, probably by my nephew, regarding one of my friends. As usual, after washing, father was sitting on his bed and we joined him in dinner. I was mostly quiet, apprehensive of the impending unknown.

After dinner I lay down in my bed, turning my side away from father's gaze to avoid him. Not that father's anger wasn't rare, but he had questioned me regarding that particular friend, newly made. Of course this boy was not my usual friend in the sense of the term, but he inquired how I got this friend. He said that he had heard bad things about him. He was a little older than me. I kept quiet throughout, remaining like a log. Father said, do I know how particular he was in choice of our outside associations? I remained mum. He said that even something bad had happened between us two. Of course, it had not happened, but could have happened,

---

* *Coir* is the husk of the coconut. In rural India, mattresses similar to futons are still filled with this husk or fiber.

considering time and the potential due to that boy's character.

I knew father was right and I had no defense, nor was it my nature to offer self-defense. I never opposed my father nor argued. He was almost always right in my eyes. Father got somewhat enraged after his questions and while sitting on his bed he took a five- to six-foot bamboo pipe, with which he smoked the hookah, and hit me with it on my back several times. I lay motionless. I could hear my mother's soft plea to him, "Leave him alone now." Father did stop. The hurt was not that hard, relatively, but soft, but enough on my delicate body and conscience. But that didn't bother me, nor was I aware of its pain anyway. I had some silent tears in my eyes but no one saw it since my back was to them the whole night and the light was relatively dim.

Normally mother never interfered when father would deal with anyone and us children. But after all, she was our mother. This was his first noticeable "punishment" of me in my life till he was alive. Only one more time, later in years, on a much more minor scale, he did "punish" me with a few slaps on my cheek. I have never regretted these a bit. I knew I was his very favorite child and he would do all for my and our family's good. I was only sorry that he had to punish me as he did. That night passed by as usual. I might have slept a few hours, never turning my side. Of course, I never saw that "friend" again and became more careful in my choices howsoever imperfectly. From there onward, mother took over to guide over my selection of "friends," but that will be later.

By nature I was a little timid anyway, in addition to my shyness, modesty and quiet nature. In the early morning, father, as usual, left for the shop. He didn't call me to go with him, nor was it every day anyway. Maybe it was because of what happened in the night, or just to leave me alone. On the one side, I felt relieved, but on the other I was very sullen to face the other members of the family who had witnessed and heard all this, except for those who might have been sleeping.

It was often the practice of father that, during the evening, he would come home after washing and he would relax in his bed, smoking a hookah before dinner was ready. Some of us children, perhaps three or four, would sit around him and later eat with him. During those times he would give some abstruse, very difficult for our age, arithmetic sums like multiplication and division to us. We were to mentally solve them and on fingers, but not on paper or with pencil. These were difficult even for adults. Fractions, he would choose, which were very odd and intricate, not whole numbers. Mostly we would be unable to do the math problem, though relatively I was good at arithmetic and sometimes would succeed. Others wouldn't succeed at all. We were small boys. The sums we failed to solve he would then explain how to do it easily. He would teach us to break the fractions into two or three convenient "wholes," and each multiply or divide with the other number, breaking the same way and then adding or subtracting as the case may be. It used to then look easy comparatively, though it needed practice. Perhaps there is no need to go into details about it here, to show examples. Where father learned all of this and how, I don't know. He never went to school but even in school, on paper, we had easier sums.

I have several times looked back on my life with my parents and always I have received the same response that, knowingly or not, my father and mother were my first Gurus in this life. It's probably the same truth enshrined in Hindu scriptures, while enumerating a small list of "gods" or "Gurus," in this instance they have included the father and mother: *Matri Devo Bhavā, Pitri Devo Bhavā,** although I consciously didn't follow that dictum, nor did I know about it at that juncture. Respect and obedience, yes, but of parents being gods and Gurus, I was not aware.

Father, though not himself a carpenter or mason, had fair knowledge of these things. Our big "mansion" was built like adobe, with thick walls that were warm in winter and cool in summer. Later they used bricks and adobe mortar, and when cement came in the market (he himself became the main wholesale dealer of cement) the brick pointings or mortar was done with cement. Some floors in the house that were covered with bricks were eventually covered or paved

---

* *Matri Devo Bhavā, Pitri Devo Bhavā*, lit: "Mother is God, Father is God."

with cement too. When A/C electricity later was available the whole day in our town, the D/C generator was replaced by it—howsoever faulty, sporadic and undependable. Soon every room had an electric bulb and a little later ceiling fans were added for the summer. But the hand pump and outhouses remained the same throughout my childhood and teenage years—almost unchangeable, classics.

Looking at it from present standards, one would like to demolish the whole complex and build anew, but then it was a haven for us. Only one room, for which solely two elder brothers were responsible, being somewhat educated, was connected with the outside door and what you would call "modern" in those days. It was called a drawing room and mostly used by my next elder brother. Later he and I (when I grew up a little) shared it, and then me, after his untimely demise in youth. But primarily it was meant to be for visitors and guests. It had a kind of sofa, an entertaining and dining set, a few chairs, a dining table, a wall mirror, a cupboard displaying some "modern" crockery and cutlery, a dressing table (!), and a closet cupboard used by my brother and later by me.

This drawing room had more windows than the whole house combined, and curtains too. When guests came for overnights who were not so close to family, we slept inside the main house. Sometimes business-related guests came too, including some foreigners. I would be one of the main ones to help in hospitality for guests. They often knew the Indian language, though my eldest brother could speak to them in English. Often such dinners lasted late into the night.

Later on when mosaic tiles came into the market, father brought some assorted tiles of many designs and colors that were leftovers from the main stocks and therefore quite cheap. He helped the tile masons to somehow make a pattern and put these in the drawing room. To everybody, it looked great. Who knew the secret anyway? After all, they were mosaic tiles and colorful too! Many neighbors, relatives and friends came to see it and marveled, and some got quiet too, perhaps wishing they had the same!

By the present knowledge, one would say that the whole house was not well ventilated, or even within the scope available then. It was not quite hygienic either, except for the courtyard and terrace, but who cared, so long as there were more well needed rooms for a huge family! Primarily it may have been father's background knowledge and limitations that were responsible for it. We had never heard of architects, contractors, et cetera. It was your property and money to build or do as you like. We had not heard of building codes. If there were any, we were not aware of it. The whole town was built that way, which by today's standards would be haphazard. Perhaps some government buildings and schools, built by the English, were done according to some designs.

There was another section of town that perhaps would be called "elite" for the court judge, a few attorneys, and few teachers and other more educated people. But we had no strong connections there, nor frequent visits. They might have had better-designed houses. Only occasionally I visited there because one of my close school friends lived there. He was a Muslim and the only son of the court judge of the town. But that will be later.

Mother: what can I say about her? She was an epitome of a mother as far as the human part of this life was concerned. If I say all, it would fill volumes! In many ways, she was like my father: simplicity in dress and dealings, and totally illiterate. On one side, she was very shrewd—more than father. Her eyes were like a hawk. On the other side, she was so loving, helpful, protective and confidence-building in us—we could confide in her where we would shirk to go to father. Nothing would escape her gaze or knowledge, even if you tried your best or worst to hide. Yet we would feel relieved once whatever we did was over. She would eventually mend well despite what we did.

As told earlier, she was also from humble origins, but not as "poor" as father's family. She was polite and understanding. Many ladies—friends, relatives and neighbors—came to her for counseling and for settling disputes in their lives. Much of her help to others would be unknown to us children, but occasionally a few things would come out. With eventually twelve children born to her (two died in early life), mother's every day and whole life was busy with house chores from morning until night when she went to sleep. She never had a holiday. She was not a person to go for an outing or socializing unnecessarily. She also never went to any restaurant and only once she went to a "talkie" movie when all insisted that it was a religious movie. It was of Saint Gyaneshwar. Throughout the movie she had tears many times, though much of the language, being Hindi, was incomprehensible to her.

On another occasion, she had attended a school drama when my eldest brother studied there. I was not born yet but heard about it later. Brother was good at school drama and an amateur singer. He had a good voice and played manly roles. Mother, until that time, had never seen a drama on stage and was not at all familiar with such things. Whatever the story was and my brother's role, I later heard that at one point he was supposed to be bitten by a snake and swoon. Mother was sitting in the first few rows of chairs and there was a large audience—students, teachers, parents, et cetera. When that scene arrived and brother was bitten by a "snake," mother literally got up, cried aloud and was starting to run toward her son on stage, saying: "My son, my son is bitten by a snake!" Of course, those sitting nearby got up and caught hold of her and told her it was an artificial snake. This pacified her, but perhaps this was her first and last attendance to a drama. In every other way, she was so intelligent! Later her son told her that he had heard her cry but continued his role. What else could he do?

Mother seldom fell sick but if she was bedridden for a sickness or a new delivery, we children were lost until she again got up. It was not that the other ladies of the house—the daughters-in-law, aunty, elder sisters, et cetera, would not look after us or our care, but they were not *mother*. She did attend marriages and funerals in her friends' and relatives' homes when needed. Mother had relatively good health. I don't think she ever even visited our father's shop.

Although a lot of the family laundry was done by our neighbor washerman, a Muslim, the cost for this at that time, including ironing and delivery, was per one hundred clothes pieces. Even still, a lot of the laundry needed to be done at home. Mother attended to all this with the help of daughters-in-law as they came one by one, and probably some growing daughters as well. Three times a day cooking was done on a wood fire. Father didn't believe in having maidservants to assist, as he said, "We have so many family members and should depend on ourselves." This was another point in which some called him a miser. He said we should not live like aristocrats, although money was there and hired labor was cheap. Later on a maidservant was allowed who would assist in washing the huge amount of kitchen utensils and do a few other chores, but that was part-time.

With so many beds to make daily, mother and the other ladies of the house carried on, in addition to looking after so many children. Often someone would be sick daily in the big home. Mother could be angry at times but that was the least we could expect!

All laundry at home was done with one hand pump, filling buckets. There were no machines of any kind in those days. With hand brooms, all floors were swept. The only machine we had was a sewing machine, run by hands. Mother was a basic tailor and would sew some of our clothes; later on daughters and daughters-in-law helped her. Only a few clothes like coats and knickers were taken to a professional male tailor in the town.

Throughout the years, we children never had to even think about our health. It was taken care of by mother, mostly at home by herbal medicines. If need be, an ayurvedic or a homeopathic doctor would be called, which was frequent in such a large family. We were totally dependent upon mother. Without her nearness and presence, we would feel lost. Almost religiously, every night when we children would be in bed after dinner and mostly asleep, after finishing her chores mother would bring a bucket of milk and bowls and go to each bed, raise our head with one hand and holding the neck with the other, pour milk into our mouths, then let us go back to sleep. Many times, the next morning, we didn't even remember that we had had milk the last night, though I suppose many times we never got up from sleep in the first place! Milk was a must for children, as she saw.

Mother was known to have great luck with money—her palm showed that. Some even said that father's luck in business grew after he married her. As would be expected in a Hindu family and from a devoted and faithful wife, mother remained a "shadow" of father and would always stay in the background. But she was always a "queen" of the house. Any time that father was at home, even he would, as if, depend upon her. If she were doing something else while he was at home, he would be restless until she was called to be there near him. Many times when we had to ask her something that generally would be for father to attend, she would say, "Why don't you ask your father?" As we were shy or afraid to do so, she would quietly solve it for us.

Mother was a known great cook, especially non-vegetarian, more so in mutton dishes. Guests, relatives and friends would often try to find excuses to come in order to eat her mutton preparations. In those days, guests were always impromptu: *Atithi Devo Bhavā.** Our family was non-vegetarian and about five days a week would be non-veg in our home. Even then, when it would be a vegetarian meal, though very well prepared, we children would eat less, at least by one chappati. Milk was abundant and in those days there was hardly any adulteration. Our home had a cow, *Lachmi* (Sindhi for *Lakshmi†*) and mother would take all her care, including milking twice daily. If somebody else went to the cow to attend to her needs, she would almost refuse to oblige until mother went to her. Our cow had a name and was as good as a family member. In the afternoons, the cows would be sent with a hired cowherder to pastures to graze, then her "room" would be cleaned by someone in the house. When she came back from grazing—of course, she would know her own "home"— she would come running, calling *baa* (*maa* or mother), and entered herself from the big gate of the house.

Mother often collected cowdung and on a secluded wall of our house outside, would press the cowdung here as cakes. After they dried, they would be used at least as kindling along with wood for the cooking fire, for heating and for bathing water in winter, especially for weak or sickly family members and those recouping from illness.

---

* *Atithi Devo Bhavā*, lit: "a guest is God" or "a guest is as welcome as God."
† *Lakshmi* is the Vedic Goddess of wealth and prosperity.

Butter and buttermilk, from fresh milk, were made by hand, mostly by mother. On occasions of our school exams, and on auspicious holy days, we children especially would go to the cow, take her "bush" of the tail and caress on our faces as seeking blessings. She would comply quietly.

The whole of our family building had one very large main gate facing the road whereupon even a horse could enter, though we had no horses. There was a small gate on the other side on a street that was generally used more. Although in those days beggars and mendicants were not many, still daily they would come, some even regularly, on the side of the smaller gate. Mother would never refuse anyone or turn anyone away. Though money as alms was not much in vogue, grains, molasses, et cetera, and sometimes used clothes were regularly given. Sometimes there would be sadhu minstrels who would sing with their tambouras for some time. Occasionally cooked food was given too, possibly leftovers. Regulars often would call politely, "Maa," and she would go to the gate.

Mother, by ordinary standards, would not be called beautiful. She was a little dark-complexioned compared to father, who had relatively fair skin. But mother's personality would never allow anyone to even think about this. She was a good mother, and that was it. She was mother first and mother last, and that was her beauty. We called her "Amma" or "Ammi."

Very, very rarely, when some business relation or guests, both local and a few "foreigners," would get more familiar with father and our eldest brother, they would be brought inside the home, as compared to coming inside the drawing room. They would like to meet mother. Even when she had grown elderly, as per her earlier village custom, mother would meet them with half-covered face with a veil, and not facing them directly, would stand by to serve them. Guests, especially foreigners, would fold their hands in *namaste** and bend respectfully forward a little to give her credit and say, "You have been the backbone of the house, and indirectly, the business." She would

---

* *Namaste:* "the God in me bows to the God in you," a traditional greeting in India.

mostly keep quiet or rarely, at the most, politely attribute it (in broken Sindhi) to her husband. Somebody would interpret to the guests in their language. It is possible the business guests might have done this out of business policy or just human courtesy, at least some, but to us it looked sincere and genuine. As I have said earlier, both parents had quite a few similarities, but outside we had never seen them touching, embracing, kissing, et cetera, at all. They, of course, talked to each other when necessary but we seldom saw them even sitting together, exceptions apart, but I am sure they were one inside. After all, they produced twelve offspring!

Grandmother from father's side was still alive when I was born. A tiny old lady, also totally illiterate, she lived with father's youngest brother in the same compound. Father was the eldest among three brothers. Grandma was easily irritated and made angry, and sometimes we children made a fun of teasing her so that she would become angry. Then we would persuade her to part with a few pennies in her pocket. She would not like to give her paltry wealth but we knew when she got angry, she would give just to get rid of us! She was well respected, but she did not play much of a role in family administration, nor did she have that capability. She was quite aged and had many wrinkles on her face. She was almost at the background but even then, being the eldest in all three families, she was a figurehead anyway.

Grandfather was already gone before my birth. He was considered to be a very religious man and was one of the very few who had dared, in those days, to go on a pilgrimage to Badrinath at 10,000 feet elevation in the Himalayas. In those days, there was no transportation at all to go there. One had to walk from home for days on end to reach there. Often pilgrims went in small or large groups. Once gone, it was taken that they may never return. If they returned, they were considered almost saints. The neighbors, relatives and friends would come and bow down to them and seek blessings and partake of *prasad** that

---

* *Prasad* is a gift or blessing from God. In Bharat, prasad given at temples is often a simple sweet but any tangible or intangible item can be considered prasad.

pilgrims brought with them. Many years later, while in my *parivrajak* (wandering monk) sojourn as a young sadhu, while in Haridwar on the Ganga banks I happened to meet a Panda (Brahmin priest who keeps centuries-long record of ancestors and their lineage). He referred to my grandfather's name in his scrolls and showed me.

Religious festivals such as *Divali, Holi, Janmashtami, Rama Navami* and *Dussehra*, et cetera, were observed and celebrated in the family, although on a small scale. Additionally, we visited the temple of the particular God relevant to the holy day in the town, and offered puja and sought blessings. Then when we would return home, mother would offer alms to beggars, who were very few in those days, servants and employees as well as some poor people. The servants also received extra gifts. We would also extend pleasantries to a few of our Muslim neighbors with whom we were in contact. They would receive our gifts happily, giving their blessings.

On *Maha Shiva Ratri*,* very early morning we boys and men from the family would go on foot to the Indus River to bathe while the ladies stayed home. While on route many miles from home, we would sing "Om Namah Shivaya" throughout. Back at home, puja would be conducted of Lord Shiva and then we would have lunch. Indispensably, the main dish would be fish from the Indus. Somehow it was almost a ritual necessary to observe; I don't know why.

Between my two uncles, the older one was with father in the same business and his two sons eventually joined, but at home his wife was not on good terms with us. Eventually a tall, thick wall was built of bricks to divide their family's assigned quarters permanently within our compound, though relations at the shop continued the same. We loved and respected this uncle and would bow down to him, as was our custom for all elders. I had heard that while young and in some kind of job in the marketplace, he was very strong—almost like an

---

* *Maha Shiva Ratri*, lit: "Great Night of Shiva," falling normally in February or March, is a holy day in honor of Shiva, the transformer aspect of the Hindu Trinity. It is celebrated with all-night fasting, chanting, meditation and ritual worship (puja).

athlete—and he carried and pushed huge, heavy bales and boxes for his earnings.

The younger uncle, living in quarters facing ours and sharing the same courtyard, was close to us. Grandma lived with him and his family. He had rice agriculture and other produce on the other side of the canal, a mango orchard and many other trees. He was mainly a wholesale rice dealer, having his own shop/office not far from father's shop. Every year, we all families and some relatives would have a picnic gathering of a sort at his garden, which was a walking distance and some went by horse carriages. There we would have a huge non-vegetarian meal and neighboring landlords, both Hindu and Muslim, would also be invited. Professional cooks took care of the food that was cooked on a log fire. A town photographer would be invited to take some group photographs, of course in black and white. He had an old camera on a tripod and would cover his head at the back with a black cloth as he took the photograph. Practically we would be there the whole day from morning until late afternoon and then return home nearly at dusk.

Aunty was a simpleton lady. She was this uncle's second wife after the first one died, so she was somewhat younger than him. She had a very golden heart, but brains?—God knows! We sometimes teased her mildly about it. She would innocently say, "God didn't give me brains, what can *I* do?"—emphasizing the "I." Frequently, for large and small matters, she would rely upon my mother. Only rarely would mother rebuke her mildly, "Why can't you think for yourself?" Then aunty would reply, "Then why would I come to you?" and everyone would laugh.

If anyone or I ever witnessed the best stepmother, due to my uncle's children from his first wife who had died, it was she. She loved all instinctively and all loved her. Once some quarrel happened between her and uncle, for whatever reason, during the daytime and I was home at that time. He hit her and she began to cry and ran, almost in a panic, weeping, to our mother. Mother took her to her bosom, pacified her and then—which we had never witnessed—went to uncle (with whom she normally did not sit or talk with much) and, like a tigress, she told him, "In our family, no one has ever taken a hand on girls or women. Who are you to do it? Never do it again!" Of course, uncle, by then, was half dead anyway and he promised he would never do it again. As far as I remember, we never saw such things again. It was his first and last; he loved her much anyway.

Whatever I had witnessed, been aware of, seen, heard, that I have written. That does not mean that other things and episodes might not have happened, significant or not. I have not researched anything in this telling. It is not my caliber . . .

School Days

Probably at four or five years of age, I was entered into what they then called elementary school. The school was not far from the home and within walking distance. A group of boys walked together to school, though in the beginning an elder would go with us. The school was in Sindhi language medium and run by the government. There was not much eventful in the early school days to mention. I liked to go to school, so there was no restriction from my side. Together the elementary and then lower secondary schools constituted, if I am right, about four or five years. These both were in the same compound, though the secondary school had a separate headmaster.

One good thing in secondary school was when I discovered the headmaster, who was known to our family and a neighbor. He was the best poet in the whole of Sindh, whose poetry and songs were in all the Sindhi text books of the schools and colleges of Sindh, in addition to his private publications of collected poems and songs. He used to be called the "Kalidas" and "Shakespeare" of Sindh. He was a very simple man, wore a white shirt and pyjama, slip-on shoes and a cap. He was a very short-spoken and quiet man. He was also a known drama writer, especially school stages and himself a director of dramas. He taught languages, but only Sindhi at that moment in the classes. As was in vogue in those days, poets generally assumed a title that would occur at the end of last line or two of each poem, fitting the meaning of the line. His was "Bewas" (helpless). Often then poets would choose humble, even self-deprecating and unassuming titles to be shorn of pride, as was not uncommon with writers of stories and novels to end with tragedies. Probably the same was true in Europe and England too? Comedy was not that common as today.

I soon became one of his favorite students and he selected me to be in one of his written dramas that played on the school stage once or twice a year. And he was the one who discovered a good musical voice in me. We had a music teacher who would teach me, not music as such, but songs to be sung on the stage. In those days, girls didn't appear on the stage and boys had to play both roles with proper respective costumes. I was one of those playing both roles, depending upon the story. Bewas, whom we called "Sai," meaning Sir, would himself teach us acting and make us rehearse. He was quite a hard taskmaster and would get angry with those who would not pick up their parts soon. Of course, he would always want us to practice at home, memorizing verbatim everything—words, gestures, attitudes, et cetera. I generally got the top role, although sometimes it was different. Whenever he visited our home he would tell my mother, "Your son is a good student and plays his roles on stage very well. I am happy with him. Why don't you give this boy to me?" Mother, of course, would reply to him, "He is yours, Kākā (uncle)." Due to his nature, personality and some familiarity of his and his family, we all called him Kākā. Though I will give details later, he eventually became one of my mentors up to the time of my schooling, right up to Higher Secondary.

Once I got the role of Parvati (Shiva's consort), and others were a king on a throne, and so on. I still remember the boy who was given Shiva's role by Bewas himself. He had a hard time. He was chosen because of his body formation and bearing, which really looked like Shiva, but otherwise was totally unfit as far as speech and acting were concerned. Our headmaster had no trouble with me as Parvati, by God's grace, but this "Shiva" got the most rebukes from him. The director's tirades against "Lord Shiva" continued almost every day of the rehearsal until the last day of the drama. Poor Shiva! He did look "my" husband, but once he opened his mouth and tried to act, he wasn't. Thus Parvati stole the show, while the opposite was supposed to happen! But who minded? After all, it was the boys on the school stage anyway. All were relaxed—actors and audience—except the director and a few teachers who assisted in the drama. They were quite tense and serious, as if this was the biggest show ever acted on this earth! Eventually it worked out, but Sai had lost his confidence.

In one of the scenes, Parvati was supposed to sit on one thigh of Shiva and converse. Afterwards for days together, I had to hear teasing from some of my school friends, enticing me to come and sit on their thighs! Of course, I couldn't do anything about it. Being handsome (in their eyes) and having a little feminine quality, I was naturally shy. Once only did I complain to our teacher, but boys are boys. This teasing, of course, wore out in course of time.

As students, we had some games in the school compound that we played during recesses. So far studies were concerned, as I have said, it was fortunate but not worth much to mention. In those days the marks were given to answer papers (like now A, B and C), out of one hundred and that determined the number in the class of the standing of a student. Generally I stood number one in a particular class. This naturally made me a favorite of teachers and sometimes, when studies were finished and there was a little time left before the next period or recess, a teacher would ask me to sing a song.

Ours being a large family, often one or more members would fall sick. In summer each year, malaria would break out. Deaths from this seldom happened, as far as I know, but high temperature (scary) and final tremendous weakness, et cetera, would as if finish the patient. It was more common among children—I was no exception to it—until after some years they got immune to it. Quinine was the only remedy and sometimes, if severe, someone would be given an injection. Quinine would be available in the British Government allopathic dispensary. The allopathic doctor would visit homes if need be, but for normal ailments, we would go to the ayurvedic or homeopathic doctor. In our neighborhood, Sai (Bewas) had a homeopathic dispensary and he himself was a doctor with one associate. Sometimes when I would visit there for medicine, I found him sitting in an easy chair, lost in musing in writing poetry if he had got inspiration then. His associate would attend to the patients. Sai was a very well respected citizen of the town and known throughout Sindh. If ever I went for medicine a little frequently or he had to come to our home to see me, if I was in bed he would lovingly reprimand, "Why do you fall sick often? What is wrong with you?" Of course, I would say nothing and shake my head down. Some time later he used to call me "sickly boy" occasionally. But on many fronts, in course of years, he taught me a lot as he did to many others in the town, both students and adults.

He wrote not only poetry but also songs and, later on, patriotic songs as well. When the freedom movements against the British started, his songs used to be sung throughout Sindh, in schools, colleges, political forums and stages on freedom days. At that time the Congress Party was in the forefront of the Freedom Movement and Mahatma Gandhi and Patel and Nehru and others were the main leaders. Technically, Mahatma Gandhi was never an official member of the Congress Party, but he was the main head and heart of it as well as of the nation as a whole, eventually emerging as Father of the Nation. Our family had told me that when I was a small boy, Gandhi had visited Larkana to give a speech, but I had no recollection. I never saw him physically because when I could have an opportunity, he was gone. But details will be later. However, as the world knows now, Gandhi permeated every inch of India, in a way.

Sai and many other leaders of Sindh and Larkana were, of course, under that spell. Sai himself was not an active freedom fighter, but through pen he inspired the whole of Sindh. Thus, directly and indirectly, almost all political and social leaders were in his contact. Sai was never arrested on sedition or any political offense since he didn't do anything to break a British law. He never wore an English dress, as a matter of principle, though he didn't wear the *khadi* (handspun cloth) that was commonly preached by Gandhi. Sai and his family lived within walking distance of our home. He had a few daughters and a son who was also a singer. It was my and our great privilege that such a great man, though only known in Sindh, was our neighbor and personally known to us.

There is nothing much to write about my school days at elementary. At about ten years of age I joined the government high school in the lower secondary section. This was a three-year course and at that time the medium was not English but Sindhi. English was taught as a subject only in higher secondary. At that moment, the school was only for boys, though later coeducation was introduced when I entered higher secondary. Girls would sit in the first one or two rows of the class, depending upon their number, and boys after that. The girls had their own private waiting and resting hall at one corner of the school building where boys were not allowed.

During this time and earlier too, I was quite fond of clothes. At one point, I had about thirty to forty shirts (imagine in those days, and for a boy!), all different designs and colors so that no one would see the same shirt twice in a month. My pyjama was white cotton always. The family had no objection to it and the eldest sister was more encouraging as she was now married and her husband and in-laws owned a cloth shop. She often bought good pieces of shirt cloth for me.

The Second World War had started in 1939 and Winston Churchill was the war minister in England. At home, the National Freedom Movement was getting more momentum, heading toward major climaxes under the leadership of Mahatma Gandhi, Patel, Nehru and other leaders at the national as well as provincial levels. I remember that at father's business, which had grown now, a "modern" office was added at the back of the new big shop (shifted from the old, smaller one). By this time my eldest brother, who had finished undergraduate, was brought into the business by father to assist in business and to converse with representatives of English companies in English when needed. It was a clever move from all angles, but it stopped brother's further education. The office was decorated in a "modern" way with a large table, some chairs, file cabinets and a small carpet under all that. Brother sat in the managerial chair and, surprise of all: a picture of Churchill was on the wall behind brother's chair. I was too young to comment but once my brother, understanding my thoughts, said, "I am doing this for business, though I know it's wrong from Freedom point of view." Whether that picture remained there all the days or only on occasions when English officials were supposed to come, I am not sure. In those days, I went there very infrequently, being busy with my school, homework, sports, et cetera.

Back home, two elder brothers and I were thinking of having a radio, which was then available in Karachi. Larkana was still a small town for such sales. For some time it was really "impossible" to approach father for this. For one, he was not "modern" at all, and he didn't want to "show" his opulence and also we would have to explain "why" we needed it. Eventually, on one occasion when father and the eldest brother happened to go to Karachi for business, I requested my brother fervently to bring me one. He was not adverse to it but who would "bell the cat"? Father had quite a large branch in Karachi, doing wholesale business in dried coconut, black pepper and other such products transported from Kochin.* After some days they returned and in the horse carriage on the way from the railway station, I noticed a huge box never seen before. It was a radio. Father was never for it! The box remained unopened in the drawing room for quite a number of days. Nobody, including the brother, dared to open it. After some time I entreated brother, and we both together "dared" to open it and place it in one corner of the room on a small, square table. It looked the most prized piece of furniture in the room! Together we hooked it up. By now our town had electricity the whole day. The radio's name was Ecko. We played it and it sounded good.

In the whole town of Larkana, I think ours was the second or third radio only. Because of my "love" of music, I fiddled around with the radio for several days to find the proper stations. Later a radio program magazine began to arrive regularly, sent by the radio company. This was in English but I had difficulty reading a few lines. I was especially fond of film music although of a sober type, sung by artists of my choice then. At that time, film music had some standard

---

* Kochin (Cochin) is in Kerala State on the west coast of South India.

and quality and lyrics meaningful; "cheap" songs had not yet entered. Brother was more interested in the news, which was primarily broadcast in the evening. When brother would return from business, he would tune into the news. I would not follow the news much, but some interest grew. At times I would hear brother comment, "They are not honest in reporting." The war was going on and he explained that the news was censored by the British press. No news came about the Freedom Movement and speeches of leaders unless it suited British interests. I didn't understand this at the time. How could the news be false? I believed the news was coming from the radio! How could it be incorrect? Father never even touched the radio till he was alive. We were careful not to play it loud when father was at home. Once or twice when we happened to play it loud, he heard it and rushed to the room to shout either to stop it or play it low.

Besides myself and an elder brother who died young, (but that will be later), I don't think any other member of the family ever touched the radio except my cousin-brother* (son of the rice merchant uncle) who would sometimes join us to hear music since he used to sing too. He had a nice baritone voice—not professional though—and would sing with the harmonium, a hand-bellowed instrument. While in my leisure, fiddling around the stations, I used to come across several stations, though many did not come clear. The radio used to work on values—3, 5, 7—and accordingly we could get the reception. Once, I accidentally hit upon some music not familiar to me language-wise and it drew my heart out. It was so unknown and unfamiliar. The voice was of a nationally well-known singer, one of my most favorite singers, but the language I guessed was Bengali! I wasn't familiar with this language at that time. It was as if I was "hungry" for this music. Afterwards I used to search out this station, but the reception was very weak. However, even a glimmer of it would attract me.

---

* In Indian languages, there are separate names for cousins, aunts, uncles, grandparents, et cetera, according to side of the family and gender. Thus a boy cousin is translated as "cousin-brother" and a girl cousin as "cousin-sister." In Hindu combined families, cousins are nearly as close as sisters and brothers.

As usual each year, on 26th January India celebrated Freedom Day according to what had been decided by the leaders. Although I was not a regular *khadi* (handloom cloth) wearer, I had kept one khadi dress* for such occasions. Freedom Day was not a declared public holiday by the British obviously, nor would any government schools close. But strikes and work shutdowns did happen as well as political meetings, processions, shouting of slogans for freedom and freedom songs did happen on the call by Gandhi and other leaders. Although the English officers did not like this, in a way they did nothing except some arrests if anything turned violent or disruptive in their eyes.

One year, my only khadi dress had been lying down for a year since it was last worn; it needed to be washed and ironed for the next early morning when I would wear it to school and join the students' strike and procession. Somehow the ladies of the house who usually did this washing couldn't do it in time. The time was short and as a boy, I got restless, in spite of their affirmative that they would do it. My sister-in-law was "responsible" for it. Seeing this, I quietly took my khadi clothes and entered stealthily in the hand pump bathroom. I had never done this kind of thing before. However, when I started washing the clothes, the sound of the pump, water flowing and the thumping of hands on my clothes couldn't be unheard in the house. It drew attention and first one lady and then a few more came to the door and knocked to open it. I couldn't avoid and what they saw they never would have expected. Everybody rushed to snatch the clothes from me and wash them. Hearing this, my mother came running too. She asked why I didn't ask anyone to do it. I said, "I did." Then mother had tears in her eyes and said, "I am not dead yet." I said, "So-and-so undertook to do it, so what could I do?" I needed them ready by the next early morning. Of course, soon someone got them washed.

As I remember, I was perfectly calm, relaxed and resigned to do it. One would expect that I was frustrated, disappointed, angry or reactionary, but not one of these was in my mind. The thought had

---

* "Dress" is a general term for clothes in India. Men's and boys' dress in the Sindh region at that time generally consisted of a shirt and loose pants.

come to me—*after all, why should I depend upon "others"? What right have I? After all, the ladies are whole day busy with household chores and their family,* et cetera. Mother and other ladies, I think, did not believe it. Being a small boy, how could it be so? As you will read in some later episodes like that, such were my openings up to my future, by God's grace, which I didn't know at all at that time. Needless to say, I was loved more for no agitation and no reaction or tantrums of any kind. I was peaceful.

At school I was especially number one in mathematics—arithmetic, algebra and geometry. Trigonometry was not my forte somehow; so was chemistry. But in physics and geography I excelled. History, though it went fairly well, I didn't do as well as in geography. However, on the whole, I would stand number one in the class, though sometimes another friend of mine, a Muslim boy, would snatch that from me. I was very well known for my handwriting and every year my notebooks would be circulated in all classes of the school for students to see. At the end of each year, these notebooks would be kept by display in the school museum, which I didn't mind. Although drawing class was not my favorite particularly, at home I used to do charcoal and pastel paintings as a hobby, copying from other pictures. They were admired, though amateurish, and a few friends and teachers would take some away. A few hung in our drawing room. As had been before, I was still a favorite of teachers in high school.

I remember once in algebra class, our class teacher entered and wrote on the blackboard a new example and asked, almost as a challenge, if any one among us could solve it. Normally that wasn't his practice; he would first teach a math example and on the strength of that, would give similar examples to do by ourselves. Somehow I felt almost intuitively, a gut feeling, that I could do it and said so. The teacher obliged to wait. No other student was able to even attempt it. After pages and pages, trying hard, I couldn't come near the solution. Somewhat frustrated and conscious of the time running out (as the period was for about forty minutes), and hurrying up I kept repeating, "Please wait." The teacher did ask about it twice, mildly, if he should go ahead and show my work. By that time the whole class and the teacher were on hold, which was their kindness. However, towards the very end, I struck upon the solution. Hurriedly completing the steps, I ran to the teacher as the bell was ringing and showed it to him. He saw it and, looking at my face, he said, "You are a genius. One day you will be a great mathematician." Although that probably could have happened, the life later took a different turn.

At sports, which were more or less compulsory, although I was good at cricket, badminton was my favorite and often I would win in the school tournament. There were playgrounds for every class, mostly for cricket, and some volleyball courts and two tennis courts. Our school was considered of high quality among many, and some even used to praise it as if as good as a college, considering the facilities, results and quality of teachers and headmasters. It had a large property around with many playgrounds and lots of trees and an orchard. The headmaster had a residence for him and his family in the premises. There was a large bicycle stand, servants' and gardeners' quarters, et cetera. In the early days, since there was no electricity, large ceiling fans used to be driven by hand in every class. Later, electric ceiling fans were provided. Being the kind of student I was, I was very fond of the school and would eagerly wait to go to school each day. Sports used to be in the afternoons, except on Sundays and holidays. The school had its own good library and a small dormitory for students, not many, who came from surrounding areas and rural areas of Larkana. Fees were very reasonable and some of the poor students were free.

Once we were in the science laboratory for some experiment in physics (what they called "practicals," as compared to theoretical science, which was taught in regular class). The science teacher was brilliant and almost looked like a college professor rather than a schoolteacher. He was quite a sober man. My nephew, who was considered a dull boy, was given an apparatus on the same table I was on. Though in a normal sense I did not much care for his company, his father had requested me to give him company so that he imbibed something from the same lessons. So often we would go and come together to school, whether I liked it or not! In such society as ours, where he was the son of my half brother, born from my father's first wife, family connections were so close and combined that whatever any one member did, good or bad, would reflect upon the other family members. Right or wrong, this was as it was, and probably that was one of the reasons why father was so society-conscious. And probably that was one of the reasons I would be choosy of my own company. But this nephew, living nearby our home and with respect and obedience to elders, even of a half brother, I could not refuse or avoid.

However, when the experiment started in the science laboratory and the teacher had given all the pre-instructions possible, all of a sudden a huge blast occurred loudly and everybody was alarmed. The teacher came running to the spot. It was on our table. The nephew had fired the glass flask without putting water in it as a part of the experiment. Luckily nobody was hurt. Anybody could have done this mistake but it was a solitary case of him. He often was so in many other matters. Of course, the teacher was enraged and barred him from the laboratory, and angrily asked me (as if I was responsible, being his uncle), "Why didn't you watch him?" I politely said, "I was busy with my experiment." He, of course, understood and kept quiet. We cleaned the mess and the experiment restarted uninterrupted.

During those years of higher secondary school, I had developed a great liking for literature beyond the school textbooks, especially of novels and short stories. There was not much available in the Sindhi language of these, but that was the only language I knew then. Mainly Sindhi literature was of Sufis and their poems and songs, some of which our Sindhi textbooks at school contained. "Modern" Sindhi literature was only the poetry and songs written by Sai Bewas. If there was any religious Sindhi literature, I was not aware since I wasn't open to that at the time. Sometime later a few translations began to appear, especially from Bengal, of Tagore, Sharat Chandra [Chatterjee] and Bankim Chandra's novels, and from central India, such as Munshi Premchand and a few others. These were high quality and I saved for them with gusto and wanted more.

Such novels, especially those from Bengal, had some social aspects and patriotic too, and some romantic but of high standard. I began to collect several books like that and made a small individual library in my room. A few shelves were put inside the thick adobe wall and then covered with wooden doors. In town, sometimes I visited a few small bookstores to find such literature if available. This was my prize collection. Only two or three translations appeared of Sherlock Holmes. These I did read but did not crave for more. At that time I was not open to literature in English. I didn't know it much anyway except textbooks at school, which contained poems by Shelley, Keats, Wordsworth and prose of Tom, Dick and Harry. My English then started in the class as a subject and ended there as I left the class except for exams' sake again. Movies, black and white, mostly were in Hindi from Bombay, the majority religious and some social. We children were not allowed to see them much anyway, only a few per year. Only once I remember did a silent Western movie come—Charlie Chaplin—and we were allowed to go and see it.

It was around 1940 that this incident happened: My next elder brother was to marry. In those days, early betrothal (engagement) was a norm. Being from a relatively rich family, many guests, friends, relatives and business contacts were invited. Professional cooks were invited to prepare food for hundreds. The family wanted to make this marriage one that the town would remember! All were very busy—elders, ladies of the house, and servants. Some days earlier, all were asked what kind of dress they would wear on this occasion. I had selected, unusually, a pyjama of silk with violet and white stripes. Nobody had ever heard of it! I don't remember if I had seen it somewhere, which very well could have been, or imagined it. Everyone insisted that I choose something else but I didn't budge. Seeing this my eldest sister said she would try to find it. Her husband and in-laws were cloth merchants in the town. Surprisingly, she brought the cloth exactly as I wanted. Now for the tailoring . . .

Normally such things were sewn at home by one of the ladies on a simple hand-driven sewing machine or by a relative lady who knew better. I wanted it a day before the marriage, which they promised. However, due to everybody being so busy, it slipped out of their memory. The day arrived and it was not ready. I got "angry" and restive about it and I would not change my mind to wear something else after their pleas. Then my mother said that she would get it done. However, the lady who could have done it right was not at all available, so another lady who did not know much prepared it in the morning of my brother's marriage day. When they showed the pyjama to me, the cloth was the same but a big man or woman could have easily worn it! It wasn't my size. I began to cry loudly and was aware that no time was there to do anything further about it.

In those days, if the mother of the bridegroom did not get a hoarse throat for some days around the marriage time, she was not a mother! And she was supposedly the busiest woman in the house. When my mother came, hearing me crying loudly, she asked with quite a hoarse voice, "What's the matter?" The whole story was told to her. With hectic activities going on all around, she became angry and asked why couldn't I wear any dress out of the multitudes I had, some being new too. But my mind was set on this one. In the meantime, father happened to arrive on the scene and learning all about it, came to me and angrily said, "Don't you know it's about time for many guests to come and the marriage procession and party and ceremony? This is not the time to make a fuss about a pyjama," and he slapped me hard on my cheek two or three times and went away. My cheek was red, of course, and I didn't say anything further. Others thought it was resolved, but as they scattered away, finding an opportunity that no one could see me, I ran away from the house from the side door.

I went as far as I could to distant streets of the town, not knowing where I would go. It seems, as I learned later, they sent our maternal uncle, who was very strong, to find me. He was very close to our business, home, and family—very confidant. We all loved him very much and he was a friend of our family too. This uncle searched for me on the streets where I wasn't. After some time, whether I got tired or not, I got "homesick" and aware that it was the marriage day of my brother. Slowly I began to inch in closer to the streets of the home so that someone could find me and save me from the "ignominy" of "defeat" and coming back home by myself. Somewhere the same uncle happened to see me from a distance (which inside I wanted) and began to run to catch me. I pretended, feebly, to run away from him. Soon he overtook me and took me in his lap and clasped me firmly so that I didn't get myself free. I gave pretended efforts of doing that, but he was very strong anyway. He brought me home.

My mother and others received me very well and I wanted that too. She hurried me to go and take a bath, et cetera, which I did, and I wore a simple knicker and shirt. Actually it was a school uniform for sports! Then mother said, "Go to your father," who was sitting on a carpet with his many guests who had arrived by then. They were smoking a hookah turn by turn. I quietly went and bowed down to him. He was quiet and relaxed and put his hand on my head. I was not agitated by then, but in a peaceful and relaxed attitude and resigned—no agony of particular dress. I thought in the meanwhile, I was wrong and shouldn't have done all this to disturb everybody. As with the episode of the khadi dress on Freedom Day earlier, my attachment to fine clothes, though unknowingly, was reducing. At this time, my body was about twelve years old.

It was probably also in the early 1940s when I was at secondary school that, one afternoon, I went with a few friends to school, as usual, for sports. We arrived earlier than usual just to loiter there amidst the trees and mango orchard. When we reached, a few students had already arrived. The headmaster's son, who also lived with his family on the school's extensive premises and was a student there, happened to be there. We all sat down near the school building to chitchat. All of a sudden the headmaster's son, who was sitting facing one wing where the science laboratory was located on the first floor (the building was E-shaped), saw dark smoke coming out from one ventilator of the lab. He immediately got up shouting and running and saying, "Fire!" Some others joined and all rushed upstairs and began to break open the doors and ventilators by thrusting their bodies and hands against them. But the doors were very strong, French style, and they could see from the windows inside that the room was filled with fire and smoke. After trying very hard (nobody had keys and they were bolted very tight) somehow they succeeded and broke open one door to let the smoke out. The headmaster's son did not seem to mind for his life.

In the meantime, quite a number of employees and gardeners and even the headmaster in his housedress arrived running. Some went on bicycle to the nearby seat of the government to call the fire brigade. Not too late, the fire brigade machine—very primitive by any means—and police arrived. They did help somewhat and the fire was put out. Inside most of the furniture, chemicals and apparatus were destroyed, but since the building was made of bricks mostly and not much wood used except doors and windows, the fire did not escalate to other parts of the building.

By that time, many more students and staff had arrived for sports. The police allowed no one to escape the premises and searched everyone bodily, but no one was suspected. We heard them saying, "It's the work of some revolutionary students of this school, who after setting fire with kerosene and phosphorus from the laboratory, which used to be under lock and key, and then bolting doors and ventilators tightly, escaped." Of course, the laboratory remained closed for a long time. Though I had great sympathy with the Freedom Movement—nonviolent or not—I had "attachment" to the school too and I did not like this destruction.

The police rounded up the suspected revolutionary students from their homes and the school for interrogation. Not long afterward, they pinned down to some who had done it. After all, these were students and not hardcore revolutionaries, so it was not that difficult to pin down. Probably this was the first time they had done such things. This was the time of intense freedom movements all over the country.

Among the arrested ones, my cousin, the son of the rice merchant, happened to be one of the culprits, though not in the forefront. I loved him and sympathized with him. He was a few years older than me. He, otherwise, was so timid and docile, passive and quiet and sang well, so that nobody believed he could do it! However, the fact was a fact. His parents and all of our family were shocked and in fear. The elders tried their best among the known police officers and government officers to get him released. No one before had done such things in our family. They were basically businessmen and had contacts with English companies and thus had some privileges, which they might lose. Finally it all boiled down to: if my cousin would apologize in writing to the British Government and say that he had done wrong and would never do it again, they would release him unconditionally.

This was like a "death" to him. Many persuasions by elders, teachers and neighbors seemed to fail in the beginning, but ultimately he gave way and came back home. He later said that he apologized for the sake of the family. After that, his head would hang down a little and he became more quiet and subdued. In a few days he resumed school again, with head hung down. But a few revolutionary boys confronted him in the verandah and said, "You are a coward. Why did you apologize? You didn't do any sin. You did it in the name of the Freedom of the country. It is the English who are criminals. They colonized this country, illegally, dishonestly, like robbers and are real criminals . . ." But it was too late for this cousin and practically irreversible. This episode basically weakened further his resolves and crippled his conscience for the remainder of his life, as far as I know. My love, friendship and sympathy for him remained the same throughout and we often met and talked and heard music together, though we never talked about the revolutionary aspect again. I was too young at that time to be able to be involved in any way.

This same cousin, sometime later, fell in love with a daughter of a schoolteacher. In those days, for the kind of business family he belonged to and the small town, it was next to impossible to get approval of this match by parents. These were the days of common social custom arranged marriages. And moreover, his parents would like a girl from another business family. So there was sadness, distance between son and parents and depression for quite some time. They tried to explain to him a number of times, giving lots of logic, family history background, et cetera, to change his mind, but on this issue he would not give up. Some elderly relatives also tried to persuade him. In the meantime, they continued life together as usual. I don't remember how long this situation lasted.

In those days marriages used to take place quite young—after fourteen years the daughter's parents would search for the groom and after eighteen years for the son, at least in such families as ours. Since time was running short and my cousin would not change his mind, most reluctantly his parents gave in and, with the understanding that, though the marriage would be arranged through the family by the parents to put a profile in the society, but later he would have to live separately and support himself. This did happen subsequently. He remained a non-businessman, though middle class, with a job throughout his life, which I suppose he didn't mind.

About this time, during secondary school, my first "opening" happened, if you call it that, which, as I looked back after years would be called "spiritual." I was still a teenager when my elder cousin, son of the rice merchant, sort of came into my life. He was already quite religious, wore handspun clothes and was under Mahatma Gandhi's influence and tried to follow on his ideals. He believed in the nonviolence movement, though he seldom took any active part in it. He ran, almost single-handedly, a girls' school up to some lower grades on ideals not only of Gandhi but based upon the example of Mirabai, a known saint of the sixteenth century. This cousin was the first vegetarian in the family and was given separate quarters in the same building compound, behind my room. Although we met often and were living close by, we had not exactly conversed a lot. He was like an elder brother to me, relatively much older than me. I respected him.

One day, a book in his hand, my cousin came to my room, which was not unusual. He was matriculate and knew English fairly well. He said that he was reading this book and wanted to share a page or two or more if I wanted. The book was in English. My English at that time was very, very poor and hardly beyond the text books at school, and I studied those just for exams' sake. I said, "I don't think I can read it and understand beyond a line or two." He said the English in that book was very simple. The book was *In the Woods of God-Realization* by Swami Rama Tirtha, written early in the twentieth century.

Swami Rama Tirtha was a sannyasin, poet and Vedantist. Earlier in life he had been a professor in Punjab. He had been quite well known, but his early demise (at thirty-two years?) probably curtailed that. Also during that time, Swami Vivekananda arose in the firmament of India and abroad so much that he might have eclipsed Swami Rama Tirtha's stature.

Either my cousin pointed to a page or two or I opened at random, I don't remember. I tried to read and he helped me to understand it. The gist was—not verbatim—that there are circles within circles of our being: ego (self), family, town, province, country, world and beyond to the Real Self. Human beings do everything for the self, for little ego. Even noble sacrifices of a mother for her son are done for this self and so on. I could catch some glimpse of it, though not enough at that time. In a way, it clicked somewhere in me, but I could not fully analyze or grasp it. But it did attract me, I remember. For the time being, it all ended there and somehow I didn't repeat or continue further, so far as "spirituality" was concerned. There was another instance in which my elder cousin took me to an early morning congregation in the town a few times for study of some scripture, but that didn't last for long as I was so busy with my school, sports, hobbies, my library and radio, et cetera.

As the World War intensified in the early 1940s, we heard that many commodities from India were being dispatched to the military in England. Larkana had never witnessed ration cards, black market or a shortage of food items before. We had never seen any other cooking oil but pure ghee (clarified butter), which was brought to town by the surrounding villagers. Even "poor" people could afford it. To compensate for sending that to England, a certain company in Karachi produced vegetable oil called *dalda*. Whether it was healthy or not, people lamented it since it was not pure ghee. People of higher income bracket could still afford ghee, but there was a shortage. Other things that became scarce were laundry powder—though relatively a small thing, but the main livelihood of washermen and, of course, in homes—cloth, petrol, et cetera. Father had some wholesale agencies of some of these commodities; therefore daily there would be long lines at the shop to fill in their ration cards. He didn't have that much staff.

Often in those days, after our school hours he would call us to come and attend to that job. We did, but I remember, seeing all this, I was filled with sympathy but couldn't say or do anything about it, being so young. We didn't know politics then. Once my brother said, "Look, we are doing this for business and not to fall in bad books with the British. The Second World War is neither in India nor is it our headache, but of Europe. But the British are colonialists here and rulers; therefore the war is thrust upon us. We can't do much, at least now." I sort of understood it. Our relatives, some school teachers, friends, some neighbors and prominent people of the town had significant shortage of such things, which they got conveniently from father's business.

It was perhaps 1942, the peak of the Freedom Movement, when Gandhi and Congress Party leaders gave a declaration for the English to "Quit India" and go home. The atmosphere throughout the country was, as if, on fire and surcharged with grave consequences. Many prominent leaders, including Mahatma Gandhi, were put in jail. Earlier the Congress Party had held elections for their President, which was normal. Subash Chandra Bose, from Bengal, was one of the contestants in addition to Mahatma Gandhi's representative (Gandhi never sought any position; he was already Father of the Nation). Subhash, though a follower of Gandhi and a prominent member of the Congress, had nevertheless divergent views as far as nonviolence was concerned. After so many decades of the Nonviolent Movement under Gandhi, people in general had become restive and quite a number wanted something else. For this, Bengal and Punjab were in the forefront. By nature, Bengalis especially didn't believe in nonviolence and were mostly worshipers of *Maa Durga* and *Kali*.* Subhash was their product, although in his heart of hearts, he considered himself a disciple of Swami Vivekananda and had said that after India was free, he would become a sannyasi. Subhash was no less a patriot of India than anyone else, including Gandhi. He was a great son of Mother India and had been educated in England and secured the highest degree of education for India then available. When the results of the election

---

* *Durga* and *Kali* are two warrior forms of Divine Mother, as depicted in Vedic scriptures. Their fierce aspects are adopted for the purpose of eradicating ego to free devotees from the bondage of ignorance.

were declared, Subhash had won and Gandhiji's representative lost. It was one of the greatest surprises that time, even for those who had wanted Subhash to win.

Gandhiji, so far, had not lost. The next morning in the papers, Gandhi declared that the defeat of his representative was his defeat and therefore he would resign from guiding the Congress Party but not stop working for the freedom of India in his own way (not verbatim). The main objection was that then India's Freedom Movement under Subhash might take a different turn—and it might have, since one of Subhash's prominent slogans was, "Give me blood and I'll give you freedom," and that we should not beg freedom from the British but earn it. Subhash, being loyal to Gandhiji and a dutiful and loyal worker of the Congress Party, gave in and declared that instead of Gandhiji retiring, he would resign from the Presidency and thus Gandhiji's representative became the President. What went on behind the lobby is unknown to me. Details apart, afterwards, Subhash was put under house arrest by the British Government for some time, under some made-up law. And one day, even though under heavy patrol, et cetera, Subhash absconded.

From then on his story became a legend and inspired the whole nation. Again details apart, he managed to leave India incognito from the northwest and reached Europe and then by submarine reached Japan. There, after much labor and efforts, he won over some Indians there and Japanese. That time, the Second World War was on and Japan was in it. Subhash created an army with the Japanese helping him to win freedom for India. He marched from Eastern India and slowly came nearer to the borders of Bengal. The British, though themselves engaged heavily with Germany, sent their army outside Bengal. They knew that once Subhash and his army entered Bengal, and then slowly, the rest of India, the whole of Bengal would rise to one man for him. He was their hero and that of India by that time. He had won earlier the Presidency and the British knew it. Then the British created what was called then an "artificial famine" in Bengal. They moved most of the rice, which was Bengal's staple food, out of Bengal to break the Bengali spirit and their spine. People began to die in multitudes on the streets, in homes, on footpaths, everywhere. It was estimated that eventually three million Bengalis died. ["This is not the forum for producing evidences," He wrote here as a footnote.] The press, as usual, was censored and the news hardly reached the other parts of India except in trickles, hearsay and by mouth. The Indian leaders were aware of it but this was Subhash and not Gandhiji's movement. Refugees from Bengal scattered all over India and even as far as Sindh, the westernmost part of India (Bengal was nearly on the eastern corner of India). Even in remote areas, like our school, on the outskirts of Larkana, quite while the classes were in session, Bengali families would arrive at the doors and beg. This is how we came to know, when the refugees told the horrors of the artificial famine. The teachers used to collect small amounts from us and then give to the refugees. We never refused. My heart was sad.

What happened outside Bengal between the British and Subhash's army we didn't know, except that they had a fierce fight. The British, it seemed, "succeeded," at least for the time being. Subhash's end remained and remains a mystery up to this day. India waited many years for his return but it didn't happen. There were many theories but it was never declared officially. He was a great hero and a legend, and remains so till this day.

On Freedom Day in 1942, a meeting was held in Gandhi Gardens in Larkana, which had a tall tower, the normal venue for public meetings. The meeting by the town leaders on the ideals of Gandhiji was held in the early morning. Many people from the town formed the audience and sat on the lawns of the garden. On a small, low dais sat Bewas to conduct patriotic songs before the other speakers would come in. On one side of him sat a boy named Narayan and myself on the other to sing songs composed by Sai, which had been put to music by a local, well-known, patriotic singer. In my opinion, Narayan had a better voice than mine and I personally admired that, but I don't know why the majority would like mine. I still remember the haunting tune he sang on harmonium:

O soldiers of the nation, soldiers of peace, soldiers of reconciliation
Do good to others, never harbor revengeful thoughts to others . . .

The last phrase indicated the British. This was my first and last appearance on a public stage for the Freedom Movement.

In about late 1941 or early 1942, my immediate elder brother, who had married only a year or so before, fell sick. First it was taken to be an ordinary illness. A homeopath and later an ayurvedic *vaid* [doctor] were called, as normally we did. Days went by but he didn't get better. They suspected typhoid, with continuous fever, but again, no improvement. Slowly other doctors came, one by one, including an allopathic doctor, but there was no remission. The biggest doctor of the town came, who was English. Everybody tried and everyone had some theory; however, nothing worked. He became very weak and thin. No one could diagnose exactly; all were worried. Months passed. Brother was bedridden.

Then some friends and relatives suggested that we take him to Karachi city where there were more expert doctors. Soon he, his wife, mother, eldest brother and I and probably one or two more journeyed by steam train to Karachi. Father was distraught but stayed back home for the time being, for the rest of the family and business, et cetera. In Karachi the family had an apartment since there was a business branch already. No prominent doctor was left unapproached, but nothing better happened in brother's condition. He was becoming like a skeleton—knees stiffened, and he lay in bed twenty-four hours. In between, father came once or twice and stayed there. He was nearly heartbroken. His son's illness began to affect him and he fell sick too. Eventually even the military doctor, who was an American, was called too, with some influence. This doctor never attended to civil cases but he came. It took him hours to diagnose and he came up with some new theory, tried to treat him but it didn't work.

By now all avenues were, as if, closed. Father's condition too went on deteriorating. One day he called his eldest son near him and told him quietly that he felt his end was near, but he would like to die in his hometown of Larkana and not in Karachi, especially near his ailing son. The eldest brother was under much pressure with the family in two places and the business to look after, et cetera. The trip was arranged to take father, mother and me home and the eldest brother stayed with the ailing brother. Back in the hometown, the whole family was in gloom. The business was somehow being taken care of by other staff and uncle. The doctors tried to bring father back to health but it didn't work and he expired. It is not easy to calculate what his age was then, since no birth dates were kept in his day; maybe he was in his seventies. In the meantime, the eldest brother was called from Karachi to attend father's last days. Mother was devastated, as was everyone, including the uncles' families, relatives, et cetera. Father had been the head and backbone of many, not only of the immediate family. The world looked gloomy.

On the funeral day, as was the custom, it was arranged for a certain ceremony. There was not enough space to accommodate the large group. Unexpectedly the municipality of the town cleared the big road outside the main gate of the house and brought in a water-sprinkler machine (very primitive in those days) to put the dust and heat down. It was unusual that for this kind of purpose they went out of their way and covered the whole road with some carpets for people to sit on. Many hundreds came, as if the whole town—relatives, friends, business contacts, et cetera. Eldest brother, being all the time with father in business and home, knew father's contacts, but this was more than that. Many faces he couldn't even recognize. Even government officers, municipality staff and some foreigners came as well. Brother was also surprised. It was more or less a public affair. Father was known as a "successful" businessman, an ideal family man, but not a public figure as such. We didn't know that father's influence had spread so far and wide and so quietly—he was so unassuming. Although only locally known, he was a great man in his own way, if we go by the definition that "a great man is known not by what he accomplishes, but what he is."

Brother had to return to Karachi to look after the nearly dying brother. In those days, as per the custom, a widow had to remain at home for a year after the death of her husband. But since mother was older and her ailing son was in Karachi, it was taken easy by all when she too returned to her son. It was obvious to everyone. I returned too, and maybe one or two more.

During those days of the intense Quit India Movement, and Karachi being a hotbed for it, I learned that there was going to be a final thrust of the people when the leaders, local and from other parts of India, would come, lecture, inspire people, et cetera. The wide, main road, not too far from where we lived, was the venue. Large rostrums were erected right in the middle of the road and loudspeakers fitted. Thousands were supposed to attend and join the march, shout slogans, et cetera. Anything grave could happen, including violence. Many police vans were posted, and fear, panic and tumultuous outbreaks were in the air. We could hear some sounds from outside the apartment. It was partly my curiosity and partly my inner sympathy and love for India's freedom that made me slip out of the home, even though my dying brother was at home. The venue was in a walking distance. When I saw the whole thing, it was something. I had never witnessed such a sight. It was overwhelming, beyond my little brain. Freedom fighters were trying to reach the stage and police with heavy boots and helmets with heavy wooden batons in hand were trying to chase them away. There was literally a sea of people, which filled the whole road as far as you could see.

In the melee, many people were being *lathi*-charged,* mercilessly; many arrested and put in vans and leaders and people shouting slogans and trying to push toward the stage to speak to the people. It was chaos—pull and push was constant. I was on one side of the road near a wall, though crowded around by people running away. If not the only one, at the most I was one of very few boys of my age. Bicycles, shoes, and many things—name it—littered all over, impeding the march of the people as well as the police. I was literally caught and squeezed into the melee, even though on one side. At one point, while strong police came running after people to chase and lathi-charge from the opposite side, I could have been easily crushed, being quite a delicate boy! I fell down amidst many cycles and there was no way to escape or return anyway. In that wall there

---

* *Lathis* are police batons with which they beat crowds, criminals or dissidents.

was a door, probably to somebody's house. As police went by, many stranded people requested the owner to let them in to be safe. Though it was dangerous at that time to open any door, the owner fortunately opened it and some went in.

I tried to get in too but by that time the door shut, because the police were returning back. Luckily, the police didn't hit me, though I was quite in their route. Maybe seeing a young boy, or maybe their attention was overridden by a more dangerous situation to tackle? But amidst all that, though I had no choice but to perish, I was knocked down on fallen bicycles. The police passed by. I was not seriously injured, but bruised only. I tried to open the door and they did allow me in. After quite some time, when the roads were relatively clear and the police vans went away stuffed with freedom fighters, everywhere seemed a war zone. Finding an opportunity, I carefully retreated home. All were waiting with bated breath and worried. They asked me where I had gone. I, without details, told them. They also knew the impending situation and were surprised how I decided to go there under such conditions. I kept quiet. Then my mother came near me, sat down on the floor quietly and said, "You know about your father's death and your brother's condition. How could you do it? I don't want to lose you. Don't do it again."

The news of father's death was kept a secret from my bedridden brother and we all knew that it would be a death knell for him. But how long can you suppress such tragic feelings? It seems the brother must have noticed this on our faces, especially when he knew that father was taken home very ill. One day he confronted the eldest brother, looking at his face from a skeleton body and sunken eyes, and asked him directly if father was dead. Brother could say neither and kept quiet. It was an affirmation for brother in bed. Not long afterward, he died too, in the night. Family members by now were as good as dead. Soon afterward, my brother woke me up and gave me the news. I was sad and numb. He said I should go immediately to let some relatives and friends know who lived in the area of our apartment. It was still dark with streetlights lit. I felt nervous and "alone" on the way and I got a strong urge for number two. Finding a dark side of one street, I relieved myself, which normally we didn't do. Due ceremony and cremation was done at Karachi. Again many came, including business contacts and some doctors. Soon after, we all returned home to Larkana. Eldest brother now was our father figure, a loving and caring guardian. He gave us things and fulfilled our needs even more than before. We heard him saying, "I don't want you to feel deprived of anything because father is gone." He filled in the gap very well. Family and business carried on, as the world does. It had to. I slowly became busy with school again.

I was in the last year called matriculation of high school. I was about seventeen. Semifinals were conducted by our class teachers (finals would be by the province) and it was a Sindhi exam, one of the subjects in which I excelled. I still remember the first question in the question paper was to choose one out of four essays. When I read them, I was attracted instantly to one: "If you were the dictator of the world . . . ?" Though technically dictators were over in the Second World War, the air was still surcharged with it. Not that I liked dictatorship in principle, but perhaps I had read somewhere an essay about a pirate who was the Pirate of pirates on the sea who eliminated pirates for the good of others. I thought the so-called dictator could be benevolent to do good for people, using his powers. Normally an essay would be three to four pages of our answer supplement, but I got inspired, exhilarated, and spontaneously went on writing without looking back or correcting. Nearing the end of the supplement of ten pages, I got aware and ended in some way.

One of our students, much elder to us and not so bright, was a student as well as a colleague of our teacher. The former helped the latter in such occasions to go through the students' papers and assign marks under the supervision of the teacher. A few days later in school, he asked me how did I write that essay? I asked why. He said the teacher would talk with me. Soon after, the teacher came to me and said, "How did you write that essay?" I said I didn't know. He further said, "Do you remember what you wrote?" I said, "Not exactly except that I wrote that a benevolent dictator can use his powers for the good of people, et cetera." He asked again, "Who taught you all that you wrote in those ten pages?" I said no one; it poured out from inside and I was very inspired. Then he smiled and said, "It's a masterpiece, beyond your age. Do you mind if we keep this in the school archives and not give to you?" Of course, I had no objection.

College in Karachi

Since there was no college in Larkana in 1946, I had to be sent to Karachi and also live in the students' hostel (dormitory) just opposite the college. Since my bent was to philosophy and literature and not to science, I entered the Arts College (Humanities). The only subject I missed very much was mathematics, which was not a part of the Arts. There was no choice; I had to accept it.

In the hostel, I had a roommate who was a brilliant science student. We became good friends. But this was the first time I was away from our family after living constantly with them for sixteen years! I had mixed feelings, and part of me didn't like it. But what could be done? We had relatives in Karachi and they would have been glad to have me, but the atmosphere there was not congenial to my studies. I visited them sometimes though.

At college, when the classes started I was lost. There were about two hundred or more students in one class. Professors came and formally lectured while the students, especially the boys, were unruly, undisciplined and shouting while the professors turned a "Nelson's eye,"* exceptions apart, when the situation was out of bounds. Though questions to professors were allowed, hardly anybody would ask. I felt the students thought that to come to a college, they had a great freedom to do whatever they wished away from home. Studies didn't seem to be their first priority, for which they came to the college in the first place. Of course there were some quiet students, especially girls, but they were a minority. In the school at Larkana everything

---

* Nelson's eye: a "blind eye," coined after the British Vice-Admiral, Horatio Nelson, who, when ordered to retreat in 1891, in spite of a naval blockade, put the telescope to his blind eye and declared he could not see the signal.

was totally the opposite—not more than thirty to thirty-five students per class, personal contact between teachers and the taught, and discipline, et cetera. I didn't know what to do. We had just to scribble on our notebooks what professors said and go home. I was lost on both fronts—home and studies. This was the first year of Arts. Being fond of studies, I had to carry on. In college, the language medium was English in all subjects, including logic, economics and civics, including other languages, except the Sindhi class.

At the hostel we had kitchen/dining facilities. There was nothing bad or wrong about it, but I had never taken care of my meals in my seventeen years! So I did not and could not distinguish what I should eat or leave off. I was not a vegetarian at this time. Probably what was the major "culprit" for me in the meals they prepared was the cooking oil or ghee, which was used extensively, but I didn't know about it then or how to conduct myself. I had non-vegetarian food in restaurants also. During this year, I got my first case of jaundice. At first I didn't know what it was. I had never taken care of sickness before. I felt weak and some pointed out that I didn't look well. And relatives, when I visited them, diagnosed jaundice, since everything looked to me yellow. Mother had to come from Larkana and shifted me from the hostel to a relative's home temporarily to take care of me. I had to take leave from college, which was no problem since I did well in exams. Maybe after a month or so, after mother took care of a strict, non-oily diet with juices and, of course, medicines, I got all right and she returned to Larkana. I went and lived in the hostel again.

At college I tried to complete the arrears. Although technically the first year Arts exams were not taken seriously; however, they would reflect on the second years'—called "Inter Arts"—final results. As usual, I studied seriously anyway and passed in higher Second class, which was then equivalent to First class in science. Seldom had anyone in the school's history stood in the First class in Arts.

In those days in Karachi, I became fond of movies and cinemas were many there. I had no special dearth of money, which the family supplied. I made a point to see one movie a week and would not let go any movie unseen. There were all Hindi movies, though English movies did come since Karachi was a cosmopolitan city. At one time I became unreasonable in personal expenses but I wasn't seeing that. My eldest brother, when he visited me next, pointed this out to me. He said he didn't want to squeeze me for reducing expenses, which he never had done, but he couldn't understand on what I spent so much since I had no bad habits like smoking, drinking, et cetera, all of my clothes were tailored and came from home, and college fees were all paid by them. He was right; I was, to say the least, "squandering" the money without much thinking, and probably this was the first time that money was "freely" available to me. I apologized and became cautious afterwards to their satisfaction.

I suppose it was the same year that the following incident happened. The hostel gate, which was quite big, of iron with spikes on top pointing upward, used to be closed at a certain time in the night about 9:00 P.M. The compound wall was of stone and quite high. This particular day I had gone to see a movie. I didn't think of the timing and when I returned, the gate was shut as usual. I didn't want to wake up the gatekeeper and wanted to avoid the news to the superintendent, who could then take action against me. So I tried, very cautiously and fearfully, to climb up the grilled gate, which wasn't a big problem, but crossing those spikes was very dangerous—at least for me! Eventually I did succeed and came inside. My roommate was awake and remarked that perhaps I had gone to a movie. I said "yes" and we talked about it a little; then I went to bed. While lying there, I couldn't sleep somehow. I searched my mind as to why? Then I remembered that on my way back from the bus stop after the movie on the main road, when I came to the footpath of our college where it was dimly lit and a quiet area, a side street, I had seen a beggar or a poor man lying on the footpath covered with a thin sheet. It was winter and cold. While lying down still, I saw that I had two blankets, though normally I used only one. I tried to sleep but no luck. I thought—*at least I have a room with a cozy bed,* et cetera. The poor man had hardly anything and was sleeping under the sky. I quietly got up so that my roommate wouldn't notice. Though the hostel was all made of stone, the floors and stairs were all of wood.

I took my sandals in hand and walked out of the room. Though my friend might have heard the sound of the door of our room opening, thinking I might be going to the restroom, he went back to sleep.

Quite silently I walked downstairs with one blanket in my hand. Outside in the compound, crossing the gate and spikes again was a problem, but so what under these circumstances! Cautiously I climbed over the gate, then went on the opposite footpath, spread the blanket quietly on the man on the footpath, and returned in the same way. Normally this wouldn't be a big deal to do, even before others, but in my case it was the first act of "charity." I had never done this before on my own. In the next summer vacation when I went home, my mother, who used to pack and unpack my bedding, luggage and personal belongings for Karachi, opened the bedding and, as shrewd as she was, commented that one blanket was missing! I certainly lied and said, "I don't know, maybe you gave me one blanket?" She, of course, didn't buy it and after a little discussion, she suggested that I had given it to someone. I couldn't lie further and admitted it. She asked why did I lie? I said that she might not like what I did with it. She asked whom I gave it to. Without many details, I told her the truth. She didn't comment further but said, "Why had you to lie about it?" The matter ended.*

---

* Gurudeva's handwritten pages ended here.

3

Renouncing Home
Early Glimpses

How long has it taken you to get this peace?
Peace was ever with me. My peace was never
disturbed. Who will disturb it?
As a child, did you never fight with a neighbor?
I am not a child.

*T*en-year-old girl in America: *Did you go to college?*

Gurudeva: I did. You know, I didn't graduate. I was an undergraduate—short of graduation. Two years of college I finished, then I left. At that point I saw: it's no good. I thought there's something more to know than graduation would give me. I'm not blaming the college. College is good for certain things, but I felt I was not going anywhere. What shall I gain? There's something more. To find *that,* I left home and went to Himalaya* and meditated. So how would I have the answers? We worked for it. Knowledge awakens. So how did I answer all the questions I heard? It's a very difficult question for me to answer. Simply, if I say I *knew,* it sounds egotistical, but that's what it is, no? How would you answer otherwise, if you didn't *know.* And what is *knowing*? It is just being conscious. I did go to college; otherwise you wouldn't have liked me. I was a musician also. Artist. You want to know more?

Yeah.

Well, it's God's grace, not me. Do you understand? It is grace of the Lord. Without God we are nothing. When you grow, you will understand, if you remember this. College has something to give, but I saw the end of it.

What made you choose Himalayas?

---

* In India, the Himalayan Mountains are often referred to as "Himalaya," singular. That is why Gurudeva's first book was titled: *Spirit of Himalaya.*

It's age-old ancient beacon light or attraction in India for the sages and saints. Himalayas are lofty. They attract. To go and be in quiet forest or cave or high natural places will give you good growth in spiritual matters. They have good vibrations.

Were you very spiritual in college?

At that moment? Not knowingly. Inside, yes, but I didn't know. But when I left and went to the Himalayas, gradually I meditated. I knew that I'm spiritual inside. That came out.

Parent: *Through to your consciousness?*

Right. That was afterwards, not during college time. In college I did as every boy and girl does who goes to college. Parents told me to go and I did. But at that point, I didn't know what I would want next. I entered the third year of college, and since it's coming up—I'm sorry to talk about myself—I was a very brilliant student. Number one. Even then, I thought—*this is no good for me.* I wasn't a dull student, by God's grace. And I loved studies—my homework was number one. I didn't want friends; I hardly had any. I was busy with studies and studies and music. And I used to read novels in those days. Beyond that, I didn't have any life, nor much friendships or parties. We didn't have those things. In spite of how I loved my studies—hours daily— I left it. I thought it has its end, going round and round.

Young girl: *Do you wish you had more friends? Like, if you could go back, would you want more friendships?*

Not now. Now you're my friends.

When you were in college, did you wish that you had more friends?

No. Even the few, one, two or three I had—not bosom friends, not very deep—I used to consider at that time that they were wasting my time. Not that friendship is bad or wrong—don't take it that way. I thought friendships were taking away my time and energy. I wanted to study, study, to attend to my studies. I never missed any one period or class in school or college except when I was sick. When other students in college would disturb the class for any kind of thing, I used to hate it. When friends came home to talk to me, I would briefly talk to them so that they would go away and I could study. I wasn't seeking friendship in a way. One or two good friends are okay, but when you have a host of friends, wasting time and energy, you'll see those students do not come out well. Their results will not be good.

With too many friends, you often end up in parties and other things and lose studies. This was my experience. I didn't avoid friends; I just wanted to study. I was very studious and brilliant. In those days they didn't have A-B-C grades; they had first, second, third, fourth and so on. I was a very successful student and singer. Later on I took up musical instruments, the sitar, et cetera. All of these were fine, but they were not giving me knowledge. And, I wanted knowledge, that's all—to *know*. As a matter of fact, in those days the first sentence that came to me was—*why don't I go around the world and read the open book of the world?* That was my own sentence at the time, when my age was eighteen. I left home at nineteen—not like dropouts in America. Drugs and dropouts—that's quite different. We call it renunciation. Dropping out is a different thing.

The very first thought that came to me—*I have to know myself, and let me read the open book of the world. That's my great knowledge.* And that I did: social work, helping the poor, working with refugees I did for some time, about two years. But then also I saw that helping the miserable, the refugees—and I was hardly nineteen or twenty at that time—was tremendous work. Even then, I got the answer that if I have not solved myself, if I have not known myself, how can I help others? That was my second discovery. First was the open book of the world, when I went to serve the refugees on the border of India and Pakistan, and so on. I'm telling you: if I didn't know myself, how could I know if what I was doing was right or wrong either? Even though it looks great to help poor people, the destitute, and refugees, still I wasn't satisfied. Then I left for the Himalayas for meditation. And that gave me all the answers.

I wouldn't egotistically claim: "I know all the answers." No, that is not the way I am saying. I have no *questions* now. If you ask me a hundred questions, I may not reply to all one hundred, but that doesn't mean I don't have answers. I don't need any. I have received the answers to all my questions. This is not a tall claim. I am just honestly saying this. I may not have answers for all your questions, but I have the answers for all my questions. And I don't have questions anymore. And *that* is born out of That.

I was lucky that at the age of eighteen or nineteen I got this hunger for searching. I have sometimes regretted—not now, earlier—why I didn't start searching when I was aged five. I have sometimes asked myself—*why at eighteen? Why not when I was five or six?* Of course, we have no answer for that. I wasn't awakened at that time, naturally not. But the time it came to me, by eighteen or nineteen, I had left home to find the answers.

Now I don't mean to tell you to leave home. Here dropouts are many in America. But they drop out for different reasons, you see? It is quite different with a sleeping bag and hippie life and drugs. That is a further waste of energy. But if you have a search, that's quite different. That makes you a prodigy. So when [this child] asked me today how did I know the answers to questions, I didn't learn those things. They came out of me, from within. It is what we call creative, not learned. Some are born musicians; some learn music and play. People like *Shine*, for example, the pianist. Did you see that movie?

I didn't see the movie.

You should see that. Some are born that way. Einsteins are born, they are not taught in laboratories and science classes. Those geniuses are a different breed altogether.

So do not drop out, unless you have a motive, and high motive— that would be different, but not because Swamiji did it. If you do that, you are going to go to hell. It has to have a motive and purpose. And that has to be a higher purpose.

If all your questions are answered, do you still have levels that you want to reach?

It's done. You can't see it, but . . . I'm sorry to reply in my personal way, I don't normally do that, but since you're asking me . . . I may not reveal everything. Why? It's very obvious. Because not everything I'll reveal will you understand anyway, so what's the use? I will only reveal to the extent I think you can catch it or understand it. This Consciousness is the Source of everything. Everything comes out from It. All our ears, eyes, nose work out of this. If Consciousness was not there, the nose wouldn't smell, ears won't hear, and you wouldn't be there. Call it by any name you want—God or Light. There are many names.

REFUGEE CAMP OF BENGAL AND CALCUTTA EXPERIENCES

As you have seen since years, I have been reluctant and unwilling to talk about myself. Yet it is hard to communicate with devotees and disciples on and on for years and not to say anything about me, who will be the figure there, of course, as a Guru, Master, whatever. Naturally it is not possible to avoid talking about myself. Sometimes it has come out, and if you remember, many times I would say, "Erase the tape," even though I really only spoke a tiny bit of the whole story out of reluctance to talk about myself. Although I am not a general, popular Guru, in the sense, I could have been easily, *easily*. So I didn't talk about myself in public, but since yesterday, or maybe a little earlier, a slight inclination has been in me, or I should say, less reluctance than before to talk about myself.

I feel it judicious enough to say that by God's grace, I am not after my self-advertisement or name and fame. To me that is trash. If the truth shines by itself, well and good—I will not suppress the truth— but to advertise myself just has no value. This has kept me from talking, even though there are a million details and anecdotes, stories, high achievements and spiritual things that would benefit some people, I'm sure. Since years I have been choosing and selecting and reducing the group to hear me for the simple reason—I am telling you my secret— to come down to my real ones, the genuine souls who are *with* me inside, to whom I could open my heart one hundred percent.

There are three stages of describing this life. One, as an ordinary descriptive story or biography, as you call it: I was born in such and such year, at such and such place, went to school, college, did this, this, this and these were my friends; my parents were like this; my sisters and brothers were like this; I met these holy people and did this and that. Then I went here and there, I had a Guru or no Guru, I studied and then I realized and came back to the world to enlighten everybody. That is one description. And if I were to go by this biographical way, literally it would be very engrossing and enthralling, which by Ganesha's grace I could do! But this is just a surface touch, skin deep, a descriptive history. The historical way of looking at things is not, I'm sorry to say, the oriental way. If you were to judge through a historical viewpoint, it will not be the oriental, spiritual way of looking. Does that mean India has no history? Now it has, since occidental people came and wrote the history. Sages such as Valmiki did not write history, they wrote epics. They knew that the kings and battles are not the only part of the history, that the sages and cultural side is needed for a perfect history. But it depends, as I heard people in America saying in earlier times, upon who writes the history. That is worth thinking about. When sages wrote the epics they were not one-sided historians or Indologists. This is the difference.

This is my second—if you call it—dilemma: I did not want to give a historical biography. What if I become great in the world one day and everyone knows me, or after my death? Then who writes the history makes a difference. An ordinary history or biography I do not value much, not only about sages and people like me, but even about nations and governments. It is a really shallow view of things. Therefore historians often differ from each other and discuss so much. They just have viewpoints. To some, Alexander the Great was a great chivalrous hero, worthy of worshiping or something. To others, while having so many qualifications and attributes, he could still be a conqueror, an invader and an exploiter. Maybe he was better than Hitler but that does not cancel that he was a conqueror, invader and killer. It depends who is writing the history. Therefore I've avoided this first kind of biographical sketch, just to mention years and times and dates.

The second way of presenting my life is a deeper one, what we call a *marma** way of writing, as a sadhubaba, a seeker, a disciple who went through various stages of practices, achieved this and this and this. And great things can be told in this marma stage that would be very inspirational and provide guidelines for many seekers. Lord Krishna's life or Jesus' forty days in the desert or Buddha's five years of sadhana are given in this way. They did tapasya—penances—meditations, searched and avoided temptations and so on, but as we know now or look back two thousand, twenty-five hundred or five thousand years, we know they are Prophets, Incarnations. Krishna went to Kailash and did tapasya practices as if to become Realized. The sages told him, "You do not need to do these things, Lord. Why you are doing this?" He replied, "I am doing for you." Now, although it satisfies everyone to hear what the Lord did for us—who is going to reject the idea?—but actually that is not perfect truth either. Did Krishna tell a lie? No, that was simply the way people understood him, so he said that way.

What is the truth? He did not have to do this, even for others. He did so that others would also do such practices. If he did not do this, some might say, "Oh, the Lord did not even do this, why should we?" If he had worn only one shoe, people would have started wearing one shoe also and the second foot naked. He did it to create an example. He could have done his mission in spite of doing for you. So what is the implication? I am coming to a third stage now. What if he already came Perfected and Enlightened, as a Prophet? He did not have to do these practices stage by stage. And then which stage of the life sketch should I give? What if the second stage proves not to be me? But if I say this—and this is a crucial point—some will say: "He's another fake Christ coming, one of those Jesus freaks, you know . . ." So the only method left to me was to keep quiet about myself. I could not be nonsensical. Revelation does not destroy logic, normally not, but logic proves the revelation. Whatever I may speak or write with literary acumen, very great competency, rationality and invoke Ganesha to come to my aid and write for me, even then, which

---

* *Marma*: "a deeper or vital meaning."

stage should I describe? That has been the dilemma. If I am giving the first stage, I am not me. If I am giving the second, I am also not me. And the third I may be—and if I am—it will be considered a blasphemy to many people. So I kept quiet. Whichever it is among the three, this is where the problem is. However, since your curiosity is not extinguished yet, I will tell a little more.

I have said that at one point I could have entered politics in India. Up to that point, I had no revelations about myself and my mission. Now this should not mean that I was ignorant; there is a stage that these things open up. When the Prophets, Self Realized Beings or high grade Masters take a five-elemental body, some of the limitations and conditions of the earth and body do play on them from birth. Then at the age of five years, ten, fifteen or twenty, they get revealed. The age is not the same in all.

When by God's grace I left home, there are too many details, millions; you will have to stay on till twelve o'clock in the night. When I left home, renounced as we call it, my idea was not clear why I was leaving. One thing was clear: I was not confused. I am just looking back and telling you the story. At that time, I was not confused. I just had—I'll relate to the present—the thought that I love people in general and I want to do something for them. Buddha's sentence, "To help miserable mankind" was uppermost in me. I was not thinking spiritually, politically or socially; I was just doing it smoothly and peacefully. I had no struggle in me at all. I did not go through that at all. It was smoothly revealing or unfolding in me, creatively.

I renounced home and came to Calcutta in Bengal. I do not want to go in too many details, but that first fifteen days I had only two meals and I was sleeping on the footpath. You may ask: "Swamiji, why didn't you directly go to the Himalayas or to a Guru?" My idea was not clear yet. I wasn't confused either; I just was drifting into something. And I had left college and everything. Before leaving home, my earthly mother had tried her worst and best to keep me from going, not only because she was attached—that's apart. She had ten, twelve children, I think. Normally they would have liked me to run a business with my brothers, earn money and make a home. And my mother, though she was a pious woman, she was not out-and-out for her children renouncing and leaving her. She was not ready for that. And I was too young yet, in a sense, to explain to her logically and lovingly. I was not yet opened up. I was drifting, not aimlessly; it was smooth and peaceful. So when mother had tried everything to keep me with her, "Whatever you need: if you want to distribute money to poor people, I'll give you, no questions asked." I told her, "No, I've not come on earth only to help poor people. That may be a good action, but I'm not born for that."

And I did not know at that time what I was born for; I was eighteen years of age. She tried her pleas: "We won't ask you questions. Go to the business as many hours as you want and help your brother." And I was at that time qualified to help him because my father was dead and another middle brother was also dead. I was the only one to go and help him and I was still in the college. She said, "At least finish graduation," but I said, "What shall I do with it?" "Oh, it will help you." I wasn't sure that time about anything. Naturally she tried everything she could but I told her, "No, it's not for me." I had one stepbrother who was blind, and he said, "Why don't you say what you want?" I said, "I wish, brother, it was clear to me. It isn't. The only thought I have is to help miserable humankind in some way that I could serve." At that time I was only thinking of India, no doubt about it. And my patriotism was uppermost too.

Then when I was in Rajasthan, in Ajmer* town, mother came there to give her last, best shot. And when everything failed—for her at least, not for me—she did the last, worst thing, which I wasn't expecting. In India, sons bow down to their mother and father as well as to elder brothers, uncles and elders. This is very common in every home and we did it all the time. When all else had failed, mother wanted to have privacy with me in her room. Here to have a private talk is common but in the Orient or India, there is nothing like that. She did ask me to speak with her privately and she closed the door.

---

* Ajmer is located in central Rajasthan, 130 kilometers southwest of Jaipur, on the Ana Sagar Lake, created by a Maharajah in the 12th century.

I did not know what she was going to do—slap me, or God knows what! Earlier she used to sit on the ground but later she had a little fall so her shoulder or something was affected and she could not sit down on the floor. So she sat in a chair and I sat in a chair too.

She said, "You have refused all my suggestions," and without asking me, spontaneously she put her hands on my feet, which no mother does in India, to make me please not go. I said, "Mother, I'm very sad to see this. You're sad and I don't want to hurt you, but this one thing I can't do. My one foot is already out. Ask me anything else." She said then her last wish. She had met in Ajmer somewhere a traditional Brahmin, an astrologer and palmist who used to live outside a ruined temple. He wasn't well known or a great advertised astrologer but he was a saint as well as astrologer. She had faith in him. She thought I would refuse this proposal when she asked me to come with her to him. I said okay and when I saw him I was really attracted. He was a good saint, a Brahmin with a little golden turban and so on. He was sitting on the dirt ground and we sat there too. I do not think he was after money. He looked at my face or brow and my hand and he didn't say many words. Mother was expecting probably that he will say something to make her happy and I had bated breath waiting to hear what he would say. Not that I had no faith in astrology or palmistry and so on, but I never thought about these things at that time. I was a young man, a young boy rather, making my own destiny, so I did not care for this.

For some time he studied me, my fingers, this, this, whatever he did. Then he looked at mother and said, "Don't force him." I'm repeating his words. He said, "Don't check him," meaning: Don't make him stay. He added, "He will be either a king or a Buddha." To me he said, "This life is not for you." Of course, mother's whole hopes, as we say in an Indian proverb: it was as if ink was strewn on her face. She got terribly disappointed; there was nothing she could do or say. I got a little delighted, but seeing mother's face I kind of curbed it. I thought—*I won't show my happiness.* She was just there; it wasn't a private meeting with him. By king the Brahmin, being a traditional astrologer, meant a prime minister or president in today's world. I am telling you this because, unfortunately, if I don't tell you the real facts, I am not telling about me. But clearly it is in my horoscope and later on was confirmed when I began to consult with astrologers more, and still do sometimes.

I saw this later in a refugee camp, when I began to do something, though not from a political point of view—I did purely from a view of helping relieve humanity's pain and misery. But what came out in some months only, I still remember. They had a mobile court on the station platforms after I had hijacked the train, or rather myself and Ranjit, "Tom Sawyer and Huckleberry." I was a different personality at that time! I could easily be so tomorrow, if I want to act that way, but that is not "me." I remember that when they held the court, the judge said, "You broke the law," and I replied, "What are these rules or laws for—the maintenance of refugee security and their sustenance and helping them to find a home?" He said, "Correct." I said, "What do you call that, obeying the letter of the law but not the spirit of it?"

And he said, "Yes, but the law we cannot break." I said, "Look, all platforms were full with refugees, thousands of people, and so many people dying, children crying, no food, no milk, and so on. And I knew another train was going to come at 2:30 A.M. I had no space for more refugees . . ." I was the superintendent and had forty-five volunteers under me, which later on reduced to twenty-two. I'm coming to why I'm telling you this story. I had the very least amount of volunteers, but still day and night everybody was working. There were nine organizations on the platforms, including the Red Cross, YMCA, Marwari Relief Society, East Bengal Medical Unit, and Congress Party. The YMCA supplied a few beds and medical assistance, Red Cross gave milk powder, Marwari Relief Society gave some blankets, clothes, snacks and breakfast, the Bharat Seva Sangha, which is now an all-India organization, gave rice and dal and other food. I was not a Congress Party man, but I was given that duty to sign the papers for camps and so on, so I had high authority. So when the judge was questioning me about the train, I said, "Look, new refugees were coming in the night, cholera was rampant, millions of flies flying around, unhygienic . . ." you know—it was hell, living hell, if you had seen it. I wasn't concerned about the hell; I was just working madly day and night with the other volunteers. So I said, "Look now, your train was standing on the tenth platform and you were looking to the rules and laws, and you refused to send the train. I was seeing the camps that there was going to be a tragedy that night. I had to take the things in my hand"—I did say that.

The judge asked, "Who are you to take things in your hand?" I said, "I don't know, but I thought to help these people." And I was the only non-Bengali in the multitude of Bengalis. The reason I am saying this is because there is a racial thing there too. Well, eventually the court heard me and ultimately decided to let me go. But as a parting shot, the judge said, "But never—this is a warning—never do it again." Then I said a memorable line, which later brought a senator, actually, from East Bengal. I said, "If you people and your government stop playing dirty politics, which create directly or indirectly these millions of refugees, I won't break the law." I said this and all were stunned. Of course, he let me go. He thought, there's more trouble there, I think.

As I looked back later, I knew if they had arrested me that thousands of refugees, who really loved me and knew I was giving my blood and heart to them, would have smashed their offices right there. But at that time I was not thinking of whether they would have released me. However, the judge let me go anyway. I told him, "I could play politics with you, but I'm not a politician." Later when a senator came to the railway station, they stopped the train just for her to see me, as she had heard all this. She wasn't angry. Only one year back, India was liberated; Mahatma Gandhi was dead. I had inside a secret wish that I didn't tell anybody because my spiritual side was not yet fully opened; therefore I was thinking patriotically of India's poor. I had a secret wish, after Mahatma Gandhi's death when no one was filling that seat, to fill that vacuum, not inside the government but outside the government. Therefore I was a volunteer.

I didn't have any money; there was nothing I needed, just one meal a day and a place to lie down in the tent. So when this lady senator came, who was over the refugee rehabilitation center, she said, "I've

After return from Himalayas, on His mother's request to wear worldly attire,
Mumbai (Bombay), June 1960

Uttarkashi, outside of hut where He had stayed during sadhana days, c. 1965

Bombay Airport, departure for second visit to U.S.A., 1974

coat like what we called a *babuji*.* He was attracted to me, somehow, and I was in poor shape of dress, like Mahatma Gandhi, exactly like that, and he said until I found a job or my solutions, he wanted to rent a room and live together, just to give me a kind of support. I didn't have any money. I got jaundice; that's a big story.

Calcutta at that time was too crowded, dirty and unhygienic. Now it's worse, and that time it was bad enough. This was in 1949 or 1950. He engaged or rather rented a room in not only a poor area but a very noisy, dingy, unhygienic area. Don't take it seriously but it was one of the dirtiest spots he chose. I had no choice at the time; I was too poor to even think about these matters, and he was polished, daily shaved and would go to office. In that time—call it my subconscious or whatever inside me began to come out—I began to pray or meditate on my own. I had not even read books of that kind nor had I come up to that point. I had not come in contact with any holy man or great man or sage except some political leaders I had met. So in the evening during sunset or so, we divided that one day he would cook and one day I would cook, which I never did. I hated to cook. So he used to cook our meals outside the room on a coal burner. The room was one; we slept in the same room.

During that time I had started some music lessons, like sitar and so on, just to find the way and cultural side. All this happened within a few months. And in the same time, I had started praying. Nobody had told me, but on my own, morning and afternoon, I would say very brief prayers and then meditate. There was an understanding between this friend of mine that whenever I was in the room meditating or praying, he would not open the door, and that door was just two planks, rugged. I used to turn off the light, which was only a single naked bulb hanging down into the room. We didn't have any furniture, just a cement floor, and we just slept on a kind of mat. I used to daily pray and meditate for some time in the evening and he used to cook.

---

* *Babuji*: a colloquial term for a rich or educated man who emulates Westerners, especially in dress.

He didn't like to cook either, but between the two I was the worst, so naturally he ended up doing it every day, unfortunately. But he loved me very much; we were two good friends.

One evening I was meditating inside the room—this he told me later on; I wasn't aware at the time. I wasn't seeking; I had no goal to speak of, and I was not focusing on anything, just praying to Divine Mother. I started praying to Her because Dakshineswar, the Kali Temple, was only a mile or so away, and I was feeling the vibrations of vicinity of Divine Mother on the Ganges. I began to pray to Her because I did not know any other God yet, though I didn't know Her either. Dakshineswar was about a mile away from this dirtiest area that I would never go to again. I did not care for that but rent was cheap, dirt-cheap. I did not regret the room; I regretted the locality. I'm holding back, but anyway . . . So, what happened was, that evening was my first revelation in spiritual aspiration. I was just praying, knowing nothing about God or Goddess yet. I was not choosing Divine Mother either, but I knew there was some Kali Temple in Dakshineswar, so She is kind of nearby, so I began to pray to Her. And all of a sudden—I won't go into details—my first Darshan—tremendous, *tremendous* floodgates began to open. I forgot where I was—the room—everything. I won't describe the experience. That was my first "close encounter" with Divine Mother and Light and everything—tremendous, tremendous. I was not ready for that, in a way, but I took it in good stride, I think. What happened that night changed my life, in the sense, and soon after, the next year, took me to the Himalayas. That experience finished that possibility given by the astrologer of being President or whatever. It was trash to me anyway. To some this may be over your head, but this is the story where my spiritual journey began.

I was hardly nineteen or twenty—somewhere in between—and that young man with me was, I think, one or two years older, or perhaps twenty-four. During that meditation, many things—everything—was revealed to me: my mission, revelations, everything, but I will not describe that now; maybe one day with a few near ones. What happened was, later my friend came and sat down while looking at me. I said, "What's the matter, Sushil?" His name was Sushil. He said, "I'm sorry, I opened the door today. You had forbidden me." I said, "What did you do? I didn't see it." He said that it was dark inside—the doors didn't clap this way; a little bit of leakage was there and he knew there was darkness inside, as he had put the light off. He told me, "I was cooking and all of a sudden, through those two panels, I saw light inside shining, very vibratory. I got curious that I had put the light off, how is the light on there? So I opened the door slowly, peeked in, and you were something else."

I knew what he was talking about because I had the revelations, so I kept quiet. I didn't confirm or deny. He said, "You were something else. I'm sorry I came in." I said, "No, it's okay." I didn't talk much; I wanted to avoid him. He started talking about food and that to me was talking about hell. I controlled myself and did not reveal what had happened. I went out, to avoid him, and then something else happened on that very crowded, dirty, place of tramcars and roads. Here I was, walking through garbage with bare feet, like a kind of cowdung, and things began to happen right on the road. This is where my political career, if ever it would have happened, ended. Thank God or not—God knows which way, because I wanted to help India at that time, filling in Gandhi's seat. I knew and had told that Senator lady that all these rules and laws are wrong; they should change. These are all from colonialist rule. And secondly I added, which she wasn't prepared for: "They don't know India's *karmas*. They don't know India's vision and how to take India to fulfillment, and therefore I won't join this government. They don't have any vision of India. I want to take India to the right place." I didn't talk about world or international; at that moment, my limits were India.

Whether it was right or wrong, God knows, but this was my first revelation. It was in Bandaghat, hardly a mile away from Dakshineswar. Of course, then I came in contact with the Ramakrishna Mission and visited Ramakrishna's room in Dakshineswar. That's how it started, right there. This Mother, you know, She's kind of something. She spoiled me. That's how my life changed to spiritual. And my friend—whether God planned it that way or not—he was a fine, healthy young man, and while still living there, after some months he died of meningitis. We all tried our best—doctors, whatever we could afford. His parents came from their village, his brothers; he didn't have sisters. We were keeping ice on his head, everything, and trying our best. Doctors came but gave up hope; they did not have a cure at that time for meningitis. His mother and father were very sympathetic to me actually rather than I was with them, and he died in that very room one night. I was very sad to lose him. I wept when he died.

Then after years, when I was in Himalayas, I thought maybe God didn't want to reveal my identity to anybody, and this boy happened to see. That was one explanation. God didn't want him to carry anywhere who am I. A second interpretation came to me later: maybe this boy having my Darshan—whatever it was that he saw—it gave him salvation, so that his life on earth was over. So that's the story of my spiritual awakening. Everything was revealed—whatever I have to do. Somehow Divine Mother caught hold of my neck, and since then I've been trying to make myself free from Her—I'm not able to yet. I tell Her, "Why don't You leave me? " but She really caught me. That's how it started. I just prayed in a simple way like a child. I didn't know this whole thing was going to happen . . .

This boy died, so I left the room and slowly moved to a southern rural area outside Calcutta where I stayed for some time. There, again, I began to have revelations and revelations and revelations. There was a small river there and a small hut that belonged to one sadhu, Bharati Baba, who is dead now. He gave me a room free and I stayed there for some time. Things began to happen: revelations and mantras and visions and I just could not hold them; I was overwhelmed. The only course left was to go to the Himalayas. While staying there—it was called Tollygunge—some small glimpses came that one day I may have to go to America. That was the year 1950, I think, but I did not want to entertain that thought. And this is how the spiritual life started thoroughly.

Details are so many. It would take an encyclopedia to describe my life. Alone that Vision, if I tell you . . . I had not done any practices or meditation per se. The subconscious would not bring that much up either. And I was not talking or mixing with anyone. I had no more friends; ate one simple meal each day. In that place, Tollygunge, I used to go by bus from the town sometimes, and those non-government buses generally have a mirror in front. People are crowded all the time and now it is worse. One day I was standing, holding the rod, and it was crowded. From the bus stop it was a dead end and I had to walk about ten minutes to the rural area to my hut. I was a perfect Bengali by that time. I had picked up the Bengali dress—everything Bengali. Nobody could recognize that I was not Bengali, which was my inner thirst, in a way. I was standing in the bus and lights were on and my face must have been visible in the mirror. At the end of the bus line, I got down along with one tiny older man who had white clothes and looked like a saint or a sage with a white beard. He was elderly, in his seventies or so, and I heard him as if calling me from behind after we got down. He said, "Wait a minute, who are you?" It turned out that he was an aura reader, a psychic but also a saint. He was a disciple of the great yogi of Puri, India, Yogajivananda, who this man later told me was on his deathbed. This gentleman had a musical instrument shop in downtown Calcutta but more or less he was on the spiritual path.

He described to me that, as he was looking in the mirror in the bus, "All of a sudden, I saw something in you. You're not an ordinary man." This was the time I was having revelations and I was walking like an ordinary social being among the people. I did not have a sadhu dress yet. He said "I saw something in you, your face and head. I want to talk to you . . ." And I was avoiding everybody during that time except God or Divine Mother. We became great acquaintances later, and so on and so forth. That locality where I stayed was where the father-in-law of Ravi Shankar lived, Mr. Nandi. And the story went around a little and Ravi Shankar's elder brother, Udhay Shankar, the dancer who is no longer living, and his wife Urmila Shankar, a great

dancer, probably still living but an old lady—these acquaintances
started. I wanted to avoid them, however. That is why I stopped seeing
them and went to the Himalayas.

I played sitar at that time in the evenings. I was not a great player,
an amateur even among amateurs, probably. In the next hut there
was a middle-aged homeopathic lady doctor; she was renting, I think.
She came one morning and said, "When you were playing your sitar,
what a beautiful music." I said, "Last night, even *I* was amazed at how
I played sitar, because I have not practiced and learned that much."
It was as if I was listening to my own playing, which I had not practiced
that much. Even while playing, I knew that either somebody else is
playing, or my future me when matured was playing. It was in me—
music perfection. What she described the next morning was that she
saw me facing the window overlooking the river and the window had
those rods like a cell. And while playing, two snakes were dancing
outside the window. I said I didn't see; there was darkness. They were
dancing while I wasn't even an accomplished sitarist.

So many things began to happen that if I go on describing, the
whole day will be spent. Primarily the inner spiritual things had begun.
I had not even practiced reciting *Om* at that time. I had a mattress
of hay on a hard wooden bed. As I look back, I didn't feel anything
bad about it. It was perfectly all right, even when the hay had
solidified like stone and I was lying in the nights on my back to sleep.
And Om began to ring in me throughout. I was not repeating it; it
was a kind of salvation. I wasn't surprised either, but I did not want
to get up. And if a thought came to me—*what's the time now?*—
without getting up I would see the clock showing me the time. I would
wish and things would happen. Bharti Baba had done some practices
and he understood that some things were happening with me. He
came in once. He said, "I don't want to ask you details, but don't tell
anyone."

One day a man came, smoking a cigar, a *cheroot*, wearing a pant
and coat, very fat, tall, kind and middle-aged. I was in such a corner,
as if the world would not know I was there, and all of a sudden, this
man walked into my hut with a small briefcase. Without asking me,

he came and sat on my rickety, ancient wooden chair. He sat there and would not say anything. I asked, "What's the matter, sir? Who are you and what have you come for?" He said, "I've come to give you a certain thing." I said, "What is it?" and something happened again. After it was done, whatever he told me and did, I had no choice but to agree with that. Then he got up to go. At the back of the hut were a few huts of fishermen with a fence in between. I had no contact with them. This man, instead of going back from the way in which he had come, wanted to go from the back, as if through the fencing and the fishermen's huts. For courtesy sake, I came out to see him off, and as he reached the fencing, all of a sudden I saw that he vanished. I do not know whoever he was. These things are many that I could tell you, how I began to awaken. It took me to Himalayas. That's it.

A Tiny Form of the World Mother

This event took place in 1950. The Hindu-Muslim riots in East Bengal had taken a very ugly and horrible turn for the second time. Displacement of Hindus from East Bengal had begun on a massive scale. Close to the border of West Bengal are two villages, Baranpur and Bangaon. Passing these two stations Hindu refugees were arriving to the nearby railway junction of Ranaghat station. All the six platforms of Ranaghat station were jam-packed with Hindu refugees. Here nine organizations were working round the clock taking care of the refugees and helping to resettle them. Among these were the Bharat Seva Ashram Sangh, the Congress, the Red Cross, the Marwari Relief Society, the YMCA and Government Hospital, et cetera. Some were distributing food, some clothes, some milk and some medicines. Some were taking care of the ill and diseased. The main work of the Congress relief at that time was to make a list of refugees and to shift them to temporary camps. In addition, they were coordinating the work of all organizations. I was working as a volunteer for the Congress.

Innumerable refugees were coming and being moved to temporary camps. There was an epidemic of cholera and other diseases. Daily there were a few deaths. We had to arrange ambulances for the ill and hearses for the dead. Also we had to cremate or bury the dead.

Together with this, we had to arrange and distribute food, milk, et cetera, and do general cleanliness and other such works. In short there was endless work. There was no sign of a stationmaster, ticket collector or any other railway officer or worker. We had no fixed times and arrangement for food, sleep, et cetera. Sometimes for two to three days we did not get time even to bathe. Everywhere there were swarms of flies and foul smell. There was nobody from the station to keep it clean. Day and night forty volunteers were working but it seemed as if nothing was being done. Usually every night around midnight we used to get a little relaxation. At that time I used to go to my tent and wonder how and when this terror would end? How long we could carry on working like this?

During one such night my eyes opened suddenly. It was around 3:00 A.M. All around there was death-like silence. That night it had rained a little. Slowly I came out of the tent and went to the platform without any particular purpose. I looked around and it seemed as if after the end of the Mahabharata War when Kurukshetra was covered with corpses. Here and there, everywhere human bodies were lying as if lifeless. However hard we tried it was impossible to provide sleeping space to the endless refugees, what to say about baggage. Dim lamps were burning here and there. Sometimes suddenly a child's cry would be heard. Otherwise, there was silence of the grave. Gloomy, listless and pale faces seemed lifeless. In spite of being calm and steadfast by nature, my heart brimmed over and my eyes became wet. What could be done? As a coordinating superintendent, I had a number of responsibilities.

In the Congress tent I had only one companion, Ranjit Kumar. All other volunteers had left. The cooperation between various organizations was diminishing day by day. Ranjit was a lion in work but when he spoke, people felt he was being authoritative. His heart was clean. He was renunciation personified. A thought came to awaken him and show him this piteous scene. But somehow my legs did not retrace the steps. Without any purpose I started moving amidst sleeping refugees. I had hardly reached the middle of the platform when there was a sudden voice from somewhere, "Superintendent

Sir! Have you not gone to sleep yet?" I turned round and saw a little girl of around twelve years giving water to an old woman. First I thought she might be her daughter, but when I inquired, I came to know they were not mother and daughter. In the child's small hand there was a small water-pot from which she was giving the water. She was wearing a white sari with red border and her hair was loosely open. On her innocent face there was a calm, blissful, sweet smile. She looked like *Devi Kanyakumari** personified.

Slowly filling a glass with water she said, "There is nobody to give water during the night and nobody to look after the ill. Therefore I thought to take up this work."

I asked, "What is your name"?

"Mukti."†

"When did you arrive here?"

"Two days back."

"But you are allowed to stay here for only one day; next day you have to go to the camp."

"My mother and other relatives have gone to the camp. They were taking me also. But I don't know why—seeing so much misery—I just could not quietly go away. I felt there was work here for me. My mother brings food once every day." Seeing twelve-year old Mukti's

---

* *Devi Kanyakumari* is the Virgin Goddess Whose temple is located at the southern tip of India (Cape Comorin) in the seaside town of Kanyakumari. Legend has it that a demon was wreaking havoc on the inhabitants of this world and Mahavishnu asked the devas (angels or shining beings) and humans to request *Parashakti*, primeval energy, to vanquish the demon. Answering the prayers, Shakti appeared as a young virgin at Kanyakumari and commenced penance with the desire of marrying Her consort, Shiva. Although the wedding was arranged by Narada, the groom's party never reached and the disappointed Goddess decided to spend Her life in Kanyakumari as a virgin. Kanyakumari is also the site of the Vivekananda Rock Temple, built on a large offshore rock to which Swami Vivekananda swam in 1892. There he received a vision from Divine Mother to take the liberating message of Vedanta to America. It was from this vision that he attended the First World's Congress of Religions in Chicago in 1893.

† Mukti, from the Sanskrit: "Liberation."

heart so thoughtful, merciful and peaceful, my head bowed. Seeing the presence of the World Mother in this tiny form, I was infused with renewed energy, as if all weariness just vanished. I felt the one thing lacking here was now fulfilled.

I asked her, "So, have you taken anti-cholera injection?"

"No! I do not feel it necessary, and if it is not God's will, is it possible for the injection to save oneself? If God protects, who can kill?"

"But even then one should take precautions and then leave it to God."

Mukti remained quiet. I then told her, "Tomorrow get yourself vaccinated or go and join your family in the camp. There is work there too."

She replied, "All right, let the number of refugees coming reduce, then I will go to the camp." Slowly I returned to my tent. It was about 4:00 A.M. Usually the first train with refugees arrived around 5:00 A.M. Some time later, Ranjit woke up and I told him about Mukti. He was delighted and said, "I am inspired and will have her darshan." Then he went for a wash.

Our daily routine of work started at 5:00 A.M. It must have been around 10:00 A.M. Work of volunteers was in full swing. Thousands of people, and everywhere long queues. Then one volunteer from the East Bengal Refugee Association came looking for me. His name was Ganguli and by nature he was very talkative. From far he called out, "Superintendent Sir! Just stop a while."

I was in a hurry and told him, "Quick, say what you want."

"Come, I will show you something."

"See! Ganguli don't waste time. If it is necessary, I will come."

"It is more than necessary. Your coming will be fruitful." Taking my hand, Ganguli took me to a hospital tent. Sitting on a patient's bed and applying wet strips of cloth on the patient's forehead was Mukti. I hurriedly asked, "Mukti! Do you not even rest during the day?" Mukti smiled a little and remained quiet. Ganguli was dumbfounded. He said, "How did you come to know about Mukti?" I told him about last night's incident. He said. "You are more fortunate than I am, as you had her darshan first."

From afar, Mukti put a finger to her lips and indicated to us to be quiet. The patient had a high fever, and without any more talk, we went outside and got busy with our work. Again I felt infused with new energy and, together with this, freshness of life. Day by day such incidents multiplied. All were coming to know Mukti and in four to five days she had become an idol of worship for volunteers. "Blessed are the parents who gave you birth . . ." At that time I remembered Florence Nightingale.

Days passed. Nobody ever saw Mukti sitting down, neither did they see her drooping with tiredness. Always she was wearing a white sari with a red border. When it got dirty, her mother would bring a similar one and give it to her and ask, "Won't you come to the camp today?" Every time her answer was the same: "Okay, today I will come." In such assurances, many "todays" passed, but Mukti did not leave or go outside the station platforms. Like virtuous *Sati,** she was absorbed in her sadhana. Sometimes you saw her giving water or milk, sometimes advising or directing someone, and so on and so forth. Looking after the sick was her specialty.

The whole day Mukti's face was lit with a smile of selfless love. Her selflessness was totally natural. One day her mother came to me and told me that if I order her, maybe she would come to the camp. In spite of her mother's repeated efforts, Mukti just avoided going one way or the other.

There was no doubt that this *tapasvini,†* who was a personification of peace, renunciation and spotless selfless service, used to cut all our bondages without saying anything. With whomsoever she spoke or dealt, it seemed as though she had a close relationship with that person. Her limitless love was matched by her pristine purity. Whenever there was talk about Mukti with Ganguli, his eyes would fill with tears and he would exclaim, "Why can't we be that selfless and that spotless!" I told him: "She has come to teach us that only. She does not teach us

---

* *Sati* is a form of Divine Mother as Parvati, the Consort of Shiva, who did great penances to win Her Lord, Shiva.

† *Tapasvini*: "female ascetic."

by words, but by her work. What more can words convey? She is an incarnation of Shakti [Divine Mother] and *bhakti*."* It was about a month since Mukti had arrived. Then one Sunday around ten in the morning, Ranjit came running towards me suddenly and said, "Mukti has fallen victim to cholera." I felt as if a thunderbolt had hit me. There was a queue of refugees in front of my desk collecting coupons to go to the camps. I got up immediately and put Ranjit in charge, telling him, "You take over and I will go and see her." I rushed to the hospital tent and saw Mukti lying on a bed, eyes closed and trembling all over. Her mother had reached already sometime before. She was sitting by her bedside. Ganguli was helping the doctor with injections and medicines. His unblinking eyes were on Mukti and filled with tears. I went close to the bedside and called in a little loud voice, "Mukti." There was no answer. I tried two or three times but there was no response; she did not open her eyes. Ganguli called her in a still louder voice. Then she slowly opened her eyes. Somewhat she recognized me and tried to smile, but she could not. I put my hand on her forehead and tried to steady her. The doctor softly told me, "Her case is very serious." Injections and medicines were being given. Her mother and Ganguli were crying all the time. After an hour I came back to my tent. Hourly this continued—my coming and going to her. I had never experienced such a blow before.

Neither had I ever become so restless. That afternoon around 4:00 P.M. we all had gathered by Mukti's bedside. Her body had become motionless but the face had the same blissful smile and was radiating love and peace. The doctor went outside wiping his tears. Volunteers were standing like statues. There was only one sound in the whole tent and that was of Mukti's mother crying. In an hour everything was ready for the cremation. About two miles to the east of the station there was a river. Volunteers lifted the bier on their shoulders and started walking toward the banks of the river. Following them were innumerable people. From the day we had started the relief work, a number of deaths had occurred due to cholera. We had buried or

---

* *Bhakti*: spiritual devotion.

We called these souls digambaras, meaning: "sky clad, space clad," all naked. We call them "ornaments of the Himalayas." They are not aware of their bodies. They don't know what oil, soap and shampoos are. If they wanted to eat they would eat. As a matter of fact, since this story has come up—I'm sorry, I may have to erase again—but it's a true story. Of course I'm avoiding details. Ramanand Avadhut was "responsible"—if you use the English term—for making me realize the Mahavakya, *"Aham Brahma Asmi."* It's long story. If I tell you, it will be a full Satsang, a lovely story, enlightening. But it will be only for a few ascetic disciples. It will be good to tell them, not in general. It is too private. Now ultimately, spiritual stories are not private, but you cannot tell them to everybody. You have to be an ascetic disciple, very confidential, to hear such stories. And I have not written an autobiography or biography of a yogi. If I do, Ramanand Avadhut will occupy one of the most prominent places in it. There are others, of course, but the major were two.

In human terms, you could say Ramanand Avadhut helped me. At one point I wanted to make him my Master—in 1955 or 1956, I think. He said, "I'll be glad to have you as my disciple, and that will be my privilege. But within two years you will be your own Master. You don't need a Master." Even then, for two years he helped me very nicely. He was responsible for making me realize the Mahavakyas, those great sayings of the four Vedas:* *Aham Brahma Asmi, Tat Twam Asi*, et cetera. I was on the threshold of, as we have been talking about, the "veil of unconsciousness." I was feeling myself on the threshold of a breakthrough to that Mahavakya, deeply meditating in the cave at Gangotri at about 10,000 feet elevation. Ramanand Avadhut lived on the other side of the Ganges. I was also in a cave. We had a rickety

---

* The Vedas, the most ancient world scriptures, have been dated as old as 8,000-10,000 B.C.E. The Vedas are divinely revealed wisdom (*sruti*) and thus not attributed to any author. The Vedas as we know them were compiled by Veda Vyas (c. 3100-3500 B.C.E.) during the Avatar of Sri Krishna (see footnote on page 5). The four Vedas include the Ṛg Veda (the earliest), Atharva Veda, Sama Veda and Yajur Veda, each divided into four sections: Samhita (hymns), Brahmana (rituals), Aranyak (forest treatises) and Upanishad (philosophical texts).

wooden bridge over which we could cross the river. At nighttime we
didn't travel, but this particular night I went. We didn't have clocks;
we just went by sunrise and sunset. We had one meal per day, that
also by begging. I had one or two blankets. I don't think he had any.
And my body was very young at that time.

Sometimes in the afternoon I would go walking in the forest, just
to have a walk, not talking to anybody for *months*. We didn't have
running water or heaters—none of that kind of paraphernalia. I had
only one vessel for water, that's it—no matchboxes or candles or books
even. I was a young avadhut myself that time. And there was no
electricity there. Now I've heard that Gangotri has electricity in
summer. At that time they didn't have, and we didn't have flashlights
or any kind of "emergency supplies." Daily we would wash in the
Ganges with water only. That was it. Tomorrow is tomorrow—we'll
see what comes, nothing beyond it. That was our state of mind.
Money, we had never heard of. Just once a day, at eleven o'clock, we
would beg for food. That was all. My hair at that time was matted,
and now I comb it, and so on.

For days and weeks I was trying to make this breakthrough, to
realize this Mahavakya, a Vedantic practice I was doing at that time.
All the devotional stages—Chaitanya, Krishna—were over. Hatha
yoga and even raja yoga were over. I had practiced Patanjali's Raja
Yoga fully, but not talking to anyone. All this happened year after year.
Then I reached the Vedanta and stumbled upon the Mahavakyas. It
is not achieved by intellectual understanding. It is realization that
"I am Brahman."* I was trying to make this breakthrough in my
consciousness. Days passed peacefully and sometimes I wouldn't eat
a meal even. There was a neighbor sadhu in another cave. Sometimes
he saw that when the time for begging came, I wouldn't be out of the
cave. He wouldn't disturb me, but a few times I found when I came
out later that some meal was lying down outside the cave. He would
do that. He was Nepali. It would be stone cold by then, so cold, boy!

---

* *Brahman*: the infinite Consciousness or Supreme Being according to Vedanta;
the ultimate impersonal Reality or Source from which everything emerges.

The dal would freeze. Anyway, he knew I was doing something, but we didn't discuss anything. Quite a number of days would pass without any meal, and if you didn't beg at that particular time, 11:00 A.M., the community kitchen would be closed later.

I couldn't make a breakthrough. Inside something was telling me to persist and it will happen. I didn't doubt this, but somehow that particular early evening, my thought went to Ramanand Avadhut—*why don't I go to him?* He had said that he would help me, and after two years I would be my own Master. Without much thinking, I went to the other side of the Ganges. It was very dark. At that spot, the Ganges is not one river; there are tributaries, and in between, big boulders and stones. But who cares at a time like that? You're mad! It is a long story. The temptation is there to tell you everything, but something is holding me back. I did reach his cabin—not a cabin as you know like on Mt. Lemmon; this was a simple, rugged, wooden cottage, and no lights. Somehow I reached.

Fortunately a fire was burning inside and he was awake, sitting down. Either he was expecting me or he was naturally so; they didn't lock the doors. And knocking would be useless, as the sound of the Ganges is so loud that a knock on the door wouldn't be heard. I opened the door and he said, "Come in, So-and-so, and sit down." He sat on one side and I sat against the opposite wall; in between was the fire. I kept quiet. He was very compassionate to me. He said, "Something is bothering you, it seems." I said, "Yes." He said, "What is it?" I said, "I've been trying now for weeks and weeks to make a breakthrough in this Mahavakya. Nothing else attracts me: hatha yoga, raja yoga, all the devotional paths, even Tantra and Kundalini.* Everything I've

---

* *Tantra* and *Kundalini* are two specialized systems of God Realization. Tantric practices use ritual and meditation to unite the devotee with the chosen deity. Kundalini yoga is a systematic approach to awakening the kundalini, which normally resides in the base of the spinal column. Through various practices, including purifications, pranayama, mantra and meditation, the initiated adept gradually raises the "serpent power" of the kundalini from the base chakra upward until it reaches the crown chakra, the *sahasrāra* "thousand-petalled lotus," resulting in full Enlightenment.

gone through and mastered . . ." He knew that, somehow. I told him that all this I had processed year after year, then I got into Vedanta. It was not that I didn't know Vedanta philosophy, but it is one thing to know philosophy and another to *be* whatever it is. And then I had come to the last rung of this Mahavakya. I was peaceful—I wasn't disturbed—but he read on my face that something was bothering me. I said, "I'm not able to make a breakthrough." And then he did what he did. I won't describe it. It opened up my Consciousness. That was the end, in 1958, I think.

So that is kutastha. In Krishna Ashram I have seen this, and a few others too. Another holy man like Krishna Ashram was Paramanand. He wasn't as old as Krishna Ashram. Paramanand was in his seventies or eighties. Paramanand lived in a very austere way. He was naked and he had made a wooden, box-like thing so we could touch him, in which he could hardly move, just to sleep. I went to him and he talked. At that time my dress was not like this—very off-white and tattered. Somehow somebody had given me a very thin sweater that was ragged too, like refugees. So one early afternoon I had gone to him. Some of you may remember that I have said in Satsang that there are five sheaths or covers over the Spirit, Light or Consciousness— the physical, vital, mental, psychic and spiritual. Knowing these sheaths is among the practices in the Himalayas. I have not spoken much about these things because it would be beyond you all—how we, one by one, shake off these five sheaths on the Spirit or *Atman* and be free so that we reach the Spirit. These are all practices, very technical ones, not just "thinking."

I had a shirt—not clean as now you see; I'm spoiled in America. But that time I had ragged clothes and hardly any shoes. And I had that thin, ragged sweater. I was sitting and this *Paramhansa** was looking at me. He had shining eyes. I didn't ask him—he blurted out, "We are busy in removing five sheaths over the Spirit and you've put three more on it!" I was just *shocked*! He was referring to my

---

* *Paramhansa*, lit: "great swan," a term used for Realized or Liberated Souls, who float unaffected, on the ocean of samsara (rebirth).

undershirt, shirt and sweater. I can keep you busy the whole night with these anecdotes and experiences. I've not written those books, because already there are books of these experiences by others. So I have thought—*why to imitate everybody?* But when this happened, for the time being I was stunned, as if by chloroform or something. And I couldn't find what to respond. I couldn't fight with him, but if I had to answer, I couldn't find any answer. I could see his logic. I was really shocked. It took me *three months* to get over this statement. We were practitioners, right? It was not a personal vendetta. You are doing practices and now this holy man has told you this. You start working on it, like a mathematical problem. And I had to get down to the bottom of this statement.

After about three months—not that he was wrong—I went to him again. I bowed down to him, of course. We do that to seniors in the Himalayas; whether you are more enlightened than another sadhu, whether he is lower than you in consciousness or higher, it doesn't matter. It is etiquette. Age-wise we bow down to the elders. So I bowed down to him and he said, "What's it again?" I still had the same three extra covers. I called him Maharishi. I said, "Maharishi, I'm telling you what I feel. Not that you're wrong or right; I'm not judging anyone. When you try to remove your five sheaths over the Spirit, do you tear them apart like skins or what?" One is physical and then vital (which is emotional), then mental, psychic and spiritual. I asked him, "Do you really take the dress, as if that skin, out of every sheath and get the Spirit to shine nakedly? Or do you simply get over them, transcend them by getting into Consciousness, not remembering about those five sheaths?" He said, "You're right." I said, "Therefore why have I to take the three dresses out? I just transcend them." He looked at me. I said, "You are trying to transcend the five sheaths without tearing them apart, and I'm trying to get over eight dresses, covers, without taking them apart." He didn't say, "You're right." He just looked at me.

When later I reached Benares, where I was very associated with another holy man, this story came up. This holy man knew Paramanand in Gangotri, somehow, and he asked, "What was the encounter?" I told him what Paramanand had said and he asked, "What did you tell him?" I told him what I said. He laughed a lot. Well, he did say, "You're mischievous." I said, "The question is, I'm not saying he was wrong, but since you don't tear apart all five sheaths to get the naked one inside out, why should I do this? As long as I'm feeling kind of cold, I should wear something, no? Or I may have a sense of shame yet and he doesn't have any; he's all naked." In Himalayas, if you're naked, they respect you more, somehow. You're digambara—more qualified because you're able to live naturally in cold and heat without shame, without any kind of hesitancy. When you look at those sadhus who are digambaras, you don't feel anything. It is just natural. So I said to this other holy man, "Till I get over these things—feeling cold sometimes—what can I do about it?" He said, "You're trying to save your skin." Well, what could I say? I said, "The body falls sick?" He said, "What does it matter?" I had to think again. When he said, "What does it matter if the body falls sick" I had no answer.

The body falls sick; it is natural. It's young; it grows old; it dies. What's the big deal about it falling sick? He spoke like this and I had no answer. So I again went for about fifteen days and meditated upon it. These things used to happen a lot. I knew these were people talking through their experience; these are not bookish people. Then I went back. He said, "What answer did you find now?" I said, "Look, there are two ways. One way is as you are describing: what does it matter? Another is that, as long as the instrument is there, I want to keep it healthy, just like you keep a house or cabin or cave healthy. It's there, so you keep it well." He kept quiet. Experiences like that used to happen.

What I'm telling you is not one-twentieth even. I avoided writing a book about my experiences with Himalayan Masters. Some others wrote such books and I thought it would be an imitation. There are many, many experiences. I remember one sadhu named Vishnu Dutt, in Uttarkashi, no longer living. He was digambara too. At that time there were no buses, roads or electricity in those areas. We sadhus walked for miles. We had a blanket or two that we would roll up and tie on our shoulders and we'd travel by foot. We had no socks or shoes or any such things in those days, just simple sandals. Vishnu Dutt was another kutastha sadhu, like Krishna Ashram. He would stand in the Ganges' icy cold water. I couldn't even touch the water at that time and he was naked all twelve months. He would stand up to the hip in the Ganges daily—*hours*—looking at the sun. We have seen these things.

Somebody told me that Vishnu Dutt is very great; go and see him. I was visiting everyone, so I went quietly. I tried to draw his attention, just to have his glance on me, but I couldn't get it! He was immersed in himself. He stayed on the other side of the Ganges from where I stayed. He would go from his hut to the Ganges and back. Sometimes he had a little booklet—I suppose it was the Gita; I'm not sure. He would show that booklet to the sun. Whatever his intention was—to catch the solar energy—God knows. I would see this in the morning. There was no one else there and the Ganges was very pure at that time, not polluted. And I would watch what he was doing, where he was going. He wouldn't tell me to go away or not; he just wasn't affected—kutastha. He wouldn't talk. I wanted him to raise his eyes, just to glance on me a little bit. I couldn't dare to go near his feet and touch, but from a distance I would bow down. He didn't even acknowledge that—whether you bow down, don't bow down, stay there, go away, go to hell or heaven—didn't matter to him.

I tried to draw his attention. A few months I went regularly near him but failed. Somebody told me later in Uttarkashi, in the winter, "The very fact that you were able to go daily for a few months means he was pleased with you or he would have played such a game, you couldn't have gone there." I said, "He didn't even look at me." He said, "Don't worry about that. Looking is sensual only. That's the eye looking at you. He doesn't care for the body. But the very fact that you were able to go daily for a few months means he had a grace upon you. Otherwise, he would have played in such a way, his occultism or whatever, that you couldn't be there." They were great ones in that region in those days.

Now when you're talking about kutastha, the Great Silence, from the outward sense, it is as if you are blocking your mind, keeping quiet, nailed, frozen. A Vedantist would say, "What is the use of this? Mind is just hypnotized, in a way." But it's not; it is a step of practices. If you see it that way, it's not wrong, though it's not the Ultimate. The Great Silence is where you're kutastha—log wood type—but you are also a Conscious Being. In the kutastha stage, the mind is not Conscious; it is a part of the practice. Some people have condemned the practice of kutastha, but then controversies have always existed between philosophers and yogis. In the Himalayas these controversies or philosophical discussions go on all the time. Since ages or thousands of years these discussions have been there. Each holy man in Himalaya is and was a character by himself; no second copy. They just do not care for the world—*nothing.*

Some have practiced the Great Silence and some have achieved it. It is beyond hypnotism or self-pacified mind. It is something that they work upon—*paripurna.** In the perfect stillness of the mind thoughts create bubble-like vibrations. These impositions over many births include memories and feelings. Any kind of vibration is considered a tension in those practices—*any* kind. Even music is a tension, though pleasant, but they consider it is a tension. Even the roaring of the water of the Ganges, the rustling of the Himalayan pine trees or the barking of the dogs is considered a tension, what to speak of memories, desires, and self-impositions, which are called *upadhi.* Also among these are *sphurnas,* which refer to when a certain thought all of a sudden comes up—instinct and the like. All these things, those who practice kutastha begin to silence, not hypnotize or suppress. They begin to solve these and let go, let go, think about, and let go. And they go on silencing, subsiding and relaxing these thoughts or vibrations without thinking about any profit or consequences. What will happen if this happens, what will happen if this does not happen—they don't worry about it. Whatever will happen is not wanted. You understand now?

It is a very great practice. Not all do it. By God's grace, I've gone through many things. If I would write, it would be an encyclopedia. Not that various yogis who have written were wrong; they have

---

* *Paripurna,* lit: "supreme Perfection"; a method of perfecting one's practices.

written their own experiences. I could have written an encyclopedia but that is not my aim. I've gone through *many* things in a short time—everything, as if jumping from one realization to another until I reached the Mahavakya, which was the acme. However, in this Great Silence, they don't reflect upon consequences. What will this produce, what will that produce or not produce? We don't want those consequences either. So everything is let go. They go on subsiding, subsiding, "I don't want it," if it is a deeper-rooted thing. They won't analyze even. They longingly want to get into that Silence, which is not a self-hypnosis of mechanical quiet. And so, therefore, nothing attracts them. Not only so, nothing repels them either. They have found the truth or mystery of nature in only two forces. I'm talking through practices now; philosophy is different. They have discovered or realized that only two forces make up nature, where nature or Mother Divine works. One is attraction; one is repulsion. For these Great Silence practitioners, neither are they attracted nor repulsed. Even if you are eating raw flesh, they won't be repulsed. And if you are hearing great, auspicious music, if gandharvas or angels or fairies are singing, that won't attract them either. They are not repulsed by any dire thing they see. There are no vibrations. They know that all vibrations are tensions.

These sages who practice kutastha are too great for America or the Western hemisphere; even for many Indians they would be unreachable. But those who are in Himalayas—we have our own world, and therefore I never wanted to come back. But that is a separate story. Somehow I got caught up in this world, and I regret that. Not regret as a human being, because Mother won't like it if I regret. She'd say, "*Boy*, you don't like My work?" And I keep quiet when Mother spanks, you know. I told Her many times, "You can create many sons, Mother. You can make anybody do this. You should leave me alone." She said, "I chose you. Why are you arguing?" I said, "I'm not arguing. You could have done through somebody else. Why I had to do?" Anyway, that's it.

I've gone through this Great Silence and I've not lost it even now. With all the vicissitudes, crises, depression, sadness, everything—I've not lost it. *It doesn't leave you ever.* It's just glued in. Ramana Maharshi

was that. He had reached the Great Silence, definitely. And so, when
you come to these practices in Himalayas, or wherever, there are no
exceptions in this. We normally think, even if we are not attracted
or repulsed, but *what if* this thing happens or that thing doesn't
happen? Then what? At times there are exceptions, but these sages
will not say that. Something greater is there: God's creation. They see
the bigger panorama. These earth things are to them *very* tiny,
insignificant, and not worth tension. The modern man would not
like to hear this, but they keep quiet. They work from there, here,
wherever they may be; under a tree or in a cave.

So when this state of Great Silence comes, nothing in the world—
profit or loss—nothing is bothering or not bothering; nothing is mine
or not mine, enemy or friend. You take away their bowl, their blanket
or whatever they may have and they don't get bothered about it. They
won't tell you, "Take the cloak also." He won't worry about it. *He*,
I'm saying, because mostly these sadhus have been men, not women,
so what can I do about it? And so, day and night they meditate, what
they call *akhanda dhyan. Dhyan* is concentration applied into
contemplation, to choose one ideal, which is equivalent to meditation;
akhanda is non-fragmented or continuous, not only continual.
Continuous meditation they practice to get into this Great Silence.
I've gone through all this. In Buddhism they call it the void, *shunyata*.
It's the same thing. And I have gone through the Buddhist ways too.
And whenever these sages practice this for one year, ten years, this
birth, they're lost into that. They have nothing to do in Himalayas;
nobody bothers them. If they want to eat they will come to the charity
kitchen at 11:00 A.M., take a few pieces of unleavened bread and thin
dal soup, like yellow water. If they don't go at that time, they don't
eat. It doesn't matter.

Oxygen and sunshine are there and they are connected with their
heavenly bodies in such a way that they get nourishment from
ethereal prana. And I've gone through this too. That is still helping
me; otherwise, I would have been finished in America. And so, day
by day they live upon the least. Now I hope you don't stupidly do
this, like *Imitation of Christ*! Don't copy. This needs great Gurus and

preparations and high previous births to sustain you. It is not as I am talking. Don't do it by yourselves; it is 440 volts—worse than 220! It's not easy. It needs a very, very great caution in doing these things.

I have concentrated upon the sun. I am not taking the credit—it is God's grace, Mother's grace. And that is why people have noticed my eyes shining and the unusual great eyes that I have. It is the blessing of the Sun god. I have done this concentration, called *trataka*, on the sun. Do not do this, please! You will turn blind if you do not know how to do it. Your question on kutastha kind of stirred me up for the Himalayas! I wish I could go back. That is why you see some gaze and radiance in my eyes. It is due to that practice of concentrating on the sun. And from that kutastha you lose all attractions and repulsions. Likes and dislikes are much lower than that. I practiced that for months: not liking anything, not disliking anything. I brought it indirectly in your "A" and "B" meditation classes*—"no imagination, no resistance"—though probably many do not understand what I am saying in that because you have to practice these things.

I was a great practitioner from God's point of view. God's grace, Mother's grace—I couldn't have done it alone. So when the mind is not swayed by this or that, left and right, it begins, like a pendulum, to come back to the central position to stabilize. And then you drop into that Silence. Beyond the silence of mind, of speech, of thought, the Great Silence is where you are totally Conscious, though you have no speech, thought or mind. In Sanskrit, *man* is "mind"; *amana* is "mindless." Mindless does not mean a lunatic, crazy or senseless. In mindlessness, the mind just does not exist. So this amana is also practiced.

In akhanda dhyan, whether they sit down to meditate, lie down as if to go to sleep, or walk to the Ganges for bathing, all the time they are meditating. They do not talk to anyone. I have gone through this. And you do not want anyone disturbing you. Nowadays there

---

* Meditation instruction and classes in two levels (A and B) were initiated by Gurudeva in the American ashrams in the late 1970s.

are electricity and roads—buses have reached the Himalayas. It is a mess! The real holy men have gone to the higher places beyond Gangotri to ten thousand five hundred feet elevation, to Tapovan. I did not stay there. At that time Gangotri was very, very quiet. You did what you wanted and nobody disturbed you. It was a kind of scientist's laboratory, without an actual laboratory or any apparatus, only one's mind and body. And those who stayed there did not care whether they bathed one day a week or not. It is so cold with pure air anyway. You do not get diseases there. But nowadays things have changed.

For all these attractions and repulsions, the left and right swayings of mind to subside, and thought, speech, mind to become mindless, it takes time. It may take years, months or decades until you drop into that. Ramana Maharshi had that experience. In that Great Silence you do not focus on anything. It is focusless focus. In other words, it is non-pinpointed one-pointedness—all a vastness. Some great sages, if they choose to be like Vashishta or Vishwamitra, and want in that silence as a pool of consciousness to see anything through clairvoyance and clairaudience, to see even into the galaxies, the focus is there. Not that everybody does so. Some reach into Great Silence and then they're lost into that. And then the body lasts for a few weeks or months and then dies. But some, if they want to, choose to focus into that "TV" of the Great Silence. Therefore they can see things afar. I am not talking about clairvoyance and clairaudience at the moment; that is a little lower. Krishna would be in that category, of course.

When you reach that Great Silence, so placid and stabilized, you never lose it again, whatever else you may do or not do. If you remember in some depictions of Krishna, where he is in the battlefield with the two armies arrayed against each other and he is the charioteer of Arjuna's chariot, in spite of war raging all around—the great Mahabharata, one of the greatest wars ever fought—in these scenes Krishna is relaxed and smiling. He sees the things and does what is needed. He only could do this if he had reached the Great Silence, not otherwise. They say that Guru Govind Singh, the Sikh Guru, did the same. He fought wars, but they said that in the battlefield, he always had a benign, sweet smile while fighting. I cannot vouchsafe for the authenticity, but that is what they say and claim. But Krishna's demeanor, of course, we know.

This Great Silence is knowing, wordless speech, noiseless sounds, everything possible. A Himalayan sage in a cave or one under a tree—not everyone, of course, one who has reached that high level—can direct or regulate anything around the world without even moving. It is an immobile movement. They actually practice this: how to talk without talking, how to see without seeing. There are very many such practices. You could stab them and in kutastha they won't utter even "umm . . ." Not that you would do it, nor you should, nor would you be able to. This kutastha is not for common people. If hippies hear this tape and take drugs and dance all night around a campfire, they will think that's yoga. This is quite different. It needs a lot of practices. It is not the result of one birth; you must understand this. And if he's an Incarnation or Prophet or Enlightened Being, then he's already so, except he begins to do a few things on this earth. Krishna did these practices. He went for austerities and meditation at Kailash. The sages asked him, "You're the Prophet, the Incarnation of this age. What need do you have to do these practices, meditations, prayers, yoga and renunciation at Kailash?" Krishna gave a famous reply, "I'm doing for you people." The Prophets do not do for themselves. They have already perfected kutastha and so many other practices. But still, when they take the five-elemental body, as Ramakrishna said, "When Brahman takes birth and enters the body, made up of five elements, it also weeps like any other being which has taken birth." So naturally these great Souls do practices even if they do not need it.

While taking the five-elemental body you are an ignorant, unconscious being again. Naturally, you have to get out of it. But such Beings do not take much time to get out of this trap. In very little time—like if you put a crow under a basket, as soon as you lift the basket it flies up like an arrow. The Prophets and Realized Souls do like that. Their practices are not boring. They are already Realized—*Nitya Siddha*—Perfected Ones. But still they do practices. They jump upon practices and realize everything. They just go through them and then they know what their mission is. Whether it was Rama or Krishna or anybody else. They did not practice too long—even Jesus or Buddha.

Buddha's whole practice period was about five years. He had only two teachers, two Gurus you might say, and then he was his own Master. Rama's sadhana was with Vashishta, in early teenage years. Krishna's case was the same. In sixty-four days he mastered all forms of knowledge, all the talents. And Jesus went for forty days into the desert. He was tempted, and so on and so forth. Not many days do they take. And they get their True Self realized. But for others, a lot of practice is needed. When this Ramanand Avadhut told me, "In two years you will be your own Master," on one side I was happy he was saying this. I thought—*thank God!* But on the other side, I knew what he was getting to. I asked him, "Avadhutji, why do you say that?" He said, "You'll know soon." And I believed him. Somehow you don't argue with sages. Arguing too much is a kind of modern humbug. We do not value this humbug, but we don't say this commonly, not to hurt people. You may ask a question, of course. Then you have to keep quiet and not argue, not say, "Come on, tell me."

Again, do not copy without learning. By God's grace, my every practice took a very short while and I came to the conclusion, then transcended. This Great Silence is not something they achieve as per a new thing; they just realize back that Silence from where the creation happened. That Great Silence is eloquent—wordless speech, noiseless sound. All faculty senses emerge from that Great Silence. In Tantra you learn this *very* well. And I practiced that too. I was lost in those days. I don't know why I was found again. It is kind of a tragedy to me. If Mother had not told me, I wouldn't have listened to anyone. I didn't. I told Mother, "Why don't You send someone else? You can create any number of sons that You want. You're not impotent." She said, "I have chosen you, that's it." What could I say?

These practices are not to judge. "Tell me in how many months I'll be kutastha." An American would ask in that way. It may take one day, it may take you the whole life—nobody calculates these things within time and space. You just do it until it happens. You are lost to the world; it doesn't matter. Nobody looks at you. You just care for you—that's it—until you reach. And there are *innumerable* such practices. Each sadhu or holy person chooses what he wants to be. Some are lost in scriptures scholastically, and they discuss aphorisms with each other every afternoon. They are happy with that somehow. There are all kinds of holy men. Ramana Maharshi hardly spoke; he would just gaze and you would get peace. In his presence people sat and found peace. He didn't have to talk even. And Ramakrishna, without a break, went on talking, talking, talking . . . In between he would smoke.

I've seen great occultists. I didn't go through that much, though I have respect for occultism as I would have respect for any power. I didn't go deeper into that. Whatever emerged or unfolded automatically in me was fine. I didn't want to practice occultism, not because it would be wrong, but I thought probably I won't need to, so why to acquire it? What has unfolded and is unfolding, I do it incognito. You would never know. You will never know what I do. I wanted to do in that way, what they call in Sanskrit *gupta shakti*. *Gupta* means: "hidden, incognito." That is also one of the practices—how to do occultism or use powers without demonstration and show. In this—not that I had to curb my temptation—some sages or holy people could get temptations to demonstrate and show such powers. Naturally, I did not want to do that.

A Paramhansa is a different Being. In this Great Silence, there is Pure Consciousness and the Source of everything—the Source of all senses, all perceptions, all motion. They simply control two actions of nature, attraction and repulsion, called *anulom vilom*. Once they master that, they are Master of the Cosmos. It is just centrifugal and centripetal, those two forces only. It is not a suppression of mental activity that makes you reach the Great Silence. It is letting go and clearing, without thinking. If you are thinking and analyzing what the consequences will be, you are missing the point. Nothing has any value for the Great Silence. Whether you are a king or a beggar, whether you have any loss or gain, health or ill health—these thoughts you do not entertain. I have gone through all this.

REALIZATION

A woman repeatedly asked Gurudeva to tell how His Realization happened. She again brought it up after He tried to distract and not answer her.

Seeker: *That's why I asked you, how did it ever happen to you or how did it ever . . . ?*

Gurudeva: Oh, you remember the question. You mean astrological date, time, and day? Okay now, let me not play more with you. When it happened, I saw it was always there. I had never lost it. It was always there. So, what date should I tell you, which age or timing?

The Realization has always been there?

I saw it was always there. I had never lost it; I had just forgotten about it.

How did you recall it?

It was always there; do you understand? It is beyond time and space. Which time and space will describe it?

I was just wondering how—

How, I can tell you that. I was longing for it. I was suffocating for it. It was squeezing me. I couldn't live without the Light. I had no other job in the world. I had no other wish in the world. I had no other position, day, time. I didn't know when the sunrise and when the sunset happened. I didn't know what the date is today. I didn't know whether my father or mother is there, or children are there—well, I have no children, but brothers or sisters or friends. I never remembered anyone; no correspondence. Not mechanically, but I just didn't remember. I didn't know people are working for livelihood and bread and butter; it was poison to my ears. I knew that life is only for God. Nothing else. I didn't know where is America or India. I didn't know where people are. I didn't know where ferocious animals are. I didn't know where the food would come from. I didn't know hunger, though I would eat at times. The Himalayas were there; the Ganges was there. I knew this, nothing else.

And the day would pass. I would long. I would think, *One more day is wasted* . . . But which day—I didn't know whether it was Monday, Tuesday, or May or June or August. Whether it was 1973 or 1958, I didn't know. I was there and somebody else was there whom I wanted. Nothing else. I didn't see anybody else—only me and Thou. And days passed, or months passed, or years passed; I didn't know . . .

Sometimes people would ask: "Don't you remember your home?" These questions were like news from Jupiter—bolt from the blue! "Don't you remember your home?" I said, "Well, you are reminding me. I didn't know." This was the case. I was in my sleep. So if somebody shook me, "Won't you get up?" I said, "No, let me sleep." Sleep, meaning, in my absorption.

And one day the Light just came. I was not satisfied with that Light, the first glimpse. I thought—*no, this is the first shadow, the first reflection only. I wouldn't be satisfied. I want full, unending* . . . So it happened. And then I saw everybody has Light. Nobody is ignorant. I have never seen an ignorant person. I have never told anyone, "You're ignorant," because I know he is not ignorant, she is not ignorant. He knows . . . everybody knows. Nobody is ignorant. I've yet to find a child or girl or boy or man or woman who is ignorant and doesn't know. When I look at their eyes and I say, "You know," their eyes say, "Yes, we are hiding simply."

Were you saying that your Realization didn't come all of a sudden? It was something that—even though, of course, you had it all along, but the fact that you were searching for it—you came into it gradually?

It is not a gradual process. The path or road is gradual, no doubt. There are steps. But reaching that Realization is instant. Let me put another example. Supposing there is a ladder going up and there are twelve steps on the ladder. Though you are going towards the top as you go step by step, but on each step you are not gradually realizing. That will be when you reach the last step. So the eleven steps are simply taking you to the last step, reaching which is instant. On the eleven steps, you are still ignorant, meaning, forgetful. So that is generally called "going towards." But at each step, you are not gradually realizing. Realization is not gradual. It is eternal. It is unchanging. It is either there or it is not there. Another example is that from your home or Phoenix you came here. Up until you reached the door, you had not seen me, though you had traveled so many miles. But at each mile, did you see me? No. That was instant—when you came inside the door. Realization is the same way. Though you were coming toward the spot where I was, but reaching that spot is not gradual.

The Spirit is a simple, tiny center—invisible. We call it *Jyoti*. In the center it penetrates. Even if the whole sky is filled with clouds, if there is one tiny pinpoint, the whole light shines through. Tear it open—the whole floodlight is there.

INITIATION

Devotee: *You said you would talk about your particular Swami order last night, only we forgot.*

There are two kinds of sannyas. Have you heard of Shankaracharya?* He lived in the eighth or ninth century. He organized the kinds of sannyas. Before that time, Shankara himself was not among the ten sects. He organized these throughout India. In his day there were recluses and monks throughout the land, but without any particular denomination or order. He organized them into ten orders, among which there is Giri, Puri, Bharti, Aranya, Saraswati . . . Shankaracharya also opened four centers in India: south, east, west and north. The northern one was in the Himalayas, and is even today. The ten sects

---

* Shankaracharya, who lived in eighth century India, was a child prodigy, a Realized Soul and one of the greatest philosophers the world has known. He purified and consolidated the various schools of worship within India and brought them under the umbrella of one philosophical principle, Advaita. He renounced home at the age of fourteen and within a short lifespan of thirty-two years, restructured all the seventy-two forms of religious practices into acceptable norms and laid stress on the six ways of worship based upon the Vedas. He wrote many commentaries, including those on the Brahma Sutras, the Bhagavad Gita and the Principal Upanishads. He authored the Advaita treatises, *Vivekacudamani*, "Crest Jewel of Discrimination," *Atmabodha*, "Self Knowledge," and other works, as well as many sublime poems in praise of various Vedic Deities.

were divided into these four centers, with two or three in each. It was called *vividishya*,* according to Sanskrit, which means the Guru initiates you into that recluse, which we call sannyas. These ten sects refer to the mountains, oceans, rivers, towns, knowledge, the forest, and others, because he saw such tendencies among the recluses or the monks. Some monks like forests; some like rivers; some like mountains; some like knowledge or learning; some like cities. So seeing these temperaments, Shankaracharya divided the recluses into ten orders. For example, *giri* means mountains. So if I'm a lover of mountains, I'll be initiated into the sannyas of the Giri Order. And if you are a man of much learning—you like learning—you'll be in the Saraswati Sannyasins.

On the day you take this initiation, there is a fire worship and particular mantras and a ceremony or ritual performed. On that day the Guru will tell you, "Your life for the world has ended. From this day onward your life is for God, whatever He wants you to do." This initiation is called vividishya. Most monks fall within these ten orders, but there are a few exceptions, which are not even one percent. The exceptions are those who have *vidyut sannyas*,† the eleventh order as if, which is not called the eleventh though. It is a separate sannyas altogether. Nobody initiates you. Vidyut means lightning. This sannyas is taken when, due to previous births, you have done so much that you have already reached this stage of "nothing to do with the world." Your life is for God. Then by certain suggestions or circumstances, that opens up in you all of a sudden. You may be in the house; you may be in the mountains; you may be in the city; you may be anywhere—whatever your mode of life may be. This opens up in you and it is automatic initiation—vidyut. Very few souls have this kind of initiation.

Nobody gives this to you. The day it happens, you are at liberty to change your name or not, to change your clothes or not, to follow the rules of monk's life or not—it's up to you. This nobody sanctions;

---

* *Vividishya sannyas*: step by step renunciation; renunciation of the seeker.
† *Vidyut sannyas*: "lightning" sannyas; renunciation of a Realized Soul.

it is self-given, like the Buddha had achieved. Shankaracharya had the same, as did Sri Ramakrishna. In the ten sects of sannyas, the name is changed the day of initiation and that monk has to wear a particular color of clothes; he has to follow certain rules and mode of living to whichever degree he can. He has not to touch money; he has not to do this; he has to do that . . . But vidyut sannyas, when it happens, it is up to you. You can wear even this [white robe] dress or you can change to an ochre robe. Your name you can change or you may not change it. In the other ten sects, generally the suffix *ananda** is given, like Vivekananda, Paramananda, et cetera. In this eleventh type of renunciation, that is not the case. The same name can continue or it can be changed. You do it yourself.

This sannyas happens to some very fortunate ones. I happen to be that. I'm not particularly following any order, but again, it is my choice. I did change the name, but not in the traditional way. There is no ananda in my name, and even if I continued with my previous family name, I had liberty to do that, but I thought to change it. For one year in the beginning, I wore ochre robes; then I changed to white. My mother asked this and I did it to fulfill her wish. Buddha also had no "ananda" with his name. In this kind of sannyas, whether you keep a beard or long hair or shave everything, it is as you like. Whether you live in the family, whether you work in an office, whether you live in an ashram has no binding on vidyut sannyas. It is self-given. It opens up in you. This is how it opened up in me.

Something was there previously. I was also to have been initiated into this by my Guru, but before he initiated me, it just happened—all of a sudden. Then the one who I had considered my Master said, "Now you are the Master. It is up to you to change your name or dress or not, whatever you wish." Before that, I didn't even know this type of sannyas existed. I had not come across it in the scriptures because it was not in the books I had read. But really when it happened, the other monks told me, "Yes, it is there"—meaning, sanctioned by the scriptures. It comes in a flash, not by

---

* *Ananda*, in Sanskrit: "bliss."

understanding, just by a flash. And there is no ceremony in that initiation. You may do the ceremony or not; it is up to you.

PLANNED BY GOD

As far as the purpose of my coming is concerned, I was not conscious of that. I didn't plan it myself through personal desire or future planning. It was totally a Godly calling from when I was in the Himalayas up to the year 1959, when I lost the spirit of working among the people or among the world, even in India. That was the culmination. Spiritual seeking was over for me—no craving, no desires for any thought of things. Even the thought to do good to others, to help or serve others, lost meaning for me and I had concluded, in a way, that all searching was finished for me. I was fully satisfied with my Enlightenment, with my peace and joy, which I realized, so unbound and unlimited and infinite that to bring in any sort of desire, small or great, would be to ruffle that infinity, to make it limited. I thought to keep it so pure and untouched that any tinge of mental activity should not come into it. With this view, I had ascended to the higher altitudes of the Himalayas, the forests where even other people or mountaineers did not go. Without any kind of provision or pre-planning, I was lost in those mountains and valleys at altitudes of more than 15,000 feet above sea level.

For about six or seven days I was in that wandering. Of course, many wounds and cold and rain and hunger—all these things were with my body, but I was not conscious of this then. I was in a sort of giving up of the body, without food or any kind of other requirements of the physical sheath. And on the sixth or seventh day, I fell unconscious one evening. I don't know how much time passed but when I came out of it I saw the world in a different sense, a calling inside that I should come back to the world although my personal search was over. I knew I was fully satisfied, in peace and joy, but that this should be shared with people and other creatures, because Oneness means all together. I knew that I could not separate myself from other souls. We are seemingly so many multitudes of people and animals and trees, but

Spirit lies in everybody, God is in everybody, and our satisfaction or anything should be shared with others. Our Perfection should be demonstrated or lived before others. And what we realize or acquire should be shared with our brethren.

And with this view at such a young age—I was thirty years of age when I got this calling—I felt that I still had ample time, a big span of life left to do work for others. And this voice, this Light, was so clear that there was no room for doubt. On the seventh or eighth day I came down to the lower altitudes of 10,000 feet, but then found myself, in a sense, crippled. My whole body was wounded in those mountain heights and I was totally changed due to that intense cold and hunger and thirst. It took me one month to recover and then I came down to the plains of India. Six months I loitered in some parts of India, South India especially, because that was the portion I had never visited. And in the beginning of 1960, I came to the state of Maharashtra, the city of Pune, which was meant for my headquarters. I didn't go to anyone for any help or any demand but things happened, as if pre-planned—well, planned by God. Not only finances, not only men, but also the choice of spot for the ashram, the choice of the doctrines or beliefs and many such things that otherwise are the outcome of the intellect or the thinking of the mind—these came to me quite intuitively. And up to now I have never thought about these matters.

After one year of working in India, collecting some young men and old men of real simple and pure spirit who wanted to dedicate themselves for Light and wisdom, heavenly prayers and divine joy, we gathered about ten people as inmates for the ashram, and many others came as daily and occasional visitors. After some satisfaction in Indian work, the calling went on that simultaneously I should take this to other nations too, and the United States was the first among them. Of course, there were questions in India about this, but intuitively I felt the reason was because the United States, as far as spirituality is concerned, and among the nations other than India, stands first, at least in spiritual hunger. This brought me to the United States. The arrangements were always done by God. I have never exerted my brain for it. I have never exerted my physical energy for that. All things happen by themselves. And when I came to United States—you may say quite unknown in the social or human sense of the term—I found in three months that I had more than a thousand friends, real ones, which I can call friends—not only known people, not only acquaintances, not only those hungry for spirituality, but really ones who were, as if, waiting for some message. I don't mean my message. I don't put it in that way. Call it a message of the Divine, a message of God, a message of Truth. People are *ready* if we can really give them the right Spirit.

5

The Prophets Pure Spirit Embodied

Like wanderers you search outside your Self only because you miss its subjective nature. Therefore Prophets and holy men come to awaken you to the great treasure within. This treasure makes your existence not only worth living—it transforms this earth into a heaven and still further, renders life eternal.

*T*here are always subtle forces that we do not see. Because everything doesn't happen right away, that does not mean the process hasn't started. People do so many bad things—crimes and other things—but God doesn't just come and cut their necks. They may think that if nothing happens, it is okay to do these things, but the process has started. Everything in creation percolates from the High Command, but it becomes so limited, so short-lived or transitory that although everything comes from the Supreme, it becomes partially satisfying so that often we call it by the opposite name: evil, vice or sin. As a matter of fact, it is only a portion of the total Supreme, so it doesn't last long. Where it ends, the opposite reaction begins. So pleasure brings pain, happiness brings unhappiness, union brings separation, birth brings death, up brings down, and so forth. This is simply because, in your conception, perception or forgetfulness, you block out the transcendental—Brahman, the Almighty. Your perception is so gross that you forget the other side, although it is not actually disunited. The Supreme is still connected, but within our limitations and our externalized life, That percolates through the pipeline and we become unconscious; it gets snapped. It doesn't get cut off totally but we become unconscious of That. So the bliss or joy of that supreme Brahman becomes happiness under limited conditions and shallow pretexts. And when those conditions end, the loss of happiness creates unhappiness. Unhappiness is not an entity or a condition; it is simply loss of happiness.

So the Great Silence, as they call it, percolates into this, our limited peace. Actually, loss of peace is war, but that may not be very comprehensible to many without a lot of commentary. The loss of light is what we call darkness. Darkness itself has no existence; it is merely the loss of light. That other side or condition does not actually exist. So loss of peace brings disturbance in the mind, and disturbed minds, because they are not harmonious and balanced, will create war. Try to understand this. It is not that they want to make war or fight or quarrel or clash. No two people or nations would like to make war, but when peace is lost, minds get disturbed, disharmonious, imbalanced and quarrelsome, wars are the outcome.

The wisdom, the knowingness of the supreme state of Brahman or God percolates to us in our unconscious, limited lives as certain things we know or study. Loss of knowledge is ignorance; ignorance is *not* the existence. Loss of life is death. Now this will be difficult to understand because we see somebody dying. According to yogic language, life is synonymous with prana, the life-force or *jivan shakti.** When the prana is completely depleted, then death occurs. Death is not a thing that creeps into us or overpowers our life. In the ultimate analysis—according to Vedanta as well as the devotional path to the Lord, at least as far as India is concerned—they do not, in the scriptures, fear death.

Let's make it more clear: there is no darkness in the universe except as the other extreme of the light. When the light gets so distant, so obscure—talking in space-time language—we see the other side as darkness. But there is light there too. Probably it is so faint to see or measure that we call it darkness. This can only be explained in relative language. There is a very high-grade spiritual term in which we say there is no darkness, but I think that will be jumping too soon. In the same way, we say that nobody is a sinner; there is no such thing as badness, et cetera. God is all goodness, but when that percolates into our unconscious life and conditions, that goodness gets so limited, so short-lived, the loss of goodness becomes badness. So when you are

---

* "Prana is a higher Light than even the sun or moon, which fades before the Light of prana, *jivan shakti.*" From "Receiving the Light," Satsang of Swami Amar Jyoti, published in *Light of Consciousness* (Truth Consciousness), Volume 12 #1.

bad, I know only that you are not good, that's all. That may not sound like a great solution, but that is the truth. Goodness prevails; badness does not. Truth triumphs; falsehood does not. Why? Because these seeming opposites do not exist. To us, on the relative plane, darkness, crimes, sin, badness, unhappiness and wars seem to exist. It is your loss of harmony and balance that makes the other side possible, but even so, the other side does not really exist. It is conceptual only.

Let's apply this to God and man. As a man, man is not God, sure; man is man. But God is within man—that is easy to understand and accept. It is not so much that God is not in a man or woman, but the lack of God is what makes us human beings. I'm using very simple arithmetic. Your unconsciousness of God is making you a human being, virtuous or not. It is not that the Kingdom of God is not within you. Your unconsciousness of the same is making you feel miserable. So the full Totality of the supreme treasure, the Bliss, the Great Silence, Enlightenment, Immortality and Lordship—all those great wealths— when they percolate through the pinhole of our ego, become limited due to our lack of consciousness. This is the whole secret, the whole tragedy and comedy. You have not lost the light or joy or awareness or your Godship or Lordship—not over others but Lordship within you. When you *be* as you truly *are*, you are Lord; not being as you, not theirs or yours or mine, just Being. Then that pinhole, the ego, gets punctured—so much the better! The Totality is our treasure and wealth eternally, if you just could be That. Then there is nothing to worry about, nothing to think about, to tax our brains. Some years back I had once said, "You twinkle too much . . ." Recently I was reading— nothing new, but sometimes when you discover it, it is new—that what we call moonlight is actually sunlight; the moon is simply a mirror. When I read this I thought—*my God, it's such a simple thing!*

These are habits. We make ourselves believe in darkness, in badness, in crime, sin and vices. We make our minds believe these things through autosuggestion, hypnotizing ourselves; brainwashing, as they call it, in such a way that we go on harping upon certain titles, habits, and things: "That's the way it is! My grandfather did this; my mother did this; my neighbor did this! This is the way I have read and heard and seen. This is the only way it could be! And that's what's supposed to be at this moment!" That is where we make limits. In old days and even now in certain rural areas of India and Pakistan, the washerman still carries huge loads of clothes tied on the back of a donkey to the canal or the river for hand washing. Their only vehicle is the donkey. And it is a well-known allegory that the washerman and his donkey are eternal companions. One without the other would mean nothing. So there is a proverb that if that donkey sometimes goes astray or is left untethered or something happens—the children chase it away—that donkey will always come back to the washerman's home. Leave it anywhere you like! In other words, our minds' habits, self-hypnotism, brainwashed beliefs, true or not—that's immaterial— have been nurtured such that those thoughts and self-impositions will always come back to that. Whatever else you imbibe, such as new thoughts, you will come back to the self-imposed impressions or *samskars*,* which are recordings on the mind.

The mind is like a record, only there are some subliminal sounds called the subconscious. This self-suggestiveness forms subtle, subconscious recordings that, regardless of how many times your mind pops up for something new, as long as those samskars are there, you will come back to them unless you erase them. Since the percolation from the Brahman, the Spirit, onward until it came to ego and the externalized world, we have formulated these recordings on our minds. Each time you want to play anything else, you will come back to it. Wherever you leave that donkey, he will come back to the washerman's home because that donkey's whole life has consisted of going from the washerman's home to the canal bank and back again. That donkey has never seen anything else. Whatever mind has seen

---

* *Samskars*, "mental impressions," are tendencies on the mind like ruts in a road that keep us falling again and again into ego-identification or ignorance. Gurudeva explained that there are primarily five samskars: lust, greed, attachment, anger, and name and fame (power). He said that ego, which is manifesting all five samskars, can be a samskar by itself. Thus, He said, each embodied soul (not including Liberated ones) has between one and maximum three samskars in a given birth, and that samskars are what keep souls in the cycle of rebirth.

and adopted is the way it will run around. All our philosophies, individually speaking, are just our individual expressions. We are just playing our own records. Unless we erase them or re-record them, unless we really clear and purify them, we keep playing the same tunes. And the more we play the record, the more it gets muddy or creaky. The voice that previously was clear becomes more hoarse and coarse like an old person's throat. The mind gets creaky until, according to Patanjali's Raja Yoga, we clean our slate, until we dehypnotize ourselves and purify our hearts. Then all those great divine treasures: the Bliss, the Great Silence, Enlightenment, Immortality and Lordship, will begin to flow. You will relax. You will have peace. You will feel joy unspeakable. Wisdom will awaken in you intuitively. You will not fear anything, including death. You will not dominate anybody nor will you be a victim to domination. These treasures will begin to emerge out.

Raja yoga has suggested the ways for this cleaning, erasing and purifying. There are two: countersuggestion or absolutely affirming "not this." Either you do not accept it or you make a counter-suggestion. You see, when we have become externalized in gross bodies, we have become what we are in this present context. Despite that, everything is not lost. If that were true, if we would lose everything including being conscious of the Supreme Lord, then we would say that God did not leave us any opportunity to come back. That would be a great allegation. But He created Realized Souls, Prophets, scriptures, the paths, the yogas, and so on and so forth as the salvaging methods to scoop us out of our unconsciousness. As they say, "He comes to save the sinners." Lost souls are saved. Then there is raja yoga and other methods, but purification is the best of those. The whole method of raja yoga is how to purify not only the mind and heart but the entire nervous system so that the prana, or God's Consciousness, can journey through our body, this three-dimensional form, without having to transcend the gross life.

The intention is to percolate or transmit that Divine Consciousness into whatever we are *even now*. This has been called the supramental descent of Divine Consciousness or New Age Consciousness. Whether we call it God's mercy or not, look at the beauty: He is not saying,

"This is a junkyard—just leave it"—not necessarily, unless you wish to, which is also okay. For those who think Swamiji has said, "This also can be made Divine; you don't have to leave this and go there, so stay on that," that will be spiritual materialism. What I am saying is that both are possible: the transcendental and the immanent. If we want to keep this body, this nervous system, flesh, blood, bones, and our prana or life-force, we have to simply purify them.

According to raja yoga, all these samskars or recordings on the mind are to be erased and made clean first. The first method is countersuggestion. For example, instead of thoughts of competition, you suggest to yourself to be forgiving; instead of fear, you suggest to yourself expansion of consciousness; instead of greed, you bring in thoughts of being charitable; instead of being miserly, you bring in thoughts of giving, magnanimity. The other way is to give unto God everything: our jealousy, stinginess, good, bad, greed, charity, everything. "All is Yours, Lord." Both of these ways lead to cleanliness. If you do want to exist as you are in the gross body and externalized world as we call it, which is not separate from the inner world, then bring in the Divine Descent. Clean the nervous system. See that your consciousness travels freely through your every pore of the skin and every nerve. See that nothing remains hidden in the corners of your mind and heart from the Pure Consciousness. Clean it thoroughly.

That is the Divine Descent into the earth consciousness. And then ego gets purified. When ego gets purified, it becomes a direct instrument of the Lord. It remains as a form but very pure. When body, mind and prana play the very pure and expansive function, that is Life Divine on earth, the Golden Age of Consciousness. Do not think the Golden Age will just drop from the sky and nobody will be poor and that's it! This is not about being poor; I am talking about being *pure*. The more you hatch on your greed, the more you are resisting. Resistance is a quality of *tamas*,*

---

* In yoga, the three qualities of mind are called *gunas*, which consist of *tamas* (*tamo-guna*), stagnation or inertia; *rajas (rajo-guna)*, the active or overactive quality; and *sattva (sattva-guna)*, purified energy.

or inertia. Resistance is a force of darkness against the Truth. Truth does not fight; the dark forces fight. Truth shines by itself. It has nothing to lose, so it does not fight. Tamas—inertia and greed—or *rajas*—ambitiousness and arrogance—are what cause us to fight. These are disharmonies and disabilities of mind. We are always seeing the disabilities of the body but there are disabilities in mind too.

God does not fight. He is Self Existent, Immortal. Why would He fight? We may see Him fighting in the forms of Prophets, yet that could be seen in different way. The lack of harmony and balance and un-Divinity makes the Prophets fight to overcome that darkness or demonic force. The Prophets come just to make harmony and the balance possible again. To us it looks like fighting. It seems like action but it is actually reaction, to put the things in right place. Whenever imbalance or disharmony exists, the Prophets bring in harmony and balance by whatever methods. To us it may look like peaceful methods or warring methods, but as a matter of fact, he is just putting things back into place. It depends on how you look at it. When unrighteousness prevails, when injustice prevails, when untruth increases, when darkness or falsehood seem to increase, the Prophets and Enlightened Souls use any methods in order to bring back the righteousness, the justice, the Light as it should be.

When children make a mess in a house and turn it helter-skelter with bed sheets under the mattress, pillows in the bathtub, pictures hanging upside down, toys on the TV, clocks upside down, curtains half out of the hooks, and like that, then mom comes in (I always think daddy should not come in, as he is going to slap the children). So mom comes in, and what does she do? If she's a good mom, of course, and God is a good mom and dad, what does she do? She just puts the things where they belong. Would you say she is reacting or fighting with her children? This is the same thing the Prophets do. But to our limited view, it looks like, "Why should Krishna fight and kill? Why should Rama fight? What about Moses?" We are ignorant, and on the top of that, we judge the Prophets! Confusion worse confounded! They just set things right, to bring in harmony, to bring in balance and then they say, "Now it is yours, children. Take it!" Once the Prophets set it right, they give the keys back: "Come on, carry on. I will come again after two thousand or two thousand five hundred years. In the meantime, make any mess you want!"

Whether the Prophets choose a method of nonviolence or violence depends upon what is needed at that time. If the children have made a worse mess, mom may slap them. When mom came in, Joan went under the bed and Jack went into the box! They are such self-imposed "stupids"! How can they believe that mom won't know that Jack is in the box and Joan is under the bed? But they hide in such a way, thinking they are quite clever. That is what we do, but which Master, God or Prophet doesn't know us? We may hide anything we want; we may pose to be something else, but those who are seers, what can we hide from them? Mom may be smart or not, but her home she knows! And how long can Jack and Joan remain quiet successfully? One or the other thing they will do in those few minutes and mom will know where the mouse is. We may hide or pose other than we are for a few hours, a few days, a few years, but eventually we will do something that will expose us. On one side, the seer already knows it, and on top of that, you are giving leakages anyway. It is no magic or occultism; falsehood cannot hide eternally and truth cannot hide, *ever*. It is self-shining. Falsehood has no existence; therefore how long can it assume to be what it is not? Reality never assumes, because *it is what it is.*

You can force yourself to be in darkness for one year, ten years, twenty years, one birth, two births, ten births, but eventually the leakages come out into miseries, suffering, pain and afflictions that you do not want. And how long you can be stubbornly ignorant either? So the time comes when dispassion and sobriety are born, when you have to face the Reality, to face yourself and stop hiding from yourself. Whether it comes in years or months or births, there are sober moments when your mind or a voice inside tells you: "This is the way it is. This is the truth." We might again ignore it, hide from it or let it go, but we do get that kind of communication—*many* times. From where does it come? You may call it the inner voice, God's voice, your Master's voice, your True Self or your own intuition. The name is immaterial. Ultimately, because we are already joined with Brahman, the Supreme Consciousness, it will percolate through some loopholes within our ego. That ultimate connection, the yoga, the link, is always there. We may ignore it, but that voice is trying to call us back. When we have lost the connection, when we are forgetful or unconscious or deliberately, stubbornly blocking it out, God sends radio waves, the communication to reach us in our quieter moments when we are really relaxed and silent. When our silence is very eloquent, throbbing and pulsating, we receive these communications that tell us where we belong. They may even tell us: "This is not where you belong," or they may say: "Bring that Light into your life, matter and mind."

Matter or the body is physical, gross. The mind as we know it is astral. In our life and mind, therefore, we need to bring that divine Light into descent. He will supply all if we make the conduit correct. The divine Voice will call us back: "Come home." But if we are stubborn and egotistical, we will reject or lose it again. Those who are great advanced lovers of God say, "Lord, whether this is heaven or hell, I want to come to You. My brain doesn't understand Divine Descent into earth consciousness." Ultimately, all is vibratory phenomena: the gross body, the thoughts, feelings, emotions and life-force. That is why it is called an illusion or dream. Dreams are vibratory. Some prefer to live still in vibrations as they *are* with the Divine Consciousness manifesting. That phenomenon makes it possible for the Prophets to come. See the connection. Theoretically speaking, if all were wishing to go back home, to live with the Lord and be one with Him, Prophets have no need to come. It would be all empty here! But some go and some do not. Even among those who stay, some are well meaning or positively motivated, the rest degrade and become more gross or solidified. They become materialistic again. And that is why, to establish righteousness, divine law, justice and also love and peace, the Supreme Entity sends or comes as Prophets or the Sons of God.

What is a Prophet? It is not only one who makes prophecies, such as Nostradamus. In English this word is used but the right word is

Avatar, which means a Son of God, Incarnation or Direct Descent of God. Jesus, Buddha, Krishna did not come just to make prophecies like Nostradamus. Their mission is far beyond that. They are the harbingers of the new age each time. They come always at the juncture when one age is closing and another age beginning. The Lord comes to set things right, to harmonize, balance, uplift and see that righteousness and truth prevail. Why is the Prophet called an Incarnation? In the Bhagavad Gita, Sri Krishna says: *Yadhar yadhar he dharmasya, glanir bhavati bharata, abhutanum adharmasya, sambhavami yugae, yugae.* Yugae, yugae, meaning: "from age to age."*
If the Lord would leave where He sits—I don't mean to imply He sits at one place, that will be real torture to the Lord; He is everywhere. But let's say the Lord in heaven, beyond the Formless, Brahman, pervading Consciousness—if He were to leave that and come here on this planet as a Prophet, that place will be empty. And if that is the right place for Him or Her, then in the meantime He has no deputy to fill in. So how does this phenomenon work? He sends His Son. Naturally, He should have a family there. And if He has a family, why should He have only one Son? After begetting, should He be impotent? Then He is lesser than even a human being! And if it is *not* a family, what is the phenomenon then? I'm not deciding for you. You think for yourself. If you can give the answer—so much the better. I'll tell my answer, of course, but you are not bound to accept it.

What is a Prophet? Who is the Son of God? Does God leave one place and come here in a different form? That will be very three-dimensional. In other words, for God, does only this planet really exist? Are other planets and galaxies all dark or empty or devoid of God? And does God come only to this planet every time we make a mess and then correct it and go back to heaven? Is that the only work

---

* Translation of the full shloka: "Whenever there is decay of dharma and rise of adharma, then I embody Myself. For the protection of the good, for the destruction of the wicked and for the establishment of dharma, I am born age after age." From the Bhagavad Gita, translated by Swami Chidbhavananda, Sri Ramakrishna Tapovanam, Tirupparaitturai, India.

He has? And are we so important? You think if mom came in that room and slapped Jack and Joan or set things right, that is the whole house? There are no other bedrooms, bathrooms, kitchen or attending to relatives, in-laws, neighbors and telephone calls? Is there no other world existing for the mom, just those two kids?

Who is that Buddha of whom the *Bodhisattva** takes form? How does this marriage of the Spirit and mind take place? How does that Supreme Lord conduct through His Prophet or Prophets to set the balance and harmony, without which the creation would not function? How does this take place? Does the Lord leave His abode and come or does He send His emissary or Son or some kind of deputy whom He trains well, or something else? How would you reply? It's a difficult question. Who awakens us in the mind sometimes? The Guru does, but inside sometimes it happens by intuition. Great voices we hear; some dreams we see; in our great moments we get an idea. How does that phenomenon work or happen?

At the outset we can easily and safely say that if we were not already linked constantly, this would not happen anyway. Is it, therefore, sometimes when you remember, when you are in a relaxed attitude, peaceful, that the connection is perceived consciously, and that time the communication takes place? How does the Lord take the shape or form of this Spirit embodied as a Prophet? Now the reply is not really new except that we have to see it: God is omnipotent. He can assume any form He will. And wherever He takes form, He does not have to leave that Absolute aspect. He can take millions and billions, an infinite number of forms simultaneously. Yogis have proven this capacity in their own yogic life, which I'll touch a little later. When He comes, God only assumes the form on the dimensions and with the circumstances and elements of this earth. He formulates this without leaving His abode, His throne. And He can do that in billions of forms simultaneously, not one after another. Throughout galaxies and billions and billions of existences, in the twinkling of an

* *Bodhisattva* is a Buddhist term for Enlightened Being, a Buddha, who comes to earth again and again to help souls achieve Liberation or Nirvana.

eye He can do that. That is what we call the Prophet, Son of God, Spirit embodied. It doesn't have to be one Son; that would limit God too much.

That is what the whole phenomenon is about: within our own conditions, limitations, dimensions, our own five-elemental world, our four directions or sixteen; within the same existence of the sun, water, fire, ether and so on, earth, He formulates and takes shape. Yogis have proved this; they can appear simultaneously at three or five different places without leaving where they are visibly sitting or walking. Just as scientists prove many things with their laboratory apparatus, yogis have proved this. If a yogi can do this, then just magnify what the Lord can do. His powers are infinite. He could do that in billions at the same time. This will explain, for those who are conversant with Krishna's *rasa leela*,* how, as many *gopis*† as there were, each one saw and experienced Krishna simultaneously. This may be allegory to some, historically apart, that he could be so many forms, so that each gopi thought, "Krishna is with me." When he can do this in sixteen or twenty-four forms, the Lord, being most Supreme, can do in billions. Now this will give you the perfect answer that I am coming to: if this were not true, how would God be in everyone? You see? Whether you keep three water troughs to capture the moonlight or sunshine, or a million, a billion, or trillions, still the light will shine in all the vessels. That is the capacity He has. Not only capacity: He's omnipotent. We can easily see from this how the Kingdom of God is within everyone; God is in everyone; Spirit is in everyone.

So God does not have to leave that Absolute Manifestation when He comes as Krishna, Jesus or Buddha. And that body, that force, that power of the Prophet, whatever it may be, accordingly He manifests. We think that Jesus manifested this way, Buddha this way, Krishna this way, but there is no use to distinguish. At different times

---

* The *rasa leela* is the divine dance of union enacted by Sri Krishna with the pure-hearted gopis in Vrindavan, approximately 5000 years ago.

† *Gopi* means milkmaid. The gopis Gurudeva refers to lived in the village of Vrindavan where Sri Krishna grew up, near Mathura, India.

and in different places the Prophet does differently. It is useless to compare. They do according to the needs of that time. Comparison is only our human frailty. Those who make comparisons feel they are sitting on the seat of judgment over the Prophets. In the first place, they cannot even remove their own headache! Then they get tired, frustrated and negative and start abusing the Prophets. They cannot have their own peace and on top of that, they are comparing the Sons of God! They learn a few things in books; some people have told them certain things; they have believed certain things and now they are great. There is a proverb in India that a mouse found a piece of turmeric root and thought he was a grocer! When he was walking with one leg up, not touching on earth, he was thinking: "How great I am! I have a turmeric piece in my mouth!" Yeah, we twinkle too much!

When you repeat the name of God or the Prophets, be humble. We really do not know that much. We are judging from too far beyond our jurisdiction. Even if you judge them, you cannot implement it. You are just impotent. The Prophet is a direct descendent of God. He comes for the devotees, to uplift us and to save the sinners. He comes to establish the law of justice and righteousness, to make harmony and balance, to make some sense in our living. It is up to us to listen to the Prophets. It is their word that we have to follow rather than just worship, rituals or ceremonies: "We had a great day. We had nice food, nice decorations, ribbons and balloons tied up . . ." And that ends the matter. We have to follow their Word. They come to make balance and harmony, to make our life worthwhile, to give us sensible living, to give us some kind of spices to live where we have made a mess, where we have disharmony, imbalance, anger, anxiety, fear, worries, losses, insecurities. Therefore we worship them. But we have to follow their Word.

A Direct Descent of Lord Vishnu—that is Krishna. The Father in heaven comes as Jesus. He may come again. His name may not be Jesus and should not be. If He plays with the same name, the same costumes, the same play, who is going to see it again? Once or twice is enough. You would not like to go to the same drama again and again. So it is as Direct Descent. When the ego is pure, even though it remains as ego, it is a Direct Descendent of the Spirit, the Light, the Consciousness. He comes from age to age to promote the evolution of humanity from one level to a higher one, so that Truth prevails, the harmony and balance remain. On one side we make a mess: disharmony, worries, conflicts, afflictions, quarrels, divorces, whatever. We can't even live together, many of us. On the other side, when the Prophets come and do these things, to help us and remind us what is our true abode, our sweet home from where we have descended, our true origin, we resist. And then we sit on the seat of judgment. Therefore sometimes they give their own life for us and sometimes they bring the stick. "Now, no more!" And then Moses is born and Krishna is born. "Enough is enough!" God or Divine Mother works in both ways. We cannot, in the first place, even solve our own mind and problems, and on the top of that, we blame them! This is our plight. We have to recognize this.

As God's law has been established from age to age, again it will be done. Justice shall reign supreme; truth will prevail. If you do not participate consciously, things will be done again anyway. Those who lovingly, cooperatively, willingly and sweetly participate, they hasten their release, their Liberation. That is what the Prophets do. They tell us: "If you have seen me, you have seen my Father," because it is a Direct Descent, pure Spirit. And they tell us, "You are also that." All the Prophets have said this. Buddha repeatedly said, "You all can be Buddhas." Jesus said, "The Kingdom of God is within you. God is within you." Krishna said, "Brahman is within you. You are Brahman." They remind you: "Look at me. As I am, so you could be." Do not look just to beards and robes. Even if you make them into a crutch, they tell you, "No. You are also That which I am. Thou *art* That." They try to remind you that you have forgotten. That is their work. *Therefore* we worship them, because they are the Supreme Lord embodied into the conditions we are in so that we could communicate with them.

Coming as a Prophet does not decrease His being God. Understand this. It is pure spirituality I am talking about. Only because He does not look like I imagine: golden-hued, one-mile-long body radiating light without limit and, you know, not sneezing! How come God sneezes here? Why does He get hungry or old? What else could He do? He is communicating with you within your own limitations. There could be no greater mercy. If He comes one mile tall, first of all you would have to remove all your electric wires and cables. Second, if He speaks to you from one mile high, you will hardly be able to hear Him. Third, if He touches you for blessings, you can hardly rise half a mile. What I mean is: if He really came as He is, how shall we communicate with Him and how shall He communicate with us? Don't we sit down on the level of a child just to make our faces level? Is this not His mercy and greatness that God does this with us? If mother or father puts his lips against his baby's lips, is he being lowered or diminished? No. He is being great. He meets the child on its own level. It doesn't take away his daddy-hood.

So when you utter and talk about Prophets, such great Ones, be humble. It is very sacred; it is divine Spirit embodied. You may not see it because you are tied up with your own limitations, and you are seeing him in the same limitations, more or less. Naturally, you are blinded by that. You cannot see what he or she is. But if you gradually enhance your perception or consciousness, you will be able to see. If he carried his halo visible around him, ten feet diameter, everywhere he went, you could see it. But then every door would have to be ten feet wide and carpentry bills would go up! Moreover, you have to have special eyes to see that dazzling radiance. We see only to the limitation of our own eyes. Therefore we worship the Prophets as God, though they do not necessarily look like that. Movies portray them like that, but they did not look like that when they existed on earth, believe me! What the movies and artists project is not exactly as they looked. They looked very human, I tell you. Jesus was very human. Krishna was very human.

They just test and see what is going on on this earth when they come. They do not have to experiment on and on with the same thing. They know it. We do the same thing over and over a thousand times and are still not fed up with it. We like ruts. Even if the wheel gets stuck in the ruts, we take it out with muscular arms and then fall again and again in the same rut. But the muscular arms do not follow us all the time. Weaknesses do come in. Old age comes in. We cannot do much afterwards. So whenever you utter the name of the Prophets and Enlightened Ones, bow your head down. I'm not telling you anything new. Because we are talking about Prophets who are Spirits embodied in the bodies as we are, in our limitations and conditions, we naturally look at them as we look at ourselves and judge them. But that is not the whole fact. If a Prophet did come in his own pristine purity, he would knock down anything or everything wherever he would go. If he bangs against a pillar, the pillar will break. So he kind of knocks his own head; the pillar remains intact. Within our own limitations, they justify this, but they also do feats. Jesus healed; he took the ghosts out of those haunted bodies. Krishna did a lot of things, very colorful! He killed many demons and saved the downtrodden, protected the simple ones.

They do miracles if they want, but they do to the extent it is needed. Do not think they couldn't. They could have done anything, but they only do what is needed for us. If so-and-so, the next Prophet, doesn't do what an earlier Prophet did, it doesn't mean anything. Why should they do every time the same thing? According to circumstances and times and climes, they do things. There is no way we could judge them. We should not judge even our fellow beings, what to talk of Prophets. If we do not understand them, that is our problem. Ask rather for the knowledge to Know. Increase your wisdom so that you could understand their play, their leela. Raise your consciousness. Then you will know better what they are doing. With muddy unconsciousness, how can we judge those Divine Beings? We are hardly able to rise beyond the third *chakra*,* touching fourth chakra and then again coming down. And we are judging the supreme seventh chakra! Even

---

* *Chakra*: "wheel" or "circular motion." According to yogic science, the seven major centers of the spinal column, from the base to the top of the head, are called *chakras* because the energy at each center moves in a circular motion.

if the seventh chakra descends down to third chakra, we hardly can understand them.

If you do not agree with something, raise a question; but otherwise, who is going to tell you clearly like this? I am not professing bowing down. That is not my mission. But just by the way, in the context, that is why in India we worship Realized Souls as God. Do you understand? Their pristine purity is Spirit embodied. They are worthy to be worshiped, as God would be. We do not see God directly, in a sense. When you raise your consciousness and vanish your ego, then of course, you would. That is how it happens.

We may reject dogmatically anything that doesn't suit our prejudice, but that is not truth. If he were to really come in his own Light—very great, dazzling, full Light—we hardly would even be able to see him. Our eyes would be blinded. How much capacity can our brains handle? Therefore raja yoga teaches how to purify your nervous system and brain cells so that they could behold and sustain that power of Light, the power of God.

That is why they teach how to purify your heart and mind. Otherwise the Prophets give you wisdom and impure minds begin to think and say as if they know better. It needs a very pure heart, a very pure mind and nervous system to sustain God's Vision. It is 440-watt voltage. You have to carry that kind of current. And just ad infinitum: ten thousand watts or like lightning. How much power does a lightning bolt have? What power would God's Light have? And how much purity should the nervous system have to handle it? That is why He diminishes Himself: to suit our communication. We see Him as being the same as we are but that is not the whole truth. That is just a manifestation according to our rate of vibration, as we exist, in order to communicate.

We worship the Lord so that we also become Him or at least *see* Him. And He is not separate from us. Right from the Spirit, Brahman, to the grossest point, all is connected. There is no gap in between except our own unconsciousness and forgetfulness. It is never separate. The very conception of separation brings pain and agony, but when He comes to redress our pain, miseries and afflictions, we again resist: "Why don't You allow us to remain in our own mire?" And when He does so, if He gets detached and indifferent—"Okay, come on, tackle your own business . . ." When the boat gets stuck, again we pray, "Lord, come and save us. You said You will come. How come You are not here?" Then the Lord says: "When I come there, you say you are going to do your own things." Both human frailty and puniness keep Him away. But the time does come when this hide-and-seek with God and man ends and *He* decides. He decides and that's it. Whether you want Him to come or not, He will come to establish the law of justice, the harmony, balance and dharma.

The Prophets come to remind you of your true, sweet Home, your pristine image, your real Spirit and treasures: joy, freedom, wisdom, peace and Lordship. They come to remind you, not only help you. If need be, they spank you to make you come back to your True Self. Nothing is too great to be sacrificed for this. One day I think God should declare that He comes to save the weird ones! That's a new category in this last half of the twentieth century! Before that, this category didn't exist.

So when you pray to the Lord, when you believe in the Prophets and their words, take it more loftily, not just that "he likes me." That is a self-delusion. I am not teaching you to bow down, but naturally when you think in this loftiness, what else could you do? It is a gesture, but more internal. The mind and ego should be humbled. Without humility you will not gain *anything*, I tell you frankly, underlined! As an Indian proverb says: "If you are arrogant and proud, you will go on polishing the shoes of your Guru for ten years and nothing will happen." Whether you cook, arrange flower vases, or burn candles and incense, if humility is not there, these actions will not yield anything. They are as worldly as anybody does elsewhere. Aspiration, humility, and following the words of the Guru or Prophets will release you. This is what you are hankering after, what you are panting for and waiting for.

6

The Grace of Sri Krishna

God is not revengeful, wrathful, or punishing people all the time. If we suffer, it is due to our bad deeds. But when His grace descends, He sends us to heaven—nowhere else. Then you are forgiven. That is mercy.

Nowadays the knowledge of Sri Krishna has grown a lot. I think everyone sees his aspects according to his or her nature or temperament. The most amazing part is that Krishna has manifested practically all the aspects of human and Divine, which seemingly would be paradoxical. That is why he is called the Perfect Incarnation, because he could combine all nature's forces in such a blending and wholesome way, which otherwise only manifests in various people at different times. That he combined all aspects is the most amazing part—right from violence or warfare to the highest unconditional love, and for righteousness' sake too! To let go, forgive and forget, he did a lot, yet at the same time he dealt with evil. A combination of this kind is not only rare but impossible, in an ordinary way. Even among the Incarnations or Prophets, only some aspects have manifested in each Personality. But all together, as manifested in Sri Krishna, that is something! One would even wonder whether it ever happened, as if his life were a legend or interpolation or dramatization by a writer.

From the human understanding or philosophical point of view, one could doubt many things, and it is not up to me to justify those things. No one can say for sure, except if you were to go in clairvoyance and clairaudience to see the past. Then you could see whether his life happened as it is written in the scriptures. There are two ways to take his leela or divine play: to believe it and take it as it is written, or doubt, or not believe and leave it alone. There is no other choice, except for those high yogis, the supreme omniscient ones who could probe into the past and see it as it happened. But such beings are always rare. And even if they would reveal what they saw in their deep meditations, again it is up to others to believe it or not. So again, it comes to how you take it.

If you are a man of faith, a believer, you will take what is written implicitly— call it blind faith or not. But if you are skeptical, doubtful or critical-natured, then naturally you can go that way. But I do not think you can arrive at any place by that method, because what will you investigate? There are no remnants or ruins left that you could probe into. Historically there are sometimes sculptures or statues, ruins, books or manuscripts available for research, but we are talking about five thousand years back, and those were controversial times too. There is nothing physical remaining from Krishna's life that you can go and investigate—no manuscripts, no buildings or statues even, though lately they have found some ruins under the sea on the western coast of India. This is believed to be the place of Krishna's capital city, Dwarka.

My own finding in this kind of discussion is that, even if something did not happen and we believe it happened, since it is written in the scriptures, and if it is noble, divine, uplifting, supernatural or beyond what we could do, then at least by believing in it I am making that existence possible for me. You see my point? Let's say so-and-so was not perfectly truthful but I believe so-and-so was perfectly truthful; I, at least, gain by this belief, even if it never happened. We are never losers if we have faith. This is not dogmatism or blind faith; it is simply a spiritual principle: what you believe in, one day you will achieve. Therefore I always value faith, not because I am a holy man but because I know that faith has its own virtues and values. Even if I put faith in a stone, if I believe that to be God's Image, whether the stone is God or not is immaterial—I'm going to get God. Whether God appears in the stone or within my heart does not really matter. Eventually—because God is everywhere and in everything created by Him or Her—whether the stone will become God or is God is immaterial to me. As long as my faith remains that it is God, I will gain His Realization.

Intellectuals or debaters might say, "But God didn't appear in the stone; He is in your heart." I say, "So what! As long as I am getting

His Vision, that is enough!" If they ask, "But then, if God can appear in my heart, my soul, within me, why shouldn't I search there?" My answer is: "Who told you that searching in the stone is not searching within one's own self? You are making only a symbolic concentration point in the stone image. What is wrong with that, even if God might appear and split the stone or not?" They sometimes show how God appeared out of a stone and the stone got blasted. It inspires me!

The fact is that whatever you imagine, one day it will happen. If I want to see God one day blasting as Light out of a stone, what is wrong with that? Is it imagination? So what! If imagination is going to make it a reality, that is fine with me as long as I get God's Vision. You may ask, "Is it not your own making, what you are imagining?" You are imagining something that is the highest Supreme, so you are making it a reality. You are making it Real in the Supreme sense. You are creating a certain Vision. Even if it is a creation by you or me, what is wrong with that? Don't we imagine how to be happy? And when you become happy, is it realistic or not? Intellectuals do not understand that logic can be used any way you like. I am producing logic now; let anybody on the whole earth come and refute this! I am not challenging, but this is a fact.

What if I am making my stone appear as God? Is it a great magic? Yes, if I were creating a devil or darkness or something degrading, that would be different. But this is God's Vision. I value faith, not because it is unreasonable, but because it is *very* reasonable. It gives me Realization of the kind I want. Is it only my creation? Yes, but in this world, do we not talk, act, achieve, lose and gain all for "me"? Don't you and I do this all the time? So in this case, I am achieving Enlightenment for me. Okay, fine, it is my imagination, but I am achieving it. It is mine. What is wrong with that? And if that satisfies me—my curiosities, anxieties and all desires—why shouldn't I do that? Whether it is actually imagination or not, we will find out later on. When the product of our imagination comes and manifests Reality, is it too late to understand whether it was by imagination or not? On the contrary, it is most easy at that point. When imagination takes the shape of Reality is actually the easiest time to know whether really it is imagination or not, compared to the earlier stage of ignorance and unconsciousness, in which we can caricature anything we want. When that Reality manifests, you are capable of knowing whether it was imagination or not, because your concentration is full and one-pointed.

So, coming back to Krishna: whether he is taken as a human personality, an Incarnation or the Supreme Godhead is up to anyone to believe or not. And then when Krishna may appear in the way you have concentrated upon him, that supreme Vision you have achieved. At that point of Realization, you are One with your Lord; you are yourself Supreme to judge what actually it is. So I do not think the faithful are ever losers—on the contrary—even if they achieve what they imagine. Many people do not achieve what they desire in this world. If you can achieve the imagination of Godhead, what more could you desire, ever?

Right from childhood through teenage, young adult, middle age and so on, we go through many stages of life. In romantic periods, we fantasize about so many things, and all of us wait for our fantasies to come true, don't we? Many of our desires, thoughts and imaginings are fantasies, but don't we want them to actualize? When we do actualize them, don't we take it as a reality? If you wanted to be a millionaire and you did achieve that—skyscrapers and all that— would you take it that it's a product of your imagination or actualization? You would feel, at least for the time being, happy about your success. So when the supreme desire, the supreme aspiration— call it imagination—you actualize, you Realize, what's wrong with that?

This kind of discussion has been raging through ages and everyone concludes that what he thinks is right. Scholars, philosophers and theologians each come to their own particular conclusions through the way they think and do and see. And then they put Q.E.D.—*quod erat demonstrandum*—and everyone of that kind is very sure it is perfectly right. But when you compare the notes of those successful books or lectures, you will see that they differ so much with each other, and everybody is right in one's own eyes. Therefore we see that they are only talking about different aspects, different levels, different stages and different angles of seeing and understanding.

One very beautiful point has been given in the scriptures: that in addition to all the angles and aspects of your own imagination, understanding and meditations, when you Realize—if it is only some aspects—you will see the perfect True Reality as it is. God Consciousness ultimately descends in its own Reality, which is called grace. Whatever we do, whatever we try to accomplish and put efforts, ultimately the success is not so much dependent upon what we do but the actual grace descending to us, giving the full impact, a kind of "rubber stamp" that it is true. Even if it is your imagination, it does not matter. It produces grace for you, and you will not receive it until grace is upon you. It is not something that, in the direct proportion you have done, you will receive. That would be karma on the lower stage; what we do we get back. But ultimate Reality, ultimate Godhead comes to us after we have exhausted our efforts and karmas rather than through them. Then grace descends in that vacuum, and *that* is Reality. Therefore, even if it is imagination, where it ends you do not really get it actualized. It is grace, when it descends, that caps or crowns the whole Realization.

If some Realized Souls would get together in a conference and discuss these matters, they would differ also. One would say, "I have seen Him. What you are talking about is not intellectual. My God looks like this." And another one might say, "I have seen my God like this." Now who is going to decide after that? So there is no way of putting this into one language or way of expression. Ultimately therefore, it comes to this: even after meditation, imagination, worship and devotion, when He or She appears, it will be through grace rather than because of your efforts. Imagination is transcended when you are given the ultimate Realization.

Therefore this grace has a kind of double meaning, though that is not accurate, but just to express it better. What is the genesis of grace? Doesn't grace mean when my ego is exhausted? And isn't egolessness indispensable for Realization? Grace would not descend unless ego finishes or ends. In other words, if grace is the ultimate, crowning experience, it would be when? When the ego is gone, right? So that alone explains that grace is a must, ultimately, because as long as ego is there, grace will not descend anyway. This is from the ultimate point of view. Grace in the ordinary relative world descends in many other aspects, like giving you a car or money or health or something. But that is on the relative plane. From the Absolute, Ultimate, Realization point of view, grace means annihilation of ego. Ego seeks, but at the same time, it is a block to its own Realization. That means the grace will descend. And when that happens, who was imagining in the first place? Let's put the question backward now: who was imagining toward Realization? It was ego, right? So when ego finishes, imagination finishes. Then automatically grace brings the Reality. It is pure mathematics. Even if you imagine something and that actualizes, then ego is not seeing that; it is no longer there. And when ego is no more, imagination loses its existence. Therefore the Reality will appear right away, even if your imagination was different than the Reality.

Let's say if you were imagining Krishna as the Blue God, he may appear brown when he actually comes. You might say, "But how can it be? When I imagined and meditated upon Krishna as blue, why won't he appear as the Blue God?" Logically this is true, but Reality does not work that way. Reality may assume the form of your imagination, that is true, but that is only a passing phase. Through that Blue God that you imagined, something will appear that is really Real. If ego were the supreme imaginer, it could actualize something and beyond that; then there would be no Reality left for that seeker. But ego is not supreme. When you come so near to one-pointedness and concentration, near-about Reality, even though coated with your own imagination, there is not too much distance left between the Reality and your imagined reality. God may appear to you the way you imagined, no doubt about it, but then He will show you His true Reality.

Many do not understand this at all. They condemn worship and rituals or imagination as a self-imposed form of God that you create, as if it is wrong. This is not true. If you have given up everything else for the sake of realizing That which you are imagining and longing for, do you think the real God is too far to hide from you? You see my point? Your mind, desires, ego, possessions and sense of possessions, what to speak of your weirdness, negativities and the ego inclusive—if you are ready to give up all these or have given up to a point, do you think God would still play fool with you? Religions may say, "Well, this is what you imagined. Take it or leave it!" The real God will not say this. On the contrary, He might say: "Okay, now you have given up everything. You have vacated your mind. You have purified your heart. You have surrendered your ego. You have done everything you could within your power and this is how you wanted to see Me." But He may also say: "This is not the end. There is Reality behind your created reality. Because you have equipped yourself with all the powers and concentrated focus, all the virtues worth having, realize your True Reality."

The only factor that remains is how *you* wanted to see and how it may be in Reality. That is called *bhṛm*, according to Sanskrit, not Brahman, the Supreme. This is *bhṛm*, meaning: "illusion or self-conception." Then the grace of God demolishes the illusion at that point. Not because it was wrong, but because it reached you to the nearest point you could reach, as far as ego is concerned. This is where, in Krishna's life we find so many aspects that were possible for him to manifest and satisfy different souls and their aspirations, as a demonstration of the Almighty right here on earth. To each one, Krishna was complete. They saw his manifestation as complete. Even though each saw only one or two or more of Krishna's many aspects, for each one that was Krishna. This is the beauty of Perfection, not only of an Incarnation of God, but Perfection *in Itself*. When various souls approach Krishna in a certain aspect or aspects, he does appear that way. It would seem as though that is the only Krishna, because they do not have a comprehensive view, but when Krishna manifests, he manifests totally to that person.

Krishna's devotee, Arjuna, is an example of this grace. He took Krishna in a certain way as he knew or according to his stage of evolution or level of consciousness. But when Arjuna reached that acme of his Vision of Krishna, Krishna did not manifest only as Arjuna had envisioned him. That is how, in the very middle of the battlefield, the Lord revealed His Universal Form, *Viratswarupa*, to Arjuna. Actually Arjuna did not ask for this Vision. He did not know prior to that whether Krishna existed beyond what he knew. Not that Arjuna doubted—he didn't—except that he could not conceive beyond his conception of Krishna. He had a certain view of Krishna as his maternal uncle, his spiritual guide and charioteer in the war. But when he reached that point—this is the descent of grace: even if he was not searching beyond it, even if he was not expecting it, even if he did not believe anything existed beyond what he thought, at that point, since his ego had come to its end, Krishna appeared in his Universal Form. He did this only to impress upon Arjuna that that was not the *only* Krishna that he knew. Then, of course, Arjuna's ego was finished. He transcended.

An example of this grace is when you are on a sea beach and the waves are coming and going and you are trying to play with them, following the waves in and out as they crash upon the sand. At one point you go a little further from the shore and suddenly a big wave comes and crashes over you. The force of the wave overwhelms you while you are trying to come out of it, and until the wave exhausts its force on the beach, you are inside the water, gasping for breath. After the wave has crashed on the beach, it pulls back, and once again you are above the water, feeling relieved. In this analogy, you could not have floated or swum any longer on the shore as you were at first doing, playing within your control. In the same way, up to a point, you search for God or the Goal, but when you really reach your Goal, that may not be the end and that *isn't* the end.

In Krishna's many aspects we find this happening overwhelmingly for others. In childhood, he challenged Indra, the god of lightning, thunderstorms, clouds and so on. The people of his town or village were rural folk who depended upon rain for their livelihood, so they worshiped that aspect of Divinity. To test them, Krishna told the villagers not to propitiate Indra, and it enraged the rain god so much so that he took the retaliation of flooding the whole Vrindavan and

Vraja* where Krishna lived. The villagers were fearful that Indra would submerge the whole area. They did not know or even imagine Krishna's capacity. He was a small boy only, but when Indra took retaliation on the villagers, Krishna told them, "Don't worry." This was unimaginable and overwhelming for them. And then he raised an entire mountain like an umbrella over them and held it on his baby finger. Then they believed.

Most people understood only one or two aspects of Krishna. Arjuna, to whom he was maternal uncle, did the same. Before the Mahabharata War, Arjuna went to him for help; yet so did Duryodhana, a Kaurava, who was on the evil side. Duryodhana, who was like their commander in chief, believed that Krishna had a large army of horses, chariots and great fighters. This prince was very mundane and worldly, so he recognized Krishna in this way. But Arjuna believed in Krishna differently. He believed that Krishna is Supreme, the Godhead—"If he is with me, I have everything!" Arjuna thought, "What if he is not with me but his whole material wealth and power are with me, as Duryodhana believes? Then I have nothing." Each one's imagination and belief is different, though the personality of Krishna is the same.

When both princes went to Krishna for his help, he was lying down asleep. Duryodhana was haughty, proud, arrogant, selfish, power-mongering, with bloated ego, and so many things. Arjuna was, of course, a human being; he was not a Realized Soul. But he was humble. He was understanding. He had some virtues of obedience, faithfulness, and so on. So when they went to Krishna, there were two chairs near Krishna's bed, one at the head and one at the foot. Duryodhana, that pampered and spoiled child, had arrived there first. He felt that he was the most deserving and walked in, as in the Indian expression, "with fists on his hips," showing how great he was. He went and sat on the chair near Krishna's head. Later Arjuna entered the room and sat quietly at Krishna's feet.

When Krishna opened his eyes, his gaze first fell on Arjuna and he

---

* Vraja is the district where Krishna lived as a child.

asked, "Arjuna, why have you come? What do you want?" Duryodhana then protested: "I came first! You should ask me first!" Herein lies competition in the worldly sense. Arjuna kept quiet. Duryodhana was teaching Krishna etiquette—whom should you ask first—and he was the one who came to ask from Krishna! Krishna smiled—he had a beautiful, bewitching smile—and gave a very simple, humble reply. "Duryodhana, my eyes first fell on Arjuna. I'll ask him first." What is the symbolic meaning of this? The one who remains humbly at the feet of the Lord is seen by Him first, before those who are haughty, proud and arrogant. Try to understand this; there is a *lot* of philosophy behind these occurrences. And why was Duryodhana afraid? Because if Krishna asked Arjuna first, he thought he would be the loser: "What if Arjuna asks from Krishna what I want?" Actually Arjuna was not even thinking of those material things. He only wanted the help of the Lord.

Duryodhana got insecure, competitive, afraid and haughty: "What if Arjuna asks for all the armor, wealth, treasury, chariots, horses and army? Then what shall I get?" But instead Arjuna said, "Lord, I want *your* help. I want *you*." Krishna divided himself from his world. The Lord, He Who has created and given us everything and will take away whatever it is to be taken away, here He divided himself from His creation. Krishna told both princes: "On one side are all my warriors, chariots, horses, armor, matter, wealth, treasury, everything. And on the other side am I, alone, and I won't even fight. Which do you want?"

This has great philosophical meaning. Though the Creator and His creation are otherwise inseparable, if the Lord is with you, His creation is also with you; otherwise not. It is logical, practical and realistic, but with our mundane values, consciously or unconsciously, we have always divided God and His creation. Now Krishna is saying the same thing: "On one side am I; on the other side is my creation." What does it mean? Can the Lord really separate Himself from His own creation? Here lies the whole answer of Vedanta: that this dualism of God and His world, the Creator and His creation, exists only in our relative, ignorant dualism. Since both Arjuna and Duryodhana had this unconsciousness, they would see Krishna as separate from his world. Krishna was just reflecting their ignorance back to them, not because Krishna and his army were separate. The Creator is always one with the creation. In our mundane values, we make these distinctions: "This is heaven; this is earth. This is God; this is creation . . ." Therefore Krishna kept the two separate.

Duryodhana only wanted Krishna's material wealth, his possessions and army, so he just grabbed it. He thought: "Whether Krishna is with me or not doesn't matter." But he did not know that he was losing everything! If God is not with you, you have *nothing*. Arjuna knew this. He said, "I want you, Krishna. You are my Lord. If you are with me, I have everything." Here lies the difference between the believer and the nonbeliever, the faithful and the faithless, the spiritual and the mundane, the selfless and the selfish. If Arjuna would have even decimal one percent thought cleverly, "If the Lord is with me, eventually His creation is with me too; His possessions will be mine," Krishna would have vanished right away. But Arjuna did not think that way. He was very pure and simple-hearted. He had faith that without Krishna, what good would it be to have his army or material wealth?

Arjuna was the greatest archer and warrior of his day, the best of Bharat, the ancient land of India, but even then he had never seen a charioteer like Krishna until he witnessed him in the battlefield. Krishna was not supposed to fight or kill anyone as a charioteer, but his maneuvering alone—the angles, up and down, the directions—made every enemy come in a tight corner for Arjuna to kill. None knew beforehand that, as a charioteer, Krishna could be so potent to turn the whole chessboard of the battlefield. Even this maneuvering of the chariot was a case of grace. Arjuna's faith brought it. He never knew that Krishna would win the entire war for him. He knew that Krishna is the Lord. He knew, "If Krishna is with me, even if I die, it doesn't matter." That is what Arjuna meant, actually.

By all logistics—the sizes of the armies, the invincible warriors on the Kauravas' side, such as Dronacharya, Bhishma, Kripacharya—one would have easily surmised that the Kauravas should have won and the Pandavas would have been finished, especially when Krishna had vowed not to use any weapons. But this was the simple faith of

Arjuna. He loved Krishna, and even if they were defeated in battle, even if they lost everything, I do not think the Pandavas or Arjuna would have regretted it, because they had God with them. They had love for him and they were satisfied with the situation, even if they were defeated or killed. Fortunately they won through Krishna's skill, but the point I am making is that each one—devotee, friend, countryman or relative—could imagine Krishna's aspects only up to a point. When they reached that point, Krishna was not the same as they had imagined. That is why we call him the Supreme Godhead, the Perfect Incarnation. He did not leave them only to the point where each could imagine or believe.

Another example is the rasa leela, Krishna's full moon dance with the gopis, who were the milkmaids of Vrindavan. Earlier on there were some jealousies among the gopis, which is normal; they were not nasty or bad or negative. Sorry for saying, but jealousy is a kind of ingredient of women's nature, so it is not particularly wrong or bad; it is just that if you are born a woman, you have to be jealous, to some extent. It may be a virtue or vice, but it is a part of your nature. So, to a point, that aspect of a woman is agreeable, and Krishna knew this. He did not want to take advantage of their jealousies either. So what did he do? He did what the gopis could have never imagined. In their deep love, they saw, "he is our everything—beyond mother, father, husband, children, countrymen . . ." However, it was one thing to love him; it was another to get his personal love, to have him as one's own, one for one. The gopis thought, "Krishna is ours, but Krishna is only one, and we are so many . . ." So Krishna created this rasa leela dance, and in that he assumed a form for every gopi. When Krishna assumed this immortal dance, it was the most perfect ever played on earth, I think, apart from the fact that the gopis were very high souls who in their previous incarnations were great sages. Krishna assumed a form for every gopi, and each one saw that Krishna was totally with her. The gopis had reached their climax of love, of devotion, of caring for, searching for and missing Krishna, and at that point, when they had exhausted their egos, grace descended and they were melted in Oneness with their Lord.

Desert Ashram, March 1980

Singing with tamboura in His room at Rishi Ashram, Manali, Kullu Valley (India), 1979

Divali (Festival of Lights) at Rishi Ashram, Autumn 1981

Divali at Rishi Ashram, Autumn 1981

Gathering with children at Desert Ashram, 1984

Guru Purnima (Disciples' Rededication Day), Countryside Ashram, Rockford,
Michigan, July 1982

At a guest inn outside Leh, Ladakh (India), October 1983

With monks at Thikse Gompa, Indus Valley, Ladakh, October 1983

wanted to touch Krishna's feet. The Lord was born on earth and that river, personified as a goddess, would not miss that opportunity to touch the feet of the Lord.

There are thousands of these episodes throughout Krishna's life in which something was achieved beyond that which could ever be imagined, once the ego's possibilities and potentials were exhausted. Now it so happens that when the Lord is born as a Prophet or an Incarnation on earth, the counterpart is always created. That counterpart is called *Yoga Maya.** *Maya* is illusion, the shakti, the power, and yoga is the union when you realize the Divine. So the divine Illusion, the divine shakti, the divine power is also born of the Lord when He incarnates. And that very night in Gokul, a town on the other side of the Yamuna River, a well-known cowherd man named Nanda Baba and his wife Yashoda had a baby girl, who was a form of Yoga Maya. This always happens as a balance so that when the Lord is born, He plays His part on the earth, using His divine energy to accomplish that.

On the night of Krishna's birth, Yashoda and Nanda were asleep, and even they did not know when Vasudeva brought Krishna inside their home to exchange him with their newborn baby girl and take her back to the prison. Yashoda did not know that Yoga Maya had been born to her, nor that she had been exchanged for Krishna. She thought Krishna was her own child. She was under this impression throughout her life. She never knew that he was not technically her own child. Yoga Maya was brought back to the jail and when she was brought inside, she began to weep. Then the guards woke up and went to tell Kamsa that the child was born. The wicked king was expecting the eighth child to be a boy, but when he saw the girl, he didn't hesitate. To him, whosoever was the eighth child must be killed. He had, by that time, killed every child they had given birth to, like the story of Moses when Pharaoh had the children killed. When Kamsa took the baby up to smash against the stones, instead she slipped out of his

---

* *Yoga Maya:* the "eternal potency of the Supreme" or divine shakti.

hands and rose into the sky, and from there she gave the *akashvani**
or prediction of the future to the king: "The One who is going to kill
you to establish righteousness and justice is already born. Now you
cannot do anything . . ."

When Krishna was a small child—there are many stories, hundreds
and thousands—one day his mother, Yashoda, wanted to punish him.
Gopal, his childhood name, which means "protector of the cows,"
was a very naughty boy. He played mischief with *everyone*—men,
boys, grannies, small girls and teenagers. On this occasion, he had
eaten charcoal or some ashes outside, as children sometimes do. The
other boys told on him and his mother wanted him to tell the truth.
She tried to look into his mouth herself but he was holding it closed
tightly. Finally at one point she pressed his cheeks like this, you know,
and his mouth opened. And inside she saw the three worlds—the
earth, heaven and the nether world, manifested in his mouth! She
got scared and swooned, saying, "Gopal, what are you doing? Close
your mouth! I don't want to see this. I want to see you as my son!"

She never wanted to see the divine part of him. If anyone came
and said, "Your son is an Incarnation or Prophet," she would say,
"This is humbug! Don't talk like that! He's just my son, Gopal." She
just wanted only to see that way, but then she exhausted the acme of
her motherliness through him. She was one of the best mothers one
could even imagine. Not just a mother because she bore a child—
anybody can bear a child; any tree can sprout a seed. Yashoda was
the very perfection of motherhood. And if someone came to tell her,
"Your Gopal is so great. He did this . . . He did that . . . Two big trees
he threw apart and two demons came out and he killed them . . . He
drank the whole forest fire and extinguished it to save our cows." Many
stories they would come and tell her, as she did not witness everything,
but she would not believe it. "Don't talk like that about my son," she
would say, as if what they were telling her was like a curse or evil.
"My Gopal is not like that. Don't say like that," she would tell them.

---

* *Akashvani*: a "celestial voice," from the Sanskrit *akash:* "space or sky"; *vani:* "words
or speech."

They would tell her these things about the greatness of Gopal but she would reply, "No, he is just my simple Gopal." She wanted to see him only as her child. *Therefore*, from that point onward, Krishna took over. Every time she would end somewhere, he would go beyond it to show her more. One day she wanted to punish him because he had broken the milk pots that the gopis carried on their heads to sell the milk. He used to throw stones at those earthen pots, and the gopis would go and complain to Yashoda that her son— "Kanaya," they called him—was doing all those things. And one day she got so fed up that she wanted to punish him. She tried to tie him to a pillar inside the house, and every time she brought a rope, it would not be long enough. She would bring longer and longer pieces of rope and every time they would prove short. She would get exhausted and he would go on doing these pranks.

The point is: he wanted to show her that her son was extraordinary, not only up to the point that she was seeing him as a mother— attachment apart, because attachment to God or Krishna would not end as attachment ever; God will lead you through attachment to faith and devotion and Realization, even if you are attached to Him. It is not the same as being attached to other mundane relationships. Yashoda went on denying all the time, trying to maintain her motherliness for the son, which was her wish to have. Even if somebody had told her that he was not her real son, she would not have believed it. Nothing else did she believe or want to see. That perfect concentration, the total loss of herself unto Gopal, made her one of the greatest mothers who have ever lived.

There are so many stories of this kind. For example, Radha was the foremost gopi. She was the personification of unconditional love, of divine love, of the highest love ever experienced. And Radha was not even Krishna's wife. Why would the love of Radha-Krishna remain immortal all these thousands of years, and growing more and more? Even Americans and Europeans worship their immortal love. That is because it was so unconditional, so unalloyed and selfless. If you consider in the social, human sense, it was illegitimate love, actually, especially in those days in India when orthodoxy was rampant; it was not a permissive society where it did not matter if she was your wife or not. This was five thousand years ago in India, when faithfulness, chastity and loyalty of a woman were most valued. And in those days, Radha was the wife of someone else. But even then, her love was so perfect, so full and supreme that she did not want anything in return.

Radha is considered to be an Incarnation of Lakshmi—the Goddess and consort of Lord Vishnu in heaven. And Krishna was everything for her, so much so that they say, if you were to go incognito while Radha was lying down asleep and put your ear on her pulse, you would hear, "Krishna . . . Krishna . . ." Now it may be poetry, allegory, or whatever, but love was in her very blood and in her every breath. She knew only Krishna, not even Radha. For her, Krishna existed and no one else. But Krishna did not end there, even though Radha would have been satisfied with only Krishna. There were some quarrels among them, little seesaw battles sometimes, but not as we do. It was more in a loving manner, like when you rebuke somebody or you kind of quarrel but inside you are not leaving each other. They had this playfulness sometimes and Radha always won because she was blameless.

I wouldn't go into too many private affairs of Krishna, but Radha was constantly the personification of love, dedication, selflessness, full faith, and egolessness for her Beloved. Krishna did many mischiefs with Radha, but even then Radha's love was never affected, fluctuated or reactionary—"If you're like this, why should I be like this?" Radha never thought this way. Can you imagine? And she was *constantly* so. Not one day till she lived did she waver. Years later in Dwarka, Krishna had six queens and many others also, and often he spoke of Radha to his wives, and they would say, "We would like to see Radha one day."

If we judge from the human point of view, Radha proved better than Krishna as a lover. At times Krishna was faithless and fluctuating with her. He was naughty. But Radha was constantly loving, selfless, giving and one-way, never thinking of what she would receive in return. We can imagine that as an ambition or purpose to achieve, but we cannot achieve even twenty-five percent of that selflessness! Even then, Krishna was the Lord, not Radha, though she was his consort. And toward the end of their days in Vrindavan, at one point Krishna was unfaithful and Radha gave him a hard time. Not that she loved him less; she just would not see him. Then Radha's friend, Vrinda, came and said, "Radha, after all, you're a woman. Just give up, okay? He is now apologizing. Forgive him. He is waiting outside to see you." Radha replied, "No, he's very selfish. Now when he wants me, he is repenting. Otherwise he doesn't care for me . . ." and so on. It's a beautiful play.

Even then Radha would not give up. Not because she did not love him—that never decreased—but in the play, she did not want to see him. And according to the scriptures, Krishna was pleading and Vrinda was pleading with Radha to forgive him, and in the end, when this play went back and forth many times, Radha gave up and agreed to see him. But when Krishna finally came and sat at her feet to apologize, she did not like that. She said, "You are my Lord. You should not sit at my feet." You see: this is Radha's side. It is the unconditional aspect of her love and selflessness. If you ever could realize this love, you will be purified with that most purifying path of devotion—unconditional, *at any cost*, without blemish, one-sided dedication of love. But Krishna did not end there; he went beyond it. He promised Radha, though she did not ask for it: "Until the earth remains, your name and mine will exist immortally together. And whenever people speak my name, your name will always be first." Therefore we say Radha-Krishna, not Krishna-Radha.

There are other stories of his leela with Radha. When the other milkmaids were jealous of her, they went to Krishna and said, "What have you found in her? She is a married woman, you know," and this, this, this. "She's even older than you." Actually she was older than him in earthly age, not probably otherwise. They asked him, "Why are you caring for her and doing so many things for her?" And to teach them, he arranged for one gopi to go in the afternoon to Radha's home when she was having a siesta and listen to her pulse. The gopi listened secretly and heard Radha's pulse beating, "Krishna . . . Krishna . . ." Even in sleep she was repeating that, leave aside waking conditions.

Our minds play havoc. We want to sit in meditation and see how it runs around. Just compare that with Radha, and where are you? How much concentration do you have? This is the immortality of Radha. And Vrinda, the girlfriend of Radha, was also a gopi of Krishna. Because she was the liaison to bring them together when they were quarreling, he gave her a boon that the whole forest where that romantic play had happened would be in her name. That is why it is called Vrindavan, and it will be immortal always.

The great war of the Mahabharata epic, the famous Kurukshetra War, lasted about eighteen days. And during the fourteenth or fifteenth day of the battle, when invincible warriors were falling like giant redwood trees—Bhishmapitama, Karna, Kripacharya, Dronacharya—Krishna knew that they were doing their duty, although because of various loyalties and obligations they were on the opposite side of the battle than the Pandavas. Some of them knew that Krishna is the Lord, but still they were fighting against his side. Not many of them surrendered unconditionally saying, "The Lord has come. I have no other obligations and commitments. Let me surrender." From the worldly point of view, they were fulfilling their duties, but from the spiritual point of view, the divine point of view, they were failing in surrender and in giving up the ego. Therefore they were defeated and many were killed. But even then, Krishna's grace was with them. He knew that some of them were, in their hearts, his devotees, but they were playing their roles on the other side because of obligations. So every day, whenever such great souls died, Krishna would take his retinue in the evening when the fighting stopped—they fought only in daytime; no bombs in the nights, that is treacherous—to the opposite camp to those who were dying or dead, to bless them and send them to heaven. He would touch them with his hand, resulting into *shaktipat*.* He did that with every enemy, and not only so; each

---

* *Shaktipat*: "transfer of divine energy."

time he would stand near that dead or dying warrior and proclaim his virtues and greatness. He was the enemy but Krishna transcended that. And they could not believe that Krishna would bless them to go to heaven when they had fought against him.

They had done their duty and obligations to the extent they could, and at the same time, they knew inside that Krishna was *right*. Even some, such as Bhishmapitama, the grandsire of both sides, had said many times to his own people that, although he was fighting on the wrong side, he knew that Krishna would win as the Divine, for righteousness and justice. Bhishma was only paying back his dues to those who had served him and the kingdom earlier. He knew the other side would win. On the day that Bhishmapitama was wounded mortally, if he had left his body at that time, he would have been reborn as a human being. According to yoga, there is a southern and northern portion in our body and mind complex, and if Bhishma's breath had departed from one of the exits on the lower half, he would have been born as a mortal being again, which he did not want. He was a great yogi and he wanted to be liberated, so he had to leave the breath from the upper half of his body, which they call the northern half of the body-mind, in order to get Liberated.

Astrologically, he was mortally wounded about four days short of this northern half. If he had waited four days or if he had been killed after four days, he would have gone from the upper portion by uplifting his own consciousness. So whatever the astrological calculations were, he had to remain alive those days in order to be liberated. Bhishma had hundreds of arrows piercing his body and, as written in the Mahabharata, he was impaled on this bed of arrows. He was a great yogi though, and he had never married. He had only fought against the Pandavas because earlier the Kauravas had taken care of him. He wanted to pay back dues, that's all. But he understood what is right, what is wrong, what is justice, what is Divine. He knew everything. He was a very *dharmic** person. So in order to attain

---

* *Dharmic:* living by dharma or righteousness and truth; a person who lives righteously, established on truth.

liberation, for four days his death had to remain pending, and Krishna made it possible. He told everyone, "Do not kill him. Leave him alone there four days, wounded." Bhishma actually wished to see the whole war up to the end. Krishna told him: "You won't die in these next four days." He allowed him to lie in the battlefield and watch the war until it ended, and then he died and got Liberated.

This grace, you see, is different than you can imagine or try to achieve. Grace never comes without faith. It is not a matter of reason. It is not a matter of theology or philosophy at all. Even toward the end of Krishna's life, if we describe him as a human being, he had a very difficult time. His own Yadava dynasty was destroyed. And eventually he was disheartened, as per the human nature, and wanted to go into a forest and meditate. He was at that time about one hundred twenty-five years of age. He wanted to meditate in the forest and leave the body and go back to heaven. When he retired to the forest, a hunter saw the sole of his foot from a distance. Krishna was lying down with one leg over the other, and there was a certain light reflection from the sole of his foot. From the distance, that hunter thought it was a deer and shot a poisonous arrow. Now Krishna could have saved himself; he had fought and easily defeated so many in his lifetime. But at that time, he wanted not to live because of the wickedness that was happening all around. So that poisonous arrow became an excuse for his departure from this world.

Krishna knew that the end of his Incarnation was the advent of the Kali Yuga, the Iron Age, the most degraded. According to the cycle of ages, the Kali Yuga follows the Copper Age. Krishna's main aim was the victory of righteousness over unrighteousness, of virtue over evil. Some people have doubted or questioned why, if he prevailed with righteousness over unrighteousness, justice over injustice, right over wrong, the world was not better after that. The idea is different: he wanted to establish God's law, whatever the age may be. Therefore the last king of Krishna's dynasty, Parikshit, became the first ruler of the Iron Age. Krishna's purpose was to give the understanding that Light always prevails over darkness; that justice always wins over injustice; that right prevails over wrong and virtue over vice. That is always the game when the Prophets come. You can see this in the modern age too. When this is done by God's Prophet, His Incarnation, the function or mission—beyond to make the world golden—is to establish righteousness, which still helps, even now.

In India they have week-long readings of the Srimad Bhagavatam, the epic retelling of Krishna's life. It takes seven days, reciting six hours daily, to finish the story. Even then, it is never finished. So it is hard to put into one Satsang everything about Krishna's life. Each aspect is so great. In Dwarka, Krishna wanted to establish the Kingdom of God and he did that. They say that it was all golden. But the point is: he could not ignore the rest of the national politics of India, which was a possible war raging between the Pandavas and Kauravas. He then came into the national scene from Dwarka. His main aim at that time was to establish the Kingdom of God in Dwarka, and he did that as long as he was there. If you read the scriptures in detail, it is written that while looking after the kingdom, the politics and administration daily, he would go once if not twice in a chariot with other horsemen around the city to see if the people were happy, if they were being taken care of, if justice was being meted out to them. He checked to see if they were in want of anything, for which they could not reach him inside the palace; they could approach him on the chariot to appeal or complain.

That was his busy life—leave aside the romantic side and sixteen thousand queens! You and I would be finished with two even! But it is said that these women were the captives whom he had freed from an evil king named Jarasandha, who was an accomplice of Kamsa. Jarasandha's two daughters had married King Kamsa. Both kings were wicked, but they were very, very powerful. Jarasandha had sixteen thousand kept ladies, and so after Krishna killed Jarasandha—it was a long battle—those sixteen thousand ladies told him, "We have no other one. You are our Lord. We will go with you." He said, "Come on," and he took them all to Dwarka and looked after them there. It is not as simple as you think—maintaining sixteen thousand wives!

You need so much food, jewelry, clothes and rooms. And later, so many "Krishnas" were born, which became the Yadavas, and they said that each one looked like Krishna.

As Krishna's heirs, they became an invincible dynasty, and when so many things in his own dynasty went wrong—they became very wicked and selfish—Krishna was worrying about it, in a way. His own descendants thought their grandpa, Krishna, would just excuse them or take it easy because they were his kin. But, no! Injustice was injustice, unrighteousness. He did what none could have ever imagined. He arranged such a plot that the Yadavas got drunk one night on the sea beach and quarreled and fought with each other until they were all killed. Krishna allowed the whole dynasty to be wiped out rather than allow injustice and unrighteousness to exist. After that, the whole of Dwarka was submerged in the ocean. His capital city was lost. And Arjuna took Krishna's wives and remaining children and other faithful ones back to central India.

With all that life and making the golden kingdom of Dwarka, he still had time to go to people, to hear their complaints, any kind of shortages. That he had such welfare tendency, to build the Kingdom of God—therefore people loved him, actually. They not only loved him; for them he was God Incarnate. He was not simply a king. He happened to be a king; he could have come as a mendicant. People wanted a righteous king but he went beyond that. He gave them what only the Divine One could give. But he always told them, "If you are occupied with material things only, that is not going to give you happiness and peace."

He gave wisdom. Therefore we, including myself, consider that Krishna's greatest contribution of his whole life—though every day, every minute was great—was the Bhagavad Gita.* He taught that if you are worldly, thinking only of possessions, attachment and greed,

---

* The Bhagavad Gita, lit: "Song of God," is the most beloved scripture of India. It is a dialogue between God and His devotee given on the verge of Mahabharata War by Krishna to his disciple, Arjuna. This revered treatise comprising eighteen chapters expounds the yoga paths of action, wisdom and devotion culminating in Liberation, and appears as the sixth of eighteen books of the great epic, Mahabharata.

you will not be happy. You have to be wise. Your karma has to be karma yoga, selfless action. You have to have devotion to the Lord. Acquiring possessions is just transitory. The Gita, therefore, we consider is his greatest contribution. Krishna's whole life is the greatest contribution, no doubt about it, but among all his many manifestations, we consider the Gita the greatest treasure that humanity has ever received. And it is still living now, not only one of the scriptures of India, but the ultimate wisdom. I am not being an evangelist. If I were an evangelist, long back it would have been different. But that is not my aim. I am saying this about Krishna very impartially. The Bhagavad Gita is the greatest wisdom and Krishna's greatest contribution to humanity.

Great powers he showed—omnipotence, magic, even love, but the greatest is the Gita. If you read it very carefully you will see that he not only harmonized devotion and selfless work with wisdom, but he gave the way of salvation out of all this. Krishna himself was a great king, but he knew that salvation is not in these riches. It is not achieved through possessions, materialism, jealousy, competition or ambition. He gave the way out of these, the release, the Ultimate, *Kevalya*, which they call the Absolute, Brahman. He showed that Brahman resides and pervades in everyone and that everyone is in Him. Therefore, to Krishna, the sinner and saint were not even in his vocabulary. He, no doubt, protected the good and the righteous, but even then, when he sent the evil ones to death, it was always salvation for them. His killing alone became a liberating force. He was not taking revenge simply. It was not a reaction or retaliation. He knew, in the case of the wicked, that their way is through destruction, and then they would be Liberated. They actually *wanted* their ruin and destruction. They had become evil to invite God's wrath. That is the way that they chose and he gave them what they wanted.

The good, the devotees, the faithful ones, he constantly protected. His famous line in the Gita is: "My Incarnation is only to protect my devotees." He said that clearly. This does not mean devotees in a sense of those following his religion. It was not that way at all. By devotees he meant devotees of God. So it was with the villagers of Vraja who invoked the wrath of Indra, or against the wrath of Kaliya, a poisonous snake that inhabited a lake nearby, or against the many demons who came to defeat him. He was always protecting his devotees against these evil ones. But to those who asked for a slap, who asked for destruction, who otherwise would not yield, grow, change or learn the lesson, he said: "Okay, I'll give you tit for tat." Both ways he did very perfectly, but ultimately both good and evil got salvation. He did not tell the wicked ones: "You are evil! I have nothing to do with you. Go to hell and just rot there eternally." He said: "Now you have paid the price. Go to heaven."

This is the beauty. This is grace again. They did not ask for it. Duryodhana, who was the cause of the whole Mahabharata War, did not ask for heaven. He just wanted to kill everyone on the Pandavas' side and rule his kingdom. And when he was dying, even then he was blaming Krishna. Still, Krishna knew that Duryodhana had played his role well, and he told him: "Now you've paid the price. Go to heaven." He did not send him to hell. This benevolence, this mercy, this grace we cannot imagine. Only God could do this. At the most, as humans we would say, "He got his own kind of tit for tat; it is not *my* wrong. He asked for it." It is only God who can send such a one to heaven.

We never understand the extent of grace, that God does not harbor any revengeful attitude at all. Once you have paid the price: "Now okay, come on, let's go Home!" It will be like that. Nobody is sent to hell once you have done your duty well. Whatever bad you do, you just suffer for it. So Duryodhana suffered for his wrongs. Kamsa and others also suffered, but afterwards they were having a nice dinner in heaven, all sitting together, whether it was the Pandavas or even the Kauravas.

Yudhisthira, the eldest brother of the Pandavas, was not aware of this. When he was shown that the Pandavas had gone to hell, even for a short time, he told Indra, the lord of thunder and lightning, "Release them to heaven. I'm not going to go to heaven without them." Indra asked him, "Why?" He replied, "My brothers are in hell.

I cannot go to heaven." Indra said, "But they have their own deeds to pay off." Yudhisthira replied, "Until then, I will live in hell." After showing the vision of the Pandavas in hell, Indra told Yudhisthira, "I was testing you, how true and faithful you are. I will send them to heaven." I am not comparing any two religions, but try to understand true spirituality. God is not revengeful, wrathful, or punishing people all the time. If we suffer, it is due to our bad deeds. But when His grace descends, He sends us to heaven—nowhere else. Then you are forgiven. That is mercy.

Why is Krishna called the Supreme Personality? He is such a perfect Incarnation, right on earth. Where he seems complex or paradoxical is only because human nature is complex and paradoxical. How could he play straight with complex people? You have to play complexly in order to teach a lesson, to change a person or to do good to people. So Krishna dealt perfectly with both: "These are my devotees; I'll protect them. These are not; I'll destroy them, but only to teach them a lesson in order to send them to heaven." And this is exactly the whole meaning of Krishna's leela, which is sometimes incomprehensible, but to me it is very easily understandable. There *couldn't* be any other way. It cannot be the same stereotyped, classical way for all people. It has to be different with different kinds. When they learn the lesson, they also understand. That is the way they are asking to learn. The mean, the wicked, the selfish, the evil ask for the hard way, but in the end, God is merciful. He does not hurl us into eternal hell. On the contrary, since you have paid the price, now you are free.

7

Lord Buddha
The Embodiment of Peace

You cannot think of Buddha without thinking of peace in the world. Whenever peace may come or whenever it has been thought about, Buddha's name has been inadvertently or advertently felt, along with compassion and kindness and so on. There was not a single exception where Buddha did otherwise.

You have to know the previous history and tradition or background of a Prophet in order to understand his mission. Originally Buddha, who lived about two thousand five hundred years ago in India, was not considered to be one of the Vedic lineage of the Ten Avatars of Vishnu. But eventually after Buddha's life, most of India became Buddhist, so much so that Buddha's name was everywhere. Seeing this, the religious leaders, saints and sages of the remaining population held conferences and decided that Buddha should be written as the Ninth Incarnation of Vishnu.

During Buddha's life and directly afterward, he was considered to be a moralist, an ethical great man, but not necessarily an Enlightened Being or Realized Soul. The Brahmins in those days were something like the Pharisees during Jesus' time, though it was not exactly the same; there were a lot of differences between the Pharisees and Brahmins, but for want of better comparison, they were like Pharisees. These Brahmins, who were the scholarly people, meant to say that Buddha was a great ethical and moral force. He had thousands of followers. The Brahmins agreed that what Buddha was teaching was perfectly all right, but they found him short of Enlightenment, or of being a Liberated Being. And this being the controversial point at that time, the Brahmins, part of them priests, part of them pundits, and part of them holy, saintly people, could not find in Buddha's sermons and teachings that he was propounding the mysteries of Ultimate Reality.

Actually Buddha did not speak much on those subjects. His famous sermons were on what we now call ethics, like right speech, right action, right thinking, and so on. So if you take his teachings out of context, it would appear that they were on ethics and morality only, but on a very sound basis. Priestcraft at that time in India had degraded to professionalism, commercialism and exploitation, so when Buddha gave his teachings, it was like "water on the desert." It quenched the thirst of those who were exploited by the priests who were playing havoc with the general population. And these were the very priests and Brahmins who were denouncing Buddha for not being, in their eyes, a Realized Soul, because they wanted to keep a hold or monopoly, as if, on Reality. At the same time, these very ones were not really religious.

This is a subtle history of the conditions of India at that time. Without this background, it may be hard to penetrate into the nuances or to understand Buddha. The priests were, in a way, successful in denouncing Buddha—not as a bad person or wrong or anything like that, but just limiting his mission to being a great moralist, a good man, a great leader of society, having done good to multitudes of people, but not getting into the deeper mysteries of the nature of Reality.

For some years this went on and it was troublesome. So much so that often the Brahmins, priests or pundits would go to Buddha's Satsang and ask him questions in such a way as to attack him or expose him to the public, that he did not know anything about Reality or ultimate Truth. And whenever they asked him such questions as, "What is ultimate Truth? What is Reality?" Buddha would hardly reply directly. In today's rationalist, skeptical age, one could say that he was avoiding these questions, but that was not the case. His famous reply to such queries was: "If you are sick, what good will it do to talk about a medicine or manufacturer or label or where the bottle is made? First try to get better and then we can discuss these matters."

The Brahmins would misinterpret this reply as: "He doesn't know; he is avoiding the question." But Buddha's point was: you are sick; your mind is disturbed; you are restless; you have no peace, no relaxation. First keep your mind sane, sensible and relaxed. That was his reply often: first drive away your disease, try to make your mind healthy, and then ask such questions. Perhaps throughout the decades of his ministry, which was about forty-five or forty-seven years, he never got an opportunity to preach Ultimate Reality to healthy minds, because sickness of mind does not go away so soon. So probably he never replied to this question. And this was another "tool" in the hands of the priests to denounce him. Those same priests and pundits went on babbling and bickering all the time about Reality—day and night, anywhere, they would talk about Reality—and here was Buddha, the Enlightened One, and he would not talk about Reality!

Gradually Buddhism declined in India—it traveled to Korea, Japan, China, Tibet, Burma, and other parts of Southeast Asia—but Buddha remained. And ultimately he was recognized and accepted as an Avatar of Vishnu. Religion during Buddha's day had become so degraded and the priests had become so exploiting that morals were much needed. If a Perfected Being or Prophet like Buddha preached morality more than anything else, it was only because those things were needed at that time. There was no other choice. It was the same as when Krishna and Rama in their days fought battles and wars. Buddha did not fight. He was nonviolent—perfectly nonviolent—compassionate, kind, generous and magnanimous.

The mission changes from Prophet to Prophet. In each Prophet's mission, what is most deficient at that time is what the Prophet gives, to fill in the gap. Not that on the spiritual path morals such as Buddha preached have no play, even if you are trying to attain Enlightenment. Actually, on the yoga path there are do's and don'ts and ethics always. Ten commandments, eight commandments—they are always there, minimum eight. Buddha emphasized the aspect of do's and don'ts, which not only help on the spiritual path but also help make society and human life healthy. Buddha stressed much upon ethics, which no other yogi, mystic or Prophet had done earlier. Enlightened Beings, advanced yogis and sages had dwelt upon morality somewhat, but not primarily. Buddha was different in that.

Those who have honestly studied the life of Buddha will have no two opinions about his Enlightenment. When he renounced his kingdom as a prince, his one craze, his one longing was to be Enlightened, and it took him about seven years to reach

Enlightenment. I have never understood how, with this previous history, the priests and pundits canceled his Enlightenment. Buddha was not thinking at that time of morals or helping people or anything else, as per his biographies. It was only after his Enlightenment that he began preaching. Before reaching Realization, he had become a skeleton under the Bodhi tree in Bodh Gaya, which is in east India. He not only fasted, which anybody could do, but he was nothing short of death so that, in the end, he had even given the famous vow: "Let this flesh and body and skin and bones dry up and be finished into dust, but I will not get up from this seat before reaching Enlightenment." That was his last vow.

And whether it is poetic or figurative or realistic—God knows—but it is written that birds used to bring leaves to put shade on him, and ultimately he swooned there under the Bodhi tree. Then one day a lady named Sujata, from a nearby village, brought him a dish of kheer, a kind of rice dessert made with saffron and milk. Sujata was a cowmaid of that village. She had made this kheer and forced him, in a way, to drink it. There is a description in the Pali canons, the Buddhist scriptures, of how that bowl of rice pudding was made with great devotion and purity. It was very sanctified food. Today you would call it "energy-giving," having protein and carbohydrates, et cetera. I do not think Sujata thought of those things.

Buddha ate this kheer and it gave him a lot of energy. And that very night when he sat in meditation—it was a full moon night—he got Enlightened. He was only a little short of Enlightenment; he was advancing into that, but he had swooned in between. So the energy from the kheer pulled him up and he went into *samadhi*—Superconsciousness, Buddhahood. When that Light travels up, Consciousness shines. They have called it Illumination, Liberation, the Thousand-Petaled Lotus radiating Light all over. It is not only from one body. When you reach there, you see that It is everywhere. The Light is pervading, Consciousness is pervading, in you, around you, every space, every particle. That is how Lord Buddha, on that full moon night, got Illumined. Therefore we call him Buddha, the Enlightened One. He became Light, just radiating. Nobody was there though, fortunately. He was emaciated, a skeleton, and Light shone in him, because it is not by bread alone that thou shalt live. There is the Word of God within you. There is Light within you, Consciousness that sustains. We have to believe this.

That Consciousness, the energy that sustains you, is the Source. If you reach there you will find everywhere it is so. Around you, in you, are all galaxies. That is what is sustaining you. Lord Buddha was lost in that Illumination, not only a static position of Illumination but gradually that Pure Consciousness began to open up all the mysteries of the Universe. For forty days and nights—at least nights—he would see all the mysteries of nature through that Light, and he knew everything. I don't think he sat continuously for forty days; he got up, went here and there, and again sat in samadhi. But he was in that Light throughout. Buddha traveled within, everywhere, and saw and remembered five hundred of his earlier births. Actually it is not Bud-*dha*. In English it is written with an "a" but it is actually pronounced *Bud*-dha. There are three words that go with Buddha and with any Enlightened Being: *Buddha, Shuddha, Mukta.* Buddha is Enlightened; Shuddha is the Purest; Mukta is the Liberated One. In Sanskrit, these three go together.

And at the end of forty days, he got up. Some mission, some voice, some knowledge called him—he himself was now the Knower. He slowly walked, unknown, with no destination, no plans, no tickets, no reservations. His Enlightenment was where we now call Bodh Gaya. At that time the nearby town or city was Gaya. They now call that region Bodh Gaya: Bodh from where that Bodhi tree is. There is a Buddha Temple there, of course, and that Bodhi tree is maintained, though not the same probably; it sprouts again and again.

Buddha began traveling, as such Beings do, because they have nothing else to do—no rented apartment to give up, no bed, no children, no bank account to close or transfer, no change of address or writing to friends and relatives. Buddha just walked. And in those days there were no buses or cars. After his Enlightenment, Buddha lived about forty-five years on this earth. Right up to age of about eighty-two he traveled, and eventually he traveled only between the four centers that he established, staying three months at each center. These four places are still famous in Buddhist literature. Among them is the place near the Nepal border where he attained Enlightenment. In summer he would be in one place, in winter another, in spring another.

Buddha's way was a clean-cut life path. He did not display too many powers, but there have been stories where some miracles and magic and healings happened. He converted people but not to religion. He did not introduce Buddhism as such. No Prophet ever introduced a particular "ism" or religion. Jesus did not introduce Christianity; Krishna did not introduce Hinduism; Buddha did not introduce Buddhism. Their disciples and followers did that. They named the religion after the Prophet, but the Prophets themselves did not create any religion. Buddha converted, as you would say, sinners to virtuous. He made them to come on the path.

A famous example was a notorious robber named Angulimal— *anguli* meaning "fingers," *mal* meaning "murderer"—"murderer of fingers." His one craze was to cut a finger from his victim's hands and add that to a strand of fingers he wore around his neck. Angulimal was very wicked and powerful and people feared him. And as the story goes, he had already collected ninety-nine fingers and was looking for the hundredth, the last one. And it happened that one day he was walking on a road and in front of him he saw Buddha walking with one or two disciples. Angulimal had heard of Buddha but such robbers or murderers would not know much about a Buddha; if they knew much, they would be converted.

Lord Buddha used to go daily in the late morning to beg alms. He did not keep anything with him. When Angulimal saw that whosoever this was, he was not afraid of him but peaceful, relaxed, as if sailing on the road, he asked the disciples, "Who is he?" They said, "You don't know, sir? He is the Lord Buddha." Angulimal said, "Who is that?" They replied, "He is the latest Prophet . . ." or something like that. "What does he do?" They said, "He begs his alms and preaches and he has disciples, and that's it." Angulimal said, "That's it? Well, I think he can spare one finger easily." So he told Buddha: "Stop!" People were terrified of Angulimal and if he would tell you to stop, you would shake all over—and Buddha didn't. He just kept walking, quietly. Angulimal again told him: "Stop!" and he wouldn't. Then Angulimal rushed in front of him and said: "Didn't you hear me?" Buddha raised his hand peacefully. He was a figure of peace. As an example of visible peace—not only feeling peace inside—no one is greater than Buddha. He was solid peace, as if peace embodied. He was not affected at all by Angulimal. The robber repeated: "Didn't you listen? I *called* you." He looked at Buddha and said, "Why didn't you stop?" Buddha told him, "I have stopped. You are the one who is still wandering." And as the story goes, that changed Angulimal.

When these great Prophets say something, it has meaning. You can go on babbling to your children a hundred times and they will not change. When Buddha said: "You are the one still wandering," it opened Angulimal's eyes right there. He understood. Later on he became a disciple of Buddha. Such stories are many. People sometimes call these miracles—they want to see magic—but the Prophets do not see changing a person as miraculous. Buddha's healings were also many. But one healing that he did not do; even then, to some it was magic. This occurred before he was Enlightened beneath the Bodhi tree at Bodh Gaya. Today Bodh Gaya is the biggest Buddhist center in the world and worth seeing. But this occurred earlier when he was staying in the Rajagiri Hills. This area is also in northeast India, on five hills where he meditated and where he used to go for begging alms down into the village. By that time he was already famous as a great saint, a great holy man. Many had faith in him that he could heal and other things, and probably he had done healings too. In this village was a lady whose only son, a small boy, had died. She had tried all doctors before that and nobody could cure him. When the boy died, she was so devastated, she would not believe her son was dead; she did not want to believe it. And so when people saw that she was mad or crazy, somebody told her, "There is one holy man on that particular hilltop . . ."

She was crazy but she had full faith that he could revive her dead son. She took her son's body up to the hilltop where Buddha stayed and she wept and wept and pleaded and tumbled down at his feet saying, "Lord, save him," and so on. Buddha did not discuss much in those days. He told this lady, "Okay, you leave him here and go back to your village. Go to each home and ask for one grain of mustard from each family, but only from those houses where no one has ever died." She was so crazy, she thought it would be easy. Weeping and wailing she went back to the village, and everywhere they would offer her not one mustard seed but one thousand if she wanted. But each time she asked, "Was anybody ever dead in your family?" They replied, "Yes, of course." The whole day up to sunset she walked to every home, but she found no home in which no one had ever died.

She came at sunset time to Lord Buddha and said, "I went but there wasn't any family or home where nobody has ever died." He told her, "When that is the fate of everyone, why are you asking differently? Why don't you accept it?" And she was changed. He did not revive the boy, which normally would be the magic or miracle. It depends on how you look at miracles. Buddha did not say this to her—this is my wording—but if he would have revived the boy and she had her son again, no doubt she would have been very happy, but even though she did not get her son back, her life got spiritualized. Her soul evolved. Which is greater? We look to outer things. Not that outer healing should not be done, but it depends on how we define healing or miracles.

Before Enlightenment Buddha had fasted a lot. That in itself had been considered a great qualification, and there was news for miles and miles through villages and towns that this holy man did not eat anything. Here you may not understand but in India it is different. Not that people do not fast there, but to fast for so long as to become a skeleton was unusual, and somehow that kind of merit had attracted five disciples. These disciples would not leave Buddha. They were around him all the time, learning from him, hearing his sermons. But after Enlightenment, when Buddha began to eat a little—what wrong was there in eating anyway?—one by one these five disciples left him. To you it may sound peculiar but if you knew the history and traditions of India, the consideration of austere people, mendicants and ascetics, you would understand this very well.

So the five disciples left, which was no big deal for Buddha. So much the better! After Enlightenment Buddha began to walk and walk and walk, and one day he reached Benares on the holy Ganges. Buddha's fame had spread ahead of him. He was going to be a Prophet but nobody knew at that time. He was hardly thirty-five, thirty-six, or thirty-seven years old at that time. The year of Enlightenment, I think, he was thirty-five years old. At twenty-seven or twenty-eight he had renounced. Benares, which is also called Kashi or Varanasi, is a city that is thousands of years old. In Buddha's day it was a central place for pundits, priests and holy people, the stronghold of orthodoxy.

Buddha got much opposition there because he was not preaching Ultimate Reality. He was preaching good conduct and good medicine—meaning peace—to avoid sickness of the mind, imbalance and restlessness. He was also preaching against corruption, exploitation and degradation, and those priests and pundits would not like to hear that. But in India, as you know, they do not crucify— thank God! At the most they malign or use malicious language. So Buddha went into the outskirts of Benares, about seven miles outside of the city, to a place called Sarnath. Now it is a great tourist and pilgrimage spot; thousands of people visit and there are hotels, inns and Buddha temples.

In those days Sarnath was a quiet village site. Buddha went there and began to preach, and somehow those very five disciples who had left him earlier found him there and tumbled down wholeheartedly—body, mind and soul—at his feet and asked forgiveness for deserting him. Buddha—I don't know if he said it this way—told them, "It didn't make a difference for me whether you deserted me or not." That is how his mission started. Sarnath is the first place where he preached the dharma or dhamma, as it is called in Pali. There he preached the Four Noble Truths and the Eightfold Path in which there are eight morals that are very helpful on the spiritual path: right speech, right thought, right action, et cetera. He also gave the famous: *Buddham sharnam gotshami, dhammam sharnam gotshami, sangam sharnam gotshami,* meaning, "I take refuge unto Buddha [Enlightenment] unto dhamma [dharma, religion or ethics], and sangam [association or institute].

His whole preaching was to drive away sorrow, actually. The Four Noble Truths is to admit there is sorrow, to admit that there is a cause of sorrow, to admit that the cause is desire, and that the elimination of desire will eliminate sorrow. Therefore Buddhism came to be known as the religion of desirelessness, which certainly, if you misinterpret it, you will wrongly understand. Buddha did not mean that we must give up day to day or basic needs; he meant we should give up extra desires, superfluous, greedy, exciting and selfish desires. Those cause sorrow. When he said, "If you do not want suffering and sorrow, eliminate desires," this was misunderstood in later centuries to mean that we should live without *any* desires. That means you cannot bathe, change clothes, eat, sleep, earn or plow the land, or what? That was not Buddha's meaning. It needs another Prophet to explain these things.

He was preaching to avoid superfluous desires. He gave it clearly: there is sorrow; there is a cause of sorrow; desire is the cause of the sorrow; elimination of desire is to eliminate sorrow. I do not see how it can be ever rejected or disproved. Only we may not like to hear this because, if we could avoid sorrow while having desires—if some Prophet could somehow scientifically bring that kind of formula—it would be really nice. Anyway, the highest aim of Buddha's life—we can name it as a mission—was to help suffering mankind, to eliminate their sufferings. He saw that the cause of suffering is desire. There are no two views about it, only how you understand it is your problem.

Apply this wisdom to anything; it will work. Normal, healthy eating does not cause suffering, but overeating or wrong eating will create health problems. Having some money for your upkeep is fine, but when you are greedy, you are inviting sorrow and suffering. His disciples follow this now as a disciplinary curriculum in monasteries and schools in order to get to be Buddha, to be Enlightened. But overall he always said: "I'm not the only Buddha. You are all Buddhas too." Like Jesus' "the Kingdom of God is within you," Buddha said: "You are all Buddhas. I cannot be Buddha for you or eat for you. You have to eat to appease your hunger." There are many such sayings of his in the famous Dhammapada, which is like the Bible or the Bhagavad Gita.

In Sarnath, Buddha started with those five disciples again and many more came, but he did not stay at one place. He traveled the length and breadth of India the rest of his forty-five years. Among his arch disciples was the most famous, Ananda. There was, of course, Angulimal, and also a famous dancer-actress who was among his great female disciples. Buddha used to take his disciples with him— hundreds. At one time they said that even two thousand used to wander with him by foot. In those days there were no highways like today, and there was nothing on the roads except people, horses, bullocks and oxen. And wherever they went, they would stay in groves, under trees and near villages. Many of his disciples would go for begging alms and the villagers would feed them; then they would travel again farther. Buddha did not establish four centers originally. He used to travel and rich people or kings would reserve gardens and areas for him to stay with disciples; hundreds of thousands of disciples would come and stay. They also arranged *bandharas* or community kitchens to feed them all. It was simple food: one or two dishes like rice and dal or *kitchari* cooked in very big pots on a wood fire. They would put rice, water, chili, salt, dal, potatoes—everything in one dish, and then sit in a line on the ground, each with a banana leaf plate, and eat together. There was no dishwashing. You have to see how they do this even today in India to feed large crowds of holy people or the poor. Food was in no shortage in Buddha's days. Kings and rich people would pool their wealth and provide for the renunciates. And many kings and princes became his disciples. They followed his way of nonviolence.

One day Buddha was passing with his disciples through a village and he knew that one butcher was there who used to kill sheep. They did not kill cows but sheep, goats, lambs, and so on. Buddha could not stand violence but he was not revolutionary or radical. He would go and tell the king or rich people to buy those animals and then he would release them. He changed many kings' hearts. They would go to fight with another king and Buddha would go with his disciples and remain outside the castle or palace until he got an audience with the king. Kings already knew him, revered him and respected him. They knew he was an ex-prince himself. And he would preach to them on peace and nonviolence. He was a model of nonviolence and peace. He would affect anybody at that time, visibly. He would preach against battles and wars and they would stop fighting. Many times he did this. It depends on how you see miracles. And this was two thousand five hundred years back—long before we had the idea of peace movements. He was a one-man job, with his disciples.

When Gautama was a boy in the palace, an astrologer had told his father that either he would be an invincible emperor or a great Prophet. The astrologer had said that when the prince would learn about miseries, he would renounce. Buddha's father knew this prophecy, so he was trying to keep his son from seeing anything bad, such as disease, old age or death. He surrounded his son with everything that was pleasant, charming and nice, such as perfumery fountains, singing minstrels, delicious food, et cetera. None were allowed to talk of disease, old age or death around him. Palaces were shielded with high walls in Gautama's day, so he never knew, up to eighteen years or so, that there is misery in mankind. Underneath he had some kind of untold pathos. Sometimes his father or mother would see him becoming sad without reason and they would ask, "What is wrong, son?" But Gautama did not know either. He could not put a finger on it because it was a future premonition. However, that sadness would pass by very shortly each time, because no episode was there.

Gautama had a cousin in an adjacent palace. One day when they were both teenagers this cousin was practicing archery and shot a bird. When it fell, it landed in the compound where Gautama was living. He had never seen a bleeding or suffering creature. He took the bird and asked his own physicians to nurse it, to make it all right. In the meantime his cousin Devadatta came to claim the bird. Gautama said, "I won't give you. You will harm it." This was the first little glimpse of suffering that Buddha saw, but the story is different. In the meantime his cousin tried to claim the bird, so they both went to their kingdom judge in the palace and he heard the boys. Devadatta said, "I shot the bird. I as the hunter am the claimant." Gautama said, "But I have saved it. The bird is mine." The judge gave the bird to Gautama, saying: "You saved him. He is yours."

Gautama had a loyal and faithful charioteer from whom he used to ask questions. One day he asked, "What is behind these walls?" His charioteer was avoiding such questions because the king had told him not to tell the prince what was outside. There are many details but the story goes that Gautama got crazy and demanded: "I want to visit my city." The news went to his father. He shuddered but could not refuse because Gautama had become a young man by then. The king announced to the whole city that the prince would go around the city in his chariot, visiting. He ordered that no one old or diseased be in sight, and that no funeral procession or pyre be visible. Everyone was supposed to be happy, gay, and the city decorated with colorful festoons on the trees and music playing. Everyone should be in new clothes, dancing, singing, and showing the world as the king wanted his son to see it.

They controlled everything that they could and Gautama was in his chariot seeing everyone happily greeting him, and he was happy. But somehow, from somewhere—it was a big city—an old man crept in among the crowd watching Gautama from the road. Gautama saw him and asked the charioteer, "Who is he?" He had never seen an old man. He said, "Sire, he's an old man." "What is an old man? I have never heard of one." The charioteer tried to divert his attention, "Forget about it, Lord . . ." In the same way Gautama saw a diseased person limping among the crowd. The authorities had ignored the rules or were a little lax and eventually Gautama happened upon a funeral procession. He asked, "What is that?" The charioteer responded, "It is a dead person, Sire." "People die?" Gautama asked. "Yes." Gautama asked, "Everybody will die?" The charioteer responded, "Yes." "I will die too?" "Yes, Sire, unfortunately."

According to another account, they say Buddha saw these three things in a dream. But whatever the truth be—I believe the first one—when he came back to the palace, he was all morose, thinking, "One day I will be old . . . one day I will have a disease . . . one day I will die." Nowadays everybody sees sickness and death. We see old age and get old. We do not get affected in a dispassionate way. But Gautama was different. Like a scientist or great yogi, he pondered, "If I will grow old and diseased and then die, then what I have and am enjoying is not the truth. There must be something else."

When Gautama's father heard what his son had seen, he got very sad. His mother was weeping. They knew the astrological prediction might come true. They wanted to divert his attention. They brought a famous beauty, Yashodhara, to marry him, and after some time they had a son, Rahula. In the meantime, Gautama forgot; but underneath his thoughts would go to what he had seen. He thought, "If death, pain, misery and old age are there, how can I enjoy life?" And on one good night, unnoticed, he left home or, as we say, renounced. Again he took the help of his faithful charioteer, and whatever ornaments he had on his body and silk clothes, he gave those to his charioteer as fees and left in mendicant's garb. That he wore for seven years until he attained Enlightenment.

The reason I am telling these stories is that Prophets and great sages each work in their own way. We cannot question why they do this and that. According to each age and time, the way is different that they work with everyone. Krishna worked quite differently; Rama worked quite differently. In Buddha's sangha, he had all kinds of disciples, and his disciples also quarreled among themselves, no doubt. They were of all hues and colors. Some were very poor, some from middle class, some from rich families. And it is written that three times in his life Buddha threatened to leave them and go. He got fed up. Now you might ask, "How could a great Prophet like Buddha get fed up?" I say, at least it was only three times! It wasn't daily! So you have to see his greatness. Only three times he got extremely fed up. That is quite a tolerance. It could have been every week. And each of these times the disciples apologized, wept, repented, asked for forgiveness and vowed to behave.

When Buddha was born, they say he emerged from his mother's right side, and he used to sleep also on his right side. When he left his body, he was also lying on his right side. And all three: birth, Enlightenment and what they call *Mahaparinirvana*, when he left his body, occurred on the full moon, which in Sanskrit is called *purnima*.*
Also, his mother, Maya, gave birth to him under a tree; he got Enlightened under a tree; and he gave up his body while lying under a tree. There is a great significance in these things.

Buddha was around eighty-five at his Mahaparinirvana. He had declared that he was leaving the body while he was lying down in the night. Thousands of disciples from various parts were sitting quiet, pin-drop silence, and all of a sudden, Buddha heard a little sob. Thousands, of course, were weeping, but quietly. Buddha was leaving the body after forty-five years that he had lived with them, wandered, preached, changed lives and brought peace and consolation to millions—*millions*. In one lifetime, hardly anyone has done that. And at the moment of his departure from this world, he heard a sob. They say Buddha was rising to his Infinity or Absolute Consciousness but he came back for the time being.

He asked somebody sitting nearby, "Who is sobbing?" The disciple said, "Ananda." Buddha was surprised. Buddha's highest disciple was Ananda. He called Ananda near him where he was lying and said, "Ananda, out of all, *you* are weeping?" Ananda said, "Lord, you are going . . ." Buddha said, "I did not know, Ananda, that you loved my body. You are weeping for my body. I'm leaving my body. I'm not dying. That means, all your life you loved my body only?" Now don't copy literally Ananda, or Buddha's words. Those who have not risen that high might say, "Why should we weep for the body?" This was a different lesson for Ananda; he was a very high soul. Then Ananda got quiet. Buddha told him, "Ananda, you will be the beacon light, the torchbearer of this whole message. You are going to teach that Buddha was a body, or what?" Then, of course, Ananda understood, and gradually Buddha then left the body. Some of you might have

---

* *Purnima:* full, perfect.

seen photographs of the Ajanta cave sculpture in which Buddha is lying down on his right side with disciples all around him. The sculpture is twenty-seven feet long.

Of course, he was tall, handsome, graceful, gentle, kind, and the most compassionate. He was peace solidified. Many who would touch his hem would just relax. It was not just words; it was so. I often wonder why the Brahmins of his day ignored all the other aspects of Buddha and called him a moralist simply, as if he was only a social reformer or something like that. Eventually, fortunately, they included him as the Ninth Incarnation of Vishnu, the Tenth being Kalki— whoever that may be.

You cannot think of Buddha without thinking of peace in the world. Whenever peace may come or whenever it has been thought about, Buddha's name has been inadvertently or advertently felt, along with compassion and kindness and so on. There was not a single exception where Buddha did otherwise. In some others, even in the life of Krishna, you might say, "At one point he did this way . . ." But in Buddha's life, we do not find where he did other than peacefully, compassionately, and with kindness. For any blade of grass, he was ready to give up his life. There was no compromise in Buddha's peace. So much so that, years and decades later, the famous Emperor Ashoka, who had fought a war for thirty years with his enemies, became a Buddhist and shunned war. He became nonviolent. In his constitution, Emperor Ashoka declared war a crime against people, and he stopped war right there. He even carried Buddha's message worldwide by creating great pillars, epitaphs, caves, carvings and manuscripts to proclaim Buddha's message. As far as peace, nonviolence and compassion are concerned, Buddha is the acme and remains a great force even today.

8

Jesus and the Quiet Revolution

Jesus wanted to give life in totality, in fullness. It is not that he could not have been a politician or social reformer or cultural ambassador. He could have been all this and much more too, but he knew that would never give true salvation. The Kingdom of Heaven is what he wanted to give, in its own fullness and glory.

Prabhushri: What would you say was the significance of Jesus' birth?

Devotee: *Partly, that he was born in a stable. He was the most humble, though he's the greatest.*

Would it have made a difference if he had been born in a better place? He wouldn't have been great?

It was not for him so much. The way they explained, the Jews apparently were expecting someone great.

To rule them or something?

But he wanted to show that greatness lies somewhere else, meaning humility and harmlessness.

If materially he was to be the savior of Jews as the king of Jews— which he didn't accept to do—then that part of the prophecy was not true. That is, Jesus himself rejected it. And if we were to say he was a Prophet of the Age—which spiritually speaking he certainly was—then the Jews did not accept him as a Prophet. Jesus didn't accept what the Jews wanted and the Jews didn't accept what he wanted. Both canceled each other, in the sense.

If he embodied humility and simplicity—having come from a simple birth—and therefore he was great, then in his own land he wasn't accepted that way. How do you take it? How then did the prophecy come true? Eventually he was known as a Prophet, but from the Jewish point of view, or Israel or the Middle East, he didn't become their Savior. Now the world accepts him or other nations accept him, but in his own birthplace, among his own people, they didn't accept him in that way. So how was the prophecy fulfilled, in the sense?

Well, I don't think he failed the prophecy.

No, he didn't fail, that's true.

They didn't recognize him.

Normally in cultures or nations or religions, when a prophecy is made, the Prophet comes true to the prophecy, though still some may not accept him. My question is: how did it happen that Jesus' own community or the Jewish people would not accept him at that time?

I would guess, because of the idea that they projected on him at that time. They were expecting something different, and what they wanted didn't happen.

But then Jesus said what he had come for, what he would do or what he had done. Why did they not accept his word? I'm talking from the community point of view. If the bulk of the Jews would have accepted him and some Jews wouldn't have accepted him as a matter of controversy or dispute, then also it would be okay. We have this in some other Prophets as well. But here it seems the whole Jewish community did not accept him, except a few individuals. The point is, how did this happen? Did he change the drama after he came? Or was the prophecy faulty? It seems as though three things are not correlating: either the prophecy should have been different, or the people should have been accepting of the way it happened, or Jesus should have acted differently. Therefore the tragedy happened. There was a kind of confusion. The prophecy, the people and the Prophet were not in conjunction. And in that kind of melee, poor Jesus was crucified.

Let us come down to that humble-born babe. You see in this simplicity and humility, his humble environment, all the portents that he would be a revolutionary. Revolutionary can mean rebellious if on the wrong way or goal, but it can mean in the right attitude as well. Jesus' humble birth shows his revolutionary nature—as if nothing doing with the Pharisees, nothing doing with power-mongering. That is what he stood against. So, in simplicity, in humility, there was an inner revolution born, which was Jesus, who presented this in his own way without being a politician. When a Prophet or great Soul like Jesus does or says something, or acts and lives in a certain way, he has a homogeneous outlook. The Prophets do not divide philosophy, politics, astronomy, et cetera, from religion. It is all combined together. Therefore, in any area he touched, Jesus was revolutionary, not only in whipping the money changers but in regard to priestcraft, the Pharisees, and the very education. He would stand in the synagogue and preach his truth, having nothing to do with what other priests taught. He was not competing either. In all these things, you can see his revolutionary nature—and that landed him in trouble!

We sometimes forget that humility and meekness are not just passive, static conditions. *Truly* humble and meek ones are like a razor's edge. Be sure about it. They are not just weak- and meek-lings. Inside they are sharp, razor-like. I have always found that the *truly* humble are the great ones. You can take examples from history and you will see again and again. Krishna, though he became a king later on, as was his lineage, was born in a jail or prison, in very humble surroundings. His parents were not criminals; the criminal was the king who imprisoned them. Jesus never became a king and Krishna did. Krishna lived a hundred twenty-five years or so; Jesus lived only thirty-three years. In Krishna's life, apart from being a king, he was very revolutionary. In the same way as Jesus, Krishna was against the priestcraft of his time, against power, wickedness and unrighteousness. Prophets do this, which is revolution, but in the right direction.

This is the main difference: when ordinary people employ rebelliousness, revolutionary attitudes, or so-called independence, they don't know that they are really in bondage, though they say, "We are independent . . ." So we have to understand that humility is not simply being forgiving, toleration, let go or not retaliating. It has its firm basis in right revolution. Prophets would not give this up. Be sure that, as we talk about the relative world or relative life, everything is relative. If humility or simplicity would be one-sided only—as an end in itself or fulfilling one's own objective—then it would be lopsided and turn into weakness. Gradually it would become passivity. It will drive you to inaction. Therefore the wrong kind of humility and meekness, if it has no inner strength, will often fall into disrepute, weakness or passivity. You have to stir such a person every time to get up and do something. That is really the decaying process of humility or simplicity. If it were only a one-sided virtue, it wouldn't encourage, inspire or elevate you to reach higher. You would just lie down and think: "I'm humble. What can I do? I am meek and weak, God. I am nothing, You are everything, so let me go to sleep. You are awakened anyway! You take care of me and even if I am sleeping, do it for me. I have given up everything unto Thee. Whatever my strength, courage—everything is now Yours. Neither have I retention power nor losing power. You understand my plight. You know everything, God. I know nothing. And now it's up to You! I don't say it is Your fault if I don't do anything now that I am surrendered to You, but inside I mean that."

Such souls lose the whole meaning of humility and simplicity. These virtues rightly applied and rightly lived transform you like a butterfly from a cocoon. And born out of that is real Consciousness. Humility and simplicity are very useful virtues, but not to be used in a selfish manner. If we only see the utility sense of virtues, it will make us selfish, seeking virtues as a commodity. True virtues are relaxing to the mind in such a way that, when the mind gets settled and peaceful, the Consciousness begins to awaken. *That* is Christ Consciousness—just as from the humble and simple Jesus, Christ was born. You could call it a second birth.

If we understand this we will see that there could have been a middle portion of Jesus' destiny as king of the Jews that he avoided. He preached instead Christ Consciousness or the Kingdom of Heaven. He gave glimpses that he could have been a ruler, in the material sense—whether it was the whipping of the money changers, or stopping the mob from stoning the woman, or speaking against the

Pharisees. Such incidents of political and social reform he touched very briefly in the ministry of three years or so, but it showed the possibility in him, the potential of becoming a king if he wanted to. Not because this was a tenor of social reform or political revolution, but also at the same time, he showed the success that he could have had. However, he declared that he didn't come to rule the earth. That middle portion he did not exercise much. Why he didn't, he knew best. But that is a fact, as per the Bible. So it's not simply that such Prophets and Holy Ones become humble and simple, just to be great. That greatness is for them a byproduct. Others think he or she is great.

We often choose from a Prophet's life and quote certain portions. If I am a scholar, I'll choose scholarly things. If I am a politician, I will choose the political part of Jesus Christ. If I am a priest, I will take out some theology. If I am an astrologer, I'll see his stars at birth and death, why the crucifixion happened, what stars and planets were conjunct, et cetera. Each one chooses an aspect of a Prophet's life and decides the whole person on that basis, which is not the right judgment. Those are fragments only. We have to take all homogeneously, the whole person as one entity, and then we will understand better.

Understanding the totality of a person is actually the domain of religion. Religion should envelop all these things. If we understand this, then our outlook on life should be religious. Otherwise our outlook will be political or social or cultural or national or religious in the dogmatic sense. This is where the problem happens: we do not take a religious outlook comprising all things together. A musician, otherwise, becomes just a musician. We see lives as departmentalized, fragmented, and that is an incomplete view.

Jesus wanted to give the life in totality, in fullness. It is not that he could not have been a politician or social reformer or cultural ambassador. He could have been all this and much more too, but he knew that would not give true Salvation. The Kingdom of Heaven is what he wanted to give, in its own fullness and glory. If we see this we will understand that Jesus had no need to be king of the Jews. If the community wanted him to be their king, it was only because, at that time they were under the bondage of the Romans. So their wish was to be liberated from that angle. But the way he preached, what he said and did, he was giving the message of Liberation in the larger context. And let's assume they had followed this. Then maybe some other way might have opened by which the Romans might have given them material liberation. But he didn't take the crusade of earthly liberation. He wanted to give Liberation for the Kingdom of Heaven, the Kingdom of God on earth, or whatever you call it. Naturally this was no consolation to the ordinary people in the street, especially when education was very low among the Jews at that time. Even if they were sophisticated, literate people, it would still be doubtful, because they would say he knew nothing, that he was impractical in worldly matters, not a politician. What did he know?

There are many, many complex issues within this discussion, and though we have liberty of speech more than it was in Jesus' day, still I think the complex strings underneath are twisted and pulled even today, in different ways though. But don't think Jesus or the Prophets could not handle these things. If they wanted to, they could and do. Prophets choose different ways. They know that the world is not political only, nor is it social, cultural, or so many nations. It includes all these but is so much more. So the Prophets show us life as it should be.

How would you solve your life's problems ultimately, in spite of whatever reforms you are seeking now? This attitude of wholeness is what the Prophets think about: that it is one thing to seek a solution to certain kinds of problems, but ultimately you are beset with life's every department and have to solve life's problems as a whole. Then what is the answer? Is more money the answer to all life's problems? Is good health a solution to all your problems? Will some kind of position or status give you all the satisfaction you want? Ultimately when you go on analyzing in this way, you come to the basic question: how can life as a whole be satisfying?

What would give you ultimate satisfaction? What virtues do you need? What way of life should you follow? You cannot avoid truth, for example. Knowing this, the Prophets show how life can ultimately give us peace and satisfaction—that godly life, call it religious life, that innocent, harmless, truthful life. Knowing this, Jesus thought: *Why go through politics?* I can't talk on his behalf; at least, being non-Christian, I have no authority. Some may say I am speaking of Hinduism. I say, whatever that is, is it true or not? Put a label on it— that's your problem. It is because you have been giving labels that you have *created* problems. The cut-short way is going straight to the truth. Since the ultimate solution will be by these A-B-C virtues, or by these methods, why go into other jargon? Then we will understand that Christ Consciousness is simply Liberation of the soul, Liberation of Consciousness, or, to quote from the Upanishads:* "Lead us from unconsciousness to Consciousness . . ." From the very gross nature, lead us to the refined, Light-full nature. Ultimately this is the answer.

It is not so much a particular community. There were Brahmins and people like the Pharisees who defied Krishna too. It is not that every Vedic man or woman or even every Aryan accepted Krishna fully. But on the whole, everyone knew the prophecy that was given about his Incarnation and had accepted him, barring some. And he himself knew what he was doing. Rama had the same situation. He had high reverence for Valmiki, the poet who originally wrote the Ramayana. A prophecy was made and Rama's whole life was written in advance, as this epic. But at two junctures Rama had a dilemma. He was going to do differently than what had been written. He was a Prophet and Lord Vishnu's Incarnation; there was no reason why he could not have done it, especially under the circumstances, which in each instance was the best thing to do. I for one would say—okay, let him do it, regardless of what Valmiki had written. Let him rewrite the history if he wants to. But, as per the story, to respect the views of Valmiki, Rama did according to the Ramayana, to make the full prophecy come true.

---

* Upanishads, from the Sanskrit, lit: "sitting at the feet of a Realized Master." Next to the Vedas, of which they are a part, the Upanishads are the most revered and ancient scriptures from India, a compilation of various realized sages' revealed teachings on the immortality of the soul. There are Thirteen Principle Upanishads, recognized today, although the original teachings, passed on orally through thousands of years, numbered in the hundreds.

Something went wrong somewhere in the life of Jesus. Either the Prophet did not do according to what the people or prophecy wanted, or the prophecy was somehow faulty. In this confusion, it brought about tragedy. We cannot rewrite that history, I know, and it's not something the intellect can solve either. But at the same time, there is a simple, reasonable logic that applies to support the truth. Truth cannot be unreasonable; at the same time, it is beyond reason. This purity of reason can and should support the truth. This being the case, we have often forgotten what is the ultimate significance of Jesus' birth. If he had limited himself to being king of the Jews, then he would have died a great hero, a great liberator and independence-giver, but is that the only purpose of a Prophet? Would he be a Prophet by just liberating his people?

Let's go back to Moses: if he had simply liberated the Hebrews from the clutches of the Pharaoh and left them on Mount Sinai, would he have been considered a Prophet? A liberator of people, whatever greatness or heroism may be underlying, eventually cannot be a Prophet unless he is more than that. He must be a liberator giving wisdom, consciousness, an elevated awakening into the Kingdom of God; otherwise he is not a Prophet. If Jesus had solved the purpose of being king of the Jews, and then one fine morning or good night had gone to sleep and never got up again, many people would have been happy that he had done his job; the prophecy was fulfilled and the Romans made to go back to Rome. "Here we are in our own liberated land. Let's build a temple to Jesus the King!" If that had happened, I don't think Jesus would have been taken as a Prophet. A Prophet has to give the people liberation from bondage into Consciousness, into the Kingdom of God, Christ Consciousness. It has to be beyond political freedom.

At that time they had no concern about bloodshed and fighting, and then here comes a meek one, talking nonsense—give the cloak also to the coat-robber. It is very difficult to visualize the aim or will of the Prophet in relationship with our own wishes and wills. As long as a Prophet does according to our wishes, or at least some of our will is fulfilled, then he is the Prophet; but if he does not do our wishes and will, then it is doubtful that he is a Prophet. This is exactly what happened with the Jews at that time. Had Jesus liberated the Jews and then renounced and left for the Himalayas, it would have been okay. There are many things in the lives of Prophets that are not said or written clearly, or even if they are written, they are not interpreted in the same way as it was. It is as if only a Prophet can understand a Prophet. It is not within the capacity of scholars or evangelists, Pharisees, priests or so-called reformers. The trouble is that if Prophets do according to what people want, even then the people are not satisfied unless all their wishes are fulfilled. And how can you fulfill everybody's wishes all the time?

So I for one would say that humility and simplicity have the sharp edge of revolution underneath. Not that the Prophets are hiding it— it's just there. In that, there is no compromise. Take for example the life of Buddha. Though he was no longer a prince—he was a mendicant—whenever Buddha saw animals being taken to the slaughterhouse, he could not bear it. Whatever money he could collect, he would go and buy those animals and set them free. He could not save all animals—he didn't—but what he did was a *revolution* against slaughterhouses. He did not just stand outside the gates of slaughterhouses and picket. You know, the picketers of today, they have nice sandwiches, eating outside, a lot of fun, concerts going on, and they say, "We are picketing." In honorable picketing there is a sense of austerity, penance, steadfastness, renunciation and self-sacrifice. When we read about the life of Mahatma Gandhi, that was real picketing, real revolution—no compromise, to stand steadfast, a martyr. Not just having a good time.

Look at those Prophets and Realized Souls, what self-sacrificing they all did! Jesus would not open his mouth and say something— even if it would save his life. He knew that death was hovering around him. He could have said something and Pilate might have got him freed, but he would not. Whatever he had already said, if that was not enough for them to consider, to satisfy them or plead for his case, what was the use in saying more? Recently I read a quote that said: "Never try to convince anyone because, if he is a friend, he doesn't need conviction from you, and if he is an enemy, he won't be convinced anyway." Why waste your time and energy in convincing? That is what Jesus did. He did say something. If they could not believe him, what else would he plead for? The more he would have talked, the more they would have found fault with him. Already what he had said had put him in trouble.

That is the worldly way: finding loopholes to condemn someone, if you want to condemn. Worldly people are clever, or conversely: clever people are worldly. They say one thing and do another. If they want to condemn you they will condemn you either way, whether you say truth or not. If people want to be bad, they will be so under any circumstances. Even when they confess that they are bad, they will say it tongue in cheek so that you wonder if it is a confession. "Let's solve the thing together," they say, as if I have done the fault. The fault you have done; you have to correct it. Why solve it together? This is just cleverness.

They wanted Jesus to say what they wanted him to say. And if he had said that, even then they would have landed him in trouble, I tell you. So don't think this simplicity or humility is just passivity or inaction. As Sri Krishna says in the Bhagavad Gita: "Yogis are very active in their inaction, and while very active, they are very inactive and relaxed inside." That is the yogic way. Jesus knew that. At only twelve years of age, he was lost in Jerusalem. We may not exactly call it a revolution, but at least he defied the laws of society. He was born of parents; that did not mean he had to remain with his parents. He did not use the word attachment, but that is attachment. Despite social customs and parental understanding, in his own way he knew what he had to do.

You may be born of something, but you do not have to be attached to it. This does not mean that we have no duties to our parents. That is quite a different question. But Jesus' family was much larger than Joseph and Mary. He could not condense himself into one small family unit. He knew that. He could not contain himself into a small bottle. At the age of twelve or so, he just flew. He broke the bottle. I don't mean society is wrong or family life is wrong, but at least he did not want to be attached to it. He had a larger call. And then whatever he did, where he went in those twenty years, from thirteen until thirty-three years of age, the Bible does not say, but some others have written about it.

Jesus did not come to give the kingdom of earth. He knew that nobody rules over anybody, so he said: "I have come to give you the Kingdom of God, not of earth." He said: "As it is in heaven, so be it on earth." That is true, because heaven and earth are married together. They have conjoined in oneness throughout. Heaven and earth are not two worlds, a separate subject-object. There is no gap in between. As it is there, so it is here. When we conjoin that way, then there will be peace. Put it astrologically: we will be in peace with the planets and the astrological signs. They will help us. Put it angelically: angels will come nearer to human beings and human beings will come nearer to angels. We will receive their communication far more superiorly and openly. The subtle worlds and material world will have more nearness to each other.

Jesus knew that and asserted: "I don't want the earthly kingdom." What does it matter if somebody takes away your bread? What do you lose? When your own child snatches a piece of bread from your dish on the dining table, what do you do? You feel, "He's my child . . ." therefore you let go. But this can be a worldview. It does not mean we should support the wrongdoer. But if we feel that meekness, humility and simplicity are just passivity, if we allow wrongdoers to do wrong and not do anything about it, this is not what Jesus would teach. Under the circumstances, he would whip the money changers. He would talk straight to the Pharisees and to the mob that wanted to stone the woman. Even to the followers of John the Baptist who told him, "Why don't you stay with us?" he told the straight truth.

A Prophet would never support wrongdoers or a wrong act, never in their lives. They know that supporting a wrongdoer is supporting unrighteousness and wickedness, and thereby injustice will prevail on earth. Then the good will suffer and that will defeat their purpose totally. Prophets stand by the good and the virtuous. They do this at *any* cost—even if they have to give up their life. If somebody is poor and takes away your bread, it is one thing; but if a rich person steals your bread, you won't say, "Let him have it." That would be wrongdoing. And then if you are supporting that wrongdoer, you are wrong. You are going into inaction and passivity. And therefore depressing thoughts will come to you.

Whatever meekness the Prophets may be preaching, they never sacrifice righteousness. This word Jesus might have used or not, as Krishna did, but similar words he did use. They protect the good. Jesus may not have punished the evildoer, but he would not have anything to do with that evil. He defied wrongdoers, the wicked, selfish rulers. Whether he did that with an open rebellion or just by subtle, nonviolent, loving, compassionate means, it is only a difference of method. The Prophets will not give up the principle, whether it is Buddha or Jesus or Krishna. So you understand that their goal is Christ Consciousness, how to be born into deliverance, the cream of life for which we are born.

This body-mind is a shell. In this cocoon is a spiritual entity, call it Christ Consciousness, Krishna Consciousness or Consciousness Itself. *That* wants to be delivered, to be emancipated, to manifest. That is the Kingdom of God, the Kingdom of Heaven, "on earth as it is in heaven." As it is inside, so it should be outside. It does not matter if the body is born in a stable, because the body is the animal portion of humanity, and animals are born in a stable. Even if it's a stable, the body is born in filth anyway, so what does it matter? You are not coming out smelling like roses! In that mud of maya, illusion, that grossness, out of this physical base, what is going to be delivered? That is the major point. Out of that swamp, a kind of lotus is being born. We may be born on earth but our consciousness is supposed to be released and born into heaven. The body will go back to the five elements one day. It is not the supreme Entity; it is only a shell, a vessel to hold something. The embodiment is of something that is within. That Buddhahood, Krishna Consciousness, Christ Consciousness, Pure Consciousness is the goal of life for which we have to be humble, simple, harmless, truthful and religious.

Which politicians and sociologists are teaching truthfulness, harmlessness, humility, innocence, purity, forgiveness, tolerance, patience, and let go? That is the domain of religion. But religion is not opposed to politics or sociology. It comprises all these things, only it gives a new color to them: what politics or sociology or any science should be. Religion includes all. It shows the way into every domain or aspect of life—how we should regulate our desires; how we should regulate our will; how we should not succumb to temptations.

If you reread Jesus' answers to Pilate, to the Pharisees, the priests, and even to his own disciples, you will see that sometimes he did not give direct answers, but by his counterquestions you get the answers. He kept quiet at times when anyone else would have babbled. *That* was his answer. Pilate understood. The Pharisees understood. Everybody understood. Jesus was trying to make them ashamed, but they would not see. They knew what they were doing. They were not blind. Mostly we are blinded by our own desires. It is because of our own illusory nature that we justify things all the time through our own angle, because of our wishes and desires. The Prophets see through those blinders and pass judgment. And then it has no meaning to counterquestion: "Show me where I am wrong." A sensible person would say, "Well, if this is not enough for you to understand, what else can I tell you?" It is quite possible that that very person does understand, but he or she is being clever.

When people become clever like that, will you keep quiet or what will you do? You try to teach or explain to those who are primitive, who do not know, who are just colloquial—that's okay. But the sensible person, an educated person, when he asks you cleverly such counterquestions, knowing what they are, would Jesus just keep quiet or not? Prophets are not dictators. That is why, in the last days of his ministry, Jesus mostly kept quiet, as if telling them: "Go ahead, do what you want to do." What else could he do? He could not have given a sensible, logical answer. It would not have worked, I tell you. They would have devised other means to do the same thing.

If a person wants to be clever, he will be clever at any cost, but he does not know that he is cutting his own feet. The next few minutes he will be landing somewhere else. That is what happened to Judas and to those Pharisees and also the Romans. Where are they today? We have built temples to Jesus, not to Roman emperors. Where is a temple to Caesar anymore? Where are those clever ones even remembered? But Jesus still lives. We all know that. So does Buddha. So does Krishna. It is a revolution, but the Prophets do not pose as revolutionaries, only because that is rajas. They could become clever but they don't. Even with smart people, they do not employ smartness. You cannot defeat badness with badness. They withdraw or keep quiet. That does not mean they are inactive.

If you understand, therefore, the significance of the birth of Jesus, it is a quiet revolution. Jesus' birth is a revolution against untruth, illusion, materialism, power, selfishness, greed, cleverness and priestcraft. He was a direct revolutionary in that sense: very quiet, except that he had to sacrifice himself. But probably at that time, that was demanded, in a way. He was born in a stable, as if with no history, incognito, until he grew up to be twelve years or so. Then he began to heal and do some ministerial work. By the time he was beginning to be known by the people, he was crucified.

It is a very quiet revolution. That is why it is so far reaching. I am not talking about any "ism" or particular religion. Jesus did not preach any religion. Never. Read the Bible again. Religions are created by others, not by the Prophets. In this quiet revolution, which I would term sattvic in nature, it leads to Consciousness. Unless you are sattvic, you cannot grow into Consciousness. Cleverness is rajas. Succumbing to temptations, covering up desires with eloquent references to the scriptures, that is rajas, the devil quoting the scriptures. A silent, sattvic approach of being opens up the consciousness, and that is real meditation.

Even in the short time of Jesus' ministry, his replies—if you study again from this angle—are cut-short, sharp, revolutionary. The Pharisees did not like those statements. They cut through their conscience and they could not stand it. He angered them. In the first place, they were shameless. In the second place, they were untruthful. Thirdly, they were selfish, greedy and position-mongering. And fourth, they were ignorant in the basic sense of the term. And fifth, they were puny and hardly skin-deep spiritually. On the top of that, they were sitting in the seat of judgment for Jesus the Great. He thought: "This world is too spoiled." He stood apart and would have no tucks with them, and they did not like it. That is a perfect revolutionary.

Jesus knew he was touching the soul of the people. If he would have argued and debated with those intellectuals, Pharisees, scholars, bankers or tax collectors, that would not have paid anything. It would have been a waste of his time and energy. He knew where he was touching the people—the sickly, the forlorn, the fishermen, the carpenters. He did not waste his time on the so-called higher or elite society. He just let them alone. And so many blames were on Jesus too that he did not care. If he could not have friendship or company of the Pharisees and so-called intellectual, clever and philanthropist people, he was blamed. So he went and lived with the degraded section of society. He didn't care.

In his simplicity and humility, in his incognito life, he was a perfect revolutionary. We do not see that way because the term revolutionary normally goes with social and political concepts. Therefore we do not speak of a spiritualist as revolutionary, but certainly he was. Krishna was the same. Buddha did not want to rule. He renounced the kingdom. He knew that nobody should rule over others. But at the same time, these Prophets have given the message of Salvation, the message of Enlightenment, of Truth, Nirvana, Pure Consciousness or the Kingdom of God. That was their main topic. If they had spent their time and energy with human cleverness, it would have been wasted. What we nowadays call "games of the mind" and take delight in thinking this is a very qualified thing to do—Jesus wasn't even dealing with such things. He went on healing, gathering men, and if they would not listen, better to be crucified. Better to sacrifice rather than fight against such puniness. I'm not talking about Jesus as a Christian, please, nor have I anything to do with Christianity. I am simply talking about Jesus the Christ.

9

Sri Rama
The Upholder of Dharma

Rama was the noblest of men, a nobility of human nature that we have yet to achieve in common. The highest virtues in humanity were expressed and manifested in him. That is why he is called purushuttam—purush meaning "man," uttam meaning "best"—"the best of men."

The Indian term for today's holy day is Divali, the Festival of Lights, the day when Lord Rama returned to his kingdom of Ayodhya. Though scholars will always differ with each other, the timing of Sri Rama's advent was roughly seven thousand five hundred years ago. Rama's kingdom in Sanskrit is called *Rama Rajya*. You could make it synonymous with "the Kingdom of God." Rama was an Incarnation of Vishnu in the Hindu Trinity of God and a prince of the Solar Dynasty or *Surya Vansha*. Krishna, the Eighth Avatar of Vishnu, was born about five thousand years ago into the Lunar Dynasty, *Chandra Vansha*.

According to Vedic scriptures, there is a cycle of four ages: Golden, Silver, Copper and Iron Age, the latter being the present one. The Sanskrit terms for these are *Sat Yuga, Treta Yuga, Dwapara Yuga* and *Kali Yuga*. These four ages correspond with four levels of mental development in man, the fullest one being in the Golden Age. In that age there were no Prophets. The sages were everything for the society, for the country, for the people and for the devotees. The length of each age is not uniform. The Golden Age is the longest, followed by the Silver Age, Copper and then Iron, each age being shorter than the previous one, the total being about 10,000 years for the four Yugas. Dharma is predominant in the Sat Yuga, less in the Treta, further less in the Dwapara Yuga, and the least in the Kali Yuga. The word dharma is derived from the Sanskrit, *dhri*: "to uphold, to sustain." Dharma is the law, justice or righteousness upholding our body and mind and everything on up to the planet, the natural forces, even the galaxies. Whatever disintegrates, whatever fragments or disunites will be against dharma, or *adharma*, as we call it.

In the Golden Age, dharma is fully present in the people's attitudes, conduct, character, laws and living together. There is more harmony, more peace, better health, unity and sweetness. People talk less and meditate more. Life is oriented toward the integrating or uplifting of consciousness. Most people spend their time and energy expanding into spiritual awakening. In the Golden Age there are masters or gurus and sages or rishis, but there is no particular Prophet because there is no decline, degradation or downward progression. From childhood onward, people are trained and educated in wisdom culture. When children grow up in that atmosphere, there is not a lot to teach them. The schools in the Golden Age were not like the mass scale education of today. Academic, secular knowledge, called *apara-vidya,* was combined with spiritual knowledge, called *para-vidya.*

Each age would take hours to describe, so I am cutting short a little bit. It is a very absorbing subject, not only absorbing—it reminds us that we have been sleeping mentally since eons. It is not something we gain by learning; we all had that capacity originally. Birth after birth, when thousands of years passed by, we forgot about it. That Golden Age, the Sat Yuga, is within everyone. The qualities of mind predominant then were sattva—equilibrium, tranquility, peace and stillness. At that time the books consisted of only a few manuscripts that were memorized, recited and sung in public. At that time the memory capacity was the highest. Now we have forgetfulness even among young people. The human mind sustained by ego cannot remain for long on one thing. If the mind remains on a level sustained by ego, even if it is on dharma to some degree, its tendency will be changefulness, called *parivartana sheela* in Sanskrit. It cannot stay long on one thing unless it goes upward to Enlightenment and Liberation. Otherwise it is bound to come down. Therefore relative existence is called a chakra or circular motion; it goes round and round, up and down, until you get out of the cycle of relativity into Liberation. So when the consciousness in the Golden Age began to degrade or decline, we came to the next lower age, the Silver or Treta Yuga.

It was in the Silver Age that the Prophet Rama was born to uphold dharma. If he had not come as an Avatar—you might say the Son of

God—humanity would not have had something to hold onto. If the Prophet or Avatar does not incarnate, even though humanity may have great men—yogis, sages and high beings—they will not be able to uphold dharma. Great souls also help, but the upliftment of the whole humanity is primarily the work of the Prophets. I may refer to the Bible only because a few of you are new today. The Father in Heaven in Christianity corresponds similarly in Hinduism or Vedic scriptures to Lord Vishnu. Lord Vishnu is the Sustainer, the Maintainer, like a Mother of the universe. In the Vedic Trinity there are three aspects of God: Vishnu the Sustainer, Brahmā the Creator, and Lord Shiva the Transformer. Vishnu is the one Who incarnates, not Brahmā According to Vedic literature, God does not send His Son; He comes Himself. So when He comes or incarnates, He becomes Rama, Krishna, Buddha, and so on.

Rama was born and lived on earth over seven thousand years ago. The word Rama itself has an etymological meaning: one who does *ramana vicharana*, which translates as "that which flows, pervades and travels through our blood, veins, and vibrations of mind." According to Vedic tradition, Lord Vishnu takes ten Incarnations as an Avatar. Rama was the Seventh Avatar, Krishna was the Eighth, Buddha the Ninth, and the Tenth would be Kalki, who is supposed to yet be born or is born and is somewhere. Kalki is the Prophet of the Iron Age or "Age of Machines." From the Golden to the Silver Age when Rama lived, dharma declined about twenty-five percent. When dharma declines, what does it mean? It means peace will be less, harmony will be less, quarrels will be more, wars will be more, ignorance will be more, selfishness, jealousies, competition and negativities all increase. God's worship may grow but meditation will reduce.

The Avatars come to sustain dharma, to uphold it and make it win. They will fight against evil if that is necessary. If nonviolence works, they will try that first. All the Prophets—Rama, Krishna, Buddha and others—first try to uplift dharma peacefully and nonviolently. At any cost they will work for this with love, forgiveness, patience, tolerance, understanding, mutual talking and sharing. They will send emissaries—their relatives, friends, brothers and disciples—to make those who are adharmic understand. But if all this does not work, the Prophets will not give up, and if they have to use violence, they will.

This should not be misunderstood to say that the Prophets favor violence or are violent. Many Prophets have fought wars and battles, but this was only when everything else failed. They don't *allow* dharma to decline further only to avoid fighting. Natural forces such as earthquakes, volcanoes, hurricanes, fires and other things also destroy. In the higher sense one could call such calamities the violence of God, but we do not say that, nor is it God's violence. When all the peaceful methods: sweetness, gentleness, forgiveness, mercy, toleration, patience, unconditional love, sermons, and others fail, the Prophet has to do his or her job, whatever that may be. As instruments of God, they will fight if that is required in order to not sacrifice dharma. They will sacrifice everything else—their lives, their relatives, whether it was Rama's family or Krishna's family—but not dharma, because that is the mission for which they come. This should be understood in proper context.

Why should we follow dharma? Why should we follow higher laws? Why should we follow righteousness? The ultimate aim of dharma is not only to uphold, sustain and nourish, like a mother sustains or nourishes the home or family; dharma has its own purpose. It unites, harmonizes and makes you peaceful and happy. It shows you how to live consciously in a way that leads you to Liberation, *Moksha*. Liberation or Enlightenment is the ultimate goal of dharma. If we fail to follow dharma, then adharma, the opposite of dharma, prevails. Adharma is that which creates degradation, disintegration, chaos, confusion, unfulfillment and dissatisfaction. Naturally, out of such black holes, you cannot reach Liberation. So do not think that dharma is simply to make us live a good life, to just be a "nice guy." That is only the mundane value. Dharma has mundane value too, which is to make life on the earth more happy and peaceful, worth living; but that is for the secular side, not the whole purpose. On the spiritual level, it prepares you for Enlightenment.

Now you can understand why Prophets have this headache of coming on earth to deal with mundane, low things. Why would they do that? Only to make you come out of your mundane existence, to lead you to Enlightenment. Let me divert a little bit here. We came on earth, from wherever we came—any galaxy or planets or whichever creation was made—not just to have fun in Hawaii or Argentina. We came here to learn certain lessons. Let's suppose if the Prophets' purpose was to make us live a good life, then they would be as if telling us: "Stay here; have a good life," and that's it. If that were true, then the Prophets would not be doing their job. Even if we had a good life here, we would get stuck because that is not the purpose for which we have come. So the Prophets' purpose is to not allow you to get stuck here even if you have a good life, leave aside a bad, confused, sad and sorrowful life. On the positive side, we can also get stuck and not follow dharma. Why? Because the very pleasure of a good life will keep us so glued that we will hardly think of dharma. In other words, we will again degrade. To lift us *up* is the work of the Prophets. Of course, there are also sages, saints, holy people and other great ones in a descending hierarchy who also influence our world and spiritual awakening.

In order to make dharma fruitful the Prophets have to give us some laws. Moses gave, Jesus gave; every Prophet has given spiritual laws, though there should not be too many. These laws are byproducts of the main dharma, which sustains and upholds you, gives you peace and stability; where you concentrate well, you live a life of inner joy and satisfaction. Once you get this, you seek the Light, Liberation. If your mind is not sattvic in quality, you will not even meditate properly. You will be mundane. What does this mean? It means you are on the third chakra: just food, procreation, lying down and doing nothing. You want someone else to do for you. You become selfish. These are signs of the third chakra or inertia quality of tamas, which we call mundane or worldly. To come out of this tamas, efforts are needed. This inertia quality of the mind combined with rajo guna, the activity, is what primarily signifies the present Kali Yuga.

In Rama's age there was twenty-five percent less dharma and seventy-five percent truth, compared to the Golden Age when truth and dharma are full. As truth declines more and more, we come to the Dwapara Yuga, Krishna's lifetime, about two thousand five hundred years later. In that age there was fifty percent untruth and fifty percent dharma. In the present Kali Yuga we have only twenty-five percent truth and dharma, exactly the opposite of Rama's day. It varies a little—some may have twenty-three percent truth and some twenty-six or twenty percent, but around that percentage. In this age of tamas, people are more worldly, more mundane, selfish, and centered on the third chakra. What does this mean? In the Kali Yuga, the hallmark of nonvirtue is perversion.

What was predominant in the Golden or Silver Age as a virtue becomes quite the opposite in the Iron Age, so truth will be impractical and honesty will not work—this is how the mind will perceive. Therefore insecurity grows in the Kali Yuga. In the Silver Age—leave aside the Golden Age—hardly did people lock their doors. Today you will not even consider this. On the contrary, there are more inventions and discoveries all the time: double and triple locks. I have gone to motels where there are four locks inside the room—a bolt, a deadbolt, the knob and one more with a chain. If earthquakes come in the night, while opening the four locks to go out I will be doomed!

Insecurity in Golden Age was unheard of. In all the literature of the Vedas, the word insecurity is never even used. And as we are more security-conscious now, the more insecurity is there. There is more greed and selfishness. Somebody else should do for me. If I do wrong, someone else is responsible. If I pass the buck, that is all right. In the Iron Age, this is perfectly good politics. So you can see how we have degraded. In the Golden Age, there was more sharing and very little greed. There was love and compassion, helping, sharing and giving. That is why Rama cared for the people so much. As you come to the Kali Yuga, you see that there are more takers than givers. Even when people have bank vaults with all kinds of locks, checkbooks, credit cards, traveler's checks, and no cash in the pockets, they are still very fearful and insecure.

In the Golden Age and Silver Age, the people were more truthful, compassionate, giving, dharmic, religious, virtuous, and therefore there was more peace. If someone did a wrong or a sin, punishments or rather reactions were more, actually. Why? The reactions were harsher because the people and sages did not want to sacrifice the dharma more. They were a little stern about it, no doubt. Today it may look quite cruel or harsh but in that time when they were very truthful, one minor untruth was considered a big sin. Now we are so used to untruth, it doesn't look that big or bad, unfortunately. That is why we are insensitive to these negativities. Insensitivity is very common in the Iron Age. In greater ages, people were sensitive to each other's needs and understandings. In this modern age, we are mostly sensitive to "my things." If we don't get what we want, we are very sensitive, but to the others' needs we are insensitive. It was quite the opposite then.

I recently read a quotation that said: "People are mostly merciful to their own faults but not to others' faults." Others we blame a lot, but when it comes to our own faults we are very merciful to ourselves. It should be the opposite. We are merciful in forgiving ourselves, but seldom so in forgiving others. Not taking responsibility and blaming is common. In Rama's time, it was more common to forgive others and blame oneself. If you have to condemn anyone, condemn yourself. Nowadays they say: unless you love yourself, you cannot love others. I have never heard this in any scripture. I heard it first in America, years back. I have put it through my whole computer of brain cells, heart, mind, nervous system and prana and could not find that this correlates to anything. What it amounts to is that those who love themselves end there. They do not blame themselves. They say they are perfect. In other words, this is another form of selfishness.

In the Golden Age the people were "ruled" by Seven Sages. These Seven Sages were Enlightened. Practically all of them were married because dharma was so high that there was no need to renounce anything. Try to understand: when there is no garbage, you do not need to clean anything. You renounce or give up something that is bad or low, worldly or degrading. So renunciation came much later, after the Golden Age declined. The Seven Sages were upholding the dharma in that age, and they still do, even today.

When there is a decline in dharma, the Prophet comes. Rama was known to be the best of men, the epitome of the highest qualities of the human mind, the evolution of human thought. Mankind has not reached that acme of human thought, what to say of excellence, that these Prophets embody. The best of mankind's potential they express: gentleness, tenderness, bravery, courage and fearlessness. Even the higher powers such as occultism the Prophets possess—not that they go on demonstrating these powers. When the need is there, they use them. The high vibratory science of yoga, including mantra, using the inner power of the mind, and raja yoga, which today primarily machines do, such as jets, telephones or TVs—in those days, they had these powers without instrumentation or mechanism. So you can see the higher vibrations. Machines are a phenomenon of the lowest age. There was no medium of machines in Rama's age. They expressed these powers through the mind, through mental powers, which is called yoga.

Rama had no problem renouncing anything in the kingdom. As is related in the Ramayana epic, Rama's father had given a promise to his wife of two boons when she had saved his life in the battlefield. "Ask me anything you want," he told her. At that time Kaikeyi, who was Rama's stepmother, wanted nothing. She said, "If I need these boons in the future, I'll tell you." She was a loving wife, so what boons would she need? But when the time changed and degradation and selfishness entered her mind, she demanded these boons from her husband, which in essence ruined the whole kingdom. Her maidservant had spoiled her mind, like Judas, in a sense. When people get greedy, negative, angry, selfish, and ego increases, they begin to demand what no one even imagined. The king had promised these boons in the battlefield, and at that time kings especially were servants to their promises. If you promised, you had to do it.

Rama was the crown prince and he could have *easily* denied to stand by his father's promise because he had not made this commitment; his father had. For her two boons, Kaikeyi demanded that her son, Bharat, rule the kingdom instead of Rama, and that Rama go for exile to the forest for fourteen years. Rama was the eldest son, and in those days the eldest son would be the next king. And Rama, by all virtues, was worthy of being a king. People loved him and he loved the people.

He was for the people, though it was not a democracy, but he was very great, just and loving. He was for the welfare of the people. Even Rama's father could not agree with Kaikeyi's demands, because without Rama he could not live, and he did die when Rama went into exile. When Rama heard her demands for him, renouncing the kingdom was what we call in India, *chutkiyon ka khel**—just the wink of his eye. Rama agreed to go even though his father wasn't asking him to go. To keep up his father's promise, he renounced. In other words, renunciation itself was a virtue. It was very normal, quite the opposite of today. He did not hesitate a moment to go into exile. He could have clung to the kingdom—"My father committed that promise. I am not a slave to it. I will rule the kingdom. Let him go to hell . . ." He did not say that. Nowadays they fight for patrimony. They quarrel and quarrel and go to court and use violence also. It is quite a drama—how selfishly to acquire rather than give up or let go! We teach nowadays so much to let go. In Rama's age nobody had to teach to let go. Everyone let go if it would help. Now it is the opposite: how to grab, how to make wants fulfilled, the adventures of desires—quite exotic!

Rama did not mind leaving the palace. He said, "I will be happy in the forest. I will have Darshan of the sages, the holy people, and hear wisdom from their lips. I will be actually blessed if I go." Of course, eventually his brother Lakshmana went with him and also his wife Sita. Without Rama, to them there was no life. Although they were in a physical sense human beings, Rama was inside them, one with them, whether it was his father Dasharatha, his consort Sita, his brother Lakshmana, his mother Kaushalya, or his servant Hanuman, whom he met later. What happens is that when the Prophets come on earth, some souls—five, ten, twelve, thirteen, sixteen or twenty—incarnate along with them from the higher region to help their work. They are called *paarshad,* in Sanskrit. The number varies. In times of Jesus, Buddha, Krishna and Rama, the number varied. But always some come along to help the Prophet's work or mission on earth.

---

* *Chutkiyon ka khel*, lit: "as easy as snapping the fingers."

Sita, Lakshmana, Bharat and even Dasharatha were so permeated with Rama that Rama was their very Soul. So when Rama went into exile, his father and the other paarshad did not know how to live. This was not because of attachment or muddiness in the human sense. Attachment on the physical level is quite a different mental caricature. I'm talking about the deepest Soul, not the mental or physical attachment alone. Those who cling to each other physically and mentally like leeches, you may have seen some of them wanting or talking about soul mates. Why do they want soul mates? Mental mates they have; physical mates they have. Why soul mates? They are missing something—don't you think so? Rama is that Soul. Put any word you want: Christ Consciousness, Buddhahood or Enlightenment. Rama is the Soul of Dasharatha, the Soul of Sita, the Soul of Lakshmana, of Kaushalya, and so on.

Some may say melodramatically, out of attachment, "How can I live without him?" I say, "You also will die. Why do you worry?" But in this case, Dasharatha did die, because his Soul had gone. Before Rama left for exile, he told Sita: "You are a tender woman. You stay in the palace." She replied this famous line: "Where Rama is, there is my Ayodhya. If you are not here, this is no Ayodhya for me." Rama was defeated. He said, "Come on." And it was the same with Lakshmana. Though in the human sense Lakshmana was Rama's brother, he was truly his shadow; he could not live without him. I am not talking about muddiness. This is the deepest soul connection—*atma svarupa*: those who live with God. They are One with him. So when the Avatar comes, he brings a retinue: a typist, an accountant, a computer player, a cleaner, and all those kinds of things, and they help his work. They all suffer for the time being, no doubt, because to uphold dharma—I wish it were smooth and peaceful, just going up, but it is not. Since you are fighting evil, adharma, naturally it is not a pleasant job. It cannot be, even if you choose to do it.

The Prophets first try to make it sweet and plausible, imperceptibly peaceful, loving and forgiving, though there is also suffering and

Sacred Mountain Ashram, August 1982

Jyoti Ashram, 1992

Jyoti Mandir (Temple of Light), Retreat at Sacred Mountain Ashram, 1991

Countryside Ashram, September 1979

Chetana Ashram, Leigh (North Island), New Zealand, 1989

Visiting Shakti Dham (ladies quarters), Sacred Mountain Ashram, September 1989

Working in the forest at Sacred Mountain Ashram, 1986

Working in the forest at Sacred Mountain Ashram, August 1986

Jyoti Dham, Sacred Mountain Ashram, 1991

At the Matterhorn, Switzerland, October 1998

At Monument Valley, Arizona-Utah border, 1995

Leaving Sacred Mountain Ashram for airport to fly to India, June 1997

Celebration of Guru Purnima, Sacred Mountain Ashram, July 1998

Janmashtami (Krishna's Birthday) at Sacred Mountain Ashram, September 1999

even self-martyrdom in this working. They try to make a smooth progression upward, as in meditation you go to higher consciousness. But this is a fight against evil, against the forces of darkness, against anti-God, you could term it. Under these circumstances, if you forgive or let go, they don't let go. That is the problem with evil people: they do not let go. They do not even understand this language. They say: "Fight for fight, tooth for tooth." So naturally it comes to greater wars and battles, which to us are now enjoyable epics: the Ramayana and Mahabharata.

The Prophets will sacrifice, renounce, suffer and fight, if need be in order to make dharma prevail. To them, dharma is higher than any relationship, higher than any wants, higher than life itself, higher than anything as far as this earth is concerned. They will stand by dharma and sacrifice whatever is needed, even whole kingdoms. Krishna approached the Kauravas, the evil side, with a peace proposal, but they told him, "If the Pandavas want one inch of this land, come in the battlefield and fight." Krishna told them: "We can do that, but the whole kingdom will be destroyed. Most of the men will be killed. Women will be widows; there will be so many orphans. There will be death and blood everywhere. What will that kingdom mean to you?" But the evil side would not listen. They asserted, "As long as you are destroyed, I don't mind if I am destroyed." Their whole aim becomes to destroy the opposite party in enmity. Even if they are destroyed themselves, they don't care. When that happened, Krishna told Arjuna: "For the upholding of dharma, you have to stand up. If you have to kill your own relatives, do that to uphold righteousness." It was not for selfishness or robbery or blackmail. The Prophets did not teach these things. They taught: give up, let go, renounce, uphold dharma, then you will go to heaven. In Krishna's time there was more degradation, more quarrels, more selfishness and more intrigues than in Rama's day, though there were demons like Ravana and others in Rama's time.

Those who come with Rama, what do they do? The major consort becomes the shakti of Rama. The Prophet needs shakti, the Divine

energy. That shakti is Lakshmi, Who shares the heaven of Lord
Vishnu. Unfortunately in Christianity there is only the Father in
Heaven; there is no Mother, though Mary is there as the Mother of
Jesus. However, in Vishnu's case, Lakshmi comes also on earth to be
His shakti. In Rama's case there were two prominent shaktis, though
there are six altogether. One is his consort, Sita, who was kidnapped
by the evil king, Ravana, and taken to his golden kingdom in Lanka.
Before Rama went there to vanquish Ravana, he worshiped Maa
Durga, the Divine Mother, Who is also Shakti. So there is the Mother
shakti and the consort shakti. Durga is actually the consort of Lord
Shiva, but all these shaktis are not separate, only different aspects of
Divine Mother.

So when the Prophet comes, Lakshmi will come as his consort and
bring wealth, prosperity, power and victory. Another shakti that
comes is the mental, occult shakti: Durga. And a third will come as
the spiritual shakti: Saraswati, the Creatrix, the consort of Brahmā.
There are six Mother shaktis totally, though the fundamental Principle
is one. All these Divine powers come to help the Prophet to win
dharma. The Prophet's whole purpose in battles and wars is not to
win any kingdom or power or ascendancy to a throne. It is simply
to protect dharma, to fulfill the earth's own mission, which is to
transcend into higher dimensions.

We are all connected with each other within our homes and
towns, our nations and the world. The world itself is a soul in such
a way that it has its own inner mission. So if the Prophet does not
come to uphold dharma, the earth will go into ruin. The earth's
evolution will degrade, and God will not allow that. It is His business,
not yours and mine. The Prophets have to save the earth. Try to see
the point. They will try to see if there is any peaceful way that the
same thing could be achieved. If we can follow dharma through peace,
sharing, giving, loving, forgiveness and toleration; if we live together
nicely and meditate and pray daily, we will help the higher evolution
of consciousness. The same goal could be achieved so that the earth
evolves into the next dimension peacefully.

If today we read about E.T.s or other natural forces coming to harm us—whatever the explanation may be—one thing is certain: had we lived together in peace and giving, sharing, forgiving, loving and sweetness; had we not been greedy, violent, jealous and so on, there was no need for these forces to come and destroy us. You may ask, "Why should they come and interfere with us?" But what power do you have to avoid it anyway? By this attitude we get afraid and insecure. I say, why don't you by yourself be peaceful, sweet and good, and live together and evolve? That is what we have to be now. There is no other choice.

Earth has its own mission as a being. We are just insects on this world. Just as in your body there are viruses, germs, bacteria and so many cells existing together—thousands and millions, probably—in that way we have to live together in this world. We may be great as human beings but to the earth we are like insects. One earthquake, a minute or half-minute long, eight or nine points on the Richter scale, finishes us in no time. All our machineries, progress, money, doctors, military, police and preparations go to null and void.

You may do anything you want—I'm not challenging, I'm one of you—but you know that all the preparations we make at the time of disasters do not help. Wildfires burn thousands and millions of acres. We try our best to contain them and we do eventually, but not before destruction has happened. When hurricanes come, they try to give satellite warnings, et cetera, but when it happens, what can anyone do? We mechanically try to know the details, but when these things occur, what can we do? When death approaches, we try injections and procedures to try to keep that person alive. And he or she may hang in for a few more years. But ultimately what is the outcome? We can't do anything. I am not saying this in a pessimistic manner, but we are helpless. On earth we are like insects. Therefore good people are preaching nowadays for conservation, for ecology. Why? In order to not spoil the earth, the forests, the water, the moonshine or sunshine. Just live ecologically. It is earth's nature to evolve. Don't destroy it.

Those who spoil it will be finished. The greedy and selfish are always destroyed because they are evil, because they are disturbing the ecology of the earth. Destroyed does not necessarily mean killed. They are thrown out of the orbit in such a way that they cannot disturb any further. Their disturbance comes back to them. Unfortunately we think the earth is "for my enjoyment, my gratification." So we mine everything out of it, whether it is gold or water or petrol or uranium or timber. Senselessly we go on cutting and destroying. So eventually what happens? It comes back to us. Otherwise this energy will destroy whom? You and me again. Gold makes us greedy and selfish; poisonous water kills us; and so on.

Dharma shows us how to make all things come into balance in our lives and on earth so that we do not destroy ourselves. There is also a corollary. When we harm the earth or any institution or family, it will rebound on us. Ultimately we will not succeed. This dharma, therefore, the Prophets come to teach: "Do this . . . don't do this . . . be good." Moses may give the Ten Commandments; Jesus may give the Sermon on the Mount; Krishna may give the Bhagavad Gita and the Vedic sages may give us wisdom in order that we live on dharma to save ourselves and the earth. The Savior comes to save—if we just listen to what they have been saying. But oftentimes it proves to be like throwing pearls before swine—sorry for the language. There is a saying from Arabia. The *rabab* is an instrument in Arabia like a violin. Now sheep do not listen much. If you tell them anything, they just bleat. So the saying is: "If you go on playing the rabab before sheep, what does it matter to the sheep? Centuries have passed playing before the sheep." Ultimately, if we do not pay heed, destruction comes. Not because Prophets want to destroy. They do not want to fight. They are unnecessarily maligned by evil people. They fight when that is the last thing left, when either they take up violence or let adharma rule. They choose violence rather than sacrifice dharma, because if they sacrifice dharma, the very sustenance or foundation of the earth is finished.

I am not talking about physical life alone because this physical life is for the mental and the mental is for the spiritual. Ultimately we have to learn the lessons here and grow. So Prophets such as Rama, we worship as God. There is nothing wrong in this. They are Divine, no doubt, but because the Prophets take the five-elemental human body, often we judge or misjudge them, seeing them as human beings doing certain things, saying certain things, behaving in certain ways. We judge not only according to our social customs and our understanding but also according to our level of consciousness. When human beings begin to judge them—whether Krishna, Rama, Buddha, Jesus or others—they judge the Prophets from an ordinary human perspective. It makes a mess.

The Prophets' limitations are due to the human body in which they incarnate. In order to communicate with us, they take human bodies. If they were just flying around like angels in the astral realm and teaching us dharma, telling us to do good things and throwing fire and brimstone when we don't, then we would not be able to communicate with them. So they come as human beings in order to communicate and teach us. But in their play, we begin to judge according to our understanding or level of consciousness. This is where our blunder happens.

In Rama's case, the whole kingdom was not lost, but in Krishna's case the whole kingdom, Hastinapur, and the whole country was destroyed in the war because the evil side would not give up. They were stubborn, angry, arrogant, and so on. Today I read that among the three gunas or qualities of mind—tamas, rajas and sattva—that people who have sattva or tranquility are not arrogant. They may have a little pride only. But when it comes to the rajas quality, they get arrogant. And in tamas, do you know what word they used? They become *vain*. Vanity is the hallmark of tamasic people. In sattva they will have simple pride. In rajas they will be arrogant and haughty. So when those conditions crop up in anger, Prophets cannot do anything else but strike. Not because they want to strike; they do so because we do not leave them any other choice. Jesus tried—not that he was wrong, but ultimately he was crucified by the evil ones. What else could he do? He thought the way of martyrdom would save the world, save the sinners. That was his way, but there are other ways.

Buddha forgave also, as a monk. But for Rama and Krishna, their job was different.

Up until now in this Kali Yuga, even if there is twenty-five percent truth or dharma left on earth, it would have been zero, chaos, imbalance and total destruction if the Prophets had not come and saved the world. This must be so because after the Kali Yuga, when the ages turn back toward the Golden Age, dharma and truth will increase out of our suffering and purification. If dharma would reduce to zero, the earth would be finished. It would be hurtling around like a dead asteroid in the cosmos, something like Mars or another planet. To save this earth, dharma is necessary. And along with dharma, one thing that comes very, very closely with it always is love, because dharma is not cold justice. Please understand this: in the Iron Age the law is cold with no consideration—just punishment. It is not law.

Prophets do not come to punish. Along with justice they are loving and compassionate and merciful. Rama proved this. When he returned from fourteen years' exile to Ayodhya, he could have easily vanquished his enemies, the evildoers who were still living. Rama was powerful; he could have done anything he wanted. He was a great occultist, a great Prophet, but he did not punish *anyone*. He forgave many. He gave back the kingdom of Lanka to Ravana's brother, Vibhishana, after defeating Ravana. He did not take any revenge from his stepmother who had sent him into exile. He forgave her. Even when she asked for his forgiveness, do you know what Rama told her? "In my eyes you've done no fault." That is justice.

It is not justice when the law becomes cold, as in the Kali Yuga where you punish only. You should have mercy and forgiveness and compassion. Rama saved Sri Lanka. When the people there wanted him to stay and rule, he said, "I did not come to conquer your land. I wanted to establish dharma and destroy this evildoer." There is no forgiveness to evildoers when they stop understanding even one percent and carry on with stubbornness, anger and haughtiness. Then they have to be finished; there is no other choice. In Lanka, Rama did not kill a single soldier after the demon Ravana was defeated. And when Rama came back to Ayodhya, he had great power. All the kingdoms were under him. He was *chakravarti*, which means an invincible emperor. He could have done anything, but he never took a reaction to anyone.

Dharma has love with it always. Without love, dharma has no meaning. It has to be compassionate, merciful, nonreactionary, nonretaliatory, without vengeance. This is the beauty of dharma. Cold laws that simply punish make those persons worse brutes afterwards. Dharma transforms a person. So, along with dharma you will see that the Prophets and sages and holy people are always very loving. Not only loving but unconditionally loving. They will sacrifice their own wife or brother but they will have love and dharma uppermost. And with dharma and love, the Prophets have no ax to grind in the world. As soon as their job is done, they leave. They do not try to have therapies and vitamins and minerals to live longer.

As soon as the Prophet's mission is done—whether he is ruling a kingdom or not—he wants to go. Why? They have seen better worlds—heavens. By that comparison, this earth is nothing. This is not to undermine the earth or make it insignificant—Mother Earth is fine—but they do not remain attached. They do not die weeping and wailing. They leave very happily, relieved. So try to understand this dharma and love, and their mission to selflessly guide humanity how to live righteously. In the meantime destruction may follow, but the Prophets are not the makers of destruction. We asked for it. We were so stubborn, so egotistical, selfish, greedy and lazy. What can they do? In other words, though some destruction is involved, upholding dharma makes our future bright. We live on again to fulfill our mission. Then the next Prophet and the great Gurus and sages carry on.

Rama still lives. The Ramayana epic has come to America too, not because of evangelism but because it is the truth. It will not die. It is the inheritance of humanity, not just one religion as a missionary zeal of converting people. You do not become "Ram-ites." It just gives you your inheritance, which has been within you since ages. You may not know this. You may not know how many births you have had or who lived in the Silver Age or in Jesus' lifetime. We keep on being reborn. Naturally, we carry on the samskars, the impressions of mind, inside of the subconscious. Therefore this truth, which doesn't convert or evangelize anyone, will keep appealing to us, because that truth is within us that we are searching.

That is why the Gurus come and remind you that it is inside you. Therefore Rama and the other Prophets live in you and me. If you do not go by the outer dogmatic view only—"Oh, Rama wasn't Christian." Christianity was not even born when Rama lived! It is fine to go through Jesus or Rama or Krishna. Jesus did say: "Those who are dear to me will follow my Word." Why would he say that? If you follow his Word, I do not think it will differ from Rama's Word or Krishna's Word. But if you stick to the form of Jesus or Krishna or anybody and ignore anything else, then you are in trouble. You have to follow the Word. If you follow the Word, it will be dharma, love, compassion, mercy, peace, joy, freedom and wisdom. On these, no one differs. Therefore the Prophets live immortally. Rama is still present. Krishna is still present. Buddha is still present. They are Immortal. They do not die. We may see their body dying, which certainly it does, as the nature of the five-elemental body is to disintegrate eventually. But *they* don't die.

When Rama returned to Ayodhya in the *vimana* or aerial vehicle with his Sita and Lakshmana and other ambassadors—Hanuman, Sugriva, Vibhishana—the people were very happy. After fourteen years of suffering, the Lord was coming back. He had fulfilled his father's promise. So they cleaned their houses, painted them anew, put ghee lamps, flowers and decorations everywhere. That was the first Divali. We celebrate this holy day not only because of the Prophet's coming back to Ayodhya, but also as the victory over evil, which every mind has to fight. This victory of Rama—I wouldn't say he could not have done it alone, but he did it with great help and grace and blessings of Divine Mother. Rama worshiped Durga to invoke that shakti to vanquish the demon, because Ravana was very powerful though very evil. Therefore Durga Puja is observed as Navaratri, "nine days puja" leading up to Divali. The tenth day is Divali, also called *Dussehra*, the death of Ravana. Ravana had earned power from worshiping Lord Shiva Himself, but he misused it afterwards; therefore he became evil. So whenever we think of Divali, Maa Durga is also a part of it. The Light comes after shakti is invoked. If you don't take it dogmatically as an Indian holy day, it has its own message.

Rama was the noblest of men, a nobility of human nature that we have yet to achieve in common. The highest virtues in humanity were expressed and manifested in him. That is why he is called *purushuttam*—*purush* meaning: "man," *uttam* meaning "best"—"the best of men." He was the best that man could achieve—meaning woman also; the best one could achieve as a human being. Anything he had to do, he did from his excellence and virtuous nature. He never stooped low in order to achieve any object or the dharma. He upheld virtues and fought for them. So if you pray to Lord Rama, really believing in his/Sita's shakti and the others who came with him, you will feel and see that purity reigns. From that we have now come to the Kali Yuga, and if you compare, where are we? We cannot even feel the possibility of achieving that purity because of the perversion that is prevalent now. People say: "Leave us alone," but Prophets will not do this. If they leave us alone, it will become chaos, so they strike us for our own good! But we do not like that either. If we are humble and pray to Lord Rama to purify us, to make us noble, virtuous, dharmic and save us from egoism, he will listen.

As you might know, Mahatma Gandhi, who was educated at Oxford and Cambridge—he was not a simple villager, though he looked like a villager—at the time of death he uttered three times, *"He Rama!"* [O Rama!] It was not just because he was Hindu. Those who are anti-Hindu are always saying we have many gods and superstitions. They malign a lot. But even such a great man as Gandhiji—of whom Einstein said: "In future generations, people will not believe a man like Gandhi lived on this earth"—when he was shot, he called God's Name. Unfortunately Richard Attenborough translated this in his movie as, "Oh, God." Now, that is quite cold. It should have been, *"He Rama."* Anyway, I am grateful to Richard Attenborough. Gandhi could have uttered "Shiva" or "Krishna" or any other Name of God. In his prayer meetings daily in the evenings, he used to have prayers from practically all religions, so he could have spoken another Name at the moment of his death. But he worshiped Rama. Rama is a great power, a great shakti, strength, purity and nobility of man. If you pray to him, his Name is a great mantra. This is not something Christians or Buddhists cannot do. It is symbolic of the victory of Light over darkness.

10

God the Mother

Whether you say God, the Absolute, relative dualism, nondualism, or Truth exists—there are billions of words in the dictionary—one thing you cannot deny: you do exist. The one who is creating exists. What does it amount to? There is a point where the creation happens. That is Mother.

*P*rabhushri: Do you believe in Divine Mother?

Devotee: *Yes.*

Do you believe in God as a woman?

Yes.

Or God is only Father, or both?

Both, yes.

Has it been ever natural to you to call God as Mother or—

No.

So when you pray or remember God, which gender do you see? Male?

Both genders. I don't specify.

No, you don't. That's not your job.

God-Father/God-Mother.

I see. Or does it matter even, whatever it is?

Sometimes it's one or the other, depending on what's going on in my life at the time.

It depends whom you want: If it's money, you call God the Father, right? [laughter] And when you want mercy, God the Mother? Probably. Do you believe in God the Formless?

Yes, I've never really considered God as having a form. He is in all forms but I have never really envisioned—

257

—a particular one?

Yeah.

But you are sure He exists?

Oh, yes.

She?

Yes.

Does it relax you when you remember God in any way?

Oh, very much.

It does. Do you think much about God?

All the time.

Let me repeat the question. [laughter] If you do that all the time, you are in trouble! Do you think about God? Or do you remember Him? And which one?

Both.

Whenever you might have remembered or thought about God the Mother, what difference do you feel?

When I think about God the Mother, I become more in tune with all the living things around me.

Otherwise? You transcend those?

Yeah. Sometimes, if I'm not remembering God the Mother, it's easy to just go through life thinking about what you are going to do next, not being there with your Mother.

So, when you might be thinking or remembering God the Father, or male form, that time you don't get much aware of the living things around you? Or what is the outcome?

When I'm thinking of God the Father, it's more when I'm going inside of myself. God the Mother comes when I'm out in nature and things.

Do you feel a little separation of the two?

There are times when there is a more gentle . . . When I feel feminine qualities coming out, I feel that that side of God is talking to me more. But in general I don't separate the two.

What do you understand by God the Mother?

You mean how would I define Mother?

Not a definition, but is there any other meaning to God as Mother?

Just nurturing and compassionate.

The Being, you think? God Mother Being?

No, I've never looked at it as a separate Being, just as another side of God.

Okay, but not necessarily two things like father and mother?

No, I never thought of them as two different Beings. Two sides.

So, if you are thinking or remembering or seeing one side, the other side is definitely there then?

Oh, yes.

Even though we don't see both simultaneously? Do you believe in God the Formless?

Yes.

You do? And there, Father-Mother does not matter?

No.

How do you think—of course, we are imagining—this all came about? You, me, or whatever is all around?

I don't know.

The one talking—let's say you, me, we understand, express and explain in one or the other way. So either it is Truth or we fall down from Truth into relative duality. The simple truth is that we exist, don't we? So, this phenomenon we cannot reject. We cannot deny the one talking, the one listening, the one discussing or the one defining what understanding you have, whichever way anybody defines. Probably everybody is right in one's own angle. However we may reject or accept ideas about God—Mother, Father, whatever— but one thing we are establishing: each one of us exists. I exist. You exist. Who is otherwise talking, saying, explaining, defining the way you think it is true? We can brush off a hundred ideas and establish one or two that you or I understand best, but the underlying idea is: the one who is establishing or explaining or defining or expressing is existing. We cannot deny that. Who is, in the first place, bringing that expression out, whether by word or thought? We cannot deny that. If anybody denies, he is going to be dropped dead right here and now! [laughter] And if you don't drop dead, you are establishing your existence! Is that clear? Let's see what it leads to.

The one who exists creates. *You and I are creating.* Whether you say God, the Absolute, relative dualism, nondualism, or Truth exists— there are billions of words in the dictionary—one thing you cannot deny: you *do* exist. The one who is creating exists. What does it amount to? There is a point where the creation happens. That is Mother. Who creates otherwise? You can't say, "Oh, I understand, so that is the end of the matter." God exists, whether as Father, Mother or Son doesn't matter. Whatever ideas we express, those are immaterial in the sense of whether the one who is giving ideas is there or not, not only bodily. We certainly see the body, too, however stubbornly we may reject anything. Even bodily we do exist. But leave aside that gross part, you and I or somebody else is existent. We cannot deny this. There is an entity, there is a being, and there is a point of creation.

Why go too far into the galaxies? Here and now, you and me are just here. Every day, every second, every moment, every fraction of a moment we live to create something. Who else is the creator? We cannot say, "Oh, Truth creates this nondualism." Then we fall down into dualism. Where are we existing? Are you existing in the Absolute? Do you exist in a nondualistic state? Who can raise your hand honestly about it? Whom have you seen established in the nondualistic Absolute and condemning dualism? Have you seen anyone established in the Absolute nondualism, floating transcendentally? Why to deny what is before our eyes and ears every fraction of a second?

This is Mother. We have a capacity to deny, but are we really denying it? Are we making it nonexistent? Why to make mind egotistical just to deny what is not only obvious but which, not for a fraction of second, you can make nonexistent? Saints and holy people have split their hair to deny it. Nobody else has been able to yet. Man can conceive, perceive and ignore the plain obvious. You can put your palm up and hide the sun and say it doesn't exist. We can babble like children, but does that make the sun nonexistent? Does it make nonexistent the phenomena: you and me and a point of creation every moment, every second, every fraction of second? Are you ever without yourself at any moment? This is a very simple question. If you know it, why to deny it only philosophically?

Let's come to our senses, if we have senses, and I'm sure we have not transcended senses. Those who have transcended senses and "me," their language is quite different. Have you been without you, *ever*? Right from your darkest moment to the brightest one, have you ever been without you? You and me are the ones we have seen, are perceiving, are living with and experiencing with. Who else could be at hand to refer to? You can't go in the past birth or coming birth without being a great yogi, of course. Can you be without you? If not, then who is creating? *You* are the one creating for you. *I* am the one creating for me. And if I exist and you exist every second, then everywhere that you are, you are with you. Isn't that true?

From where have you come? Have you sincerely asked yourself who you are? We can babble philosophy and scriptures anytime, no problem. You can read a thousand books about what Jesus said, Krishna said, Buddha said. Nothing wrong with what they said. But the point of reference is which one? You and I live with ourselves— everywhere, every minute, with every experience, with everything. I do exist myself. I am not without me. So who am I? Or put it in more tangible language: who created you or me? We can deny anything we want, but let's face the facts. Who is your Creator or Creatrix? If we can find the answer to this, probably my or your questions would be extinguished. It's not so much that I can explain to you where creation came from, or you can refer to books and say, "Okay, this is it." Maybe those are right but that's not *our* experience or realization. If I could find my own Creatrix or Creator, probably these questions would be answered.

Me and my creation, you and your creation, is what we are talking about as Divine Mother. If we don't fight about words, then it is very easy to see what we mean by Mother. All manifestations, all pervaded projection, the creation, the release of rays from your Being—it is the Mother fabric. It is, as if, from you, whatever you are. When you find creation coming out of you, up to whatever degree, it is like a sheet or a fabric that is spread out. That is Mother. As long as you are existing, as long as you are doing, expressing, living, manifesting, projecting, creating, whatever—that is Mother. That is the Creatrix creating. That is the function of Motherhood. Even if we say we don't believe in different sexes of God, okay. I don't think God knows about sex even. But it is not that two sexes are different.

What is the *inner* meaning of Motherhood, Mother existence? That is your expression, your projection, your manifestation, your pervadedness, as if sheeting out. Like you hold a flashlight switch and, all of a sudden, a flood of light comes out. That's Mother! What would be the flashlight without light? It is inseparable. If you do not make a mess of the words—"Oh, God the Mother or Father, what else?" You may talk high but you are crawling here on earth, baby! Many tried to deny this phenomenon. We are putting down God, whichever Form we give to Him or Her. It is only because we are intellectual, philosophical—that greatness of the ego trying to deny the utmost, realistic, day-to-day, you-with-you, me-with-me phenomena, as if we are not here! We *are* here, right? But we are denying the very fact! And if you don't, what do you come to? Establishing the Motherhood, the Creatrix, the pervadedness, the manifestation or projection, here and now.

That is your creation, your expression, your art. That is your Being, *multiplying*. And that is your joy, the joy of creation. It is a joy to you to create. You are expressing yourself, manifesting and multiplying yourself. You are projecting yourself out, and that is the Mother aspect. There is no use in juggling around words: "I don't believe in bhakti or shakti or *takti*"—takti, meaning: "deceit." These are Indian words, of course. Do not deny what you are and try to jump up somewhere else. You cannot do that without being fictitious. You can beat about the bushes, but we understand what it means. When you come to true Reality, facing the situation as it is and as you are, we are just with this manifestation all the time. Then you will see that you are creating. Whatever you do and say, you *are* doing that. You are creating that. You can express the way you like, but that is the way you are seeing, the way you are experiencing, the way you are creating, and therefore you cannot expect that everybody else will see the same way. That is not necessary.

This is the Motherhood. She has a joyful, myriad, multiple-creative faculty. That is Her variety. Whether you worship God the Father or Mother or something else, all are joined together. It is not that the light beam coming out of a flashlight is a separate entity than the flashlight itself. It is projecting out. The term "outward" we use by way of explanation of dualism. Actually it is projecting Light within itself, but that will go to Absolutism. According to the Vedas, the denial of the very fact you are establishing is the product of ignorance. When we come to senses—that is, to realism, to face the fact that you and I *are* doing, saying, and expressing them, we are facing or becoming part of the Motherhood. Those who have denied this have always suffered. Their absolutism does not help them at that time. Even to eliminate one stomachache, absolute Knowledge does not do anything.

Therefore we say, "Mother, You are *everything*." And that is true. Who else is everything? Supposing you would ask God the Father about the creation, about the becoming or manifestation, I'm sure He will tell you: "Ask Her." Is He keeping Himself aloof, as if—"I have nothing to do with this separate thing"? No. He will simply say:

"Ask Her." If we can solve this question by our point of reference, you and me, that we exist with our Self everywhere, at any situation, any moment, any time, and it is not separable, then we will begin to see our own creation. This is where love for Mother starts. Then we are discovering the secret of my and your creation: the Mother. It is as if you left that faithful One, forgotten, separated. You missed the whole love for the creation, the love of brothers and sisters and society.

We miss that love because we have been denying unnecessarily and trying to avoid something that cannot be avoided, which exists with you and me. Because we have been denying that, the love suffers. When you come back to this very acceptance, you begin to love others. Intellectual absolutism is cold. Not only is it devoid, it cancels love itself. It does not solve any problems when they come to your ankle or stomach or head or arm—be sure about it. You may resort to painkillers but we all know that those are temporary. Even painkiller tablets you are relying upon, not on your absolute Knowledge. And that pill is Mother! Don't forget it.

Ego can play a lot of tricks. Even if something does help—an herb, a food, your dear ones where you get a succor of some kind, or some entertainment—what is that? *That's* Mother. You can deny verbally. The tongue can revolve 360 degrees—and God gave that capacity to our tongue to waggle—but that does not mean it is always talking sense. When you come back to yourself, then you will see that *you* are doing everything—sensing, believing, thinking, hating, loving, liking, disliking, eating, not eating, going or coming. The hundred thousand things you and I do every day, we are *creating*. Or put it differently: God within you is creating. Whichever way you phrase it, *that is Mother*. That is why we *love* it—it is so one with us, each one's own. It is dear to you! And that is Mother. That is maya—*your* maya. That is your film, no doubt, and that is why it is your Beloved. You *love* it. It is *yours*. Therefore we love it. *That's Mother.* That very point of connection, of creation, that *awareness* is what we are missing. This is "me"; this is "mine." That "mine" is Mother.

The Sanskrit word for this is *mamatwa*, from which comes Maa. *Mama*, "me," *mamatwa*, "mine." *That* is dear to me. That is my

Beloved, my Mother. If you establish this relationship, you will find love. This is what Divine Mother is about. It is not only that She is a nice woman or compassionate or good or loving. All that is fine, but the truth is beyond this. That is so dear, inseparable from "me" and "mine." "Me" is Father; "mine" is Mother. "Me" is the *purusha*; "mine" is *prakriti*. "Me" is my soul; "mine" is my creation. Therefore, discussing about this is futile. You can only separate in words but both are inseparable. Once you realize this relationship of the phenomena, the Lord, God and His creation, you and your own creation, then loving all will be very natural, because in that "mine-ness" and "your-ness" you will encompass everything, as far as your projection extends. That is the form of Divine Mother.

Those who have denied this have had problems, always. Philosophically you can write theses, but when it comes to your daily affairs and problems, those theses do not work. You can study and write any number of books on economics, but when it comes to your own budget, books do not do anything. You were dealing with petty cash that time; now it has to be hard cash. Do not try to separate that which is inseparable, even though conceptually you can do it. You will be deceiving yourself.

Come to this awareness, the consciousness of You, wherever you are. This spreading-out of Consciousness is the Mother. That is your creation: *Chetana*, the Awareness, the Consciousness. When you are becoming *aware*, you are establishing a loving relationship with Her. Not that your relationship was not there already, but you were not aware of it. That is why you have problems. That is why you have a dearth of love. But now you are getting *aware* of that. It is your creation, your Consciousness, spreading out like a bedsheet or a tablecloth. And with that spreading out, you can see it is all-pervaded Motherhood. You can refuse to see, but that will not extinguish it. That is Mother. It is not Mother versus Father. Though we pose questions in order to analyze and understand, it is not actually one versus the other. It is *there*.

This is your own joyful creation, your joyful projection, your joyful art. You are the artist. You are the "live-er" of the life. The life is your

Mother. You hug your life, don't you? Even if you hate Her, it is She with you. You cannot hate someone who is not with you. Do you understand? An artist may get angry with his projection on the canvas and go on applying other colors and brushes to it, but he is still *with* the canvas. He is doing it at the same time. It is your creation. You can change it, but once you come in terms and tune with your creation, with that relationship with your Beloved, your Mother, you have found the whole secret, the whole truth—*Om Maa*!

This being the fact, we have to come to a very humble sensibility, as if saying, "I surrender at the Feet of the Mother. I denied You. I ignored You. I didn't want to see You or recognize Your existence, but it was always there. I, the doer, all the time creating, was the deny-er of my own incessant creation. That was my problem, my pain, Mother. I just surrender at Thy Feet." You establish the relationship. And She says: "Okay, prodigal son. At least you have understood. Even though you denied Me, *I was there anyway*. You just created your own problem fictitiously, called ignorance, and you suffered. Now you are recognizing. Now you are seeing. Let's start again." Just be aware of you and "your-ness." That "my-ness" is Mother, baby! Don't fight over the words. I cannot talk to you without sipping a few sips of water. That's *Mother* to me. I can say: "I have nothing to do with the water . . ." You can deny anything you want. Denial is the faculty of ignorance.

She is all-encompassing Awareness. When you surrender to this benevolence of Mother—*your* Mother, *my* Mother—it works wonders. It is such a simple thing. Mother would say: "Why do you deny the very simple fact? It's all right, kid." This recognition, this Awareness is what we need. This is Self Consciousness. Forget about Pure Consciousness, which seems impersonal. Be conscious of your *Self*, that's all. Can you do that? Then you will find your creation, your Mother emanating from you and me. Then there is no denial. You will find love for all. You will be compassionate to all. You will find joy in your creation. Whatever you will do, speak or express will be joyful. In joy you will travel, sit, write, type, whatever. It will be joyful creation, once you are aware. You were doing those things already, but you were not aware of your Self being present, as a point of creation. Therefore you weren't *enjoying* it, because you were ignorant.

Don't deny the obvious. It is making you unconscious. If you are making yourself deliberately unconscious, then whose fault will it be when miseries follow? Miseries come because we get unconscious; we deny the very obvious. Just come to Self Consciousness, S-E-L-F in all capitals. Just be aware of your Self. You will see everything; secrets will open up. So, therefore, what does it amount to? *We have been living in sleep.* We are not aware of our own Self. That is Truth. Then we babble any philosophy we like. We are all projecting, creating, manifesting and releasing out of us.

Krishna said: "Surrender unto me." What does it mean? When you surrender unto God, your ego, your mind finds its solace. It finds its relaxed point, its openness. Surrender unto the Lord opens you up. It makes you aware. It is not surrender in which you lose everything, as if God won the game and you lost. It is *not* like that. Our human brains think that way, and human brains are not fully open—all the cells, anyway. With the few cells open, we think this way. If your brain was open, in full bloom, it would say something else than what it says when partially open. So when you surrender to the Lotus Feet of Mother, you just become Conscious. You know what you are doing. You know your creation. You know your art. You know your expression. You find joy in it. You know the secret that was not known to you, in spite of you doing, thinking, and expressing everything. It is not only taking responsibility for what you do and are; that involves the law of karma, which is quite a moralistic language. The very fundamental issue is: are you aware of what you are doing, saying, seeing, expressing and whatever? This Pure Consciousness, opening to your Self, to *you*, brings you to the very secret of creation, where it starts. If you are projecting out of you, that is what God said: that He created the world out of Him. You and I are doing the same thing. Why? We are made in the image of God. God is within you and me. Come back to your Self. That is coming back to your true Home.

See if you can pinpoint your Self to the point of creation where you start. Where is that meeting point of the flashlight and the light that emanates from it? Go behind the glass. You will see the bulb glass again. Go within the bulb. There is something there, tungsten wire or a metal plate with something. Light is coming from there? No. The bulb is joined to some battery, so does light come from the battery? What is inside the battery? It came from where? Go backward. How was the battery made? How was the bulb made? Where did the ingredients come from? Go back and back and back to find the source from where each thing came. Eventually you will see that the light comes neither from the battery nor the bulb nor from your finger touching the switch. Find the point of connection, the creation. Right from that glass backward you will find that all the ingredients came from some other ingredients until you come to the atoms and eventually back to original Consciousness, the Light of God. Take *any* example and you will go back to the same Source. That is the Creatrix. That is Mother.

Go on simplifying the factors and you will come to the original One. Go back to the Light and Consciousness, that point of creation where it is happening and where the other ingredients are made. Every time you go back to the Source in anything, every time you will come to the same point of creation, that is Mother. You will amazingly see if you go on tracing everything back to the Source, the billions of details apart, *that* will be the Mother. That is why we say Mother creates. She is the Creatrix.

How has She created all this? Go on tracing back and back and back, and each time with everything you will come to the same Pure Consciousness, the same Light, the same Creatrix. This is the pervadedness of Mother. Isn't this an honest thinking and exploration? It is not just babbling of the mind and ego, denying anything you want. And when it comes to one of the problems of your kid that occupies you twenty-two hours of the day and night, absolute Knowledge doesn't work that time. You are dealing with the phenomena. Don't avoid it. If you avoid it, you are devoid of love. That is why you are hungry after love. You are not aware of the

Mother. Trace anything back to the Source and it will come to this Creatrix, the Consciousness, the point of creation where you will see *you*. *You* are doing that. In other words, you are becoming aware of your own projection, creation and art. This opens up the Consciousness, and that is surrender to the Mother.

And what a joyful thing that is! You are coming back to you, to your creation. You are finding your meeting place of your Beloved. Isn't that joyful, normally speaking? That is the truth, and therefore it is loving, therefore it is joyful, therefore it is creative. Not just a creation, it's *creative*. It is spontaneous. And this keeps you in perpetual joy while living or while dying. This gives you the secret inside. It is not so much by my explanation or your thinking or understanding, but when you really reach that point, you will find the secret. We call Her Mother. There is no use distinguishing between God the Father and God the Mother. That is jugglery. And this releases you, relaxes you, gives you freedom from problems and gives you peace. That is benevolence.

Even the great Prophet, Sri Rama, before meeting Ravana, the demon, had to propitiate the Mother Goddess. For nine days before he went to Sri Lanka on the southern tip of Bharat or India, he worshiped Goddess Durga, the dispeller of darkness, to give him the invincible weapons of victory. He had to worship that energy or shakti of God the Mother. Without that shakti, the divine power, he could not even conquer the demon. That was *Durga Puja*, the worship of Divine Mother as Durga, Who takes away your malevolence and dispels your darkness and ignorance. And with that endowment of great divine powers from Goddess Durga, Rama attacked Ravana and was victorious.

So in the field of mind—the field or battlefield—where good and evil exist, where sin and virtue exist, where the phenomena exist, you can deny any phenomenon. Still, you are dealing with your mind, and that is phenomena. We forget this. We deny the whole creation, as if having nothing to do with it—relative, dualistic . . . Okay, fine. You are dealing with your mind. Not a single thing can you do about it. Your mind is over you. And within this mind, in which you have good and bad, virtue and vice, ups and downs and imperfections, you are dealing. To conquer evil, to change the bad, to dispel the darkness, we need shakti, divine power. We need energy. We need strength. And that is Mother. That is Durga. When you invoke that energy, you establish that relationship. With that power of Divine Mother, we overpower our weaknesses and come out victorious within the same field of mind. You are the doer and your mind is your field. When weaknesses overpower you, propitiate your Mother again, the shakti Goddess. She has all the weapons—not just weapons such as war materials. She has all the divine powers given by *devas* or shining beings. According to the scriptures, the evildoers, the demonic spirits had begun to trouble the angelic ones, so the devas went to the Mother and each one gave Her his or her own divine weapons. With those, Goddess Durga fought with the demons and conquered them. And the devas rejoiced after that, because when weakness is overcome, you feel joyful, don't you?

Whatever the allegory may be, it has its own symbolic meaning too, apart from its own historical occurrence. When you awaken the strength in you, you overcome weakness and then you feel joyful. This strength is not egotistical assertion. Inner divine strength overpowers our weaknesses. It is not so much that goodness triumphs over evil, but that weaknesses are erased and you are made strong again. And that is Mother reigning in you, working through you. Those who have known the secret of this Creatrix, the Mother, your own creation, know it is inseparable. Don't even attempt to deny it, except at your own loss. Problems or miseries might follow. We each live and learn from this very phenomenon. How can we deny that same thing? The very Mother who feeds us, we are denying, in a way. Without Her power, even the Prophet Rama could not conquer evil. As a matter of fact, Ravana was a great devotee of Lord Shiva and had been granted great powers and boons by Him. And there was Rama, propitiating the consort of Shiva—as if the Lord was on Ravana's side and the Lordess was on Rama's side. But the question is: Ravana had misapplied and misused that shakti in selfish, evil ways. So he was ruined by his own wrongs. It boomeranged on him; whereas when Rama propitiated the Goddess' strength and divine power for the great use, for release, for peace, for justice, it conquered.

Divine energy, if you do not use properly, will boomerang back onto you. When we get a little bit better in health of body or mind, ego comes up and again we are ruined. A little better treasury comes, greater peace of mind, strength of body, some kind of possessions, talent or recognition comes to us and our ego puffs up, normally, doesn't it? Then that power boomerangs and again we lose it. It can ruin us. But if you use it for the right purpose, a justified means, you will see that it flourishes. This is the function of dharma. The Goddess comes or the Prophets come to establish dharma, the sense of justice and righteousness. The phenomena, relativity, when established on dharma, will never make you suffer. When it goes against dharma, on the unrighteous way, on the wrong application or misuse, abuse or egotistical way, it will ruin.

This happens all the time. Then a Prophet comes like Rama to put that shakti of Ravana down again, because he misused it. Ravana was creating disharmony and loss of peace. The Prophets come to establish harmony and balance and dharma with the strength of the Goddess. It's not something like, "Mother, you be at home in the kitchen; I'll go and do it myself." So try to be aware of this minimum requirement. Otherwise our weaknesses, anger, disharmony, imbalance, sorrows, sufferings and loss of peace are often there. We know that. Which Absolute Knowledge drives these away? It may do so while we discuss intellectually, but as they say, when you bathe in Ganga, that time your sins leave you. As soon as you come out again, they hang on to you. In Satsang, we are great philosophers. When we come out of Satsang, we see the purse again; we see if somebody is in the hospital or not; we see how our son and daughter are doing. I may be okay today but tomorrow I have to again face my employer. When my monthly bills come, I have to think about them. At that time, philosophy does not work. When your budget is deficit, tell yourself God is Absolute and see how it works. It doesn't! When your

health is down or your son or daughter is troubling you or a dear
one is dying—just go on telling them, "Nothing is wrong, God is
Immortal, Absolute. This whole relative world is illusion." Try it.

This does not negate the ultimate Truth. Let me plainly tell it. But
that Truth, have you realized? Have you found it? If not, what should
you pay attention to? Here and now, what you and I are, that is where
our attention is required. Just be realistic to your point of creation.
That is the Mother. It is easy: "Mother, I forgot You. I thought I was
doing all these things. But without Your one percent of energy and
power, I could not do anything. I could not drive away my few
weaknesses. Please help me." That is surrender: opening up and being
Conscious. Then see how Mother reveals to you the secrets and truth,
which you never understood because, through intellectual jargon and
illusory perceptions, you blocked what Divine Mother was telling and
showing you. When She begins to reveal and show you secrets, it is
different than you ever thought or imagined. You will see that all your
thinking was null and void; you were just beating about your own
bushes. You will see, "I took Mother as like any other mother . . ."
but it isn't that way at all. She is eternal, divine, radiant Being. She is
that pulsating energy of Light. She is radiance Herself. And when That
reveals, you will be finished.

Before that, whatever your thinking, perception, conception, you
will see is null and void. Those were your imagination, your own
thoughts; they have no basis. When Truth reveals, you will be
astonished. It has nothing to do with whatever you did or thought
previously. That is why we say, "Mother, reveal Yourself to us. Give
us Darshan." If you ask for revelation, if you ask for Darshan, divine
Vision, do not say, "Mother, make me understand." It is not a
matter of understanding. "I'm trying to understand . . ." I say, why
are you trying to understand? How much can you understand with
your puny brain? How much can you hold in this particular bowl?
That is the mistake you are making. If you had just *done* it, you would
have seen results. By trying to understand, you are blocking it and
pushing it away. "Let me see if I got it right . . ." And then they write
down in the notebook. They can't even remember *that* much! I say,

if you had got it right, you would not write it down. You would get it. When that Vision comes, when that revelation comes, it's *radiant*. Mother is radiance Herself. This power, this shakti, this emanation is from the ultimate Source. How can you deny one or the other: the Source or the radiance? And that radiance, that Mother Vision, that revelation, when it comes, whatever you believed has nothing to do with it.

That is the Mother I worship, Thou Who art radiance: *Tejasvi naava dheeta maastu*. In Sanskrit this means: "That which gives higher intelligence to my brain"—*dhee*, meaning dhyana, "meditation" or that which makes me meditate. The *medha*, "radiance," is Motherhood. "With that strength, with that power, I meditate upon Thee." Do not think that with a weak mind you can meditate. You can try, but we all know we just go to sleep. We think of all kinds of things in meditation. The mind does not focus the way we want because the power, the strength of the Mother, is lacking. Those who have been focused, those whose mind pinpoints while meditating—they will see the Mother is with them. So when you invoke the Mother in you, invoking your strength, your shakti, your medha, your radiance—that's Mother. With that help, you reach the Lord. These two are inseparable.

11

A Friend of the Birds

The birds thought it was a sanctuary there and here is a kind-hearted man who protects the birds. The news went around like wildfire: here's a friend of the birds.

In the course of a week-long retreat at Sacred Mountain Ashram in June 1997, one morning some ashramites discovered that twin fawns had been born near the yurt, not far from Jyoti Mandir where Gurudeva's Satsangs were given. They brought Gurudeva to see the newborns and their mother, which were guarded by a number of very large bucks that Gurudeva refers to in the opening of this Satsang. It was extremely rare to have deer giving birth at the ashram even otherwise than a retreat when many devotees were around the general area. A few days later on a walk of the lower parikrama* with Gurudeva, we came upon one of the twin fawns on the roadside. It was too small to walk so its mother had it lie very still and, rolled into a tight ball, it looked almost a part of the terrain, like a large brown stone, until someone recognized it as a newborn fawn.

From the Golden Age and onward, animals, birds and humans lived very close by, nurturing each other. They did not fear each other because they didn't kill that way. So it is not surprising that here, the animals' and birds' instincts would tell them they are secure, since nobody hunts them or kills them, whether it is chipmunks or chickadees or deer. Of course, these are at least nonferocious animals, but in earlier times even ferocious animals would dwell close by each other. Buddha's story is extraordinary, of course: that lions and lambs sat together, and we know about the birds' and animals' friendship with Saint Francis. The animals could feel these souls' love. But as

---

* *Parikrama:* prayerful circumambulation or circumference of a holy place. This is the name Gurudeva gave to the perimeter road at Sacred Mountain Ashram.

the days went by and population grew, people cut forests and began to hunt and kill, often just for fun. The animals and birds then got scared and went away. So if they find the same peaceful atmosphere, they will come around again. But if you are going to feed every animal with sandwiches, I'm in trouble!

At first I wasn't even sure whether deer would come and lick the salt brick. They hesitated, even though it was so far away from Jyoti Dham,* relatively. I thought they would not come and at first they avoided, actually. They are so sensitive and telepathic. Sometimes I would see them in early morning. Now they do not run away, but in the beginning, even my coming to the glass door they would notice and not come near the salt brick. Slowly they came closer and closer, and now they're bold enough to open the maternity home. Well, of course, these are harmless creatures, but even ferocious animals could be tamed. I could do that, but the question is, I have to give time and company. And who is going to do that? Taming humans has been difficult enough.

I know that animals and birds respond more than humans. They don't have "ego syndrome." They get scared and run away for their survival but they don't have ego at all, in a sense. Humans have. Today I was in my bedroom upstairs and the sliding glass door was practically transparent, except where the net† is. And two big birds—I don't think pigeons, not bluejays either . . . What's that grayish type thing, this size [indicates with hands]?

Devotee: *Doves.*

Probably, yes. You know, they didn't know that this house was occupied. And they came on the balcony to sit. They wanted to talk to each other, or whatever. I can't even explain because of language deficiency. But all of a sudden they saw me inside, wherever I was, and they were so panicky, they flew away. I actually telepathically told

---

* Jyoti Dham, lit: "dwelling of Light," is Gurudeva's small, pyramid-shaped house at Sacred Mountain Ashram.

† In India, a screen on a window or door is called a "net."

them—*don't worry, don't fear, just sit down* . . . but they didn't come back. They must be sitting there other times when I'm not there. That two-by-six railing up top is very nice to sit on, for birds especially.

Long back, maybe a few years ago—I'm not good at these timings—the deer were coming to Jyoti Dham at nearby trees. They had come closer than in earlier years, so I thought—*since they have now come so near, kind of not fearing or something, it's better if I go and touch them or go near.* Up to about four or five feet I came and still they were looking at me, curiously. I didn't get too bold but I thought—*well, since it's four or five feet, then probably it's easy for me to go and touch them.* Boy, a few inches more I came and they ran away! Then I thought I was being too abrupt, so the next time during that stay here—I don't remember whether it was two or three years ago—I thought—*as we look at stars in the sky, if you want to look at them, don't look straight. You have to look a little to the side.* I had observed that trick with these deer. So when I passed by, I wouldn't look at them.

This really worked. Why? This is my own detachment. I passed not quite nearby, a few feet away, and subconsciously, or God knows how, probably they were expecting me to come closer. And I showed my detachment, looking at them from the corner of my eye, passing by as if I did not see them. You wouldn't believe this happened. And they began to come closer. They didn't touch me. They knew I was quite detached to them, only passing by, so they understood that I could leave them too. I had this experience once.

There is a whole system of tending animals and birds. I could do that, but then I'm occupied with humans. What can I do? Next time I'll bring androids. I like deer, particularly the deer I had seen earlier in India. When I first saw deer in America, years back, some people told me this is a deer. I wasn't used to a gray deer; I was used to a golden brown type. So for some time I had a difficulty in appreciating them here. Of course, I appreciated them for what they are, but as deer I had a difficulty, because my focus was on those golden deer, beautiful looking. They are a big size here, though. They look like bodyguards of the Dalai Lama. Yesterday when they were guarding—four males there or six, very big, huge—I was reminded of the bodyguards of the Dalai Lama; very tall and special Tibetans. These deer were really sturdy. I knew they couldn't do anything; they're not going to attack you or anything. They are harmless that way. I could educate myself about it but then I don't think I've come for animals on this earth. I have love for them but I'll leave them alone.

There was one cat that had troubled me a lot at Jyoti Ashram in Pune [India]. I had a *great* trouble in getting rid of her. I succeeded, but what a tremendous labor over a few months. It's a huge story; it will take my whole Satsang. In Jyoti Dham at Jyoti Ashram, outside my two rooms is a covered porch or verandah, as we call it. A cane chair is there with a cushion and my small table for a teacup and a mat to sit on when anyone comes to see me if the weather is permitting, if it's not too rainy, and not after sunset when mosquitoes could come. It was actually the neighbor's cat. I told the ashramites, "Don't feed her, because then it's your constant job." Now how she knew or understood that I am the "boss" or God knows what, but she would hover around while I would be inside my room. She would do her "meow," whatever they do, and I would look from my bed and screen door. First she wouldn't stop meowing; then she would pass by to draw my attention. A few days she did like that and I kept quiet; no stir. I would be lying down on my bed.

Some days later she would stand there and look at me. I'd ignore her and look down instead. In this way it carried on; there are too many details. Invariably, morning and evening she would come, give a good round, *parikrama*, and then go away. I ignored her. She saw that I was not paying attention. I didn't even know wherefrom she came; later on they told me it's the neighbor's cat. Then one day I came out to sit in that cane chair and she was sitting comfortably there. Now I thought—*that's too much.* The unfortunate part was, when it was the rainy season, she would walk in the dirt or mud and then come and sit on my beautiful, holy, sacred chair, you know? I thought—*she doesn't have that privilege over my disciples; even they don't sit there. Who is she?* I would [clap] to make her run away, but invariably, in the morning I would come out and find that the whole night she had been resting in that comfortable chair.

To her it was like a down comforter! I had to get the covers changed because the cushions kept getting muddy, and she wouldn't know that she's muddying my cushions; she didn't have that sense. If she were our cat, we might have trained her. And then came one of my Bengali disciples, and he said, "Cats want to draw your whole attention and win you away from others slowly." I said, "That solves my problem." The question was: how to get rid of her without killing or beating her. And she would not listen. Now, twice, thrice, in the morning, after some days, we had to launder the cushion covers. I thought, *that's too much,* so in the nighttime I began to put the chair inside. What to do? And it carried on. She did "meow, meow" a few other days, but she didn't leave. Well, it's a long story; she did a lot of dramas with me. I even telepathically told her—*look, Siamese, I love you, but this is not the way you should behave with me. I'm a holy Swamiji, and you just behave properly.* She wouldn't listen. She wanted to come inside my room even. I said: "Nothing doing. You're greater than my disciples, or what?"

However, the time came that we all got fed up and one of the ashramites told me a lie. I had asked him twice, "Are you feeding this cat?" He said, "No, no." What would happen was, when I would refuse, she would go behind the kitchen back door, wait there, and this kind-hearted disciple—he's actually weak-hearted and he thought he was kind-hearted—would sometimes feed her. I said: "You are spoiling my whole thing." He thought he was being charitable. I said, "Well, you're being charitable at what cost? She comes and sits on my cane chair. Every night I have to put it inside. As a trouble, I need two people to do that. And your charity is not begetting charity at all." However, we didn't want to beat her, so we asked the neighbors, "Are you feeding her well?" "Oh, we give her nice food," they said. But somehow this cat felt love in our place. I came to know later on that in the daytime she would go into the trees and eat the eggs of birds. I said, "I won't allow that! They are beautiful birds and we have an oasis or aviary of birds in the ashram. I'm not going to let this cat eat the eggs away."

So four people tried to catch her—all gunny bags, this, this, this. She was so clever that they could not catch her. Our gardener said,

"Baba, if you allow me to kill her, then I can do it." I said then, "I'm not about killing. Devise some means . . ." She'd run this way and that. She wasn't ferocious—actually she was a tame cat—and the neighbors would not care, as if they were telling us, "it's your problem." We couldn't do anything. At one point they succeeded finally in catching her in a gunny bag, tied her up, put her on the back of the bicycle and took her miles away. Next morning she was there. It's a huge story. What can I say! I don't know how she found the way.

I love animals but when they cling to me, then I don't like it. Of course, birds at Jyoti Ashram come in flocks: small birds and various— four, six, eight, ten—come at a time on the verandah of Jyoti Dham. Amazingly, they even come to the glass and look inside like this, and "chirp, chirp, chirp." Of course, they are innocent, in a sense, so I'll give them some seeds or something; then they go away. They made a habit of this, actually. They would come and call, "chirp, chirp, chirp, chirp," and I got tired. The same thing happened with others.

One afternoon as I went for a walk around the ashram parikrama, all of a sudden in the sky I heard a lot of birds making noises. I looked up and there were quite forty, fifty, a hundred crows and other birds following a certain bird. I don't know if it was a pigeon or a dove. They were trying to catch that bird, whether to hurt it or eat it or whatever. All of a sudden, as I was coming on the four-foot wide footpath, the parikrama, facing toward the east, from the west came this bird. You would not believe it. I'd never experienced these things. That bird, seeing me as some kind of security or shelter—God knows what— flew down like this, and touched right on my chest, not violently, actually feather-like, trembling. I saw blood and that it was injured.

I looked at those crows that were kind of abusing me—"Who are you to take away our morsel?" and they scattered slowly and went away. Now this bird was shaking and I thought—*if I leave him or her here, I am afraid those birds might swoop down and kind of scoop it away.* So I had to stand there, and the position where I was, the ashramites were quite far away. I don't remember in my life that I've shouted like that. I just shouted one or two names and they came running, as if I was in danger or something. This same Bengali disciple knew how to tend birds, somehow, and I said, "Go and nurse him." He took the bird near his room and by next morning he was over fifty percent better. Then to protect him from other birds, the ashramite built a box in such a way, with a little opening, that other birds couldn't go in. Outside there is a certain storeroom and there he put the box and food and water, and gradually the bird was cured. I don't think it was one hundred percent, maybe eighty, ninety or seventy percent, and one fine morning we found that he was not there. He flew away.

But in a few days another thing happened in our ashram. There is a kind of bird called a kite that lived in the trees in the ashram. A pair of kites had a baby and they made their nest very high up in a tree so that others may not trouble. Accidentally or for some reason— we don't know—that nest fell down and the baby bird fell down and got a little injured. It couldn't fly, of course, and again I was walking on the same footpath and saw that fallen bird. I thought it was an adult bird but it was a baby. The size was quite big. Again I called and shouted and somebody came. We made a very good shelter box with food and did nursing, and so on. His mother up top was watching us with huge eyes. Yeah, boy! Terrifying! But she instinctively knew that we were trying to save her baby, which we did. Slowly we put the box higher so that cats and other birds and animals could not trouble it, and we gave it food and all that kind of stuff.

After a few days, that disciple who knew nursing took the bird out on his lap and was walking around carrying it like a baby. However, the mother bird was watching. So wherever he would bring the baby near me—I was sitting outside under the mango tree in the cane chair—the mother would fly over that tree and watch us. She got aware that we were taking good care but at the same time, you know, she was the baby's mother, so she would feel it. And she got friendly, in a sense. Now among birds, what language they speak, how they psychologically sense matters, how they feel, and so on and so forth, we don't know, but they probably communicate in some way. What happened was: the news went around among the bird community. The birds thought it was a sanctuary there and here is a kind-hearted man who protects the birds. The news went like wildfire: *here's a friend of birds.* I was remembering Saint Francis and thought—*how did you do this? You tamed even donkeys.*

There are quite various kinds of birds in Jyoti Ashram. It is only one and a half acres but it is like an aviary, but open; no rooms or cages or chains. And there is a high compound wall with a four feet walking path around the inner perimeter. I know you will believe but I couldn't. What happened next was that when I would walk—if you have ever seen this or not, God knows—some birds, small, big, quite a number, would walk along with me, hopping along the top of the wall. It was amazing. I could believe it because it was happening, but I couldn't believe they could understand. And when I looked up at them, they would be joyfully hopping more! Boy, I couldn't believe it. We had a lot of play like that. If I would study and play with them, befriend them, then it would be easy. Often I don't know why I didn't do that because it is too difficult to tame humans. The birds respond very well. And these are not birds we befriended even. They just lived there and we sometimes gave them rice or seeds, but I personally didn't; others did. Water we kept and still we do. And they come and drink. Sometimes certain birds will shoo away the smaller ones. I rebuked them once. They were crows. I said, "If you're going to do that, you can't stay here in this ashram. Leave." And they really got quiet. They never did it again.

Once I was sitting on an open dais under some shady tree that now we have cut down. It was on the lawn and devotees were sitting for Satsang in the afternoon. There was a little canopy over my dais and the birds would not understand that Satsang is going on, so they congregated in that tree. Ten, twenty—God knows what—and I'm sitting and talking into this mike, and they started their dialogues. We were talking, they were talking, and it got so disturbing. About fifty devotees were sitting; it was during a retreat. So I sent the telepathic thought to these birds: *keep quiet now, if you have to live in this garden. Live and let live.* But they probably didn't get the telepathy or they didn't care for that. So at one point—not that I was really disturbed but my attention was being drawn; I was giving Satsang—I just looked up there and said in Hindi: "Keep quiet." And they really did. All of them—quiet until Satsang was over. You wouldn't believe these things. The devotees looked at me and smiled.

One other bird story was as hilarious as Charlie Chaplin could be. I think it was another kite again, though not the same bird. Again it was in the morning and I was walking toward the west, near the compound wall and some big trees. There I saw some baby bird that had grown a little bit. It was not a teenager but perhaps a preteen in a way, though big in size. It was a dark brown color with sharp eyes. What happened was: this bird was probably learning to fly but had not matured yet, and while doing so, his mother probably was watching and helping him to fly. God knows what training was going on, and on a certain branch he probably wanted to sit or couldn't catch the branch or whatever. He tumbled down. This all happened in a second while I was passing. Now in his survival instinct, he succeeded in somehow catching one branch. Probably it was the lowest of the branches. It was a big, shady tree—I don't know the name—but that branch was not strong enough for the bird to sit on, so he tumbled upside down but still holding on! And it was a kind of *Urdhva Padmasana Shirshasana**—head posture. He was so helpless.

He couldn't get up and fly because the branch was so tender, and if his mother allowed him, he was going to fall down and might get injured. And his claws were so strong, I thought—*if I catch him, he has no sense of not hurting me.* My skin is so tender that I knew if he catches me, I'm going to bleed. And there he was in such a precarious, Charlie Chaplin pose, laughable, yeah. I knew he had to be helped and I was afraid to catch him because he might catch me. And his mother was looking pitiably at me to do something! She didn't come there, partly maybe because I was there, partly because she couldn't do anything either. So again I shouted. It happened several times! And again that Bengali disciple came. He saw and he laughed a lot. Then he began to make sounds with his mouth like you do with children. How do you make those sounds? I wouldn't do that because you'll be surprised. And he went near and did like that, like with a

---

* The inverted lotus pose or *asana* in hatha yoga.

baby, and got hold of the bird and talked to the bird to come on, don't fear, don't worry, this, this, this, this. Then he took the baby down, which wasn't injured, only he was in a Charlie Chaplin pose. I still remember that. We didn't have a camera to take a photograph. Poor guy. He was scared too. He looked like a big baby. The mother was watching all this. Then at a certain place the disciple put the bird down and the mother came and she took him away.

Now, this part you have to believe. Days passed, probably weeks, and I forgot about the whole episode. Maybe one month later, maybe three months, again I was walking in that area one afternoon and, all of a sudden, some bird like a kite was sitting there, watching and watching me. I first ignored it. Then I went to other side of the walk and he flew to that side, still watching. I again ignored. I give rounds there on the stone parikrama. And this bird came again and probably, because I didn't wait, he came and sat on a lower branch. I looked at him and, boy, he looked like that very bird, that Charlie Chaplin. He understood that I had recognized him and he showed signs of happiness. They are very serious birds, these kites, and they have very sharp eyesight.

I first thought to give him something to eat, but they're used to flesh, you know; they don't eat sandwiches. So I told a disciple to bring some bread, though the bird didn't eat much. He was more interested in seeing me. I stood there and as long as I stood, he stood. He didn't leave for several hours. He was grateful. I was sick a little with either fever or cold, and I was sitting outside under a tree near the disciples' quarters. I was in my own, you might say, sad state in a sense, and all of a sudden in that tree opposite, there was a little stir in the leaves. My attention went there and, boy, he was watching me, that very bird. I called that same disciple again and he agreed, "Yes, it's the same guy." He was very loving to me. He would look at me for a long, long time and not go anywhere. I gave him food once or twice but I didn't see him much interested in eating; he just wanted to see me. After a long time he left. So three times he came that I remember, but that time I could feel he came to cheer me up a little bit. They understand so much, but I know if I go further, they are going to cling to me.

12

Divine Compassion of the Guru

If the sun would not be shining within, it could not shine outside. If love was not in my heart, I could not be loving to you. If I had no peace in my heart, I could not exude peace unto others. Knowing this, the Guru's or Enlightened Being's compassion is their second nature.

Gurudeva: Do you believe in Oneness and also in compassion?

Devotee: *Yes, they go together.*

I know you have learned that from me, to mix everything together. I don't know if it was right or wrong. I went for all together rather than one "ism." Presence is more or less on three levels. One is physical; the second is mental, astral, subtle, vibratory; the third is Vision, Consciousness, intrinsic Core, the Being, which in Sanskrit is called Atman. That Core is the soul of the Presence, Spirit, not only subtle but the very substantial Presence. In terminology these are three but in actuality they are all connected—right from the physical, gross point to the subtlest conscious Presence. That Presence is pervading and indescribable. We are unconscious that we seek the Presence with the body and mind. We want this gross and vibratory dreamland because we are unaware of that real Presence.

I wouldn't say the physical and vibratory are "unreal," as normally some explain in dualistic language. For the sake of understanding, it's okay to say this, but truthfully that is not the case. There are two ways of looking at it. One is discriminatory: this is unreal and that is real. The other is comprehensive, homogeneous, in Oneness. The physical, vibratory and spiritual are *all* real in their own way, but they are not separate. They are all connected, right from the grossest darkness to the brightest Light. Therefore, because That is real, because God is real, we are real. But when we demarcate with language and thoughts, it becomes a multiplicity. Another way of expressing is: "God is real; man is unreal." Again, for the sake of understanding we give this distinction, so that you see the difference of the various stages. But when you begin to transcend the stages in your evolution and you come to the last, infinite point, then this all assumes meaning. If we were to say: "Everything is real," then you will never go to your true Self, your true Light, your Spirit. You will miss the real Substance, the real Core of things. Therefore we say: "This is illusion, unreal, transitory, finite, limited and changeful," just to get you dispassionate, detached and discriminatory, or to say it more appropriately: to make you see the right perspective so that you could fly from this to your all-pervading Presence, God's Presence.

All this phenomena is real in the sense that it has come from the Reality, from the ultimate Spirit, the Core of Being. But in order for you to each have that Realization, we say: "This is dark; this is ignorant; this is limited; this is dualism . . ." Saying this is bound to be fallacious, because if we do not separate altogether from that true Presence, that conscious Presence, then this is also real. Herein lies the need of compassion. If this creation and phenomena were all rubbish, darkness, ignorance and illusion, then I don't think compassion is necessary. The need of compassion is due to this fact that everything is real. Why otherwise would Prophets like Buddha talk so much about compassion and really *live* compassion toward everyone, so much so that we call him compassionate Buddha? Why would he bother and not leave us eternally condemned, sinful, and ignorant?

If we were to start saying from the beginning: "This also is Real; this also is Light," you would not give up your attachments, greed and desires, and at the same time, you would be in self-deception because you do not *see* the Reality. You believe it, probably, but you do not see it. So if you start saying, "This is Real . . . this is Real . . ." you are bound to fall into self-delusion, thinking that this is Real whereas it is still unreal to your perception. That is why we say: "Be detached, be disinterested, be discriminatory . . ." so that by that discrimination you see what is Real and what is unreal; what is Permanent and what is changeful; what is dark and what is Light.

Knowing this, the Great Ones are compassionate. Not only compassionate but endlessly compassionate, because they know they are teaching an ignorant person. But when that person awakens, the Knower and you are the same. So you can understand the deepest or highest meaning of compassion. It is not the compassion of a businessman to a client, where you have the motive to get bucks. Why would a selfless Being, an Enlightened person or a Prophet be endlessly compassionate? There is no motive. I was reading a book in which a channel was communicating with some E.T.s who come to earth supposedly to save us. The channel asked, "What interest do you have? Why are you doing this in the first place, coming and doing good to the earth or earthlings?" And that E.T. said: "We are so interconnected in Oneness throughout the galaxies, the cosmos, that what you question, 'Why?' we don't think that way. It is Oneness. We cannot be isolated or compartmentalized into some part of the universe, having nothing to do with the rest of the universe."

The same is true in the family. Why do some members help others? This question could be asked from anyone—a brother or a son or wife or husband or father or parents or children, neighbor to neighbor, friend to friend. The E.T. said: "We are all connected. We are just One. We see the earth is in danger; earth has problems; earth is going through pains, and if you don't mend your ways, you are going to suffer tremendously through sickness, wars, chemicals, diseases, death, warfare—just name it. So we see that we have a way to give you, to save you, if you can listen." That is the whole truth: the Awakened Souls, Great Ones, Gurus and Enlightened Beings want to show you the way. They know you are going a wrong way or you are in trouble or you are suffering, in whatever degree. They want to help. *Why* is not a question. If at all, the answer would be compassion.

Compassion starts from being One. The Guru—*gu* means "darkness" or "ignorance"; *ru* means "dispeller" or "remover"—is the dispeller of darkness or ignorance, the One who awakens you or shows you the path. Therefore, if he is a real Guru, a *Satguru*, he never sees that you are ignorant, that you are dark, that you are any antonym of the Awakened One. He sees: "You and I are the same, One." From that premise they work. And it may be one year's work, ten years' work, a whole lifetime or lifetimes. They work from that premise because you and I are the same Consciousness, Light, Truth, God. Therefore until you are Awakened, until you come to your Consciousness, until you get Enlightened, compassion is needed. Otherwise the Gurus will have to go on beating everybody—you know what I'm saying?

Lifetimes you have wasted. The real Great Ones may rebuke but that is out of love. When the straight road doesn't work, it has to be in different ways, to somehow get ahold of you to do it. If there was no compassion, nobody could help anyone. There are limits to compassion in every being, that's true. Some are infinitely compassionate; some are ninety percent compassionate; some are twenty percent. Some lose the temper after ten percent. This is all to get you Awakened, conscious of that Presence of God. It is not that God is absent, but simply that we are ignorant and unaware of Him.

God's Presence, the Totality, is always here and there, inside, outside. But to begin as a process, as a path, as a method, we often distinguish: "Close your eyes; go within. Outside, what you see or perceive with five senses is an illusion." There is nothing wrong with that, but in the ultimate analysis, the ultimate Truth, when you truly open your eyes—your inner eyes—to the Presence, Consciousness, this distinction of "in" and "out" is lost. The gross, vibratory and the fully Awakened state are all joined together. While you come from the Spirit to the vibratory, subtle plane, the mind, and then to the physical plane, you lose consciousness of the Ultimate wherefrom this Light came. It is as if the Source of light is here, and now light is traveling up to a point, and as you go farther and farther away, you still see some light but the Source is forgotten. This forgetfulness of the Source is the cause of misery. Not because this is unreal, but because we are *unconscious* of the very Source that gives this existence meaning.

So this existence is *true*, I am deliberately telling you— *Sarvam Khalvidam Brahma*. This is the last sentence of the Ṛg Veda: "Everything is Brahman; everything is Essence; everything is Spirit; everything is God." But if we start by saying this, there are more fools than wise people in this world and you know what a mess it will be! Therefore we say: "Your father is unreal; your mother is unreal; your wife is unreal; everything is unreal except 'me'!" [laughter] As a

Guru Purnima, Sacred Mountain Ashram, July 1988

Jyoti Mandir (Temple of Light), Desert Ashram, January 2000

Griha Pravesh (Dedication) of new Jyoti Dham, Desert Ashram, December 1999

A gathering at Annapurna (Dining Hall), Sacred Mountain Ashram, June 1997

Ṛta Dharma Retreat, Pawlet, Vermont, Fall 1999

Ṛta Dharma Retreat, Fall 1998

Prabhushri Jayanti (Gurudeva's Birthday) at Desert Ashram, May 1999

Havan (Fire Ceremony) at Jyoti Ashram, Gurudeva's Birthday, 1994

Gathering with devotees in Pimpri (near Pune), December 1997

Sacred Mountain Ashram, May 1999

Aarati (worship) upon arrival at Jyoti Ashram from U.S.A., April 2000

Satsang at Jyoti Ashram, Spring/Summer 2000

process, as a method, I have no qualms about it, but again if you stick to that, then the world has to be bombarded, because it is unreal anyway. Why to worry about it? And once you bombard it, it's going to be a greater mess! At no point, by God's grace, would I like to give up compassion, whatever the situation. There is another corollary, and this is out of practice I am saying: Divine Mother forces me or us to experience things of the human being so that we understand where they are. I accept it but I don't like it.

Let's say you are endlessly compassionate or considerably compassionate or much more compassionate than the average person would be, and even so, you could think your compassion is wasted, good for nothing, because the results do not come in two years or ten years. So why to be compassionate? Through my experience I am telling you: compassion is a healing power. When from that point of view alone I maintain my compassion, it releases and relaxes me. My tensions are gone. Since God is in that person, the same Light, the same Truth, the same Presence is there, therefore what do I lose? In that compassion, my heart gets warmer, softer, more loving and kind. I am Liberated. The same applies to peace, love, joy, freedom, power, strength and understanding. In themselves these have their own healing power, apart from whether you get anything in return or not.

Therefore we stress selflessness so much, because even if we don't get anything in return, in *itself* selflessness is very healing. Peace will be with me, at least. If I love somebody and I do not get love in return, it is okay. The loving heart is within me, making me more tender, more gentle. It makes me kinder inside. I don't need anything from another person. This is selflessness in its utter meaning. We have been habituated to objectively want results; therefore we mostly think in those terms. Years back, before Americans got "enlightened," [laughter] when we would talk about Enlightenment to the utmost meaning or connotation, sometimes someone would ask, "What will I get out of it?" In the 1960s a devotee came to me in India. He had met me in America and we were talking deeply one day—he was doing gardening—and we got inspired, both of us, talking about Enlightenment, Himalayas and such things. When the conversation ended—and I think I did my best and I was satisfied that nothing more could be said about Enlightenment, and he knew that too— he asked, "What would you do after you get Enlightened?" I said, "You are your own Master, the Lord. You decide what you will do. That's up to you, whether you build ashrams or just be alone, whatever you want. King Janak was Enlightened while remaining a king."* And I still remember what he said: "You know, in America, what we would think?" I said, "What would you think?" He said, "If I got Enlightened, I'll just go and make merry and be happy, have a marriage and home and that's finished"—as if you finished the graduation course or something and get settled now! I said, "Mister, you have spoiled the whole thing." "What is wrong with that?" he asked. I said, "Not wrong with that. You are introspectively projecting from where you are standing and judging what you will do. First reach there and see what you want. Now you are deciding every program after Enlightenment. Maybe when you get Enlightened, this program won't stand or it may stand, whatever it is."

In the spiritual world, the Ultimate, that is not the language. First you reach there and *then* see. This is the Guru's prime object and only mission: to take birth for the disciples and devotees, to awaken them. But in between there are ups and downs, the slip between the cup and the lip, sufferings and happiness. The Guru is dealing with disciples' unfulfilled karmas or what we call tendencies or temperament. Those have to be exhausted, cleaned, cleared, purified, and it's a big job. In the meantime, so many experiences happen between Guru and disciples. Whether it is one disciple or a million, the process is the same.

Without compassion the Guru would not even live long. What for? A businessman has a motive at least—profits—but there is no profit for Gurus. Theirs is a "nonprofit organization." The Guru is your father and mother and friend and brother and son, your Lord and consort. He assumes practically all the roles; otherwise karmas would

---

* King Janak was the father of Sita, the consort of Sri Rama.

not exhaust. All this needs compassion. Like when a child is born: if the parents were not compassionate, the child would be in trouble. He cannot do much for himself. If you didn't have love, kindness or compassion—just assuming that word, though parents don't do out of compassion; they do out of their own attachment and love—you could not help anyone. It just would be a coldhearted mechanism. So, without compassion, I don't think wisdom can be acquired or given. It is not an objective study, like academics; it is very subjective.

But again, subjectivity is real; objectivity is unreal. When you distinguish, it's okay as a method, as a process, but it's not Reality. If the sun would not be shining within, it could not shine outside. If love was not in my heart, I could not be loving to you. If I had no peace in my heart, I could not exude peace unto others. Knowing this, the Guru's or Enlightened Being's compassion is their second nature. It is not an acquired or cultivated nature. If you are loving, you will be giving. It is one thing to plan or cultivate a culture or courtesy as an objective projection. This spiritual quality is not planned. You may plan but as you grow realistically, more conscious, your plans may all be canceled. You may have to change the blueprint every day.

Compassion of these Beings is second nature, like the sun's warmth. The sun does not project; it does not try to give to you or do good to you. The sun's second nature is to be warm, to be bright, to be life-giving. So if a Realized Soul, a Guru or Enlightened Being is compassionate, giving, loving and so on—what a patience this guy has—from where he or she stands, the Guru is not thinking these things. He is not projecting or planning to give you these things as a "be-gooder, do-gooder." He cannot *be* otherwise. That is his nature. Why would Jesus love the sinners? Virtuous ones didn't have much to do with him, since they thought, "We are okay." Sinners are the ones who are not okay, so who else would he love? Not that he does not love the virtuous—he does—but the virtuous do not receive his love because they think they are fine already.

When in the summer you jump into a swimming pool or river or bathe in a stream, the water is cool, nice, soothing. One could say the stream is trying to project its coolness to comfort you, but that is not so. Its nature is coolness. It is the same with compassion. A real Guru, Enlightened Being or Prophet cannot be otherwise than loving and compassionate. There is no choice, whether it is regrettable or not is different, because truth can also be given jocularly. By jocularly I mean that sometimes these Great Ones act differently in order to make you aware that they are not stupid. If they would not show their suffering—"God, why Thou hast forsaken me?"—then what would happen? The so-called average person would take advantage, saying, "If you are eternally compassionate, endlessly suffering, selfless, patient and so on, then let me do anything I want to you! Let me take advantage of it!" I don't know if you are catching the truth, which I sometimes give humorously, but feel sure that inside they are endlessly compassionate and giving.

They have no other motive. If they had a motive, I can understand that they could block their compassion and love and kindness. But since they are selfless, there is no other end. Deliverance or Liberation has to have pains, you know. What can you do? This earth existence is made that way, in a dualistic sense. The darkness and light are mixed up. Not every planet has this duality, but at least on this earth we have it—darkness and light, pain and pleasure. Knowing this, though everything is Light, but since there is an overlapping of darkness, we have to be compassionate until we at least reduce or modify or eradicate this darkness. That is the main reason of educating the people on earth. Unfortunately when education goes out of focus, instead of driving away the darkness it teaches you further multiplication of darkness. Then we are gone; we just keep away. Until that happens, this is the only work of your Guru or Master or Lord, to the extent that it has been praised and sung that the Guru is Brahmā, Vishnu, and Mahesh; the Creator, the Maintainer, and the Dissolution-Maker.

Many think intellectually or rationally, "How can that be?" I say: "You don't know what Guru means. He dispels your darkness, your ignorance, to make you free from earth limitations and conditions." *Therefore* we say that he is God. It is written in the Vedas very eloquently that each Guru, to his disciples, is the Avatar or Prophet, because he makes them transcend their ignorance and darkness. Now if you take it as these five feet six inches, you are not going to understand. God is not just five feet six inches! Even angels are ten, twenty, thirty feet high, but our eyes don't see beyond this. That's *our* mistake, our limitation and conditioning. This is what we see as the Guru but it is not the Guru; it is only the present physical form. Above that is the vibratory form, which works with your mind through occultism, clairvoyance, clairaudience, and psychologically from a distance. Even if it is ten years, twenty years, a birth or ten births later, the Guru will catch you wherever you are. You will not know but he or she knows. In the Gita, Krishna said: "Arjuna, you don't know—I know. That is the only difference. Now surrender."

Surrender is the English word but that is not the word we use in Sanskrit. We don't say: "Surrender to the Guru." It has been translated that way, which is our misfortune, Gurus' misfortune. The word "surrender" is not even there in Sanskrit! I never liked this word "surrender," because it came from the world wars—surrender treaties and all that. Now which disciple signed a treaty with a Guru? Objectively we use the language erroneously. The closest translation is, "Take *refuge* unto your Guru, your Master." The movements of your mind and your aspirations are to be submitted, but again, that is an English term. The meaning is: "taking refuge" or "taking comforting refuge" unto the Guru's Being. The Sanskrit word is *sharanagati*—*sharana* meaning: "to take refuge and comfort unto," *gati* meaning: "movement, motion, the life which moves." It means, as you say, "coming back to your sweet home," like the prodigal son. When the prodigal son comes back home, is he surrendering to his parents? No, he's just coming back to his sweet home. That is *sharanagati*, where all the thoughts and movements of your mind, all your signs of existence subside and become relaxed. Then you are taking refuge unto the Silence.

So when a disciple takes sharanagati unto a Guru, he is not simply surrendering in a military way; that will be nonsense. It means that all the movements of his mind, his desires, thoughts, aspirations, changefulness, calculations, planning, imaginings, known or unknown, this whole mobility of existence takes refuge unto the Great Silence,

the Great Void. That is what the Guru tries to do with the disciple, so
that whatever you are or not, have or have not, will be doing, are not
doing, and must have done are eventually immaterial. The Guru deals
with the ego to make your mind take refuge unto the comfortable home
of the Guru's Silence, the Light. And amazingly, when a disciple does
reach that Ultimate and opens his inner eyes, he sees, "My Guru and
I are not separate; we are the same." Then the Guru's job is done. This
does not mean that the disciple should then be egotistical again. He
or she realizes that they are the same Substance, the same Presence.

For example, when you sit in meditation, your thoughts, emotions,
excitement, agitation, tensions, memories, imagination, projections
and calculations gradually begin to subside and you relax into a pin-
drop silence. There you will find the Light awakens and you will not
see a difference between you and your Guru. Then you no longer see
that Guru as six feet high. That is the inner Presence where we are
One. In the vibratory world we are still two; in the gross we are still
many, but in that ultimate, conscious Presence, you will see the
Oneness, the Totality. That is all-pervading because it is One.

In the vibratory realm there are also many different entities,
though it is higher than the gross level. If you are in a vibratory plane,
you have arrived there by your practices. Then your Guru, if he or
she has left the body or is in another nation or another time context,
can still guide you even though not physically there. But if you cannot
catch that vibratory level, then it has to be a physical Presence. But
in no way, once the treaty is signed, can you cancel. He or she will
catch you in another birth also, only you may not know it. This is
not a trick; it is just the way Oneness works. Once you start, you cannot
go back. In between, ten years, twenty, a hundred or a thousand years
may lapse, but the journey ends only when you come back to your
Source. Until then, Guru's compassion remains.

Suffering will happen. Suffering is not due to the Guru's doings—
never. It is due to resistance and misunderstanding and disobedience
and disciples' karmas. If compassion were not there, the Guru or
Prophet would be back in His True Self, in *nirvikalpa samadhi*, lost
in Superconsciousness, not working with disciples. He is then in

Oneness, everywhere, without contacting you through the vibratory or gross realms. But how many are on that level to receive the higher working? The main purpose of everyone on this earth, whether they agree with it or not, whether they know it or not, is how to become free from darkness and ignorance, how to get Enlightened.

We have to fulfill the conditions on this school of earth. Then we can be reborn elsewhere where there will be all Light. Then we can grow according to the conditions on that planet. But within this planet, there is darkness and Light. Those are the only conditions we know and are born into; we don't know the comparative study. If we knew beyond this, we would see that this darkness breeds all miseries, pains, wars, clashes, jealousy, greed, attachments, sinfulness, selfishness, negativities—*ad infinitum*. Once you have conquered or dispelled your darkness or ignorance, you are free of all these things. And that is true education. In Sanskrit it is called *vidya*—knowledge, wisdom, Enlightenment. Then you are free of this earth's conditions.

Enlightened, meaning what? You are full of Light. That means you are free of darkness. It is an Awakened state and *therefore* darkness won't exist. In Christian terms, if we were to explain this, it means that Satan will have no power over you. Satan puts hurdles and blocks in your way if you are aspiring to be Enlightened, because he knows his business will not run. You have to be ignorant and in darkness in order for Satan's kingdom to exist. He, Lucifer, will even defy God. I was reading in one book—and it was even news to me—that when Lucifer left God in heaven, *one-third* of the angels of God followed him. So, I thought—*well then, we are not the only ones!* One-third of the angels left with Lucifer to help him. That is one way of seeing it but there is another side: if it were not for Satan's troubles, negativities, these products of darkness, how else shall we get purified? Fire has to burn the dross. There has to be trouble, pain, suffering—wanted or unwanted—in order to purify us.

It is a great plan of God. On one hand it is so painful, regrettable and tortuous, and on the other hand, when you come out of it, or at least out of that burning, you feel purified. Then philosophers and astrologers call it a blessing in disguise. As you will look back you will also call it a blessing. You will say, "Why didn't you tell me in the beginning?" And your Guru or God will say: "You wouldn't have believed it at that time. You would have called it a curse." In other words, if Satan had not tortured you, made you go astray or misled you, then how would you have become purified? By your own willingness you would not have accepted it. Therefore pain is a necessary ingredient on this earth. I don't mean this is true of every planet.

The true purpose of all education is actually to dispel darkness, but many branches of education have forgotten that. They have gone astray, diverted to particular goals of each branch of knowledge and ended there. The original plan was not that. Vishwakarma, the architect of the universe according to Vedic literature, did according to God's plan. Now take today's architecture. It has its own limited motive. Whether it is a landscaper, botanist, philosopher, zoologist, ecologist, naturalist, humanist, social worker, carpenter, it is the same. In Vedic times there were writings, revelations, occultism, yogic science, vibratory science, clairvoyance, clairaudience and other things, but all were diverted to the major purpose of dispelling ignorance. So all the branches of secular knowledge, called *apara vidya* or indirect knowledge, were diverted to *para vidya*, direct knowledge, to fulfill the destiny of education for Enlightenment.

Nowadays each branch of knowledge has fragmented and assumed its own personality, which ends into limitation. A frog living in a well sees only that much; he does not know the existence of the whole ocean. So these various branches of knowledge are not an end in themselves. They have assumed their own personality—individualist, egotistical; therefore they do not correlate. Everything should converge to the ultimate end of educating in such a way that darkness is dispelled rather than just acquiring more information. This leads to Liberation.

Another example is medicine. According to Vedic literature, natural medicine or healing is ruled by the *Ashwini Kumars*, the celestial physicians. These celestials act in such a way to reduce disease or illnesses so that the body and mind can be utilized to reach the Light. The medicine itself is not a cure for the disease; it is supposed to make you free of disease so that your instrument of body and mind can be used for Enlightenment, because disease is a block. They did not mean only that a body should be healthy. That the mind should have peace is paramount, but if today psychology and psychiatry end in only dealing with the mind on its own plane, solving a few problems but never connecting with the ultimate Goal, then it is limited, dead. All the branches of indirect knowledge are aimed to reach the direct Knowledge, the indestructible immortal Light, God. All the faculties of the human body and mind should be diverted there; then they have meaning; then we have fulfilled the conditions of this earth and rise beyond it. Otherwise we'll get stuck here.

Now what is wrong with being stuck here? There is nothing wrong for those who do not have a comparative study or perspective. If you are an astronomer, the purpose of studying the galaxies, planets and cosmos is to see and go beyond and beyond; then you are going in the right direction. So it is with music and art. Music for music's sake is purely an occidental philosophy, not spiritual. We say music is for the Divine, art is for the Divine; otherwise they have no meaning. Even cooking, if done for food's sake, is shallow and mundane. In the case of health, I like to keep the body healthy, not to enjoy the healthy body but because it will be a good instrument for further meditation. By keeping healthy, it frees me twice. One, it frees me from attachment to the body because it is an instrument of God; second, being free from disease is itself very peaceful. But if I were to enjoy that peace and health of the body as an end in itself, I would lose it.

Why would I want to have peace of mind? Because then I don't get disturbances and tension from others. If you just want to be in peace for that end in itself, you are going to lose it. The purpose of a peaceful mind is to be able to relax and meditate well on the Light of God, to realize the higher purpose of life. Even in the yogic and Vedic literature, when they are preaching asceticism, renunciation, martyrdom and poverty, they say that when you want to meditate, select a place where you won't be disturbed by insects or high winds or noise; find a cool, comfortable, undisturbed spot to meditate; acquire a posture in which you could sit unobstructed for a long time. So these are instruments toward something else.

All branches of knowledge, therefore, are not bad in themselves. But if you make them an end in themselves, you are bound to be limited, egotistical, and forming so many personalities. Acquire that in order to go to the Divine, to the Ultimate; then it has served the purpose. It frees you because you won't get attached to it. Second, you transcend it. Whether your Satguru, as we call the real Guru, tells you this or not, it is what he tries to do for the disciple—to free you. Therefore they attack egos. You may wonder sometimes, "Why does he do this so much? Does he want to rule or be a dictator or what?" He just knows that the ego is your block. It is a kind of assumed personality that you want to hang onto for nothing. Therefore sometimes it happens or appears that the Guru is just chasing your ego all the time, but that is his work. What else could he do—pamper you or what? That would only substantiate your ego! This is the main job or the only job of the Guru. In between, if he does not seem to be after your ego, that is only because he doesn't want to give you the impression that he is like dogs and cats after you! So he gives you respite. If he were to be, as we say in India, *godadabai:* "pushing the piston all the time," you know how the truck runs then. You have to sometimes release the second and third gear to give it a little respite. Otherwise the Guru's only job is to finish your ego and go home. But if they were to do this incessantly, you know what that means. Then you are in trouble.

Therefore compassion comes in between as an ointment. If they were to be on your back all the time, on your neck, though meaning real good to finish your ego, how many can take it? They mean that your ego should be finished, that your personality or self-consciousness should be finished, and the sooner the better! That is a blessing, but we take time. We are conditioned by time and space. In spiritual training, the Gurus and Prophets always try to teach you to go beyond *desa* and *kala*, which means: "space and time." They want to make you transcend time and space so that you go into timelessness, infinity, and eternity, and find your True Self.

Time and space create their own limitations and conditions, just as darkness breeds so many negative products. The Guru wants to make you transcend that. This cannot be done without shedding off the ego. Taking ego into timelessness and spacelessness does not work. The Prophets and Gurus and Enlightened Beings have been working since ages now for one same purpose. In earlier years I used to often hear that there is a cultural difference between East and West. We have grown culturally different, I agree, but the principle remains the same always. Cultural differences only make some things more fitting and some things less fitting. My experience—not out of theory—says that outer cultural differences are no justification for erasure of principles. Work for your ambition and you are a limited, mortal being. Work for Divine Mother or Heavenly Father and your mission is fulfilled. You don't have to have ambition. Use the instrumentation of your life, your existence on this earth, for that higher purpose, and that is exactly fulfillment. If you add selfish ambition into it, you will not be fulfilled. So when we say: "Dispel your darkness and ignorance," it is only because the whole body-mind or life's movements have to take refuge unto That, and find relief. This is Liberation, Salvation—*Moksha*.

It takes time. Certainly we exist in time and space, but that is what the Guru is doing: to get you free from these limitations and self-conditionings. How to be awakened? How to be conscious? How to not only *feel* the Presence—feeling is the vibratory phenomenon—but to be present, to *see* the Presence? It is a deeper Vision. That is what Guru tries to make you do, but your mind wants to run away all the time to save itself. It resists taking refuge because it is afraid of losing itself. But if it knew that it is finding the True Self by losing, it would be fulfilled. By that we will be joyfully doing it and not resisting. The more we resist and delay, the more we create problems, sufferings and pain. *Sharanagati* is a self-joyful surrender of all mental thoughts, any kind of imaginings, desires and dreams.

According to Vedic literature, for the disciples the Guru is symbolic of the Presence of God. Try to see the point. This refers to not only disciples but *initiated* disciples, those initiated into the path. The Guru cannot train those who are not on the path. The more you are initiated, the more you are committed to a disciple's job.

The uninitiated are kind of freelance, not committed, so the Guru cannot train them in a serious manner. If we were to go by the ancient method of testing a disciple before we start training, then ninety-nine percent will have to be rejected. But compassion saves the other percentage. Without compassion we couldn't work or teach. Being an initiated one is not like buying a membership card. It is a very real commitment. You have to be under training; you have to go through thick and thin, happiness and unhappiness, testing, trials, and so on. There is no easygoing method. Some have called it "like walking barefooted on a razor's edge." I don't think it is this way all the time, but certainly it is a great testing time. The Gurus train you to finish your mind.

The Guru-disciple relationship is working very mutually, very consciously. It is not hypnotism. That is against your wishes and will. The working is just to finish your mind and your ego. Your blessings can be counted after the ego is gone. Then you'll see, "Boy, this is all a blessing. I didn't know." But in the meantime you had your appreciation, depreciation, resistance, blocks, revolts, rebelliousness, anger, fear, anxieties, retaliations, reactions, and so on. But all this the Guru lives with. The Guru is one; disciples are many. It is not what you call "a fair fight." If it was one Guru and one disciple, fine, but one Guru against the odds, you know. But they do that, and their safety valve is compassion and kindness; otherwise they couldn't do it. The pressure would build up and without a pressure valve you are in trouble!

All this sounds very difficult, very testing, very rigorous—which certainly it is—but at the same time it has other sides. There is a soft way; there is compassion, an easygoingness, helping and guidance. Actually the higher the disciple or more worthy the disciple, the more harshly he or she is tested. If you find soft training, it is only because you are not ready for the higher way. If you go very high—I even shudder to give examples—there are examples in the Bhagavad Gita in which Krishna asked his disciple to even transcend all attachments to kith and kin for dharma's sake, for righteousness. The nearer you go to God, the more fire purifies you. Commitment is a western word.

We don't say commitment; we say it's a serious matter, a serious training. It is faith that you have to adopt. The higher you grow, the more testing or rigorous training, but God supplies higher strength also, more strength to endure. It goes both ways. Faith instills that strength by which you go through rigorous training. And he will even tell you: "You couldn't do this because you didn't believe it." If you had believed it, you would have done it. If you question whether you can do something or say you cannot do it, then there is a doubt, and you are rejected. Ultimately we are even disqualified without trying.

How the Guru knows is different. From one word, one line, one gesture, he will understand where you stand as a conscious being. Your evolution is known to him. If you were to say, "At least let me try"—what will you try? How many have said "I will try" who have done it? At least in my working, I've not seen one who tried and did it. Those who did it—they never tried. They did it! Spirituality is not an easy science, but we do not practice this all the time because people cannot take it. What can we do? The Guru's main job is dispelling the darkness, and darkness cannot be dispelled if your ego is persistent. Guru knows better than disciples; we have to understand this. Blind faith or awakened faith is no problem. He knows the way. He knows the Truth and the life. He can show it.

He cannot boast: "I know and you don't know" all the time. He knows the disciples' level of evolution. He knows what they need, what they can do or cannot do. He doesn't try them or test them beyond where he thinks they will fail. His way is to give you Light. That is exactly what *Guru Purnima** is about, not just for celebration. It is well said that "Gurus are many, disciples are very few"—meaning, worthy, deserving disciples who will do it. Jesus said the same thing: "Many will come and few will be selected." It is only because their

---

* *Purnima*, lit: "full, perfect," is symbolic of the Guru's full Realization or Perfection. *Guru Purnima* occurs on the full moon of July, the "fullest" moon of the year. Traditionally in India, Guru Purnima is a day of rededication to the Guru by disciples. Guru Purnima is believed to have been initiated by the disciples of Sage Veda Vyas who was born on that full moon day.

main job is how to finish your ego, and that is what disciples do not want. Say anything else but preserve the ego; then they are okay. But if a Guru were to do forcibly with everyone at any cost, like a crazy one, it won't work. Either he will be crucified or everybody will run away.

The greatest blessing, I would say, is this: the Guru wants you to be Enlightened. He knows you have Light within you. He knows God is within you. Satgurus work from this premise, though outwardly they do not go on saying this. You are not an eternal sinner to him. You happen to be a sinner in the meantime, but he knows Light is within you; therefore he is working for that. Very few are fortunate who understand and accept and submit to that rigorous working. He wants to make you reach your True Self, your Light, and when you do that, you will not find any difference between you and your Guru. You are One.

13

God's Presence
on Our Path

Bhavā takes you very near the Goal, more easily than centuries of meditation, I tell you frankly. That is why it is said that devotion to God is the easiest and the fastest way to God in the Kali Yuga.

*T*here's a question here. Boy! The question is—I have to start a new retreat! I'll read it and see if you catch it. The first part is, of course, American: "I have been wondering about the relationship between a number of terms: witnessing, practicing the Presence, being awake, using the consciousness. We have to reach the ultimate Consciousness and the term, I think, the feeling of *bhavā* and the love for the Guru . . ." Let's have another retreat! I'll see if I can tie it all together. It's quite a challenge to me!

Let's go from the last sentence first: the feeling of bhavā or love for the Guru. Bhavā is a Hindi or Sanskrit word. As you know, many Indian terms are hard to translate into English. The overall translation is "feeling," but bhavā is more than that. Bhavā comes from *bhavār*, the grammatical root, which means, "to be." Let's say I feel for you, but if I have bhavā for you, it is as if I am in your image, in a way— more *together* rather than feeling for you. There are many kinds of bhavās, meaning different levels and stages. You could have bhavā for the Guru, for God, or it could be for someone. The term bhavā is used more on the path of devotion, bhakti. Lord Chaitanya had bhavā for Krishna, assuming himself to be Radha. So that is called Radha-bhavā. As we touched last night, without devotion nothing is possible.

Now, witnessing and practicing the Presence: these have a very subtle difference. Practicing the Presence is to be aware mentally of what you do, what you say, what you relate to, what you see, what you observe. You are *there*. This part is not the same as knowing; you are simply present with it. You are consciously doing it, not instinctively or habitually doing things. That is called presence of mind. When you think or do things habitually, instinctively having done the same way a million times repetitively, that is an unconscious way of doing things. But when you are *with* it and aware, you are *seeing* and your presence of mind is there. If you are reading a book, your mind is there. You could otherwise read without being there, habitually. If you are watching a kind of scene, you could watch unconsciously or you could be very conscious, with presence of mind. This presence of mind is not being fully conscious though. It means your attention is there; you are with it mentally. That is practicing the Presence. But witnessing is farther or higher than that. Witnessing is when you are observant and present, but you are not *identified* with it.

In bhavā you are identified, but in witnessing you are not. You are holding onto yourself without being carried away passionately, impetuously or emotionally. You are simply observant without being identified. So you are not the reaper of any fruit thereof—good or bad, pleasure or pain. That is witnessing. Now the highest of all among these is being Awake, using the Consciousness. We have to reach the ultimate Consciousness. That is when the ego dissolves. In witnessing, part of the ego is still there but it is not being pulled or pushed or carried away, not identified. In bhavā there is a very subtle ego but it is purified. In witnessing, we do not say you are pure or impure, you are simply not identifying. In bhavā your ego is purified; otherwise you could not have bhavā, the feeling, the love, the devotion, and so on. But in awakening to Consciousness, ego dissolves. In that, you are Consciousness Itself. You are Conscious Being. That Being is no longer ego but Cosmic Being. So these are stages.

Witnessing is a practicing step. It is simply to come out of your mire, your swamp of attachments and stickiness so that you can stand apart. It is not the last stage. It is a saving device, so that you can attach upward or higher to your God, your Spirit. Bhavā helps purify the heart and ego so that you are a fit instrument of the Lord.

The term samadhi is sometimes translated as superconsciousness, but samadhi also means when your ego dissolves into the ultimate object of your meditation and you remain there. There are three stages of samadhi: *bhavā samadhi, savikalpa samadhi,* and *nirvikalpa samadhi.* Bhavā samadhi could be explained as the lowest stage, but we don't say lowest; all are near about each other. One is ice, one is steam, and one is water. Those who differentiate scholarly or philosophically, I say: "God forgive them for they don't know that they are not philosophers." If you differentiate between water and ice and vapor, you are in trouble! Of course, there is a difference in the outward appearance of each, but intrinsically they are the same.

Bhavā samadhi means you are in love and devotion of God; you are in great bhavā—not ecstasy; ecstasy is different than bhavā. Bhavā is when you are soaked in love for God, for whatever is the object of your devotion, not simply feeling but with love, devotion and faith all mingled into one. Then your whole mind, might and soul are in it. The most important aspect of bhavā is love. In that, you are a devotee and God, such as Radha and Krishna, or whatever relationship you are maintaining with God. Now when you are merged and absorbed into that and only that—nothing else—though still maintaining God and you, it is called bhavā samadhi.

Then when you *see* God in your meditation as an inner Vision, having a form and attributes and radiating His Being and you are absorbed in It, when that Vision is living with you, you are *in* it, seeing anytime that God is there, as Mirabai did, that is called savikalpa samadhi, samadhi with a form. It is not dualism in the sense of the Ultimate. It is together like water, ice and vapor. Then finally, when you realize the essential Absolute, the ultimate Substance that is in you and in your God, this is transcendence. You are not rejecting any thoughts from your mind; you are simply not there. You are ultimately merged into That which is indescribable: Consciousness, Light, Absolute. They call it *Kevalya* or Brahman, of which you and everything is. You merge into That and *are* That. That is called nirvikalpa samadhi, samadhi without form. It is as if ice has melted into water, water has evaporated in steam, and then steam comes round again to become water.

Those who differentiate too much between the three samadhis— well, we keep quiet. There are devotees who, when they are one with bhavā samadhi, if you tell them, "You and your Krishna are the same," they say, "No, I want to *see* Krishna. I don't want to *be* Krishna." That is their satisfaction! There is nothing wrong with this. The example they give is, "I want to *taste* the candy; I don't want to *be* candy." That is their language. And if you tell them, "Your Krishna is one with you," they won't hear it. And some others say, "Krishna, you and I have been too far apart. Let's be One." Then they get the Darshan of their Lord. After that Vision, all are the same. And that will be nirvikalpa samadhi.

Bhavā takes you very near the Goal, more easily than centuries of meditation, I tell you frankly. That is why it is said that devotion to God is the easiest and the fastest way to God in the Kali Yuga. In the Golden Age, meditation and austerities are the highest path, because in that epoch there is so much dharma, purity, truthfulness and goodness pervading. But with the decline of goodness, purity and dharma, impurities increase. It is hard to do austerities and sit in stark meditation. So in Kali Yuga, you can still reach the Ultimate in bhavā—love and devotion—using all your senses and karmas. But that does not mean the other paths are inferior; simply we cannot do those things too much. In Mirabai's case and others, bhavā takes you really near your God. Then those who want to merge ultimately into the Substance of all, Pure Consciousness, Brahman, that will be, as far as language can express, the end. But never take one path as superior to others. If you do that, you will not reach your own path at all.

You are dividing unnecessarily, as if you are saying Krishna's arm is better than his eyes, or his eyes are better than his head, or his head is better than his feet. And he might come and say: "Nothing doing. I am one whole Being!" The whole truth is One. This Cosmic Totality we have to realize. If we are deleting any parts as inferior and superior, we are self-deluding. This is simply a mental exercise we are used to doing in the world, so we apply it to the Highest in the same way: trying to analyze, trying to fabricate, delineate or divide. That is not correct. God, Brahman is everywhere, in everyone. Ultimately bhavā with form and God without form—we are talking about the same Totality. God is in everyone; that is the Totality.

On the path of love and devotion, God and His creatures are the Totality. The way of reaching is what differs. We choose our path according to our tendencies and temperaments. I do not consider one way inferior to the others. It is simply what suits you and you feel comfortable with. Also the impact or quality of the age partly determines the paths—in which times we live, in which country we live, what kind of associations we have, our home and the family in which we live. The social, cultural background you are born into and so many other factors determine your path. If you are born in one country, you will choose one path; if you are born in another country, you will do differently because you are born and brought up in a different culture and nurturing and religion, so you choose according to your temperament. If you are born in the Copper Age, you might think differently than today. If you are a man of the Golden Age inside you, even today you will choose a different path. You can carry your Golden Age with you and still do the things that people would do in the Golden Age.

Also, what you can do according to your time, situation, job and home, accordingly you may choose your path. If your situation changes and you have more time, more inclination and more purity of heart, you may choose a different path. Some say, "I just love work. Work is my Creator," and they are just day and night with it. Not that work is bad or wrong—God creates and works too—but the question is of balance and harmony. So supposing your heart is more pure and you want to meditate more and deeper, that will suit you. But if your mind is not pure, it has all the jargon possible, and you are trying to shun work in order to meditate, you are *nowhere*, neither here nor there. You do not get anything—neither peace of mind nor knowledge nor wisdom. So it depends upon each situation and temperament. That is why I would say the need of the Guru is there, because he chalks out a path for you under your own circumstances. But when disciples write, "This is the best way, the best path you have given for me," I say: "No, it's not the best. This is what you can do now." They think that because I suggested it, it must be the best path. Actually I gave up suggesting because of these misunderstandings. I say: "Just choose what you want." I was seeing what he or she can do under his or her circumstances—not only outer but inside the mind and heart: how much purity is there, how much sustenance is there, how much energy is left, how much inclination, how much positive or negative thoughts are there, how much a spiritual materialist the person is, and so on.

Though the person may be asking a very wise question, sometimes I find that he or she is a spiritual materialist, so I may not answer. I know he or she will turn everything to the wrong benefits. Some shun work out of negative thoughts. They think, "I will meditate," but a negative mind cannot meditate. There are so many details in this. That is what I feel the creation of the Guru is: to chalk out the path for you under the circumstances you are in, not what you think is best. This is a kind of custom-made prescription. Otherwise you can read medical books and take out any medicine. The combination of a seeker's mind, temperament, life situation, energy, previous karmas, past births, future births, and so on are known to the Satguru. They can see what, at the moment, is the most suitable path for you.

Under those circumstances you will see that temperament plays the major part. It is not that what *you* like or want to do is important, but what you can do. So to some, worshiping Divine Mother with form is suitable; for others, meditation without form suits; and for others, bhavā suits. Some copy others, however. When I spoke about the lotus and light in the heart meditation, everyone started doing that. I give ten things to see who suits what; you pick it up if you can. But normally you have to stick to one thing. However, there are common factors that apply to every path, every temperament and circumstances, such as truthfulness, faith, devotion, regular practices, purity of heart, harmlessness and such other things. These are pretty common on every path. Some people tell me, "Oh, I will meditate upon the Absolute. I have nothing to do with devotion." I say: "You will never reach. Try it. You can fool around it but you won't reach." "Oh, but devotion, that's dualism." I say: "Yeah, but are you starting from nondualism or dualism?"

There are so many misunderstandings and pitfalls in between; it is not easy to jump from dualism to nondualism. The main reason people avoid devotion is because they don't want to submit their ego, and that is a block in any path. They will not get it, whatever philosophy they talk about. In the Bhagavad Gita, Sri Krishna very clearly tells Arjuna: "Just shunning action is not Liberation." Some people say, "Because action is the cause of my karmas, I won't do anything." On the contrary, Krishna told Arjuna: "Inaction will not lead you anywhere. It is just drowsiness, lethargy, laziness, avoidance. It is just an ego trip." He didn't use the words "ego trip"—he didn't know that language—but he said something like that. He told Arjuna: "Doing action or duties according to your temperament, for the sake of dharma and righteousness, finishes your temperament and karmas. Whether you do it perfectly or imperfectly even, it does not matter." Then he added, "Even if you do something else perfectly that is not your temperament or your karma or duty, that will not lead you to Liberation."

Since you have to use your temperament anyway, use it for righteousness and justice. One cannot say, "What if my temperament is to do unrighteousness and injustice?" That will be quite twisted. That is not what we call temperament; that is quite evil. You have to use your temperament and do your duties in action. Of course, there are Sanskrit terms such as *sukarma*: "good works," *vikarma:* "evil works," and *akarma:* "inaction." Whatever temperament you may have, use it for righteousness and dharma. Of inaction, Krishna said: "Lethargy, procrastination, negligence and such things not only keep your karmas and tendencies stored in your subconscious, but on the top of that you will be kicked around in the world like a stone, without any fulfillment or success." Read the Gita again. Sometimes I add my little commentary, but the idea is the same.

So in this world, in this material age, we have to do karma or action. We have to do whatever is our duty. But see if your duty is for justice, law and dharma. This way your mind gets pacified and peaceful. And when that is there, you can meditate. For the modern age, if we can call it that, bhavā is, for most of us though not all, the easiest and most suitable way to God. For one thing, we are so hankering after love anyway, and bhavā is love and devotion and faith combined. It fulfills our urge of being loved or loving, plus it purifies the ego and heart so it is easier to reach God. Then if you want to have His Darshan—"God, I feel for You. I feel Your Presence. I feel love and devotion for You. I feel You around me and behind me sometimes, but I am not able to *see* You yet . . ."—the urge for God's Vision comes naturally.

Now don't do all these things on one day in meditation. It is not that quick. It could be instant but it's not. It doesn't work that way. It comes out naturally, an urge in you—"I want to see You." And even then, underneath, if you have any doubt whether He is there or not, He will not appear. And doubt does come mostly at that time. "I want to see You but I don't know if You are existent like that even." They don't say this but inside the doubt is there. So the first stage in bhavā is a connection or relationship at a distance. Then gradually His Presence is felt—His or Her, whatever your God is. You will feel this Presence in your mind and heart. You will feel voices giving guidance and instruction. Now don't take it that when your mind is cluttered and tells you something, God is speaking to you. How can you judge that? If it is nonsense, it's not God's. [laughter] Naturally, God could not give you guidance that is nonsense, could He? Then again you can pose a question: how to judge whether it's nonsense or sensible? I think your conscience can tell you that, whether it's weird or not. If it's weird, it's not God's.

This Presence, as we are talking now, joking or saying things— God may joke or not, that's immaterial—is the same Presence you feel. It is not only something to believe in, but it is so. You are not feeling that Presence, that tangibility, because you are not that pure. You are not actually calling upon Him or Her to that intimate action. Underneath you are not believing, as if, that it can be so, at least vibratorily. You do not believe that inside you, outside you, in your room, here and there, God is with you in your walking, that He can talk to you and you can feel His Presence. If your longing grows, in course of time, you would *long* to see Him or Her. It may look like dualism but ultimately it is not dualistic. You and I are dualistic now— we have bodies; we are in relationships; we are living and eating, lodging, boarding and traveling. All these are dualistic. So we cannot suddenly decide that we are nondualistic, as if that is a separate apparatus, which it is not. So when longing grows, you will feel, "But, Lord, I can't see You." You will begin to feel the Presence nearer and nearer.

It is not a matter of imagination, although at first you may imagine as a part of the process. It is not imagination; it is very concrete. All the saints had this experience of the Presence: Surdas, Mirabai, Tukaram, Saint Francis. Ultimately Saint Francis was so full of longing that he got Christ Conscious. He was in a cave and saw a cross and Light shining through. He was blind in the end, a bundle of diseases, but even then he had this Realization. The saints have not only believed; they have made it tangible and they know it is right. If God would not exist, you and I would be null and void. How could we exist? You and I know that we did not create ourselves. If someone's arm is cut, he cannot join it together as it was. You and I are not the creators. We may be creators of our own little world— what we are living—but we are not creating ourselves. Somebody is doing that. That is what you have to have faith in: that the Creator, He or She, exists. I would say not "or" but He *and* She exist. You have to believe it. You have to have faith. When you get more and more pure in faith, then inside your heart will tell you, "Yes, there is a Presence."

That Presence can talk to you, can give you guidelines. When you grow into that, then you long to see. When Mirabai used to worship the *Murti* [Image] of Krishna in her room on her altar, she used to do all the waving of lights—*aarati*. She was soaked in bhavā. And in those days in Rajasthan, India, there were a lot of social constrictions and limits. Until you marry, no other relationships were allowed. Mirabai was a princess, but she was in love with Krishna from when she was a little girl. Her Guru or preceptor, a Brahmin, one day happened to give a statue of Krishna to her, and she took it more real than you or I would. She took it as the real Krishna and made a little altar in her room and worshiped day in, day out, day in, day out. Nobody knew what she was doing. Before she was to be married to a certain prince of another kingdom, one day some ladies heard a male voice along with Mira's coming from her room, as if she was talking to a man.

So suspicions grew and the news went to her father and others that there was someone inside the room with her. But every time they asked or went inside, there would be no one. When one day they pressed her hard, she told them, "Krishna talks to me." This voice was audible to others, not only to Mirabai. The others asked her, "How does he talk to you? He's just a stone image." She said, "No, he comes down from his altar and plays with me." Many times they heard this, and it's not a story of five thousand years back, it was only a few centuries ago in historical time. Of course, there is a long story about how she was forcibly given in marriage and ultimately she got Liberated. This Presence is very tangible, whichever form of God you worship. When they have the Vision of God, they are soaked again. Then if they do get the urge—that's up to the devotee—for "God, I want to be One with You," they get into nirvikalpa samadhi, the Ultimate Absolute.

It depends upon how much you can do, how much you want to do, or what way you want. As far as duties, commitments and obligations are concerned, there is no shunning. Just do for righteousness' sake, for dharma's sake. You are using your temperament; the rest, your heart, give unto God. If you do not run after your ambitions, selfishness, greed and possessiveness, then you can exhaust your karmas and leave your heart unto God. That is what we call karma yoga, actually, but karma yoga can be its own ditch again. Within karma yoga you can try to seek your own position and gratification. Mind is mind, you know. Just do for the righteousness' sake. In that you may lose something materially, but then do you want the kingdom of earth or the Kingdom of Heaven? It depends what you choose. Do you look to your greed or profit or position or gratification or ambition, or do you want God's bliss, joy, love and peace?

You can choose the kingdom of this earth or the Kingdom of Heaven. They brought a bowl of poison to Mirabai because her husband was very jealous of her; he could not stand that she loved Krishna so much. And Krishna wasn't a person, in a sense. Her husband tried to dissuade her to just be a normal, sensible housewife. Mirabai told him, "I'm doing whatever you are telling me." She wasn't a liberated woman of the West—thank God! That would have been trouble. But her husband said, "All the time you are saying, 'Krishna, Krishna' and all that kind of stuff. Just be as other wives are." But she couldn't be that. She said, "Krishna is my Lord. He is everything to me. You are my husband—that's it—on the earth. I'll fulfill my duty to you," but he wasn't satisfied. He wanted the whole of Mirabai, which is understandable. And so eventually her infamy grew so much around the palace that the prince thought, and some advisors advised him, better she should be put to her end. They knew she had love for Krishna, so they brought her a bowl of poison, saying, "This is nectar from Krishna's temple," which we call prasad, consecrated food.

Now Mira had no doubts of any kind. In the name of Krishna, whatever it was, it was great. And as the story goes, when they gave her the bowl of poison—whether she knew it was poison or not—she saw Krishna's Vision in it. She drank the poison and nothing happened to her. There were a few other attempts on her life also. In India still today, millions sing her songs. She became a great poet and singer and composed many, many songs in the name of Krishna. She was freed afterwards and wandered the length and breadth of India—rural areas, cities, towns and villages—throughout her remaining life.

What you choose is up to you. Whatever your duties, your situation, your obligations, temperament and commitments, according to the Gita, we do not violate those things except to use them for dharma. "This way," Krishna told Arjuna, "not only will you be free but one day you will be Liberated. The others for whom you do work will also get benefit out of it. You will do good to others and later on you will be Liberated." Therefore Krishna urged Arjuna to fight because he was a warrior by temperament, a Kshatriya. This does not imply that everybody should go and fight. If you are not of that temperament, you should not. If you are an artist or a musician, a businessman, clerk, housewife or whatever, you have to go through that element. This way gradually your karmas will be exhausted. That is why the Gurus and Masters guide you, to show you and chalk out your path so that you can grow to a higher evolution.

Otherwise we get stuck where we are, going round and round on the same level, reaching nowhere—just having some budget, eating, living, having a few comforts and medical treatment available. We revolve around in that area only. We do not rise to a higher evolution to see more Light, to know more mysteries, to become a higher being, a conscious being, nearing God, more blissful, joyful and peaceful. There is so much treasure. Dharma leads to Liberation. It is all chalked out: the classical path. Don't think that if everyone gets crazy to see God, to meet God, to feel the Presence, then what will become of our life? We all know that all do not simultaneously reach anyway. It is a few at a time. But we should keep the Goal to grow toward. At least we can grow on and on. We may not see or feel His or Her Presence but we can grow on that path if we go the right way. We may falter, make mistakes; we all do. But keep the Goal burning and the focus in your forefront and you will progress.

There is no end to the search until you become *That*—Brahman, Consciousness, Spirit, Light. That is the Goal. Those who care for the Goal are just mad after It. Others can combine this with their duties. But see that the path you tread is righteous, where there are no negativities, where there is no greed, no harmfulness, no revengefulness, no hurting of others, no untruth, unnecessarily at least. That does not mean that untruth is necessary, but because we cannot maintain the full truth, that is why I'm saying this. At least minimize untruth. Selfishness you may not be able to eradicate totally, but you can be less and less selfish. You cannot go on doing good to everybody because your means are limited, but to the capacity you have, do good to others so that your mind gets peaceful and not agitated. We have to avoid tensions and unnecessary friction. With some, when you walk near, they throw sparks of love. You feel it. Others are like thorns; you avoid them like cactuses. You can at least modify these things and keep the thorns to yourself, not projecting them out like a porcupine. This way it does not take away your life, whatever life you want to live. Only live life according to dharma.

You may still falter and make mistakes, but learn from those mistakes. We all do. But keep the aliveness to progress. Even if you falter and make mistakes, see that you are alive to do better and not give up. Those who get mad after God are certainly the blessed ones. They are always the cream of society. They show the way to know your Self. I have talked about many paths and many sections of the Totality. Pick out whatever you want. All those paths and ways are not really contradictory; they are paths within the same campus. The Gurus choose according to your temperament. But the Goal should be burning—Liberation or Consciousness or Brahman or absolute Purity. And one day when you get that pure longing to see God, you will be blessed.

Do not disbelieve that He or She exists. God and Divine Mother are as alive and present as you and I are, and as near us, even more so. Whereas your body and mine are perishable, He or She is not, because that is One with everyone. We have to *feel* that, not imagine so much but *feel* that He or She is there, that He or She can guide you wherever you may be. While driving the car, just feel that God is around you, nearby you, but drive carefully. If it is nonsense, it is not God's guidance. Do you think God is going to tell you to drive in such a way that you fall down Sunshine Canyon? That is your mind speaking. People say, "God told me to drive this way. I was practicing the Presence of God." I say, "No, that is nonsense. God won't tell you to do this." On the contrary, He will tell you, "Be careful." Only *hear* that voice of God—"Be careful"—rather than say that God made you crazy to go down. When you are writing at the desk in your office, feel that God is present in that room with you. Don't ask Him, "God, what should I write on this paper?" That is your duty. Just feel His Presence. When you are cooking in the kitchen, feel God's Presence there. He is watching you, what kind of mess you are making or good cooking. Cooking is not only karma yoga; it is how you feel the Presence that makes it consecrated food, which we call prasad. Are you cooking prasad or cooking just for your palate? It makes a difference.

It sounds like imagination at first but ultimately it is not; it is very concrete and tangible. It may be through you, inside you, that is true, but He and She are there. Try to feel the Presence. If you cannot do deep meditation, sitting for hours, at least this much you can do. When you are walking alone, see that God is walking with you. He is taking care of all this forest that you are visualizing and enjoying. Add the thought, "He is taking care of this forest." Bring what I call "A" into every B-to-C relationship.* In friendship you may be enjoying, socializing and outgoing. Instead, as you are talking to people, see that God is present, listening, and you are keeping His remembrance near you when you are relating to people. Add A to your B-to-C in everything. Perhaps you have come to an airport and are getting into an airplane. You may think, "This is not the place for God! I'm just doing my business. Now I have to get home." Instead, take God with you. He is the airport and the airplane where you are sitting. Feel the Presence. It may be imagination in the beginning but it will work.

When you are eating food, don't just eat to live or to enjoy it. Feel that you are eating for God so that your body-mind could work for Him. Feel that it is prasad. That very consecrated food will also give you food for survival and enjoyment. As long as your body is there, use it for God's work, as His instrument. We worry, "My body is suffering. This is *my* pain, *my* misery, *my* ill health," and then we get miserable because we forget that the body is an instrument of God. Bring in that Presence. It is the same as we talk about Consciousness. Instead of using the word Consciousness, we are bringing God. Both ways are correct. God does exist and is more tangible than you and me. The Presence is more alive and intimate than you think. Apply this in everything.

---

* Gurudeva is referring to an equilateral triangle placed so that A is the apex and B and C are at the nadir, A representing the Divine, B and C denoting the duality of the world, particularly relationships. This is pictured on page 83 of His book, *Retreat Into Eternity* (Second Edition).

Sometimes we feel that exams are over, so now there is no need to study. But after exams are over, education is not over; it still continues in its own way. So when the retreat is over, don't think, "That chapter is closed; now I can do my own things again." If you do that, you are erasing the whole effect. Continue this practice in your life: God is listening; God is talking to you. Put it any way you like. Light is shining inside and around you. Wherever you go, Light is there with you. Try to feel its Presence. And then one day it will become tangible and you will long to see That, to be Enlightened. Whichever path you take, there are some common factors. Purity of heart, above all, is the greatest golden ornament. It gives you peace of mind. That peace of mind makes your meditations, prayers and worship more fruitful. Witnessing is necessary to get rid of unnecessary attachments. Do your duties according to dharma. This way, if you go one step forward, God comes ten steps forward—be sure. I wish it were otherwise, that you would go ten steps and He would go one step! Even then, it is not a bad deal! [laughter] Well, we have been since ages believing that if we take one step, He takes ten steps. Even then, it is one step we have to take. He is more eager to meet you than you think.

I would still say that purity of heart is the greatest ornament—to whatever degree we can achieve it. It is hard in this Iron Age to be perfectly pure, I agree, but we can try as much as we can. That will give a real boost to any path, whichever path you are following. And that will give you peace of mind. With a pure heart you will not feel depressed, frustrated or disappointed. Retreats and Satsangs are some of the means for purifying, but more so in your homes. Do it daily. It is not so much the practice or regular meditation that is necessary; that alone will not do everything. *Pratyahara* is necessary: whatever distracts you, maligns you or spoils you, you have to avoid in order for your practices to be fruitful. Unnecessary attachments are to be avoided. Some attachments, if we live together, may be there. It is all right to take care of your child or your husband or wife or parents, but see that it is not overly done in such a way that it gets sticky and muddy, like a swamp. The drowning and sinking part should be avoided. But in day to day life, we have to gather affection, love, and living together. In this way, your mind will relax and you can grow higher.

Carry the idea of Light or God with you wherever you go. But be careful what you are doing. Don't get in reverie when you are working with machines, et cetera. That will be very terrible. It's something like taking a tranquilizer capsule and then operating a machine. Use the presence of mind. Awareness has to be there. Don't think you are remembering God while you work so that you burn your fingers on the stove. God never tells you to suffer. He wants you to be aware, very conscious. Don't say, "In the name of God, my fingers got burnt." Suffering is our own making. He is blissful. Light is blissful. He would like us to be in ananda: "bliss," and to be wise, peaceful, loving, harmonious, fulfilled and satisfied. Those, I would say, are His attributes. Anything else—suffering, dissatisfaction or failure—is our own making.

Any misery is our own making, the cause being desire. If we do God's will—if we could hear that—there will be no suffering. Suffering is created by us. We may blame somebody else for it but that doesn't erase the suffering, because that's not the truth. Altogether in propensities or talents, we have to express and achieve things. Do your duty according to dharma and your capacity, and exhaust your karmas. Keep your mind and heart pure and focused on your Goal. Talents will grow. The manifestation will be harmonious. You will be happy. People around you will be happy. It all blends very well—this whole totality.

Somebody is singing the Lord's Name. Let him do it. Don't say, "This is an idiot because I am nondualistic." Somebody is doing the head posture, standing on the head, and we say it is kind of funny. And somebody else is doing great meditation. We may say, "He is doing nothing, just inactive, sitting at one spot, a parasite." These are all harmonious, blended in oneness. You have to understand this. You think you are doing the best and others are wrong. That is your problem. And when you do that, you are negative to everyone. And when you are negative, you lose your own peace. And when you lose your peace, you cannot do what you are doing. That is dogmatism. Someone is selling vegetables; someone is selling rice; someone is selling bread; someone is selling ribbons or kites. That is what it should be. It's perfectly fine. You choose to do what you choose to do.

In this harmoniousness you will see that every path is different, but at the same time, they are all harmonious with each other. Let others do what they are doing. Follow your path. This is the way to live. And God will be pleased with you. From where He is sitting, He takes care of all His children. We may divide here but He is not dividing from there. This totality of view we have to cultivate, that all are blending very well into one whole arena.

You can grow but not at the cost of somebody else. Grow vertically in your own self, not horizontally, overpowering others. See the point? One is competition; the other is cooperation. You have freedom to grow in your own self to any heights, to the God Almighty, but if you get into friction and struggles that pull and push, repulsion and attraction, you forget to grow vertically in *you*. Then your meditation does not happen, so you do not get to the Divinity that you are. You are a flood of Light yourself; each one of us is. The one who sees Light—he sees everything is Light. Everybody is Divine. With whom would you compete and hurt?

Others do not distract you; it is your mind that distracts. You feel others are distracting you because your mind is cluttered. It is confused and powerless and restless; therefore others seem to distract you. If your mind is focused and stable, nothing can distract you. Keep the focus: all is Divine, everything is Light, everyone has God in him and her, and be on That. You will have no time or intention even to think of others in a negative way. That is utter purity.

14

Giving God's Secrets

You can again be God. You can again be the sun shining. Do you know that the sun of our solar system is not simply hydrogen gas burning? These are scientific terms, but in yoga terms we say differently. The sun is a creature, a soul.

*I*n our individual bodies there are so many things that we do not know. This body has *everything* in it. There is a great science in it, a great universe in it, love in it, thinking in it, Tantra in it, chakras in it. There are gods and goddesses or angels in it. There are regions and regions in each body. You see dreams through this body of so many magnitudes. You can have clairvoyance and clairaudience. You can be an artist, a musician or a dancer. You can fly through the air. *Everything* is possible in this one body. Call it a temple if you like. All possibilities are in it, to the extent that you can be God, *Ishwara*, in this body.

One body can be seated in a corner or a cave in the Himalayas— this is what the yogis do and have been doing—and control the universe. It is such a creative computer, not this data-fed computer. The yogis have been given certain regions to control: the minds of people, of creatures, changes in the universe. Particular regions are given to them, just like the president controls America in certain spheres but not higher spiritual things. Those higher regions are given to yogis, or what we call maharishis. Evolution can be realized through this body without going anywhere, without talking. This possibility is in everyone.

Seeker: *Better than transistors.*

A transistor is simply a pale reflection of that faculty. I'm not against transistors or TVs or radios or telephones, but those are pale reflections of this possibility within us. If it were not in us, it would not be outside us; be sure about that. How otherwise would they get the idea to create such things? This is modern language though. In yoga terms we say that you can be Ishwara, God, in this body, and fly to any Milky Way. *Everything* is there: total bliss is there; total peace is there; total love is there within this one body. We take it for ballroom dancing; give it smoke and bottles to keep it happy, meaning: keep it forgetful of all its faculties. That is a slumbering, a tranquilizer, when the faculties remain closed. Through Tantra, mantra, yoga, meditation, prayer, repentance, devotion and surrender, you are awakened.

Once you know that Consciousness, you are a monarch, a King of kings. You are the controller of millions of people. I don't mean control necessarily in a domination sense. I mean you rise so high; you raise your consciousness through various means: Tantra, mantra, yoga, meditation, purity, discipline, abstentions, and so on. Whatever has happened has happened; it is gone. Whether you repent or not, it doesn't matter. It is gone now; it cannot be undone. I do not mean to just forget it—you cannot forget it. You have to repay; be sure about that. But by this I mean don't look back, just go forward into Consciousness.

You can again be God. You can again be the sun shining. Do you know that the sun of our solar system is not simply hydrogen gas burning? These are scientific terms, but in yoga terms we say differently. The sun is a creature, a soul. After thousands and thousands of births and thousands of years of austerities, penances and practices, he or she has achieved that life, that existence as our sun. As we have become man, he has become the sun. To be the sun shining, giving light and life to the solar system, what *tremendous tapas* or penances he must have done. His name is the sun *now*. We do not know how many names he had before. He must have been Swami Amar Jyoti also, but now he is the sun. He must have desired: "I must give light, life and heat to the regions, to the planets, to the beings." And he must have done tapas and tapas; then his soul was released and he occupied that form. For another soul to become the sun will take millions of years. Scientifically they say that so many millions of years are the life of the sun, right? But in yoga we say, he is a creature. And there will be an end of the sun also, perhaps after billions of years. He lives so long because he has done so much tapas.

It's possible for you to be a sun too. His physical age is billions of years and ours is a hundred years, supposing. An insect's life span may be one day or ten days; a bird's may be four years; an animal may live ten years or twenty years; a tree may live one thousand years. Even a banyan tree lives five hundred years. It is not a fantasy or mythology. People say, "Oh, Hindus worship trees"—but a tree is a creature. We don't understand that if there is life, there is a soul too. The sun has a life. If it doesn't, how does it give us life? If the sun can give us life, if our living is dependent upon the sun, then it has to have a soul. We call it hydrogen gas. That way, you are made of flesh and bones, what else?

What is the sun, apart from that hydrogen chemical analysis? He is a creature living his life. Ishwara, the Lord, goes beyond it. At His command the sun shines; at His command the moon shines, through the sun, of course. He can dismiss the sun if He likes to, but God does not destroy. He can replace the sun anytime and we won't even know it. We'll be sleeping in the night. He will dismiss him and bring in a new sun. What God does, we do not know. Only higher authorities know this. But we don't understand this. Of course, God doesn't destroy, He fulfills. He will not dismiss just anybody and put another one in his place. He's not that kind of shaky-fakey. God is not moody. In moods we can do wonderful things and again we can do otherwise. When the sun is there, He will not destroy it. He will allow it to fulfill its duty and obligations. There is a famous aphorism in the Vedas that the sun is also under obligation, fulfilling his duty, and will go on shining until we need him.

Seeker: *Is there a thing where there is a golden person in the sun no bigger than your fingernail? . . .*

No, that's different again. That is called *angooshtha maatrena,** the soul or Spirit. I was talking about the sun creature. But there is this

---

* *Angooshtha maatrena:* in Sanskrit, "of the size of the thumb," also called the "seat of the soul." Gurudeva said this is actually the pineal gland, which thousands of of years ago, yogis had seen in meditation and described thus. The human pineal

kind of soul aspect in us, the immortal Spirit within everyone that is called a "spark" in other languages. If we find that angooshtha maatrena within us, or in everything, then even the sun is at our command. He will obey such a Realized One. The famous mantra, the Gayatri, is to the sun: "We meditate upon that sun who gives us Light. Because of that sun, all the regions are shining. We meditate upon that and none else."* That is the meaning of the Gayatri mantra. If you invoke that radiance, the sun's power, its energy and generating capacity, it will give you boons.

Seeker: *And the moon?*

The moon has a borrowed light. The sun is connected with our soul, the moon with our mind, i.e. lunar, lunacy. Daily, when you get up, worship the sun. You may call it primitive or pagan, but it is very scientific. Pray to the sun—not with open eyes so much but in worship—"Thou art great. Thou art shining, radiant, powerful and energetic. Give us your Light and your heat. Our life is dependent upon you. Bless me that I be radiant like you, that I be powerful like you, that I will be energetic like you, that I inherit from you the life you have." You do not need injections and tablets. You can get energy directly from the sun. We are not separate. We are connected to the whole universe. Each one of us is a point, a speck in this cosmos. We are connected with the whole cosmos, including the solar system, part and parcel. We cannot disregard anything. If we do, we are harming ourselves. That is why this famous Gayatri mantra* proclaims:

---

gland was first photographed by Lennart Nilsson of Sweden and published in *Behold Man: A Photographic Journey of Discovery Inside the Body* (Little, Brown & Co. 1973). Decades ago, Gurudeva showed us this photograph (page 170) in which the pineal gland appears in the actual shape of a thumb.

* A literal translation of the Gayatri Mantra: "Om: the earthly, atmospheric and celestial spheres. We meditate upon that Supreme Light of the Radiant Divine Creator Who illumines everything. May He guide, stimulate and inspire our intelligence to the fullest."

Om Bhur Bhuvah Suvah
Tat Savitur Varenyam
Bhargo Devasya Dhi Mahi
Dhi Yo Yo Naha Prachodayata

Reciting this mantra opens the chakras and gives purity, radiance and Light. This is not primitive superstition; it is very scientific.

Seeker: *We should also be grateful for the earth and all . . .*

Earth is a creature, a body, and we are on it. How can it be only stone and mud and dust? Have we not bacteria, germs and various living things inside us? It is the same with the earth. When the earth shakes in an earthquake, we have no power. In seconds, thousands of people fall dead. If she quivers a little, her children are squeezed. We are born out of the earth and sun, water, fire, air and ether. We are the product of it. We owe so much to the earth and all these elements, so we should not pollute them. If we pollute any of these, it will poison us. We cannot just live separately. It is the law of nature. If we take care of a thing, it takes care of us. If we spoil something, it will spoil us. And then you say the world is bad, miserable. *You have made it so.* Earth is heaven. Keep everything purified and it will keep you purified.

Supposing they explode atom bombs under the sea. They say, "We are experimenting," but they are polluting. The earth takes the reaction and the results will make us suffer. Somewhere else an earthquake will happen that will kill thousands of people. Somewhere else a sea storm will come. Things happen that way. Earth is a soul, which we call *prakriti*. Each thing has a soul. In this great science, which you call primitive, the very basic laws are known to the yogis that otherwise are enigmatic, which geology or physiology cannot solve. Any one branch of knowledge cannot solve this because it is not a homogeneous view. You have to take the total Being.

Let's suppose you go to a doctor when you are diseased or ill. The doctor says this is cancer or diabetes or high blood pressure or asthma or something else. He takes that one portion of your body and treats it. Perhaps it will be okay, but then that is why often we do not become healthy, because he does not take the homogeneous whole body. When you go to a psychiatrist, he sees you from a particular angle. That is not the solution. You have to take the whole personality, the whole body, mind and soul together to give a cure. When you understand this basic law of existence, your life will be sublime, blissful, peaceful and Liberated.

We have to take this homogeneous view because otherwise we are forgetting God. A psychologist thinks, "My psychology will cure you." Does he or she remember to bring God in between? The scientist who discovers the laws of nature is simply discovering the laws of nature; he is not inventing or creating them. Any time we are going through one faculty only, we are forgetting God. When we bring God into the understanding, we are taking all the faculties together, *everything*. Your own aspirations, your desires and subconscious mind— *everything* has to be taken together in order to regenerate, to bring peace, joy, knowledge and Liberation. You have to be sublime, pure, harmless, nonpolluting, peaceful, charitable, patient, enduring, tolerant, and so on. Then your total being gets transformed.

We are all connected with everything around us—the earth, the planets. Mars affects us; Jupiter affects us; Mercury affects us; Saturn affects us. We are not separate. If we understand this we will behave so that harmony remains. "Change yourself; the world is changed." This is a famous aphorism. But if you do not change and the whole world changes, still you will be the same. These basic laws are eternal.

Seeker: *Did the knowledge of mudras come from the Vedas or do most of the people who use mudras develop the knowledge through just observing what happens?*

It is from the Vedas but was developed by the sages over thousands of years. Different sages introduced different parts. There are sixty-four aspects, sciences or arts in all. Krishna mastered these in sixty-four days. Each day his teacher would teach him one science or art and in one day he would master it. His life story is in the Srimad Bhagavatam. So much so that it is written that he would be given one and [snapped fingers] it was open in him. He was just that receptive.

After sixty-four days his Guru told him, "I've nothing else to give you now." And Krishna said, "Now be my disciple." Then Krishna began to do wonders.

He had so many queens and so many plays. He was the most charming, the most modest and most powerful. He was a great peacemaker and the greatest warrior. If you see these aspects perfected together, it is wonderful. That is why we call him, according to Indian wisdom, the highest Prophet. According to the Vedas there are sixteen phases that accompany the Prophets or Incarnations, and Krishna had all sixteen. Buddha had twelve. Rama had fourteen. That's why we call Krishna *purna*,* the "Perfect Incarnation." The greatest ascetic he was, and the greatest enjoyer of life we have ever known.

He was the greatest, gentlest, most tender and sweetest lover. None else has loved more than Krishna, yet he was the most detached. When he loved Radha, he was the greatest lover. When he left her to continue his work, he was completely detached. Nobody could ever leave Krishna, whether an enemy or a friend. He was the poorest, born in a jail, penniless, shelterless. He had no spoon in his mouth, what to talk of a silver spoon! And he became the richest and highest emperor in India. He had an invincible army, the Yadavas, who were his own offspring. They were invincible by his blessings, but he knew that they would do havoc by their power, so he cursed them and saw that they were destroyed before he left this world.

To know Krishna is something else. Commonly we think: he taught war. That is not Krishna. He used to get up at four o'clock in the morning, according to his life story. Having so many queens and children and grandchildren, he still got up at 4:00 and did meditation for two hours. You might ask, "What need did he have to do this?" But he did it for us. Before that he would do yoga and bathing and all that. At about six o'clock he would eat something. His breakfast must have been quite beautiful. He was very fond of butter, genuine butter. And at eight o'clock he would attend to business in the palace court. People would come; cases would go on. Around ten o'clock

---

* *Purna*, lit: "full, perfect."

he would get into his chariot and go around his city, Dwarka, to see who was unfortunate or miserable or downtrodden, to help them. At twelve o'clock he would come back, have lunch, rest a little, play with his children and grandchildren, and then again attend to the court for two or three hours. Then again he would go round the city for two hours, from 4:00 to 6:00, to see who had grievances or if there was any kind of injustice. At six o'clock he would come back to the palace, do meditation for two hours and then take dinner. He gave regular Satsang and there was chanting. He seldom slept in the night. He never got ill in his life, as the scriptures have written.

He died at the age of one hundred twenty years, and that also a self-imposed death. He left the whole kingdom—grandchildren, princes, princesses, queens, palaces—and went to the jungle. He sat under a tree and someone shot him on the bottom of his foot with a poisonous arrow. Krishna's feet used to shine. A hunter saw something from the distance shining and thought it was a deer. When the hunter came near he saw it was Krishna, their Lord and emperor, and he was just very bereaved. Krishna told him, "No, it's just an excuse; I want to go. Otherwise I could take this out." He could have saved himself but he said, "I want an excuse to go." He died in the forest, not in the palace. Being the greatest emperor-king, he was the greatest ascetic. When the people heard that he was dying, his queens and subjects came and they asked him, "Why, Krishna, did you do this here? You could have been in the palace." He said, "Well, ultimately from this place I will go directly to heaven." He showed them: "You are not bound by anything." He played everything to the utmost; everything he did fully. He knew how to not be bound by anything. That is why we call him *Mahayogi*—the greatest yogi.

His love is the greatest and most famous even today. He did not teach war, but if need be, he fought and fought well, successfully. He had all the knowledge of politics, commerce, science, yoga, administration, ruling the kingdom, forgiveness, love of the simple folk, everything. That is called Perfection. Doing everything, he did nothing. He told Arjuna, as written in the Bhagavad Gita: "In the three worlds—heavens and surface world and nether world—I have nothing to achieve. I have nothing to desire. Still I am working, Arjuna, day and night." His Perfection has to be understood from all facets.

If you open up you will see that everything—your soul, peace, Light, Spirit, God, Perfection—is within this five- or six-foot body, which is otherwise perishable. Again, a demon or devil is also there. All the disturbances, miseries and failures are also there. Your Guru is within you too. Everything is there—stars, the moon, the sun, mountains, rivers. Your bones are mountains; your nerves are rivers; your right eye is connected to the sun and your left eye to the moon. Each organ—liver, kidney, intestines and all—is connected with each planet. It is a great science known to yogis.

Seeker: *Is it important to understand about these things along the way— I mean, to learn them?*

No. Even if you do not try to understand these things, if you follow some other methods, this knowledge will come to you eventually, because the way is through your Being. It may not be the same language as I am saying, but you will come to that knowledge, through you.

Seeker: *Is there one thing you can tell us to have our mind on before we go to sleep?*

Whatever form of God you have chosen, just pray to Him or Her. Or repeat your mantra on and on till you are carried away by sleep. Either your chosen God, or remembrance in prayer, or a mantra, or any particular line of thought you can repeat, such as, "God, give us courage to change what we can, the humility to accept what we cannot change, and the wisdom to know the difference."

THE MATRIKAS

We call the letters of the alphabet *matrikas* or "mothers of the creation." The entire fifty-one letters of the Hindi or Sanskrit alphabet are the matrikas or Divinities. That is why the whole mantra system came up: "The Word was God and Word was with God." From these fifty-one "alphabets," this region of our universe was created. In Tantra they intuited this knowledge and formulated mantras. Each matrika has given rise to a different god, goddess, angel, fairy and all the beings of the astral and physical realms. That is why speaking truth or speaking intonations clearly is very important in Tantra. The things you repeat must be correct and must be truthful. If you speak truth, the chakra opens; if you speak untruth, that chakra closes. It is connected with everything. Normally we say, "Without untruth, there is no practical world." But then if you speak untruth, these chakras get closed up.

John Woodroffe has written of these fifty-one matrikas in his book, *Serpent Power*. He writes about how these alphabets are connected with our nerves. Don't think it is simply speech. That is why those who attend my group talks or Satsangs have sometimes felt a glimpse of Enlightenment and Liberation. Through language it is sometimes so perfectly given as a science through the chakras that the words themselves can awaken you. In the Vedas they have called this *vak*, "original sound," out of which these matrikas have come. So whenever you pronounce, pronounce correctly and clearly. If you do that, Goddess Saraswati resides in you; the Goddess of learning and knowledge opens up in you. This is called *vaksiddhi*: *siddhi*, meaning: "power," *vak*, meaning: "speech." You say it and it happens. Unbelievable, unimaginable things will appear before you.

15

Repaying the Guru

My strong wish or desire is: I want some solid souls, unconditionally, without reservations, without compromising with any other mixture, to carry my vision and work for that.

*D*evotee: *I was just remembering what you said about how that bird came back and understood and repaid you in kind. And I wondered what we could do to repay you.*

Repay me? And where shall I keep it? Even if you pay me, what shall I do with it? Build a garden house for me where I can live with birds and animals, and you come and help me. I'll make disciples out of birds and animals . . . Okay, I'll talk about it. Your question is correct—how to repay me—but it won't be material. Offhand my answer would be: if you grow spiritually, that will be a repayment to me—if you use those terms: "repaying me," because I have a problem where to keep it, you know. Even if you pay me, I'll redistribute it. It's natural with me not to keep anything.

One way is if you grow spiritually and transcend human nature. But there are deeper replies, which I'll come to. My strong wish or desire is: I want some solid souls, unconditionally, without reservations, without compromising with any other mixture, to carry my vision and work for that. That will be my first wish. It is not as though I am leaving institutions or ashrams and buildings— whatever the number be—to carry on my work; just taking care of buildings, vacuuming carpets, paying taxes, performing rituals and holding functions punctually. I am not referring to that kind of work. That is only the outer expression. And it is not because this is "my" vision, or because I have started it subtly, or I want it, but because that is the dream or fulfillment. You have to understand me properly. When I say: "I want . . ." it is because that is the way it should be. It is not a personal dream or ambition or utopian aspiration. I would

341

not want anything from anyone if it were not serving the evolution of consciousness of humanity.

Much of my work is subtle and I do not talk about it. Because I have a physical body, naturally I do physically certain things, but that is only the tip of the iceberg. If I were to declare my subtle work, it would be beyond the understanding of many, even if they would believe it. And secondly, it would create unnecessary sensationalism, which I feel just becomes enjoyable entertainment in a sense, though it gives a good impetus too; but beyond that, it does not serve the purpose. This vision needs solid—and I won't compromise— hundred percent dedication, so that I could *infuse* that vision and dream into those souls, if they are ready vessels.

I do not believe in compromises. My only compromise is compassion. Beyond that I cannot go. I don't compromise the principle. Compassion makes me, as if, do on the physical level some compromises such as tolerance and patience, but do not think these are the virtues that I've come to demonstrate. Humans want it, so I do it. Somebody may praise me for these virtues, and that is fine on the human plane; certainly these things are to be praised and practiced. But at the same time I know that because of this human nature, compromise and compassion are necessary. I have never seen in my experience that compassion is needed for imbibing the truth. But people cannot take it, so you do with compassion and kindness— not that these are bad, but we cannot live for kindness and compassion alone.

I am being very frank and open about certain things, and saying things that nobody may even agree with. If they are solid souls, I do not think compassion is necessary. It is soothing, but that does not mean it gives you the truth. It gives you a kind of respite, a gap in which to relax. Does truth have to be, therefore, harsh, rude or terrifying? No, actually not. If you take no compromises or liberties in the truth, it is very sweet. But our resistance and desires and individual natures come in the way, the lower nature that is demanding and wanting "on my terms." So we behave with kindness, love, compassion, forgiveness and whatever else could be. But when you are dealing with the baser elements in nature—demanding, unnecessarily egotistical, unreasonable, unfair, merciless, terrifying, low—you cannot give the truth. They will not accept it. They will put their own terms on the truth: what they want to do, they want you to accept it; what you want them to do, they reject. Therefore the need for compassion, kindness, let go, forgiveness. What else can you do in the meantime? But that is not the solution. I'm very frank about it. Howsoever golden these virtues may be, and I, by God's grace, could be an embodiment of that, but even then I'm saying *they are not the solution*. This is an uncompromising attitude.

So when that dedication happens, unconditionally and thoroughly, the number does not matter. It could be a few: two, three, four, five, ten, twenty, thirty or a hundred. I am not a crusader—introducing new things and making billboards about them. Such souls, if I could prepare or have, I will consider I am repaid. And there is no mundane trace in that wish. Giving that vision to those who will be ready to take it with one hundred percent unreserved dedication—that will be perfect repayment to me. If not, we come to the second stage: have a burning aspiration to transcend the human nature to the next evolution of spirituality. That will also partly repay me. Don't get stuck in your day to day frailties and human baser nature. Do not carry on the ruts of habits. Habits make you feel comfortable, in a way, and you fall back into ruts every time, like a bullock cart on a muddy road. This repayment will be second best, for which meditation, prayer and yoga are needed. But more than that, pure *will* should be there. That is very important to me. Without that, no practices will be fruitful. "Crocodile tears" and "cremation ground pathos" do not pay—"I'm evil . . . I'm bad . . ." As soon as you get to your other moods, you are a different person. Aspire to transcend the human nature, but your aspiration has to be very honest.

There are good things in human nature too. Somebody has said you are known by what you are, not by what you accomplish. I have seen often that people's talents can be very nice ones, but the person can be quite different. What he or she *is* is very important, more than what he or she accomplishes. This is nothing against accomplishments. If it were, I would not accomplish things such as creating these buildings and institutes. But the amazing complexity or frailty of human nature is that people can accomplish nice things without being nice. How does that work? Ask God Almighty. I could explain but I would be ruthless if I explain, which I don't want to do, especially in your welfare, or rather, farewell Satsang.* Farewell is also welfare, right? If I don't make humor, I get serious. I want to cut a joke at the last breath. So, in spite of this complexity of human nature, I want you to transcend it. Not transcend it to null and void but to the next evolution, which only can be spiritual.

A nutshell definition of spiritual, though there could be many explanations, is: surrender your life to the Lord or Spirit or Light. Live for that dedication and your human nature will transform. If you are expecting that within the orbit of human nature things could be better, I agree to some extent. But the human and spiritual are so opposite each other that one or the other time you will fall back into the lower aspects of human nature. You cannot remain just a good human. It is not possible all the time. However low you degrade or not—there are degrees, of course—to expect to grow in human nature to a better person, more satisfying, more peaceful, nonhurting and so on, is really very difficult. You can be so in degrees of good and bad, but you can't solve these problems. Human nature in one respect is higher than animals, but in another respect it is quite raw. This being the case, that raw material has to be refined and made more conscious. Then you are evolving beyond human nature. Not because it is evil or bad alone—it can be good too—but human nature is so limited that it will always remain unsatisfying.

Ten years hence, fifty years or next birth, you will realize this anyway. There is no good in going around in circles. People say, "I'll commit suicide" and all that kind of stuff. That is only an escape. It is no solution. Instead of trying to change or better yourself, you are running away. What a glorious end! You don't have to be bold about it, just be humble and change. Even if you try to change within the

---

* This was the last Satsang of the *Grace of the Guru Retreat* in 1997.

human orbit, it will only be tossing back and forth between various waves that eventually do not give you the solution. So this second repayment is: if you cannot be that instrument of vision, which will be my A-grade demand, at least try to evolve from human to spiritual. Now if that also is too much for you or you cannot do much to repay, then there is a third method. If you cannot be spiritual—supposing your caliber doesn't allow you—at least, this is the minimum repayment I'm asking: follow the dharma. Below that I cannot go. This will be your repayment, which means that you remain human but on the dharmic path. Because when you transcend the human nature to spiritual, you transcend dharma actually. And when you transcend the spiritual even, then you are coming in direct contact with your Guru or God, to be His instrument.

If you have gathered any deeper insight into what I've said, you will understand that when I expect, I expect the most and the best; otherwise I do not expect. Do not take my compassion, tolerance and compromise as if it is my asking. Either I expect the best or I don't expect. And then I follow the compromises or compassion as you might expect, but not as I expect. It used to happen in early years that somebody would ask, "What can I do for you?" I said, "Well then, surrender totally." "Yeah, I can surrender to some extent"—this was in the 1980s—"but total, I'm not ready." I said, "Sure, you're not ready. I understand." "But anything I can give, please tell me." I said, "That won't satisfy me. Or don't ask me; just give what you feel to give." You understand what I mean? In between I have no way. The only way is compromise, compassion, toleration, forgiveness, kindness. Yet to me these virtues, though golden and coveted by millions and achievable by only a few, when I am doing this I am not feeling great. Some people think these are a great treasure, and I understand their value too. But inside me I say, "No, this is a via media, a compromise." Does that mean I will be intolerant, unforgiving, unkind, and so on? No. I have to be this way; there is no other choice for me. But don't think this is my nature.

My nature is uncompromising. I compromise in between because you want it that way. "Isn't that what you asked me?" I said, "Because you could only do that much; therefore I asked it." Is it my wish then? No. Mine is full, perfect. So out of these three, any two you can combine and repay, provided you are using that word repayment. Anything else I will just accept. When you send your dining table and chairs, I might use them somewhere in the community or ashram. "But that's not what you wanted, Swamiji?" What shall I do with dining tables and chairs? I'll put them in a room somewhere and the mundane disciples will be happy about it. If I give them a new vacuum cleaner, they are in heaven. So my repayment or indebtedness will be one of these three. The first one that I said: those are dearest to me. The second one: those are dearer to me. The third one: those are dear to me. See what you can do. Below that I won't go.

I will tolerate but I won't go below that. That is *me*. If I can't be what I am, I don't want to be anything. This is my Vedantic Love. In spite of your imperfections, infirmities, low, high or whatever mistakes, I love you still. Knowing everything, I love you. I don't believe in condemnation, because each soul will go to hell or heaven by his or her own karmas anyway. Why have I to curse or bless anybody? Vedantic Love is when you are wise and loving. And when you are wise, you are not supposed to be egotistical; you won't be. If you are egotistical, you will not be wise anyway. And when you are wise and egoless, your love is perfect, unconditional, agape, God's love. If in my life I have been able to do that perfectly, then you will understand me, what or who I am. And if I am deficient in that, let me be not judged by the imperfect ones. Theirs are always faulty judgments.

If you do see me with a purified heart and humility, you will understand my words. The reason I have hesitated so long to talk about myself is this: that I won't be judged properly. I know that, with even my nearest disciples. As I have seen on this earth—not that my disciples are thousands or millions, but it is hard to give revelations commonly. You have to work with the raw material as it is. You can help me and my work, although "my" I am not using in the personal sense. It is God's work, Divine Mother's work. I am an instrument simply. I told you last night that I have taken to hiding behind the apron of Divine Mother. Let Her be in the front; that will be all right for me.

You can help me and my work in this way: the minimum is to follow dharma. What is dharma? Volumes can be written, but in a nutshell dharma is something that should be, not only because it is pleasant or what you like. There are things that could be unpleasant, that you could dislike, but still could be dharmic. Dharma is the way it should be, the religious way, not what you think you want but what God wants, what your Spirit wants, what your conscience tells you. Conscience is dharma. I assert: if you are sincere and honest, you will let conscience tell you what is right. People avoid it, saying, "How do we know what is dharma?" I say, "Well, if you're honest enough and sincere, your heart will tell you." It may be that you are weak, not following what is right or avoiding what is wrong. That is where dharma should be followed. It may be difficult sometimes because it clashes with what you want. You might fail, but keep doing it. Keep at least the banner of dharma before you. This is not making you Hindu or Christian or Buddhist or anything. Dharma does not have anything to do with these labels. It is very impartial for all humanity. That is why the ancient religion of man was called *Sanatana Dharma*, when there were no labels of any kind, many centuries back.

It may be difficult, but as you grow and mature into adulthood— not of the body age but mentally—you will see what dharma is and should be. It is the way of salvation and growth. And you can follow dharma without being austere and without suffering, but sincerity, honesty and humility are needed. Don't say, "I'm not egoless." Who is asking you to be egoless right away? If it happens right away, then every problem is over, but that is not the case. Egolessness comes at the end. So while following dharma, ego is still there; but if you maintain ego, you are in trouble. Just be honest, be sincere. Do practices. Ask your conscience or ask your Guru what you should do. But if you ask your Master, in whom you have faith, then follow it. Obey it. Don't tell him that he should admit to what you are saying. Then you are not being humble at all.

I am against blind following. Having faith out of your love and devotion is different than blind faith. Reflect upon the human nature: its bad and good side, its tension and peaceful nature, its comfort and discomfort, loss and gain, health and ill health, youth and old age, birth and death. There are so many things you have to reflect upon in life. And even if you get things in human nature that you like, you have to leave them behind when you die anyway, so it is very imperfect. Do you want that kind of nature to continue, only because you have comfortable habits to hide inside? Even if you are greedy for money, where will you keep your wealth when you die? And even if you are attached to dear ones, what will happen to them eventually? Either you will die or they will die. At one or the other time you have to give in, so what will you do then? How will you even use all your possessions? Are they secure enough to keep you secure for all times to come? Reflect upon these things. These are the imperfections, the raw material of human nature.

We often refer to others being worse than us, as if, therefore, "I am okay." If somebody else does wrong or bad, does referring to that make you good? It is just an escape. And then you want to be accepted as you are. I would say, "Yes, love thyself. No problem there, but which self? Your True Self or untrue, fictitious self?" No psychologist can reply to this question. Is your untrue self, your falsehood, your self-imposed self the one you are trying to love? And what will that give you, even if you do love that self? Learn to love your True Self, where you are real, where you are sincere and honest, transparently pure. Otherwise reflect upon the raw material of human nature and try to transcend. How? Through meditation, prayer and yoga. But even more important than that, it needs your sincere *will* to change, to transform. Even change is, to me, a very human, psychological word. Transformation is what I would love to see. God's love is all-inclusive. The Prophets know the totality and perfection of things, so they embrace them.

If you get this kind of reflection or dispassion to human nature, you will understand. This does not mean despising or condemning it; because when you despise or condemn something, you imbibe it. Why? Despising as well as blaming and condemnation make you related to that particular aspect. It joins you to it so that it enters into you. That is how we imbibe things around us. Even psychologically I have read that the things we fear will one day come into us. So any connection, including the negative such as condemnation, hatred, jealousy, competition and other such things, you will imbibe. Or put it another way: those negative traits must already be in you; therefore you are condemning them. We often see ourselves reflected in others.

I am talking about my experiences and my realizations. Take it or leave it, it is up to you. I'm uncompromising. Still I may love you and be compassionate, kind and forgiving. But I know what the Truth is. Therefore I am saying: be forgiving, let go. Be tolerant and not blaming, not coveting, not demanding, not unnecessarily unjustified or unreasonably demanding. Only claim what is yours. Underline this, please. I'm not saying don't claim anything and be a Lord Buddha. If you can, so much the best, but that is not your stage. You can accept the philosophy but you will not do that. Millions of years have passed away and where are we? Let's be straight: claim only what is yours. This is a very good compromise. Do not be desireless, but only desire the things that are basic for your survival.

You cannot give up your desires; I know that. Only one out of thousands or millions has done this. Is this pessimism? No, it is a factual thing. So how should we say? Let go of what is not yours. Don't covet and claim what is not yours. Allow others to have it. When you stand in the way of others, you are putting your own soul in jeopardy, turning blessings into curses. Please underline these things. When you come in the way of the fortunate luck of somebody else, you are turning your blessings into curses. I am not saying you should be totally zero in anything; I am just trying to tell you what dharma is and how to overcome human nature's imperfections and frailties.

We became human as an evolutionary process; this level we have achieved. Whatever the A, B or C grade in the exam may be—exams of the human nature, human life—now go to the next class. You can't remain in the fifth grade all the time. Even if you received only forty percent, fifty percent marks or a B or C grade, now move on. I'm not saying to be one hundred percent perfect in human nature and then to go further. You will not be able to do that. Unless you are a failure in human nature, then come and be reborn as a human—that's okay.

Then by the grace of your Lord and Master, if you are sensible enough to understand, he will make you grow beyond human nature. It's not growing out of human nature into some kind of wilderness. The next evolution is spiritual, Life Divine, lived for the Lord and your Master. Then grow to fulfill the vision.

You have to be a pure instrument. You cannot just demand and then weep and wail and scream and shatter. That does not pay anything. It is desperation only, as if not willing to change. When you are stubborn not to change, you find other outlets, but they do not help. You are then actually depressing and disturbing your own self and others. This is within your reach in human life, as you're living. You can choose any one of these ways to repay me. The third one is the way of karma yoga: following dharma. The second one is the way of wisdom but includes devotion too. The first one is the way of yoga. Take any one, two or three of these.

You think blessings are too far from you? Do not be proud of your accomplishments only. Those are talents worth praising but they do not necessarily speak of what you are. God sees what we are rather than what we do or say. What you and I say and do or accomplish may not be what we are, or it may be. As a matter of fact, I have difficulty to do or speak or express or write what I am not. If I have to do that sometimes, I feel not only guilty but also that this is not the life I want to live. If it doesn't express what I am, I can't live even. To me, accomplishments, words and deeds are necessarily not antagonistic to what I am. I can tell you what Vedantic Love is, but if you believe me and see it, I am demonstrating that. What else could Vedantic Love be? Where you are wise and loving. To me, that is salvation. My only pathos is that I want to give and many are not taking it, even after more than two decades. Some are very dear to me because they are in tune with me. Those who are out of tune with me, whatever they may do or whatever they may be expressing, it just does not matter to me. They are out of my rhythm. I cannot dance with them.

I am not asking you to repay in that totality, but since you asked, see what you can do. If none of these three you can do, then you are not repaying me at all. Then you are doing just for you, and that is not your salvation. At least start doing the third way. Otherwise you are just living selfishly and using your Master and God for what you need. It's a very terse statement probably but if I'm wrong, you can question again. I may not agree with you but do not be afraid to express yourself. If you cannot do the second best, then do the third. I did say three things. Below that I won't go—I'm sure about that. I can go up to C—A-B-C—but not D. D students are failures; they are not promoted to the next class. At least you can be honest and sincere. Is that too difficult? Just be honest and sincere and avoid being unreasonable. Or at least be humble and accepting of your faults and wrongs. Is that too difficult? The Lord will help you there. Just be humble enough to agree to your faults and not argue about them inside or thrust your demands. Is that too difficult? Can you be a little submissive and not blame others and take responsibility for yourself? If you cannot do any of these, then you are on the wrong path.

You want others to do what you want. Have you ever thought you should do what others want from you? The same old thing: judge not for ye shall be judged. Instead of thinking everybody else is wrong and you are right, why don't you think the other way around: you are wrong and others are right. In judging others, most people are right; in judging themselves, most people are wrong. Can you accept that? I've seen often that when people judge objectively, most of the time they are very analytical and correct. Can you change the formula a little? Apply that same objectivity to yourself and see what you are. This requires humility; then only can you see yourself. With arrogance, pride and defensiveness, you cannot see objectively. Your judgment will be very wrong. Others should follow what you want but nobody should impose on you. This is the way of perversion. And perversion, as I have been saying, is a hallmark of this Kali Yuga.

I'm not talking about oriental and occidental. These are universal virtues that we should imbibe. Whether you read the Bible or the Gita, they will tell you the same thing: "Judge not for ye shall be judged" . . . "Do unto others as you want them to do unto you." Are these new things we are hearing? This is dharma. Our conscience tells us this, but if we want to hear conscience, we have to have the prerequisite virtues of honesty and sincerity. Are we born with vice or virtue in such a way that we cannot change it? No. If there is a will to change, there is a way. Humility is the first prerequisite—leave aside faith in the Lord, surrender, optimal faith in the Guru, all of which certainly help. But you cannot have faith in the Guru and also be antagonistic to him. All the Prophets, all the religions and great scriptures will tell you the same thing with a little change in the words or locations.

You have to start where you are, not where others are. You cannot change yourself by criticizing and blaming others, and that is why we don't change. We are busy with criticizing others, overtly or covertly. It is difficult to change simply because we are busy criticizing and seeing how others are—isn't that true? Even if one half of that energy you employed in seeing yourself impartially, you would have changed long back. This is the transformation we want, actually. That is what I am for: total transformation from the human nature, which is quite raw. I would not say it is diabolic, but a part of it is. Because within the human arena, I do not think you can do much to solve the problems. You have to divinize it or at least rise to the next evolution.

You think we are deficient in giving you love? Love is inexhaustible, but if you go on taking advantage of love and compassion, then what? Then *Kalki** has to come—not Buddha or Jesus. Even if Buddha or Jesus were to come as they were, or more than that, I do not think they are going to succeed. Therefore we need Kalki. When you take advantage of love, compassion, forgiveness, on and on, year after year, year after year, and still do nonsense, what do you expect? Buddha and Jesus? You have to come to some senses. I'm sure the sages, the Enlightened Ones, the Prophets and Avatars will not stop loving and being compassionate, because they cannot do otherwise. But if even that has not produced any transformation or betterment in humanity,

---

* The advent of the Tenth Incarnation of Vishnu, *Kalki Avatar,* is predicted in the *Vishnu Purana* and other Vedic scriptures to be concurrent with our modern era. Kali Yuga means the "Age of Machines" or "Iron Age," the nadir of the Vedic cycle of Yugas. See the following chapter: "Kalki Avatar: Prophet of This Age."

then what remains? It will not be tit for tat or reaction. It will be another method entirely. And what is that method? Colossal destruction.

I hope we do not make the Prophets bitter against us, like *Maa Kali's* annihilation,* though Kali means good through transformation. Lord Shiva, as well, is the God of Transformation, not only of destruction. We may fear it but the scriptures are replete with those stories. That is how they forced Krishna to come out differently. He came down to a compromise of only five villages for the five princes, which, compared to the whole kingdom, was not even one percent. But ego is stubborn and hardheaded. What else could Krishna do? The Kauravas forced his hand to bring the war.† He did not want it. He was the God of Love and still is. Here in America, after five thousand years, you are asking about the rasa leela, which means what? You could have asked to be shown the battlefield, the war going on. Krishna is the God of Love. He most unwillingly undertook war because there was no choice left to save dharma.

My very principle, uncompromising, is that you cannot forgive those who do not ask for forgiveness. "Learn to forgive yourself first." I'm against this. Forgiving yourself is forgiving your ego and mind as dross. It will not pay you anything. Others we should forgive, but you cannot forgive anyone unless he or she is asking for forgiveness. One-sided, arbitrary forgiveness to anyone does not reach anywhere. It is a waste of forgiveness. He remains the same evil. What can you forgive? Those who sincerely ask for forgiveness, you should forgive. It has to have communication to receive forgiveness, and if you are not open to it, you can't receive it. Yes, if they are asking, *even an enemy you should forgive.* But if the person is egotistical, stubborn, not tumbling down from the pinnacle of arrogance, how will forgiveness reach there? If Krishna had forgiven the Kauravas, he

---

* *Maa Kali* is a form of Divine Mother Whose methods of transformation can, when necessary, be crude or terrible. Yet many saints and sages and Her near devotees describe their experience of Her as utter love and bliss.

† See footnote on the Mahabharata epic, page 8.

would have been an impotent God—not omnipotent! They not only did not ask for it, they challenged that if the Pandavas wanted even an inch of land, they had to come to the battlefield to win it. Krishna said, "Okay, let's have it"—at what cost: colossal destruction!

Did Krishna do it? No, evil did it. He tried all loving methods— compassion, forgiveness, kindness, tolerance, goodness, giving unconditionally. If it does not work, what are you asking for? You cannot give water to those who are not thirsty. To give anywhere else, whether they drink or not, is not my philosophy. You can only give to those who are ready to receive. This is actually another form of love: not to leave them to their mess and drudgery and ignorance; even through destruction to try to make them awakened. Krishna told Arjuna: "The soul doesn't die. Fire, disease or floods do not destroy your soul. The body is perishable and we will all die one day. Live for the dharma, Arjuna." Our attachments do not allow us to transform through demolition, but often that is what is needed. You tumble down a whole building with bombs inserted inside in order to reconstruct a new building. You cannot construct the new building without demolishing the old. Attachment does not allow us to do that. And we are attached to what? "That which is already perishable"— these are Krishna's words. Violence is not used at the outset or beginning. It is employed quite at the end to restore virtue and dharma and truth. That is how God does through natural disasters, actually. To us weak ones, attached ones, it sounds cruel, but only because we are weak. When Arjuna was being weak, Krishna told him: "You're an imbecile."

In this retreat I have given you a lot of things to work upon. See that you work well, with your sincere will. God is not too far; your Spirit, your Light is not too far. God is very near us, but unfortunately we keep resisting, turning away, putting away and fighting with Him. That is why I call this human nature raw material and dross. This nature has become circular, repetitive and habitual. Change that. Habit is bondage. Even George Washington's father took away the ax from him when he did not deserve it. I always believe the one who gives can take away. We fight for our rights and privileges when we lose them; we forget that He is the one who gave and He has every authority to take it away. We stubbornly claim and demand without being deserving. Therefore I said earlier: claim only what is yours. If it was one day yours and you lost it, then it is not yours.

I gave you what I want to say; now it is up to you to buy it. I will stand on my own truth. I am very well satisfied with my God. Nobody can convert me. And He is my anchor—and She, of course. I have given you frank replies that generally you do not find in books. Say anything you want. If you want to differ, I won't mind it. It will not change my truth. But how much you can do is up to you. I gave you three categories or stages. Choose any one. Beyond that, I do not promise any salvation. You can find your way and truth and life through your God, through your beliefs, which are equally true to me. So many religions are just so many paths and ways. I have nothing against them. Follow the truth any way you like. You can reach directly even, without methods or practices, which is no way, actually. When you accept that you are low or wrong, see that you humbly, truthfully and honestly see it and accept it, not as a reactionary expression. That will be repentance, surrender to the Lord. And one day you will be purified. When Divine Mother takes you in Her lap, everything is cleansed.

16

Kalki Avatar
Prophet of This Age

It is written in the Vedas that God has loved us so much that He takes the body forth, roughly every two thousand five hundred years, to take care of us. If He did not love us, He would not bother to come and save us.

*D*evotee: *I was wondering what the scriptures say about Kalki.*

Well, in a way, it's a good question. How much can I declare? Some of you might know a little history about Kalki, some of you may be unaware, so I will start with a brief introduction. According to the Vedic religion, which is now called Hinduism, there are ten Prophets or Incarnations, like Christianity has Jesus and Islam has Muhammad and Buddhism has Buddha. According to Vedic belief, God is One but appears in a Trinity or three Aspects as the Creator, Preserver or Maintainer, and Transformer. Lord Vishnu, the Maintainer, incarnates to take care of His children or human beings, His creatures. From time to time when dharma—law, justice, righteousness—and goodness decline below a minimum level, and when no other sages, holy people or yogis can help balance this decline, roughly every two thousand five hundred years, Lord Vishnu takes the body forth as a human. He comes with His special powers and bounties of prosperity, beauty, strength, wisdom, and the six wealths or treasures.

Lord Vishnu comes in each cycle of earth's evolution or human evolution. The Ten Incarnations cover approximately twenty-five thousand years. Among these Ten Avatars [*Das Avatar*] according to Vedic scriptures, nine have already come, the last being Buddha, roughly two thousand five hundred years ago. Others were Krishna, Rama, and so on. The same aspect of God as the Preserver or Avatar comes in every age. He may come as a peaceful, nonviolent Being or as a warrior to vanquish the evil, depending upon whatever humanity or the situation requires at that point in evolution. To Him, violence and nonviolence are not opposite things. He comes to uphold dharma and to uplift the consciousness of humanity.

In the cycle of evolution, Kalki is the last one among that galaxy. He is not, according to scriptures, coming as nonviolent. Not because he is violent but because the situation is such that nonviolence will not work in this age. Dharma is superior to violence or nonviolence. You may ask, "How can violence be over dharma?" We don't say violence is over dharma. That distinction does not exist there. At any cost, dharma has to prevail, justice has to be done, humanity has to be uplifted, and the Prophet knows best what methods are required. Otherwise we can ask why there are volcanic eruptions, earthquakes, forest fires and diseases. God has created all these things, including falling stars and comets, which, if they fall on earth, we are in trouble. "God did it! God is violent!" But that is a different topic. Let me just concentrate upon Kalki.

In Sanskrit, *kal* means "machine." Kalki literally means "of iron" or "of the machine." Kalki Avatar is the Prophet of the machine age. It implies not that he is a mechanical robot made of metal, but that his birth is in the age of machines. Kalki is supposed to come on a white horse, according to scriptural description, with sword in hand, though in this world swords don't work anymore—you have to have bombs and laser beams. There are, as usual, differences of opinions about his coming time. Some scholars and pundits say it is very nearby, by the end of the twentieth century or a little later, or that he has come already. Others say it may be centuries or thousands of years in the future. According to the scriptures, there are four ages: Golden, Silver, Copper and Iron, the current one being the Kali Yuga or Iron Age. And according to calculations based upon the scriptures, this is not even *peak* of the Kali Yuga, which means it is not yet in its full decline. So just imagine: if the peak of adharma, injustice, unrighteousness and untruth is much later, then what it would be— God knows!

However, I'm not declaring which is correct or not. For example, the Second Advent of Christ is predicted to be about now, or has come, or will be coming in the twenty-first century. If some theories are correct, Kalki is coming or has come or is coming soon. There are different interpretations of the scriptures. Some say he is already born and is a boy. Some say, no, he is already grown up and he will reveal himself as Kalki, just as Gautama Buddha worked as a sage and Guru; when the time came, he was accepted as Buddha. He wasn't known at birth as the Buddha.

So the time of Kalki's coming is open to interpretation, your faith apart, which certainly can make any stone an image of God. Somehow, especially in India at the moment, the following of Kalki—not only belief and faith in his coming—is like we have seen in the West about the Second Advent. It is very tangibly declared and said in such a way as if he is just coming through the clouds from heaven. But if, according to one theory, it will be hundreds or thousands of years yet for Kalki to come, what will the Kali Yuga become? I don't know. It will split everybody's hair, I think. However, I feel that coming events cast their shadows first. Why, in almost every nation and faith, whether Christian, Buddhist, Hindu or whatever, is there talk about the Second Advent, Incarnation or Prophet so commonly now? If it were to be hundreds or thousands of years from now, why would anybody bother consciously with it now? There must be some coming events that cast their shadows. So there is some truth that Kalki might come or will be coming or has already manifested.

Sometimes the manifestation is different than the body that is born. You have to understand this. For example, Christ would descend into Jesus, the Bodhisattva or Chenrezi would descend as Buddha, or Vishnu would descend as someone and would be called the Prophet, whichever way you take it. So in India, alone, there are thousands and thousands—I am surprised myself—who have started worshiping Kalki. They have created temples of Kalki that weren't there before. Through the scriptures it was known that Kalki would be coming as the Tenth Avatar, but nobody was waiting for him yet. Not many people were even thinking about him. But lately, since the last few years, thousands and thousands in India have initiated Kalki organizations and temples. They have already created, in a way, the forthcoming manifestation or birth of Kalki. Whether they prove correct or not, that's up to them, but at least they are not against the scriptures' declaration.

Buddha and Jesus are also expected at this time, so either the three are coming together, because the job is very serious—one person won't be able to do it—or the three are One, whatever name we give. But either way it will be terrible. We may imagine or believe that if Jesus Christ was to come as the Second Advent, he will be meek and humble and harmless. We may be right or wrong. He may come differently. According to some, they expect an Armageddon and— what is the word?

Devotee: *Rapture.*

Yes, according to those "rapturists" and "armageddonists"—I mean doomsday-sayers, not soothsayers—he is going to come as terrible. He will fight the Antichrist and his forces. So he is not going to be nonviolent. I don't know how the Buddhists are declaring, whether they think he is coming as the compassionate Buddha, *Avalokiteswara*. But somehow, whatever that manifestation may be, it is a great time of change. This we cannot dispute. It is a quantum leap.

Devotee: *What about his characteristics?*

According to Vedic literature there are six characteristics of any Prophet. I may not be able to enumerate all six but four or five, yes: great beauty, great prosperity and wealth, very wise, great strength, invincible, and he could be an occultist. He will be victorious, eventually, that's sure—leave aside some defeats in battles in between. Ultimately he will win the war.

The mission of each Prophet is the same: to uphold dharma, righteousness, justice, goodness; to save the virtuous, the sinners, or to demolish the evil people—either way. It depends on which role he plays. Do not think that if the Prophet incarnated like Buddha or Jesus, who forgave and suffered, it means he will come the same way next time. It is not sure. I could even say surely, he won't. Once is enough. If that had worked, then it would be repeated. Since it didn't work the way it should have worked—which is not their fault; we are duds—I don't think he will repeat the same compassion and mercy that we would expect. It looks cruel, it looks terrible, but that is the way it works, somehow. But I'll add one more thing at least: since Prophets *could* repeat the same drama in different details for the same purpose, this time, as we have been reading and hearing so much, what is needed is not only humanity's uplifting and establishment of dharma but also the evolution of earth itself into a higher dimension. For this reason, the Prophet's work is different.

Much work, therefore, is on the astral levels, because the next dimensions, the fourth and fifth, are subtle. Up to three dimensions we are on the gross level. Let me say one more thing: in Christianity we commonly hear and read, "God loves you," and that is true. Now let's take it from the Vedic point of view. It is written in the Vedas that God has loved us so much that He takes the body forth, roughly every two thousand five hundred years, to take care of us. If He did not love us, He would not bother to come and save us. The only difference between these two religious viewpoints is that in Hinduism they don't harp too much about God's love. This is not a criticism. I'm only saying that when you tell your Beloved or Lord too often, "I love you ... I love you ..." you lose the strength of love. It becomes commonplace. In Vedic literature they refer to this very sparingly, to keep the value and sacredness of God's love. Not only does God love us, God *is* love. What I mean by this, in relationship to the Prophets, is that they really love us, but they don't blow the trumpets all the time. The Avatars come ten times to save us. They demonstrate their love, not brag about it; otherwise the phenomenon is the same.

I am not disregarding the Second Advent or anything. Whether he will come as a Hindu, Christian or Buddhist—I'm sure, blindly, that he will be none of these! We may call him anything we want; that is up to us. The earth's evolution is also a part of this Advent, the ascent into the fourth or fifth dimension. Some believe it will be to the fifth directly but I don't know how humanity will jump from the third to the fifth. I doubt it. To the fourth, at least, we can believe, or even alternately: what you call a parallel reality.

Whether it is the Second Advent of Christ or Kalki Avatar or the Buddha's Second Advent, to me it makes no difference because these are God's Messengers or Prophets, Sons of God. Naturally, I have no controversy there. I wish I could give you more detailed things about Kalki. According to the scriptures he will be blazing Light. But so will be Jesus when he descends from heaven. And Buddha is already in *nirvana*, a Liberated One. They will be having halos of light around them. Roughly we translate this as auras but I think that is a misrepresentation. An aura everybody has, but not everyone has a halo. Halos are like a broader sun behind the head of the Divine Personality. Prophets are a perfect manifestation of the Divine, not potentially Divine, as everybody is. They are already so. There is a difference between normal human beings who are potentially Divine, who have Light potentially around them, and also an aura. The Prophets come already equipped with that Light, as if armored with that manifestation.

And it is a different matter when they manifest. In the Mahabharata epic, which we've seen on video*—not that everything is represented in these films, but there are clues here and there—up to a certain age even Krishna wasn't known as an Avatar or Prophet. Even Jesus wasn't, actually. Very few believed he was the Prophet in his lifetime. Buddha also was not known as the Prophet commonly, but more followers believed he was than Jesus had. At a certain point Krishna revealed himself or was revealed, and then he was accepted as an Avatar more commonly than either Jesus or Buddha.

The word Avatar comes from the Sanskrit *avatirna*, "descent from heaven." The Avatar is an Incarnation of God, not a reincarnation only. As we describe how the Ganga River descended on earth from the matted hair of Lord Shiva, that is avatirna: "heavenly descent." The word "prophet" has been used in the English language, but how this word came to be used for Jesus and other Biblical prophets, I

---

* Gurudeva is referring to a serial drama of the Mahabharata created for television in India, which He had shown to devotees at the ashrams in America.

don't know. A prophet normally refers to one who gives you prophecies, such as Nostradamus. In India, we use the term "Incarnation of God" or "Avatar."

Kalki will come and save the virtuous; there is no doubt about it. He may also demolish the evildoers—not every common evildoer but those who are real devils. The difficulty in today's warfare is that it is no longer one-to-one fighting, so that you go on vanquishing the evil ones. Bombs, terrorism and chemical warfare are such that, when they are thrown in a locality or city or part of the globe, you cannot be sure whether there are only bad people there. This is a difficulty that Kalki might feel, I don't know. So how will he destroy the evil and save the virtuous? Will he tell the virtuous to go on one side of the fencing and, please, all evil ones on the other side because he is going to bomb that side? Then everybody will jump on the virtuous side! He might feel this difficulty or he may know better. It reminds me of the story of Gomorrah and Sodom in the Bible, when Abraham heard from the three angels that God was going to demolish the city. Abraham had compassion and pity for the people, so he prayed to the Lord, because Abraham was a man of God. He begot a son when he was ninety-nine years old but I don't know how he did it!

So when the angels came and told Abraham God's message, he prayed, "Lord, but there are some good people there." He didn't talk about an Incarnation coming or uplifting the virtuous or dharma, but he told God, "You are going to destroy everybody because of some villains there?" Abraham asked, "What if there are fifty good people? Will You still destroy the city?" And God said, "If there are fifty good people, I won't destroy the city." This is how I am feeling that Kalki might feel difficulty. But then Abraham got more compassionate or weak or pitying and asked the Lord, "What if there are fifty minus five good people? Will You still destroy the city?" God said, "No, if there are forty-five good people, I won't." Abraham was a man of God, but it is a part of human nature that when someone relents or yields, you ask for more. So Abraham asked, "What if there are only forty good people?" And in this way it came down to thirty, then twenty.

At this point Abraham got a little self-conscious, thinking, "I have been asking concessions and troubling God too much." Then he said, "God, I have been really insolent to You and I have been taking too much advantage of Your leniency, but I have one last question." And God said, "What is it?" He said, "What if there are only ten good people?" God promised, "Then I won't destroy the city." Thank God Abraham didn't go further than that! But as it turned out, there were only four good people: Lot, his wife, and two daughters. Not only so but the others in the city were so wicked that when the three angels entered the city and were guests of Lot and his wife and daughters, the wicked people came right into their house to prey upon them. Lot's family got scared and then the angels, of course, saved them. They turned everybody blind in the city. Then the angels told Lot: "Abscond with your family from the city to where you will be safe and nobody will see you." After that the city was put to torch by God's hand.

It sounds wicked, cruel and merciless, but I will not go into these explanations now because then I, myself, would become a revolutionary. However, what I am trying to say is that modern warfare is different. It is no longer one-to-one fighting. It is laser beams, bombs and computerized warfare. So under those conditions, how would Kalki or the Second Advent of Christ or the Prophet distinguish between the good and the bad, the virtuous and the wicked? The angels did. Only four good people they warned; everyone else was wicked. If that is the case, and since Kalki is not supposedly nonviolent, people will come out wicked. I know that. There are a lot of wicked people on earth and they will come out more exposed, shamelessly wicked. As the time goes on, by the year 2000, you will see the exposure of wickedness and evil. You will perceive it very clearly. They will not be hiding anymore.

In Krishna's time there were so many good and dharmic people: Bhishma, Dronacharya, and many others, but when Krishna triggered the button, their evil side began to come out. Some were already evil, like Duryodhana. What I consider in this is that when the Prophet accelerates karmas, then whatever exposure is inside will come out, good and bad. Those who so far seemed meek, knowing-nothingers, may come out all of a sudden as very great, angelic people, because they will get a plank to come out angelically, which they suppressed before out of shyness or out of weakness. That is how, even in Krishna's days, he brought out the virtues suddenly in certain people who were not known before, and some known "great ones" came out evil. This is the triggering or acceleration of karmas by the Avatars. Krishna already knew each one and so will Kalki know everybody.

In Rama's life, his stepmother's maidservant seemed a good lady until she became evil. She had come with the queen from their ancestral kingdom and was devotedly serving her. But given time, place and opportunity, she came out wicked, whatever the triggering situation was. Therefore, according to Vedanta, we never take for granted that good is good and bad is bad. We never take for granted what one says, does or writes. We wait for the exposure and unfoldment to take place. The Prophets and Gurus know who is who, but they don't declare it, only because that is the way of leela, the divine play. They let it unfold by its own natural laws rather than declaring or condemning someone ahead of time.

In legal laws you want a proof. As long as there is no proof, you can't do anything. Even though you may be sure that someone is guilty of a wrong, you can't do anything unless you have evidence. The Prophets do exactly the same thing. So why don't they catch the evil ones' necks earlier? There is no proof. What will people say or think? You have to have some evidence. So the Avatar's coming, by itself, triggers the exposure, and all of a sudden evidence comes out, good and bad both, and very unknown figures could be forgiven and made angels while very known good people may be exposed as wicked. In every Incarnation this is a fact. Jesus' disciples were all good people— renunciates who had burned the bridges behind them. They threw the nets in the sea and followed Jesus, giving up everything. But how many of them proved to be real sincere and honest ones? Probably John. Matthew maybe. And the two Marys: Mary Magdalene and his Mother. Beyond these few, all others failed, in a way. Before that, they were all angelic apostles. Given time, place and opportunity—when the cock crowed three times, when thirty silver pieces were thrown—they were exposed.

He *knows*, only he doesn't expose or declare because you have to have evidence. An opportunity will trigger it. And those are the ones who are afraid of being exposed. So once they are exposed, they turn reviling, evil, vengeful, and so on. Before that, they will carry on very well—courteous, honest, everything. Once they are exposed, that's a test. They will turn inimical, revengeful and negative. You may ask, "If the Prophet or Guru knew what everyone was beforehand, why didn't he take precautions?" There was no evidence. Do you see the point? Many times we know that someone is a culprit, but we can't do anything about it. Now, whether Kalki will have a problem or not, I don't know, but I think he will have a problem.

One thing we know: he won't fight like Rama with a bow and arrow. He won't go on fisting everybody. That would be an easy way to distinguish between good and evil. Even machine guns don't distinguish; when you start a machine gun, you don't know who are standing. Now warfare has come to hydrogen bombs, atom bombs, chemical warfare, and so many other things. How will you distinguish good and bad? I really don't know. He may be laughing that I don't know anything. I'm just superimposing. He knows. God had the same problem. He gave a promise to Abraham. Fortunately God knew that there were only four good people and Abraham had stayed at ten. So God had no problem in destroying Sodom and Gomorrah, saving the four out of which one turned into a pillar of salt.

Do you know why God is doing all that, or the Prophets? Whatever they will do, we know that it won't be easy. If it was easy, they would have not taken the trouble to come, I'm sure about it. Things must be serious; otherwise why would they come? If the Jews and Romans at that time were an easy lot, I don't think Jesus would have come. John the Baptist would have been enough. But they were both difficult lots, Jews as well as Romans. So, let's see its conclusion: why would God do all this? You know the answer but you are trying to find out a new or different answer to make it more enjoyable. What do you think is the reason? One very simple word—whether you are a Hindu, Christian or a Buddhist: because He *loves* us. Out of love He will do all these horrible things? Yes, if that is the only way we leave open to Him. We force Him to do that when there is no choice left. The only choice is not to do anything. Would God allow adharma to triumph over dharma? That would be the end of the creation. It is always out of love that He does.

That is why we say that when you do practices, you have to come to a level of feelings. You have to come to love which responds to God's love, and then there is salvation. God has told us thousands of times through sages, Incarnations and scriptures, that if we had gone the straight, simple, loving, innocent way, this would not take place— the destruction and horrible things. If He does nothing and leaves us alone, is that the sign of love? That will be negligence and ignoring us. So He comes out "hard-handed." We call it hard-handed, but this is just another side of His love. And that's what He asks us to do. God is not your slave or tied-up goat or sheep in your courtyard that, because you concentrate on Him, He will just appear. Try it; it won't happen. It is not a mechanical method. Try feelings, the astral love. That is the language He responds to, not what you tell Him to do or pray for Him to give you. "Shouldn't we pray then?" I am not saying that. I am saying to replace it by loving God. If you love God, you don't need to pray. This is nothing against prayer. If you don't know how to love Him, you pray. That is the only language that binds or unites us with God. The love makes *yoga*—union.

Even in our life on earth, we have seen that animals, trees and plants all respond to the vibrations of love. Plants grow better if you lovingly tend them. Animals respond better if you have love and harmlessness in your heart. So does God respond. It's a yoga method. And if we are loving God, we will not invite destruction. This is not a threat; I'm simply saying that if He wouldn't be serious with us, we will be more in hell as neglected, ignored or demolished. Without dharma, nothing establishes or stabilizes either. So when you come to this pure love—

not attachments, please, those are sins, anti-God—you will easily see why, even in social, national, family or ashram life, everyone is hankering after love. Because that is the only *tangible* thing.

Try to practice love for thirty years or fifty years without feelings; it will go *nowhere*. "Oh, I have done everything for you. Why are there no results?" I said, "No, you did for *you*, not for me." It is like bullocks with blinders that go round and round all day squeezing the oil out of the seeds. In the evening when they stop, they are at the same spot where they started. No progress. You have to serve the Lord with pure love. If your love and devotion are missing or if you are serving the Lord in competition with someone else, that is not acceptable. Are you doing with pure love and devotion? If yes, that will draw you near Him. Do you have genuine love and devotion or have you lost it? Have you slipped down and are now depending upon your self-made practices? I know this is ruthless; I did say in this retreat that I will do rolfings—take it or leave it. You think you can boast about your doings and qualifications and God will be timid, cowed down, and accept what you want? You have to love the Lord with a very pure heart, not in competition or jealousy with somebody else or in prejudice against other cultures and religions. You cannot get near heaven if you are doing anything in competition with other religions and cultures. God won't accept it. Your history of twenty or thirty or even a hundred years of serving the Lord doesn't make you qualified at all.

Your love has to unite with God's love. That is actually what we all *want*, whether we express it or not. Isn't that what we are hungry after? Leave aside aspirations for Brahman and Vedanta and Absolute Realization. Tell me what is more tangible and more satisfying to any soul than love? What is greater than that? If that love is pure, then you are serving Him. If you are trying to serve the Lord to impress upon Him, you are doomed. He doesn't take action until there is evidence, that's all. Up to that point you are safe. Only saying, "God, I want to be near You," doesn't make you qualified to be near. You want to be near, okay, so grow into those prerequisites and qualifications. Lucifer could slip from heaven and still demand from

God, "I was in Your ministry and so near to You. I have every right to be near to You." But God might say, "Lucifer, you have fallen. You have gone astray. You have lost the way. You have become egotistical and ignorant. You have become competitive and selfish and ambitious. Don't you see your fall? Only because you *were* near, therefore you think you are qualified to be near now?" Where is the *love* of Lucifer for God? It is not a matter of rights.

God knows whether you love Him or not. It is your pure heart that loves the Lord, not as a human. As humans among humans, we do need love. We are hungry after it, and that is the only language we actually understand. God understands that language of love when it unites with purity of heart. So I consider that, failing this, there is another way: His coming out on a white horse with a sword and throwing what you call "fire and brimstones." What else can He do? We are afraid to heed these things but we leave God no choice. The only choice is to do nothing about us, and which God would do that? We never understand that ego has become stubborn, demanding, willful, asserting: "What about me?" Selfishness is rampant. Even if we repent and say, "I am evil, God," He sees with which feelings you are talking. Are you genuinely expressing this or simply condemning something without really realizing its implications? He sees through our hearts.

So I consider God's coming as a destructive Prophet or Avatar is also a blessing in disguise, a mercy. It may look harsh, but when parents spank their children or people in society beat each other, we take it easy as a part of human nature. Why then God wouldn't do that, if it is the demand or *need* of the hour? We have difficulty in loving very purely and unconditionally. We feel it is below our dignity, our constricted ego. "Oh, boy! How can I be so humble, a nonentity? By loving the Lord unconditionally, then I am nothing. I have to be something." This struggle goes on. It is a blessing in disguise if Kalki comes. I will be happy, whatever he does. That's not my business to even calculate. Maybe those who pray for Kalki to come, some among them will be evil ones too. "Oh, God, I'm your devotee since the last fifty years. I have created a temple to You in my own bedroom and also elsewhere." But He will see the deeds and heart—mainly the heart. Deeds or misdeeds can be forgiven, but not an impure heart.

Vices such as anger, lust, attachment and greed can be forgiven because they do not separate us from the Lord, but ego does. Ego separation is the greatest and only sin. The egotistical demanding person doesn't get what he or she demands. They are blinded. Humility softens us and purifies us to get out of these stubborn ruts. Humility is a very indispensable ingredient to get to the chamber of love. The proud, willful, arrogant, angry, ambitious, competitive, jealous and false cannot love the Lord even though they profess to. True humility—not just blurting some humble words—purifies the heart: "The meek shall inherit the earth." That is why some who seem good people turn out to be betrayers and revengeful after being exposed. Why? They were not truly humble.

People say, "Oh, they were so good! Oh boy, what happened?" Nothing happened. They were not yet exposed, that's all. It couldn't be any other way. They didn't love the Lord, the Master; they loved themselves. Isn't it a common philosophy, these "adventures in selfishness," which even now persist? Today they are trying to teach people to love your own self: "Unless you love yourself, you can't love others." This is quite a reversal. If they said, "Love your True Self," I can understand it, but they mean, "love yourself"—meaning ego and mind. "Learn to love your ego and mind; therefore you will learn to love others." This is a travesty of the Kali Yuga. They are trying to boost ego this way, and these are supposedly good people.

I say: if they were truly good, they would not be exposed this way. Expose the fire; it will be fire. Expose the water; it will be water. Expose the flower; it is a flower. Expose the thorns; they are thorns. "Oh, he was a flower but turned out to be a thorn!" The flower is outside, the thorn inside. If they had flowers inside, they wouldn't expose thorns outwardly. There is a common saying in the Vedas: "If you eat onion, you are going to belch onion, nothing else." Whether anyone may profess, "It's an apple," what he belches proves whether it is an apple or onion. Exposure proves it. If someone has goodness inside, he or she would expose goodness. True love of God or true love of ego will be exposed.

Love is the only language in which we can unite with the Lord. That is the meaning of unconditional love. Every other love is conditioned and therefore selfish, possessive, belonging to, attached out of insecurity or weakness. Kalki will help us or the Second Advent of Jesus will help us. That is what they come for. That is their work. You think they will come here to open factories and industries or trade unions? Do they come here to amass wealth and take it to heaven? They come and they do their job. Allow them to do that. Stand by them. Those who stand by them are the devotees. Krishna openly said: "I have come to save my devotees." It was not a political party kind of partiality. He wanted to save the virtuous.

If you want Kalki's manifestation or birth, if you want to be his instrument, you have to be pure-hearted. Not because then he will save you from Sodom and Gomorrah. If that is your inner motivation, he won't. You have to love the Lord with a genuine pure heart. Shankaracharya, who wrote famous Vedantic treatises and commentaries, lived in the sixteenth century in India. In his own company of five disciples, four were scholars and the fifth one was a servant who served his Guruji by washing his clothes, cooking his food, fetching wood from the forest, et cetera. This disciple wasn't a scholar and didn't know the scriptures. He didn't have any talents. And the other four learned disciples believed he was a dud. When Shankaracharya would give sermons or teach the scriptures in the afternoon, this guy would stand near the back door listening, humbly. He used to hang the clothes outside and sweep when the Guruji left his room. He never sat in the class or listened in a systematic way, but at times he would stand and listen if he had time. He didn't know Sanskrit even. Everyone thought he just did menial jobs—laundry, cooking and rubbing the feet of the Lord—but he was a very pure-hearted man.

Then one day the Guruji tested them. They test in their own way, not as you tell them or want them to test. Shankaracharya knew that the other four looked down on that fifth one, and the story goes that he wanted to teach the other disciples a lesson. He created a situation or a situation arose in which there was a certain question that none of the four, who were each geniuses, could solve. Shankaracharya waited until no one could give a real reply, then he looked at that fifth one standing near the door and said, "So-and-so, can you answer this question?" Before he could answer even, the other four began to laugh tauntingly. They thought, "When we couldn't even answer, how will this dud answer such an abstruse question?" However, Shankaracharya patiently waited. He asked the disciple again, "Do you have any answer to this question?"

The disciple could have said, "I don't know anything," or he could have arrogantly replied something. Instead he gave a famous reply, "I really don't know, but since you are asking me, I will try to reply." And the four got quiet. Their ears got big like deer. And then he replied—whatever it was—and all four looked at him dumbfounded. The answer was right. He had never even sat down to read the scriptures with them! Those four got ashamed, of course, and humiliated that this so-called "dud" could reply when they could not. The difference was that they were arrogant and egotistical about their learning. The fifth disciple was humble, not only because he was a servant; the secret was more than that. These four later asked their Guruji, humbly, "How could he answer this question? He didn't study like us or anything." Shankaracharya gave a famous reply, "It is not learning of books that makes one wise. By serving me, he is so humble and loving that his whole mind and ego have become united with me so that wisdom just flows through him. Your ego, arrogance, learning and books cannot reply to these things." The major part of making you wise is ego demolishing or humiliating or humbling. It is one thing to learn academics; it is another to be wise.

God sees genuine love, where ego is not involved. If you have that, Kalki is with you; otherwise not. Distinguish between real good and so-called good. Who would have thought Judas would be a betrayer? Who could have known Peter would lie about having known Jesus. Saint Francis' own disciples disregarded him and, as if, exiled him— and they were Franciscans. Who could have imagined that? You think, therefore, Kalki has no sense to distinguish? Many surprises will follow. You will see. What you thought was okay, you will be alarmed, because you never thought about it. How wise are you anyway? He waits for your exposure. As a matter of fact, exposure is a blessing, but we don't take it that way, unfortunately. We think it is quite a slur on our respect and prestige. We don't admit it when we are angry and revengeful because of being exposed. Why? Because we know it is bad; it is not showing a good side. Expose the good side—our whole blood flushes in the face. Expose the evil side—we don't want God to even touch that subject; we want Him to hide it. But if we love God truly, would we care for exposure? We wouldn't, because that exposure is in order to be cleansed and purified.

It is like a wound or sickness to be healed by a doctor. Hiding the disease from the doctor will not help. "Oh, God exposed my tumor." How will you cure it otherwise? Those who are humble would be grateful for exposure. You see my point? And those who are egotistical will turn hostile, angry, jealous and revengeful. Humility will make you grateful and humbled down. You may not like your exposure but you will accept it with humility, and then He will clear it or clean it. This is the language of the love. It doesn't sound that way but it is. The doctor means good when he does a surgery and cuts that thing out, even if very painful. He puts a balm on that again to heal it. God does the same. Gurus do the same. They may seem hurting at times, but then they put a balm on that, nicely healing it—if you allow them, humbly.

If you love Him, won't you be humble? Definitely. I already said in this retreat that I will be not ruthless but I will be more frank. Even when Jesus spoke at the table, exposing his own disciples, they asked him, "Am I that one, Lord?" They were all shuddering and fearing what Jesus might say. He was exposing them, right? Some denied him; some betrayed him; some left him. Actually Christ, I would say, only scratched the surface. Had he done more than that, he would have had only John and Matthew and the two Marys.

There is a humorous story commonly told in India. A Guruji was giving Satsang to a large gathering and, one by one, everyone left.

Only one remained when he had finished speaking, so the Guru thought, "He is the only genuine, sincere disciple hearing me still." The Guru told him, "Well, you really approved my test. Among all the multitudes, you are the only one." The remaining one said, "No, Sir. I am just waiting for you to get up so I can roll up this carpet." In India they don't have wall-to-wall, fixed carpet, so this man was just waiting there to do his job. Not many remain behind, and this is why the Prophets do not go deeper. But those who are loving and humble in the true sense will stand by him. This we are waiting for: those who will stand by Kalki. It will not be two or ten; it will be multitudes, or at least many. He can't do it alone. It is a colossal destruction.

When it comes to that, Krishna told Arjuna: "They may be your cousins and uncles and teachers, but they are on adharma and wickedness. Kill them." If he were to say all this from the beginning, nobody is going to like it. So the exposure is needed. We can profess ourselves as good, but when put against the wall and really squeezed, then our true nature comes out. The greatest consolation and salvation and easiest way to go to the Lord is with a pure heart. Then you are forgiven, totally. Even Jesus said to the woman, "Okay, you repented and now you are cleansed. Go and sin no more." Simple. What philosophy and practices are involved? Unite in yoga with your Lord with pure love and pure heart and you are saved. Kalki will stand by these souls.

There will be many surprises. Though we stand quiet, when the time comes, we will see. That is why I have often referred to a cartoon I saw many years ago in which God is asking for a volunteer to be the next Messiah. Nobody wants to come back to earth! It's kind of nailing somebody alive on the cross. It is not easy to take. If he was in a coma or under anesthesia and then they had killed him, probably that would have been easier, a mercy death. Nailing a live person on the cross—it's not easy to bear. And probably humanity is still paying the price. Afterwards we may repent and erect temples on their heads—that's different. That's another ego worship. But at that time, what did we do? After evil is done and destroying and reviling and revenge, then what can you do? There is an Indian proverb: "After the cow has been sucked by the calf, what is the use of milking it?"

So sometimes they come with forgiveness, compassion, kindness and letting go, but other times they come with full fury and do their job. Are these pent-up feelings? No. That's the only method we leave to them. They come with full fury because they have that power. They won't come with a little anger or rebuking. They have to cleanse the mess and they do this perfectly. They use nonviolence *perfectly* when they come as nonviolent; and when they come violently, they are *perfectly* violent. They won't come half-heartedly. That is the work of the Prophets. We cannot question them. We don't leave them any other way.

Before that our ego might have done any mess and got away with it, thinking, "God is not doing anything so I can do what I want." But He is listening. He is seeing. He is aware of everything. And at the right time He acts. So much so that Christians call him the Son of God. Certainly there is intimacy between him and God. They come full with *Durga-shakti*,* not as a revengeful actor. And I suppose that is the way we want Him. The best way of all, the easiest, most humbling and relaxing way is just to love Him with a pure heart. This is the secret that will solve *everything*. No problem will remain as long as you have a pure and truthful heart.

Devotee: *Master, is that pure will that you spoke of this afternoon related to pure love?*

These are two different words but they are the same thing. When you are using your will a hundred percent, why would you do that if you didn't love Him? Or vice versa: if you didn't love Him fully, why would you will a hundred percent for Him? If you are willing fully, it must be your love for Him. If you love me a hundred percent, wouldn't you do anything for me?

Devotee: *Yes.*

---

* *Durga-shakti*: power or energy of Durga (a warrior aspect of Divine Mother).

Naturally. And if you were to do everything for me, would you not do that because you love me?

Devotee: *Yes.*

It is the same thing. What do you say?

Devotee: *i think that if i am united with my Master, i don't have to worry about Kalki anymore.*

That is a good reply. You are blessed. Have faith. He will take care of your salvation. Don't worry about it. He knows it. And He loves you too. There is nothing greater than love, at least on this earth. If you have a pure heart—that's very important. *Love thy God with all thy heart, mind and might.* It means one hundred percent, right? Those are the ones we worship and look to for guidance. Lesser love would make us selfish. Love is not gratifying; it is satisfying. And that is what we are searching. Allow God to "interfere" with you—so-called interfere.

Once you love the Lord with a pure heart, you can tie up these other things: live for God's sake; eat for God's sake; look after family for God's sake; earn money for God's sake; write a book for God's sake; be charitable for God's sake; learn talents for God's sake; sing for God's sake. And what satisfaction it gives! All your problems, all your worries, anxieties and fears evaporate if you love Him with a pure heart. If you fear Him, your love is deficient. God doesn't like you to fear Him. He knows your love is deficient, and *therefore* you are afraid. So if you really, one hundred percent love Him with a pure heart, you will be free from all anxiety, fear, doubt, problems and worries. It will give you transcendence right there. You will be free of all infirmities. Then there is nothing to remove. Anger, anxiety, worrying, problematic thinking and tensions will not come to you. Pure-hearted love evaporates all this. It is instant. Instead of focusing on your deficiencies, love the Lord. He will cure all your deficiencies.

17

Devotees' Remembrances from Bharat (India)

The sole aim is how to really walk with Him as He walks with us, how to hold His hand as He is already holding ours, how to see Him as He sees us, how to make our life Divine and Conscious in such a way that the whole panorama, which was in darkness, could now be bright.

Most of the remembrances in this chapter were translated from Sindhi or Hindi, a few were given in English. They have been rendered into first person to make them as close to the original sharing as possible. To respect the devotees' privacy, names have been deleted throughout.

*M*y sister S---- went to Ajmer in Rajasthan at the time of the partition of India, right after her marriage. Her in-laws migrated from our birthplace by train to Ajmer. The rest of our family came to Bombay. When Swamiji came to India, He was in Bombay for some time and then He went to Ajmer. There He told this sister's husband, "The real thing is I don't want to get married and I want to go on a spiritual path."* So, the first information that Swamiji didn't want to marry or didn't want worldly things was given to my sister's husband, who informed my elder brother. Then my brother got wild . . .

Swamiji had gone to Ajmer in the middle of the college term. He left everything in Bombay and went there. He said, "I want to meet S----," but in mind He wanted to tell them He wanted to leave. He didn't want to create a mess here. Mother was in Bombay and wouldn't have allowed Him to leave home, so He went to Ajmer instead. Our eldest sister, P------, was also living in Ajmer at that time and He was very near to her, so He told her everything that He wouldn't tell Mother. So from Ajmer He left the family, so to say.

---

* According to Indian tradition, the family was planning a marriage for Him despite His objections.

In Ajmer He was staying at our eldest sister's house. He directed
and acted in a drama in Ajmer, the last stage drama He did. When
that was finished, one day He told our eldest sister, "I'm leaving
today. Could you call [the younger sister] here?" When that sister's
mother-in-law didn't allow her to meet Him—she said, "No,
nothing doing!"—He went to meet her at her home and told her,
"I'm leaving today." She came to know only at that time. She was
crying the whole time He was there. He had no money in the
pocket, only one shawl and, being winter, there was severe cold in
North India. She was crying and telling Him to take everything,
anything, but He wouldn't take anything except this shawl that she
had, a maroon shawl from our eldest sister. He wouldn't take
anything else, no money. He had a little bit: about five rupees and
one book, *Gitanjali* by Tagore, a shawl and a small cloth bag with
one dress in that, a kurta and pyjama. He told the younger sister,
"I don't know even where I'm going, so how can you accompany
me or follow me?" He did not know whether He was going by
train or a bus or anything.

For twelve years nobody heard from Him at all. He just went
away walking, wearing *chappals*.* That was the last time they saw
Him. My mother was there also in Ajmer before He left, but before
His departure day she had gone back to Bombay. He had told her,
"I'm not going, don't worry . . ." so she came back to us because
we children were at home; we were teenagers then. He had gone to
Ajmer along with our Mother. He was very much disturbed and
she could see that He was disturbed, so she went with Him to
Ajmer by train. She was there about three months and then He
promised her that after finishing the drama, He would come to
Bombay, so she could go. This was the last time we heard from
Him until He came back twelve years later.

> *—Related by Gurudeva's younger sister and youngest brother*

∞

---

* *Chappals:* simple rubber thongs.

When i* was small, i was going to Swamiji. i put one day a garland (*har*) on His neck. Then Swamiji took me on the lap. i was very small, with my mother, father and sister.

And what did He tell you?

i don't know. i was small.

How old are you now?

Eight years old. i like to come here and i like to see Swamiji. i remember Swamiji when i do my studies. i'm closing my eyes and sitting, then i see Swamiji that He has come in my house.

   i like Swamiji's Satsang. i can understand His Satsang. i go in Swamiji's *kutiya*† and talk with Him. i like Swamiji. Swamiji gives me prizes when He comes from outside. When i'm closing [my eyes], i'm thinking of Swamiji, then Swamiji's coming in my [house].

Now also?

He smiles and He talks to me. i sit with Swamiji, whenever Swamiji is free.

Does He put you on His lap still?

Yes.

How does He appear to you?

He wears white clothes. He has long hair.

∞

When my son K---- was two and a half years old‡ our family went with Swamiji on a boat trip and we took sandwiches. We used to

---

* This young devotee's sharing was spoken in English to the editor. For an explanation of the grammatical style of this chapter and Chapter Eighteen, see "Notes on the Editing" (page xvii) at the beginning of this book.

† *Kutiya*: a small house or hut.

‡ This occurred around 1968.

generally take these when we went on the way with Swamiji, but He never really ate anything. So we were sitting in the launch and halfway Swamiji asked me to give Him a sandwich. i was thinking, "Swamiji doesn't eat after breakfast or between meals. He has had His breakfast and He never usually asks for anything that i bring along. How come this time He is asking?"

While i was thinking this, Swamiji again asked, "So-and-so, give me a sandwich." So i gave Him a sandwich and He ate one bite and then threw it into the sea. And at that very moment, a white snake came up and caught the sandwich and then went back inside. i saw all this. The snake came up and opened his mouth and Swamiji gave the sandwich. So this time when Swamiji came,* i told Him, "We are going with [a devotee] to her home on an island." And He asked me, "Have you gone there before?" i said, "Swamiji, yes, with You, and that white snake came and You threw him the sandwich." He was smiling and said, "After so many years, you remember that?" And i said, "Yes." i tell my family that it may have been the ocean or *Shesha*† coming up to take His blessings.

∞

First when we came to Swamiji, we were very poor, because of money and my husband had some drinking problems. We would not have much to eat. So many problems we had; Swamiji has solved them. When we started coming, we couldn't say what was inside our minds and hearts, but every problem He solved, one by one. My husband also started drinking less; now he's not drinking. And the family got more comfortable financially, also. Now we are well settled. Swamiji had said: "Slowly it would be solved, don't worry."

∞

---

* In 2000.

† *Shesha* is the giant cobra on which God as Narayan or Vishnu reclines in perfect balance according to Vedic tradition.

i met with a few Gurujis but i could not get the answer to my questions. i wanted to leave all of the world and surrender to a Guruji, but i could not get the answer inside me that was right. And when i met with Swamiji, i got all the answers. i thought then that i will get *Naam** from Swamiji only.

∞

When i came to Swamiji, i was not well. i was having some physical problem and my husband also was not well. That is why i was very worried. When i came here i was walking slowly, because i was not well. Swamiji said one day, "Why are you coming so slowly? Come fast, no?" That is why today also i am coming fast, because of the blessings of Swamiji. My husband was not well. When i came with my husband, Swamiji blessed him and put His hand on his head. Then he was all right. The doctor had said that my leg would have to be cut off. Then Swamiji told me, "Oh, don't worry. It will be okay." He suggested some doctor and i went and it was all right. Swamiji has cared for us a lot. Every problem He has solved.

∞

In the image of Shiva i saw Swamiji. Inside i was saying, "If You are my Guru, i should have Darshan." Then i saw Swamiji as Shiva. This was towards the beginning, in 1977. i first came in 1975. i was thinking, "He will be my Guru only if i get His Darshan." Then He appeared to me as Shiva. And i was sorry [to have asked in this way] and obliged to Swamiji. In a dream also i saw Swamiji in *Shiva Rupa.*†

∞

The doctor had said that i was having a cancer problem and that i would not live. Two or three doctors said the same thing: that i

---

* *Naam,* lit: "Name of God," referring to mantra initiation. In the Guru-disciple tradition, receiving Naam is a form of initiation.

† *Shiva Rupa,* lit: "Shiva's Form" or "Shiva's Image."

was having cancer inside and wanted to cut it off inside. Then one
day it was decided i should be operated on to remove the cancer.
It was breast cancer. When Swamiji knew that i was having this
problem, He sent one doctor inside the hospital operating room
and said to that doctor, "Don't move from that operating room
when she is being operated on." Then at the operation time, every
doctor was finding that i was not having cancer. Then i believed
that Swamiji only had removed that cancer.

∞

When Swamiji came [to Jyoti Ashram] from Jammu,* i had His
Darshan. This was thirty-two years back. When Swamiji came and
sat, i was crying so much. He asked when i had come and why i
was crying. He said: "I have come here and you are crying. When
somebody goes, then everyone is crying, no? And this situation is
the opposite: I came and you're crying." i kept quiet and Swamiji
said, "I want to ask you a question: when God comes in front of
you, what will you wish? What will you say that you want?" Then i
said, "Sorrows, sadness—only sorrows." Then Swamiji asked,
"Sorrows? Why sorrows? In Kali Yuga, how are you saying you
want sorrows? In the Mahabharata, when Krishna asked Kunti,
'What do you want?' Kunti said: 'Only sorrows.' But in the Kali
Yuga, nobody says, 'I want sorrows.' Everybody is wishing: 'I want
this, I want that.' How did you say like that?"

Swamiji asked, "What do you want?" Swamiji meant inside, but
in front of you, God will give what you wish. Swamiji said to think
what i want and He will give it to me. And i said sorrows. Swamiji
said: "That means, in the Kali Yuga, nobody has any shakti that
they can solve sorrows and problems." i said, "i am asking You for
sorrows because in sorrow only can we take the Name of God. In
enjoyment and all that, we are forgetting God." Then Swamiji
smiled. At that time He was very sad because of what i had asked,
and in between also. Whenever He used to come here, He'd tell [a

* Jammu is part of Jammu and Kashmir state in northern India.

devotee]: "She has got sorrows because she has said 'i want sorrows.' She has wished; she has got." Now i am tired of sorrows and not having so much. i think later He will bless me.

∞

My second son was getting engaged in Nanda. My family members were going in a *Sumo** for the engagement. On a road we met with an accident. Then i saw Swamiji in front of that Sumo, standing like a statue. Everyone was very afraid and i was saying to them, "Don't worry. Nothing will happen because Swamiji is there." Then what happened was: that Sumo got dragged but my family members got no injuries. When i returned to the ashram, i told Swamiji what had happened. "i saw you, that You are blessing us and all You have taken care, whatever was to happen." Then He only smiled.

∞

When my *masi* [maternal aunt]was very ill in 1964, she asked me to bring Swamiji's youngest photo. She took the photo in her hand and told me to bring a glass of water. i went and came and she had just kept the photo on her chest. She passed away. i was very small at that time, twelve or thirteen years old. It happened within one minute. Then she left. She was with Guruji.

∞

My mother-in-law had Darshan of Swamiji. She was sitting there and i was sitting with her husband. And then she told me that she was seeing Swamiji's Darshan—"See, see, Swamiji . . ." [indicating as if looking out a window]. Swamiji had changed *Rupa.*‡ She was seeing His other form. She has had many Darshans, now also. She is very lucky.

---

* *Sumo:* a large four-wheel-drive vehicle made in India that holds eight to ten passengers.

† *Rupa:* "Divine Form" or "Divine Image."

My father-in-law got hurt. He hurt his hand. Swamiji knew that he was going to get hurt. He got twenty-one stitches, i think. He might have lost the hand. Big karma was going to happen. Guruji cut it short. He reduced that karma. He had told my father-in-law, when he had brought roses, to be careful of those thorns; otherwise you'll be cut. And the next day this happened.

∞

One day Swamiji asked me, "K-----, say what you want to say." i was quiet. Then i said: "Give me this photograph* so that it will be with me. Nobody can touch it." Then He said, "No, I'm inside. This is outside. That photograph, if I give you, everyone will ask for a copy of it. Know that I am *here* only, in your heart."

∞

My mother came to the ashram alone and was sitting with Swamiji when one man came. Swamiji asked him, "How are you? How is your health? How is your family? Is everything okay or not?" He was a very poor fellow, selling writing pens. Swamiji asked him various questions and was giving him answers. Then He said to that fellow, regarding my mother: "She's my disciple, so-and-so . . ." and introduced both of them. That fellow was telling Swamiji that he was selling pens to support his family. Then Swamiji said, "You're having pens. Show me your pens." That man then showed pens and one pen Guruji picked up and said, "What is the price of this pen?" That fellow said, "I think thirteen rupees." And Swamiji said, "Should I take this?" The man said, "Yes, keep the pen." Then Mama was thinking inside, "He's a very poor fellow and why is Swamiji taking a pen from him?" She was thinking, "He's so poor and it's not good," but she didn't want to question Swamiji. He had told my mother that He had a silver pen with which He was writing letters to everyone. And afterwards,

---

* She is referring to a photograph of Gurudeva that appears as the frontispiece of the cloth edition of this book.

within two days, my mother came again to see Swamiji and He told her that that fellow from whom He had got that pen had died in an accident. Swamiji told her that He owed thirteen rupees to that fellow and that karma He wanted to reduce of that man. That is why He had asked him to give Him a pen. Then my mother was very sorry about what she had thought. She understood that Swamiji knew that after two days that man was going to die and He wanted to take some of his karmas.

∞

Thirty years ago i was going to Ganesha's temple and crying, "Nobody is mine, nobody is mine . . ." And then i met a devotee whose mother-in-law used to come here. This devotee brought me here and i met with Swamiji. Inside i thought, "If you are really God, then you will automatically say that i am your disciple. i am not going to say it." Then He said to me: "You are my disciple," and He gave Naam to me. And how it happened is: one day Swamiji gave a message to a devotee that i could come on Friday and He will give a mantra to me. My sister-in-law was pregnant at that time and we live in a joint family. Then on Thursday night, my sister-in-law was feeling labor pains. So i was worrying "How will i go? That means You are calling me and this is happening. How will i come?" Then in the morning the pains were not there. In the afternoon we saw that she was okay, so i could leave home and come to the ashram. i felt saved by Swamiji. After i returned home from the ashram, her labor pains started again. i knew it was because of the grace of Swamiji that she stopped for so much time, and i started to have more faith in Him.

∞

Last time He was here,* Swamiji asked me, "You're not purchasing a car?"† i just listened to Swamiji. He said, "Then your son will

---

* This was in the spring of 2000.

† In India, purchasing a car (except for wealthy families) is generally a major event.

bring you here in car." i did not tell this to anyone at home or anywhere. Then two or three days back,* my son said: "Now it's time to have one car also, no?" i told him what Swamiji had said, that we should purchase one car.

∞

My father died and for eight years i was not able to remove those feelings of grief. Every now and then i was thinking of my father only. Then when i met with Swamiji and He gave me mantra initiation, i forgot about my father. My father used to ask me, "So-and-so, how are you?" whenever he met me. After meeting Swamiji, whenever i would see Him, He used to ask, "K-----, how are you?" the very same way as my father had done.

∞

i asked of Swamiji, "How will we get in joy, like Krishna? How will we get Darshan and then leave the world, and only God and we? When will be that day when we will leave the whole world, inside, not outside?" Then Swamiji told me that when we make rice, in boiling water we are putting rice, and after some time the water is absorbed. He said our karmas are also like that, in boiling water: "When they will be finished, then you will be ready."

∞

This was way back. i was in Fifth Standard or Sixth Standard, or grade, as you call it. i was in an all-girls' school and the teachers took us on a fifteen-day trip to Nepal. The whole group drove: sixty girls in each of two buses, and since we were an all-girls' school, there were only lady teachers. This was the first trip i was going on without my family but it was a school trip with schoolteachers, so i came and asked my father. Usually if we went out for even a two-day trip, he would ask Swamiji, but He was in the U.S.A. that time and there was a retreat going on there, i remember. So dad made it

---

* Two years later, the summer of 2002.

a point not to call because there used to be different timings for meditation and Satsang, et cetera. Swamiji would always think our phone calls were urgent and come to the phone. So i kept on telling my father, "Daddy, i want to go," and he didn't want to disturb Swamiji. Finally he said, "Okay, you can go," and we were happy.

This happened while on the way back. In Nepal there are two cities: Kathmandu and Pokhara, so you have to travel by bus and it's through mountains and there are no guardrailings or anything. It was November at that time, so it was snowing there. It was my birthday. i remember that i distributed sweets in the bus and then we went to sleep because the whole night the bus was going to travel. That night, Swamiji called up my father from America. Usually whenever Swamiji called, He would say, "Hello, P----," to my dad, and ask, "How are you?" He would never take single names. He would always ask, "How is everybody?" and talk generally, then say "*chango*," which means, "Okay" in Sindhi; then He would put the phone down.

That night my dad was sleeping, and at 10:30 Swamiji called and my dad picked up the phone. Swamiji didn't say, "Hello" to my dad. He abruptly said, "Where is P------?" [my name]. My dad had been asleep, so for a moment he couldn't understand what was going on, because Swamiji never spoke like that. My dad said, "Huh?" Then Swamiji spoke strongly to him: "I'm Swamiji speaking! You can't make out who I am? Where's P------?" So papa said, "Swamiji, she's asleep in her room. It's night now." Then he realized what he had said and corrected: "No, no, Swamiji, she's gone on a school trip with her . . . ah . . . this . . ." Swamiji scolded him. He said, "Why didn't you ask me?" So papa said, "Swamiji, it was a school trip with girls and lady teachers going, and i didn't want to disturb You . . ." Then Swamiji said, "Okay," and kept the phone down very abruptly. He didn't say, "Bye" or "How are you?"—nothing, my dad was a little worried. But then you never knew what was going on with Swamiji!

This was about 10:00 or 10:30 P.M., and exactly at 11:00 P.M. in Nepal, our bus rolled down the mountain. There were two sides on that road. One was a deep cliff that was about one hundred twenty feet down, where, if it fell, people wouldn't even find the bus—a deep gorge. The other side was a deep ditch and then the mountain started. Our bus rolled over in that deep ditch one and a half times and landed on the side where the entrance door was. i was sitting on the side on which the bus rolled and—you wouldn't believe it!—i didn't have a scratch on my body, though i was sitting next to the window. So what we did is: we broke the windscreen and we broke the windows and we jumped out, because we couldn't come out through the door and all the tires were up. It was eleven o'clock in the night and there were no lights on the road and it was snowing. So we came out but i didn't have a scratch, and among all the sixty girls, nobody was seriously hurt.

There was a girl who got a few stitches on her leg, one who got a few stitches on her head, but that was the maximum hurt that anyone got. All the other girls were okay. We were the second bus, so the first bus didn't even realize that we had had an accident behind them. And for two hours, till they called up and the next bus came, we were sitting on the road, on the stones, with the ice all around us, holding our bags [luggage] because our bags had also tumbled out. And all the girls kept telling me, "It was your birthday—you gave us the sweets. That's why we were saved." And i just laughed it off because i never really took it seriously. And when i came home and we got down off the train and my dad saw the bandages on a few girls, he asked me, "What is this?" It had come in the papers there in Nepal but not in India because it is a different country. So i told daddy we had had an accident. Then he told me that Swamiji had called and scolded him like that. Then everything was understood.

∞

He used to tell me: "Don't be afraid of anything, I am with you. Don't worry inside. Anything you want to tell me, tell me. I am with you only." i told Him that i am not afraid of anything but i'm afraid of death, i'm very much afraid of death, i don't know why.

Then He said, "Don't worry, don't worry. If you will meditate and sit and repeat your mantra every now and then, then I am with you and nobody will touch you."

∞

We have known Swamiji since 1981. The person who introduced us to Swamiji was Mr. K---------. He was the first person who knew Swamiji [in Pune] and was Swamiji's oldest *bhakta*.* He has expired now. Mrs. K--------- has also expired. He had diabetes and because of that his one leg was amputated. So he was without that leg and still he used to come, climbing the stairs, and sit here. Swamiji used to request him to address us [in Satsang] in place of Swamiji. It was excellent. He himself was a great ascetic. He was a teacher in charge of a really big school. He was very popular there.

Mr. K--------- was a personal friend of mine for a long time earlier on, so he brought my wife and myself to Swamiji, with a previous appointment, the first time. Swamiji had a very informal talk with us. We were so much impressed with Him—we would like to come here every day! Every week, from then and thereafter, we started attending the ashram. Swamiji used to be going for a year overseas. He was not here, but even then His bhaktas, His devotees, used to come here. They met every Thursday and Sunday, and we used to also follow the same.

i was very fortunate in knowing other swamis earlier. We used to meet and talk with them, so they created a liking in us for this agape—devotional love to God. So when we came here and met Pujya Swamiji, we were so much impressed with His high status in this agape. He took a very high position in that and He, Himself, was an ascetic, so we thought we wanted to stay with Him, meet Him, and talk with Him as much as possible.

My wife was very much impressed. At that time she had read a book in which there was a picture of Sri Krishna, and she had noticed His feet. When she saw Swamiji's feet, she saw the

---

* *Bhakta*: "devotee."

thumb* of His feet and thought it was exactly like Krishna's. So she thought, "He's exactly . . . He's Krishna."

i'm an old heart patient and i had my personal vigil also, so Swamiji took personal care to have particular food and extend all facilities to us when we came here for camp. Four days' spiritual retreat used to be held here when Swamiji used to come [from abroad]. All of us stayed here for four nights. So that time normally [my wife] should stay in the ladies' hostel, but then as a special case, Swamiji constructed an attached bathroom [in one of the ashramite rooms] on the lower floor for both of us. He was very, very thorough, and so fatherly.

[Wife] Whatever question was posed in my mother's mind, in the next Satsang it was solved. She would just think about it and without even telling Swamiji, He would answer it in the next Satsang. She felt that Satsang was for her only.

[Husband] My wife's father lived up to one hundred three years old. Her mother was ninety-six years old. They had a meeting with Swamiji and then He had long discussions with them. Ultimately they became disciples. My father-in-law would go in meditation for hours. He used to spend time in worship all day. So when my wife's parents were brought here and were introduced to Swamiji, they came very close in a very short time. They knew each other very well. Swamiji didn't allow my wife's father to touch His feet.† He just held his hands. He was a very great saint and Swamiji would not allow him to bow before Him. Instead Swamiji went just like [indicating a gesture of pranam with hands folded]. Swamiji had extremely great love and respect towards our parents. If He had lived more, then we would have come very close . . .

---

* He is referring to the big toe, which in Indian languages translates as "thumb of the foot."

† In India in general and in Hindu families in particular, "touching the feet" of an elder is a gesture of respect, as Gurudeva describes in Chapter Two. In the Guru-disciple tradition, touching the feet of a Realized Soul or Satguru is a form of reverence or worship.

∞

My husband and myself were coming to Jyoti Ashram since twenty years back but we never used to come inside. We used to come here to leave our parents for *Adhyatma Saptah,** drop them, pick them up, but we used to stay in the car only. Now i wonder how i never felt that i should come in and see Swamiji. [Husband] So sometimes on Sundays i used to drop them near the gate, then i used to go to Pune Club, play sports, and after two hours i used to come back and pick them up. [Wife] i saw that board which is there outside the gate: "Private," so i sat outside to wait. i never thought of coming inside. Then, after twenty years, the first time we met Swamiji He won us over. i cannot explain what we felt, what it was like, what happened.

It was six years back.† My son, daughters, husband and his parents and i had all come. We sat there with Swamiji and He smiled how He used to smile. He smiled at us and said, "Ah, the daughters are father's," [the father is more attached to the daughters]. Then He pointed to R---- [my son] and said, "He is his grandmother's." Until that time my daughters used to tease their grandmother that always she was partial to my son, and she became so red because they started smiling. She got embarrassed. There was a fight always in our house on this. And then Swamiji said, "She's neutral," pointing at me. Then after that day, He invited us for some function in the ashram. i think it was Janmashtami day. So after that, again we came to meet Him, after a week or so. That time [my husband] said, "It was only a week ago that we met Him, no?" So i told him, "i've never fought with you for anything, but today i want you to come to Swamiji." We had a long argument on this and finally he came. [Husband] And even i said: "Okay, for your sake i'm coming today, but don't ask me next time. i'll not come." [Wife] As soon as we entered,

---

* *Adhyatma Saptah*: "spiritual retreat week," which Gurudeva gave yearly at Jyoti Ashram since the early years.

† This occurred in approximately 1996.

Swamiji said, "You caught hold of [my husband] and dragged him here." And no one knew about this; only we knew what had happened. But that time [my husband] was totally amazed.

[Husband] The first time He made me sit with Him, in the first meeting, the first thing He talked to me about was badminton. He talked about Prakash Paducone. Few minutes He talked to me about badminton because He knew i was playing badminton. Then He said, "How is your business?" He knew that it was a little slow; slack was there. So He said: "We have about a half acre plot here, so why don't you construct something? It's a main road. You can develop shops. You can get a good price." He said: "On the first floor* you can give a Satsang Hall or something. We'll help. It is lying vacant only, so the plot will be utilized." i said, "No, Swamiji, we won't build anything commercial. Let it be like that. We'll do farming or something. We'll plant trees, make gardens and all that. We need that place for the ashram," and He smiled. He said, "No, but we have to construct something there." i said, "No, Swamiji, we will not construct anything." So He smiled for a minute. He waited, then said, "Okay, there will be something and you're going to do that." It was in the first meeting that He told me this; then He changed the subject completely. So after six years, i knew what He was telling me that day . . .†

And even two or three years back, i was not aware that there were some bathroom repairs, renovations, tiling and all that needed at Jyoti Dham. Later i heard that they had had a lot of problems: the tile man would come and go; the plumber would come and go. Swamiji had a terrible time getting that work done. Someone told me later that if at that time i would have come forward, i could

---

* In India as in Europe, the "first floor" of a building is above the "ground floor," equivalent to the second floor in the United States.

† This devotee was the builder-contractor in charge of the construction of Gurudeva's *Samadhi Sthal*, the Temple that enshrines His *Asti Kalash* (Sacred Remains). The Samadhi Sthal was constructed later in the exact same plot this devotee describes at Jyoti Ashram in Pune, India.

have done this work. But Swamiji never asked because, maybe, as someone else said, He had kept me for this Samadhi [Sthal] work. He never bothered. He never told me. Nobody did. i was not even aware that these works and problems were going on.

[Wife] Once we came to see Swamiji about four years back. That time my son, the youngest, was in the Fifth or Sixth Standard [in school] and quite chubby, big tummy, and all that. He came with us to the ashram wearing a white-colored tee shirt with some cricket player's photo on it. Swamiji was sitting outside and saw him from a distance, and He called him: "R----, R---- come here." He asked him, "So what are you wearing on your shirt? You want to wear his tee shirt or you want to play like him?" R---- said, "Yes, Swamiji, i want to play like him." Then He touched his tummy and said, "Then what is this big pouch? How you can play with this?" R---- smiled and He said, "Tell your father, India's Camp is going on in Pune Club. You go there and see how the players train and be fit and all that, if you really want to play this cricket."

Very small things He used to know. He knew that [my son] loves food. He really loves eating very much. The first time he came, Swamiji asked him to sit next to Him during the *priti bhojan** and He, Himself, saw to it that he was eating without being shy. Then before going to America, when Swamiji went the last time, He called me and asked me, "You are non-vegetarian?" i told Him, "Yeah, we are, but nowadays i don't like to cook non-vegetarian, so we make vegetarian food only." He told me, "No, for R----, if you don't like to cook, you get from outside and give him." That was very shocking to me, really. [Husband] So every priti bhojan, my son was there and Swamiji used to ask, "R----, how is the food? You like it? Go on eating."

[Wife] When Swamiji was leaving India the last time, i said: "Don't go now, Swamiji. Please don't go." He Himself was telling me, "Actually I don't want to go, but I have some work over there so I'm going." He used to say that. So i thought, "He knows

---

* *Priti bhojan*: sacred or sanctified food shared by devotees.

better." i was really feeling—i don't know why—i was feeling that, "You don't go." So He said to me: "I'm going this time but I'll come back here and then I'll never go anywhere. I'll be here only, with you only." Those were His last words, just before leaving. And that time we didn't realize the meaning. Every time it happened like that: we never realized the actual meaning of His play.*

∞

His leela in the last year was to reduce the karmas of all His disciples as well as mankind in general. He let His physical body suffer so that our karmas would be reduced. He has purified all of us through His suffering and His love for us. He grew progressively weaker in the last year, so much so that He could hardly speak in the last three months. When we reached the United States on 1st June, He was very, very weak. He exchanged messages with us and blessed us. He blessed us with His Darshan when He was sleeping. His leela in the last year was such that He wanted to protect most of the disciples by not showing us His suffering. Other than three to four disciples in the United States, He did not meet anyone else except rarely. He washed away most of our karmas and we can only repay Him by following with complete dedication the path to God that He showed us. At the end, on the 12th of June, He went into samadhi for thirteen hours. When He awoke that night, He uttered the holy Name of Maa twice before going into final Mahasamadhi.

On the 13th of June 2001, at around 2:15 A.M. i felt a hand touch me and wake me up. i got up and looked outside the window to see a huge storm. i realized that it was now time for our Beloved Gurudeva to leave His body. He used to say that it takes a great

---

* Eleven months after His departure from India on July 4, 2000, Gurudeva took Mahasamadhi in Colorado (U.S.A.). His Asti Kalash (urn of Sacred Remains) was brought back to Jyoti Ashram in Pune, India by devotees and, a year later, on June 13, 2002, enshrined in a beautiful white marble Samadhi Sthal at Jyoti Ashram.

wind to take away a great soul. The storm became absolutely quiet as soon as our Beloved Guruji left His body. One of the devotees sitting and meditating near Him after He had left His body heard a heavenly voice say, "Don't shed tears. Remember all that I have taught you all these years. I am happy where I am and I will always be there to guide you." This, i think, was a message from Him for all of us.

He always had a way of asking a question when you least expected it. i remember quite a few times He would be standing, surrounded by throngs of devotees in Jyoti Ashram in India. He would pick me out from the crowd, look at me in that special way He had, and ask me: "Where are you, -----?" My lips would answer without thinking: "i am right here with You, Swamiji." Today my lips are again asking a question without thinking: "Where are You, Swamiji?" and He is looking at me in that special way He has and answering, "I am right here with you."

18

Devotees' Remembrances from America

You are a walking universe and Truth is within you. It is within your power to control, erase, divert and rebuild your thoughts. And ultimately, when you become convinced that you are your own barrier, then you will have the courage and kindness to give up and transcend ego.

18

Devotees' Remembrances from America

$\mathcal{M}$aster, on your Birthday,* the day we are all blessed, i would like to share memories of You. One of my favorite memories of You is the walks You would take devotees on during the Retreats. This was one summer/spring Retreat at Sacred Mountain Ashram. i had heard that a mother deer just gave birth to two baby deer. i wanted to see them so much, i took a couple of walks by myself looking for them, to no avail.

The next afternoon, Master, You took us on a walk. We were just walking, then suddenly You picked up the pace, walking strong and fast up the hill and, around the corner, there was a newborn fawn lying by the side of the road. Master, You were about one foot away and we were about three feet away. You said not to go any closer as the mother and other baby were close by. i was awed that this wild animal known for its shyness didn't even twitch a muscle. She just lay there, opened her eyes and looked up at You, Master, with the peace and love of an old friend.

During a different Retreat, Master, You said, "When you get home, you'll see everything will look flat, as if one-dimensional." i didn't pay particular attention to this because You said a lot during the Retreat, until i got back home to Tucson. i walked up the stairs of the balcony and looked out at one of my favorite views of the desert and the Tucson Mountains. Everything looked flat. i couldn't believe my eyes. i kept looking and looking. It was God projecting onto a screen, like a movie. It was a giant movie screen. i laughed and laughed and thought to myself, "You are

* This remembrance was an offering on Gurudeva's Birthday, May 18, 2003.

right, Master. You are the Perfect Shower of Truth." And i could feel You chuckling and twinkling Your eyes.

i loved to watch You laugh, smile, take such care when You gave everyone fruit or some gifts. The first time You gave me a fruit—an orange—i was so excited and happy, i jumped up to go receive it. You were beaming Light. The whole room was filled with Light. Everyone and everything was Light. i felt i was walking on and through Light—toward You.

There are so many beautiful times with You. The point of these three are that i know Your Love, Truth and Light are all-pervading and will shine forever.

∞

During one of His visits to our home in 1973, He said to me: "Whatever I do has meaning. When I step out of the building, whether I turn right or left has meaning. Whether I use my left or my right foot has meaning. Everything I do has meaning." At a later stay before a retreat, He was standing with a small group of us, ready to leave the house. All of a sudden He took me into His arms and asked, "Do you want Me to take you to My Father's Home?" It was the most precious moment.

∞

At the first Tucson retreat in 1975, He asked me to sing for Him. He showed me then that He knew me completely, since for a decade my singing had been extremely secret. . . . Nearly all of the fifty retreat attendees requested an interview. When my turn came, i asked how to repeat a cherished past experience. He told me to remember it and it would come back. As He spoke in His soft voice that always seemed to come from the far reaches of the Universe, i felt that He had no edges and was "endless." Later, from one of His Satsangs i understood this impression was a sensing of His Universal Form or Viratswarupa. There was absolutely no force or push in Him, just an ocean of soft expansiveness and Love.

Once while He was walking i asked Him if He was the One i was waiting for. He responded, "Don't you think I am your Guru?" For months i had been pained with extreme tension in the neck and shoulders, which no remedy would help. One day after that, several people were outside standing around Him. He was exuding such sweetness and the mood was very heavenly. He looked at me and then motioned over a gent, asking him to massage His shoulders. As He gazed lovingly at me, every ounce of tension and pain melted out of my neck and shoulders. In my heart, i knew that He was Jesus, the One i had waited for.

A few months later in another retreat, in Satsang He gave me the Vision that He was Jesus. Nearly levitating with pure joy after this, He called me and two others to Him. From the blissful looks on their faces, it seemed they too had seen His Vision. He asked all of us, "Did i speak untruth today?" Soaring in bliss and ecstasy, we all weepingly said, "NO!," because He *said* nothing about His Identity. Later, we three alone were helping in the kitchen, and one of them revealed that Gurudeva had appeared to both of them as Sri Ramakrishna!

∞

In the early days with Swamiji at a weekend retreat out in California, Swamiji stepped outside after the meeting. A little later when I emerged from the house, He was already talking to a group of local devotees. Not feeling a part of that group, i stood about twenty or more feet away. Then i overhead Him saying that He was going on an extended trip and didn't expect to be back for three months. This made me sad and i thought to myself, "There will be no chance to see Him for three long months!" In one leap He was suddenly at my side and, looking directly into my eyes, said, "P----, I'll never leave you."

∞

Swamiji looked at me with His shining eyes so full of love and fun and said, "Pathologist or pathetic?" pronounced "potetic." i was

asking His permission to drop out of my first year of residency in
pathology. My parents had raised career children so this was a big
step for me. i may have mumbled something like, "Oh, come on,
Swamiji, i can do something," but inside i felt scared. i was $9000
in debt from medical school so i really needed something, but i
knew a residency program was incompatible with the new spiritual
direction i wanted to take. Later He said to me, "Think,
J---, think of what you can do." i said something like, "Maybe
i could teach," but inside i was thinking i didn't have a teaching
certificate, so probably it wouldn't work. Strangely enough,
i ended up with a job that required teaching on a junior college
level without a certificate. Once i mastered the mechanics of the
job, i began to learn a lot.

When i was controlling, identified and proud, i had all manner
of problems at work, frequently humorous, sometimes bizarre.
When my work threatened my spiritual practices, however, i could
just tell Him, and my problems would melt away. Gradually i
came to realize He created the job for me to expose my flaws,
allow some expression of my inner tendencies, and give me a little
money. However, He was so humble and unassuming, never
claiming the credit, that it took me years to catch on. As He
explained so sweetly to me once: identification with my job role
was wrong, not so much because it limited me and caused
suffering—these were the byproducts, no doubt—but because it
was fundamentally untrue. Truth was the highest. He was the
Truth and this was (is) what He wanted for me. Jai Gurudev!

∞

i'll always be awed and blessed and amazed that He ever walked
the earth and that i ever had a chance to meet Him and be in His
care. He transformed my life. He took me from chaos to peace. He
healed me on every level. He truly did literally give me life. i went
through an episode where a doctor said later that she hadn't
expected me to live and also that she was surprised i hadn't
become a vegetable from what i had gone through. And to have

gone through that and recovered is all His Grace. My survival is His Grace, my recovery is His Grace, that i'm sitting here speaking is His Grace.

What first drew me so strongly was His love and compassion. i was really surprised, just after meeting Him, that He cared so much, that He showed such concern. And it wasn't until many years later, until recently even, that i understood that that's the way He was with *everybody*, all the time. With everybody He met everywhere, He had the same love and compassion and gave everybody every opportunity. i think all of us know how immensely patient He was—superhuman patience and tolerance. i know there were many things i did and attitudes i had at times where i was afraid He'd send me away, and He never did. He once said something to me: that He would forgive anything. And who cannot love in the face of that kind of love? He's given me so much that i just hope and pray to live what He taught me the rest of my life and to see Him again someday. Because i'll always miss His beautiful physical Presence, that golden Presence, and His loving smile and laugh. No one laughed like Swamiji.

∞

My mother had some early exposure to eastern religious philosophy, as her mother and father had attended the Parliament of Religions in 1898 in Chicago. So when *Autobiography of a Yogi* came out, she acquired a library copy. Noting her intense involvement in the book, i asked her about it; and begging her to read it out loud to me, she explained she would have to interpolate a bit for me (as i was only ten or so), which was fine with me . . . About this time, when it happened that Paramahansa Yogananda made a visit to Seattle, the Unitarian Church in our small town invited Him to take a ferry boat ride to our town and thus speak to a gathering, which He accepted. My mother hearing of it asked if i might want to go and hear Him speak; i consented until she said a neighbor friend would be going also, a lady of much chatter of little import. My mother was disappointed and, as i came to find out, she had a motive in wanting me to go. They attended and the next morning, when asked about it, she said she was quite impressed with Him, and had asked if He might be the Spiritual Master i kept referring to. He had said, "No, his Master will come into his life when he reaches forty years of age . . ."

Going back now to age thirteen: summer had come and as usual we packed up and left for the family wilderness retreat—primitive in all ways. Bringing with me a library copy of Yogananda's book that had so caught my fancy at age ten, immediately dove into it and didn't stop except for food and sleep. Early one sunny morning i had finished the book with heavy heart and eyes filled with tears at not having been born in India where one would grow up with such Holy men as discussed in the book. Briefly expressing my distress to my mother, i left to go down to the beach. Just short of the beach i stopped at a small ravine amongst the tall Alder trees where light was somehow percolating down through the foliage overhead, when before my eyes appeared a large image of a temple complex—black/white and gray—as a photo mural looks. While staring at it, thought i must be visually recalling a photograph from some book, but couldn't bring any to mind; and for years after sought that image in any book that might contain such a photo. It wasn't until years later, when Swamiji pointed out in a photo some rocks where He had meditated across from the temples of Gangotri, that i could see that if one were sitting where He had indicated, that it would match this image exactly; the temples there and the granite boulders along the river being black/white and gray.

Proceeding to the edge of the high bank above the beach, in an opening like a large cave that looked out over the waters to the distant mountains, decided to sit in the lotus posture there, with the thought of bridging the distance somehow westward to India. While doing so the thought came that "maybe if i can't go to India, India might come to me." Within a few seconds a bright light began to form above the beach about thirty feet out in which appeared a young man in white with long black hair and a beard, sitting on a white asan/dais with a motif of two rows of inverted lotus petals, one above the other at the topmost edge, the lower one in ochre-gold and the upper in pale blue. A voice spoke saying, "This is your Spiritual Master. His name is Amar Jyoti," and the image began to dissipate. My first thought was, "my father is right—i do have an overactive imagination," and proceeded to get up and dismiss the whole thing as just that. But i hadn't taken but a few paces before realizing i was chanting out loud, over and over, "Amar Jyoti." Stopping, i chided myself and moved on only to commence the chanting again, and this stop/start routine went on until i finally gave in to it and chanted it with some kind of conviction all the way up the hill to the house. My mother had apparently seen me emerge from the woods and was at the doorway when i approached. i asked if these words meant anything and she said that there was a French word, la mar—the sea, and i said no, it was Amar—Amar Jyoti, and told her what had happened.

A week or so later we had gone . . . to town for the day and the two of us went back to the library. When we arrived my mother said she wanted to talk to the head librarian while i looked around. When she returned to me, i had been standing looking at the west end of the large room at the late afternoon sunlight steaming through the windows. The librarian was also standing nearby with a large pleasant smile that one seldom sees from librarians. My mother asked, "Do you remember those words you mentioned, Amar Jyoti?" "Yes." "We looked them up in a Sanskrit dictionary and they mean Eternal Light." Was delighted to hear of it and turned and looked back to the sunlight coming through the windows with a smile on my face . . .

A few months before i turned forty, i was increasingly concerned and intense about matters of a spiritual nature, and with frustration one day confessed the need for a spiritual teacher. Within a day or two of turning forty, we were asked if we would like to meet a swami from India. We accepted the invitation to attend and on the evening of the gathering, while driving there, found myself saying out loud, over and over, "i will not follow another man." My wife said, "What are you saying?" "i don't know . . . i'm just going to meet a swami," and under my breath to myself saying, "i hardly know what a swami is." Somehow we were the last to arrive and i made some pretext to finally drag in at the last moment after subduing my feeling of apprehension. Entering a small dining room where all kinds of snacks were laid out, there was Swamiji, serving Himself. Without thought i put my palms together and bowed slightly with a feeling of respect. He looked at me expressionless but fixedly without a word, eye to eye. i became engulfed in a golden light, with body consciousness totally gone, and i knew that He was seeing all of what i was, even the most vile of things. Somehow i knew He would never use anything against me . . . Not like my intrinsic caution, i was quite at ease . . .

∞

In 1978, Sacred Mountain Ashram had moved to a new location at 10,000 feet elevation up in the Rocky Mountains, just four miles from the Continental Divide. i was a visiting worker there during August, and on the morning of my forty-fourth birthday, i was assigned road-raking duties. This was hard, dusty work—filling in ruts and scraping down high places with pick and rake. By lunchtime i was somewhat irritable and harboring a bit of self-pity. But a rest after eating helped, and as i came outside, i saw Swamiji sitting on a bench, alone. Miraculously, there was no one else around—a very rare occurrence when Master was present!

i came over and touched His feet, feeling deliciously revived. He then placed His hands on my head for a while, and a most wonderful joy flowed through me. i don't recall how long we remained that way, but eventually a large truck filled with 10,000 catalogs pulled up and many of us were called to help unload it. As i worked, tears of joy were still flowing from my eyes, and for several hours, this joy continued to fill me. It was a taste, i believe, of the Golden Age, working, but with no weariness; inhabiting a body, but living in it so lightly—and in Bliss! This was certainly a birthday present i would never forget.

∞

When i think of my Gurudeva, a flood of images comes rolling in—images of His Beauty, His Mystery, His Power, Grace, Omniscience, and above all—His Love. i see Him as Mahadev, a lion among men, a whirlwind of powerful energy going through the ashram cleaning closets, both internal and external. "Why is this here? This is unnecessary! Why are you cluttering? Clean this out!" Objects fly and ashramites scurry. But after the storm, all is clean, peaceful and beautiful.

i see Him on His asan,* dissolving walls, pulsating with white-blue Light; sitting at the helm of a ship that transports us out into the Universe; or standing on the horizon, robes whipping in the wind—so delicate and fragrant. Then striding gracefully, peacefully, purposefully—a Prince incomparably majestic and beautiful among unevolved humanity.

i remember all the times He read my thoughts or knew of things i'd done and so discreetly and tactfully let me know. And the many times He gave me a well-deserved rebuke, then came to sit quietly near, inundating me in a silent flow of Love.

i remember the silent night, one year ago† when ashramites were repeating the *Mahamritunjaya Mantra*‡ twenty-four hours a day. i had just finished my turn from 11:30 P.M. to 2:00 A.M. and had dozed into a light sleep when i was awakened by a sudden howling wind that had come from nowhere. Trees thrashed furiously outside while the wind moaned through the cracks in the window. Around 3:05 A.M. the phone rang. It was Sita speaking through tears. The wind stopped as suddenly as it had come. As we drove down the mountain from Sacred Mountain Ashram a few

---

* A simple cloth padded seat where Gurudeva would sit with devotees formally or informally.

† June 13, 2001, the night of Gurudeva's Mahasamadhi.

‡ *Mahamritunjaya Mantra*, Sanskrit: *maha*, "great," and *mritunjaya*, "victorious over death." This ancient mantra to Lord Shiva is recited for good health, release from bondage and the attainment of Immortality.

minutes later, all was silent and surreal. Broken tree branches lay strewn across the mountain road, across Boulder city streets and all the way to the hospice. Wearing the guise of a frail mortal body that had taken on our sins, our Beloved Mahadev had left for His Home in that familiar whirlwind of powerful energy.

Later that summer morning, while driving back to the ashram where He now lay covered with roses, i saw a small patch of dark storm clouds gathering over the mountain. Just as i pulled into the driveway, the clouds let go as the gods showered His beloved Kailash with a beautiful summer blanket of snow. Once again, after the storm, all was clean and beautiful.

Six months later as i struggled with the sense of loss, struggled with overwhelming problems that i would have normally taken to Him and wondered how i would ever find my way again, i had a dream: Just as i left a room and turned down a hallway, Beloved Gurudeva suddenly stepped out of a room and into my path. He was radiant, beautiful, and full of health. He looked at me mischievously and then proceeded to give a stern but loving Satsang on one of the problems i had been wrestling with. When i woke up, i had the answer. This and other dreams reassure me that still He reads my thoughts and comes to sit near—if only i'm quiet enough.

∽

On New Year's Day in 1976 i was permitted a first visit to Sacred Mountain Ashram. Master had just moved to Gold Hill. i stayed in the common room with a sleeping bag. Although i offered to "help," they didn't give me anything to do and i just sat around, crying as usual. Then after a few days, Prabhushri asked if i would do one thing, and i eagerly agreed: to shovel snow from the upstairs deck. When i got there i could see that the deck was pretty big, and the snow was so wet and heavy i could hardly lift the shovel. It was hard work and i thought, "What if i get altitude sickness from all this exertion?" Then the thought came, "Well, let me just repeat my mantra (not the one that Master gave later) and get on with it." Soon the snow became so light and fluffy that even a small movement of the shovel made it fly right off the deck. The job was quickly done. Later, when i told Master about it, He said, "God is higher than altitude sickness!" Years afterward He told someone, "That's when she got converted."

Not long after the first visit to Sacred Mountain Ashram, i went with a friend to visit a priest she thought highly of. When there, i asked for an adult baptism. Somehow i wanted that but he refused because of my association with Master. i was devastated and couldn't stop crying. Back home by myself, i sat there sobbing, with Prabhushri's picture in my hand. Suddenly the picture came to life: He was moving, and i could even see some perspiration on His brow. He was looking at me quite seriously. i was dumbfounded and stupidly tried to get the picture out of the frame so Master could "get out." Then it all faded away and was a "photo" again. i stopped crying and as far as baptism went, that was the end of that.

At Desert Ashram, Master had me doing bookkeeping (me, who couldn't balance my checkbook!). i used to work at the desk in the little office room, right outside the door to Gurudeva's interview room, crying over the account books. One day i was sitting there with little piles of coins and bills all over the desk, trying to make something come out right, but to no avail. All of a sudden, Master's door opened with a bit of a crash, as usual, and He stood at the desk. Without saying anything, He rearranged a few of my piles. Right away i could see my mistake and that He had corrected it. He just turned and calmly went into the main hall.

Another day, i was sitting at the same desk. Prabhushri came out and i stood up. With quiet and beautiful grace, He folded His hands, leaned them on top of the filing cabinet, and laid His cheek on them. And there, before me, stood the dazzling form of Lord Krishna. His beauty was staggering. It lasted but a moment or two. i stood there open-mouthed like a complete dolt. Prabhushri was acting as if everything was quite as usual and saying something about the work, and i just tried to answer Him.

Often i would see a halo around Master's head. It looked so much like the halos seen in the paintings by the old masters; at first i thought i was just imagining it. So i would look away, look back, that sort of thing. But it was a halo for certain, sometimes a glowing disk of golden-white light, sometimes a fairly thin circle of intense light, sometimes streams of light radiating from His beautiful form. Surely we see such things only by His Grace, and if there was the capacity in us, what else He could show us!

At Desert Ashram my little room was across the hall from Master's interview room. i used to just sit and gaze in His direction. One day, all at once, i saw a vision of the head of Christ crucified, and an image of Master, and the two images fused into one. There was a great feeling of love and the thought: "i have loved You for a long, long time." Tears came. The message was unmistakable. Master had said in Satsang that we would never recognize these things unless He by His Grace gave us a glimpse of them.

Prabhushri sat with us to view the television presentation of *Jesus of Nazareth*. It was in several installments. Sometimes, just before it began, we would see a minute of the preceding commercial. One time it was people dancing to rock and roll. Master observed, "That's very good for opening the third chakra," and added in His special way, "provided you're already on the second." We laughed and laughed. Gurudeva gave us the gift of love for all the Prophets—Jesus, Krishna, Buddha, Rama— especially these, although He also included Moses as a Prophet. It enriched us so much.

During Retreat, Prabhushri allowed those present to ask questions of Him. At an Annual Retreat in Michigan, someone asked why at all it was that we ever left Perfection. The thought crossed my mind, "That's a very good question," and i heard a very fine, male voice within saying, "I wanted to play." Thus the question was fully answered forever.

Master rebuked me for treating C------ badly when we were at Countryside Ashram before an Annual Retreat. Another Retreat was about to take place, this time at Sacred Mountain Ashram.

Walking past the main lodge, i saw Master standing upstairs on the balcony by His room, looking down with the sweetest, heart-melting look. i looked back lovingly. He sweetly waved and i waved back. Master then melted away and standing there waving at me was C------.

At Satsang i often saw Light streaming from Master's precious form, a golden radiance that began to reveal itself around His body, but afterwards expanded to fill the space all around Him. Behind Him would appear lovely pastel hues of pink, blue and gold. Once the golden light became so effulgent, it almost seemed that Master was dissolving into it. When i told Him later, He said, no, it wasn't time for that yet.

Once a devotee, in imitation of Swami Vivekananda, asked Master, "Have You seen God?" In great humor Master sweetly replied, "Why should I tell you?" Everyone burst out laughing. So often, so often, Prabhushri shared with us the most warm and wonderful, gleeful laughter.

One day i was looking at a small catalog of gemstone jewelry, thinking how nice it would be to have something like that. Just for fun, i read the descriptions and had a little conversation with myself about which one i would choose, deciding that a small rose quartz pendant would be best, since that stone bestows devotion and loving kindness. Of course, i never told anyone. Not too long afterwards, Prabhushri gave me a small box and inside was that very same pendant. i was overwhelmed and stammered my thanks. Master walked out the door and remarked to S---, "She likes it."

Sri Gurudeva sat with us in meditation during a solar eclipse. The whole time i was seeing, inside, beautiful visions of the Master. It was a shock to have to come out of the meditation and go to the next part of the program. i wanted it to go on forever. Such is the amazing Grace of the Guru. All this is His Grace.

∽

i remember one time He went to Price Club—He loved Price Club; it was one of His favorite shopping places. He'd get that big dolly

and push it. He liked to push it! Of course, we didn't push as well
as He did, so He'd get behind the thing and push. We were standing
in an aisle and a little boy who must have been about two or three
was there with his mom at one end of the aisle. The boy just looked
at Gurudeva from across the aisle and then, as if a light or
recognition went off, he came running and threw his arms around
Him. He was pretty small and came up to about Gurudeva's knees
or so, and after hugging Him tightly, turned his face toward
Gurudeva's and lovingly gazed upward at Him. Gurudeva gently
laid His hand on his head. The mother was a little freaked out
because the boy had just taken off on his own, so she came over
and was gently pulling the boy away. Gurudeva was real sweet,
trying to get the mom to relax and telling her she had a nice boy,
very loving, sweet-natured. It was the most beautiful exchange.

Everywhere you'd go with Him, children always knew Who He
was and that He was their own; they always recognized Him
immediately. You'd often hear them asking their parent, in a child's
whisper loud enough for everyone to hear, "Is that Jesus? I think
that's Jesus." In all kinds of places such things would happen.

He blessed so many states in America when He traveled. Places
that you'd never really think to go into, He always managed, and
would buy things that He didn't really need or weren't that special.
It was His way of blessing the person, by getting something.
That was always something He did to give His blessings to the
shopkeepers. This was their livelihood and He wanted to increase
their bounty, so He would most always get something. That
was how He was with all of us. He always said He never saw a
distinction between disciple and nondisciple. The world wasn't
divided that way to Him. It's His creation, so it was all part of
Him. He was always that way, so incredibly loving, whether it
was a waitress when we would stop and get tea or something
somewhere, and He would just be His charming Self. He was
always so charming. And that smile would melt a stone anywhere.
He always "gifted" wherever He went. He didn't have to do
anything; He would just be there and everything would light up!

He was then to me what He is now, my conscience, guide and the righteousness within me. i wish to remember His patience and toleration, His amazing Faith in the Light within me. i wish to remember how, out of His immeasurable Love, He let me know His Presence. He dove down into the ocean of samsara and communicated with me there. One of His methods of lifting me up was gentle exposure. He would ask about certain samskars, but never judge. Though He was exceptionally tolerant, i could tell He was not pleased. His lack of pleasure affected me, decreasing the related behavior. Through His grace i began to see these actions differently and be ashamed of their adharmic quality for the first time.

Going into a person's mind, He found the things that would charm and fulfill that person beyond words, and then do those things and make them fall madly in love with Him. Or perhaps He was Charm itself. He was a servant of His devotees. My wish to have a child this birth was unsatisfied. He knew this, and wanted to be that child to fulfill me. He would make Himself very, very small, a child of five to seven years, and ask me what to do about things, while vibrationally nestling in my arms. These moments were unspeakably, amazingly sweet and fulfilled motherly wishes. Who could imagine a sweeter child! His softness and intimacy were beyond imagination. Soon after, He would again be His Omniscient Self, and i would ask Him what to do.

i was working with a gent, moving heavy furniture under the supervision of Master. Sometimes Master would physically help lift; other times He would seemingly just observe and occasionally direct, although He was doing more than that. At one point we were arranging ourselves to lift and position a heavy bookcase. The gent was at one end of the bookcase and Master told me that He would be in the middle and i at the other end. He said, as an explanation of that arrangement, that i was stronger than Him. i knew that was not true, but i was not going to argue with the Lord! Even as I searched for the meaning, i said, "If You used Your powers, it would not be so."

His remark had nothing to do with physical strength, of that i'm sure. It seems He was saying that my resistance was stronger than He was willing to overcome, only because He will not force His Will or Love on anyone. His Love is soft and tender, not aggressive and combative. He waits patiently for us, never considering the possibility of "force." The only "force" He uses is His Love, which is stronger than any other force in the cosmos.

∞

It was the last flight of an all-day journey from Tucson, Arizona to Rutland, Vermont. As we sat in the six-passenger plane flying into the beautifully large crimson sun, i wondered what Prabhushri was doing just then? It was about 7:00 P.M.—was He having His evening meal yet? Would we get to see Him so late in the evening?

After we landed, S--- picked us up from the small airport and in no time we were opening the door to the ashram of Ṛta Dharma Retreat.* And there He was, waiting for us, with His beautiful and radiant smile. He looked so healthy and we were so relieved to see Him. He asked if we were hungry, but we said we just wanted to see Him and be with Him. But He insisted and then He Himself brought out many dishes of food for us. It was a time of Durga Puja and there He was, being a Mother and feeding His children. Even though we weren't hungry, we ate almost everything He brought out. He stayed with us the whole time.

Throughout the retreat, He gave His Darshan so many times and even took us on a walk around His heavenly paradise there. During that week, He gave brief discourses on meditation and talked about His possible future plans, even a two-week Meditation Retreat, and

---

* Ṛta Dharma Retreat (*Ṛta Dharma*, from the Sanskrit, "eternal law, cosmic law") was founded by Gurudeva in Pawlet, Vermont in 1998, the last ashram He founded. Unfortunately, due to zoning restrictions, it was not able to be retained after 2002.

about other centers like Ṛta Dharma in other states in the U.S.A. He also spoke about Divine Mother and how they relate to each other sometimes. It was so sweet that He shared this with us.

One evening we were able to sit in close proximity with Him for two videos. i was sitting behind Him, yet He radiated so much love that my heart and mind were filled to the brim, and He'd turn around to glance at me often with the sweetest and most innocent smile. It was so touching.

After the video, in the context of Vedanta, He spoke about politics and religion, and how the world one day would recognize the spiritual wealth and heritage of India. Then He began talking about, "What if? . . . What if? . . ." and He took us up with Him into a time-space capsule, into the future or another dimension, which left us all wide-eyed and spellbound. He poured out words of intriguing, mind-expanding and fascinating wisdom. It was so stimulating that i could hardly sleep that night . . . knowing of our potential, if we could just tap into it—into Him!

It was so fulfilling for our hearts and souls to be meditating day and night, every day, knowing He was so very close to us physically, and on the last night He sat with us the whole evening of meditation. It was so powerful. He gave us a little glimpse . . . to see and feel His magnificent Presence as Isvara.

∽

In Vermont at Ṛta Dharma Retreat there was a lot that had to be done with the main building. And one time there was a problem with the plumbing and it affected Master's quarters. i'm not exactly sure what the problem was but one of the ashramites came to fix it in the morning and he worked and he worked and he worked and he worked and he couldn't get it. And after lunch he came back and he worked and he worked and he worked and he still couldn't get it. And finally he went to Prabhushri and said something like, "Master, with your Divine Wisdom, how would you get this fixed or what would you do?" And Master said, "I would call a plumber." The plumber came. Ten minutes later it was done.

∞

On several occasions, when Master was working intensively on someone and they were being kept away, "behind the scenes," He expressed His love and concern for them in little ways. With one devotee He was working on and who was having a hard time being positive, He would inquire about her, how was she doing? What was happening with her? . . . How was her health? . . . And so on. He wanted to give her something that would help her health but, since He was not communicating directly with her, He gave her this gift "on the sly" by asking someone else to give it to her but not say where it really came from. Since the person was having a hard time being positive, she almost rejected this gift from the Lord.

With another devotee that He was working with very intensely but not speaking with directly, He said very compassionately that, while she had her faults, she was "with Him" and had given Him all she had. He said, "She gave me all she had, which for her was a lot since she doesn't have much. Others have given me big amounts but they have a lot." Though she had her faults, she was dear to Him for her giving.

∞

Master affirmed to me years ago that He would "speak" to me through the "little animals," which i love. i have learned many lessons through animals and nature, and i observe now, usually aware that there are beautiful messages for me, if i observe and listen closely enough. The day after i heard of His passing, i was feeling rather low and i was staring out my back kitchen window, shortly after a rain shower. (This window He had also stood at fourteen years ago when He visited our home and, with His hands folded behind Him, He had said quietly to me, as He looked outside, "And so you seek yoga . . .")

On this day i realized there was a good-sized unusual bird on the ground, insistently and persistently working at freeing a worm from the ground for its dinner. It was determined and actually in a very vulnerable and unusual position—in open space. It kept watch over its shoulder and was determined to get what it was after. The interesting part was that it was not like any bird common to our yard—it was speckled on its front with a black ring around its neck and red under its beak. I thought it was a woodpecker and wondered why it would be after a worm on the ground.

Later i went upstairs to meditate. I have the small calendar Aphorisms book by Master on my altar. I was still on the page of June 13th—i needed to turn the page to the 14th, which i did. There, on the left side of the new pages was a picture of the identical bird! i immediately knew that whatever was written beneath the bird picture was a direct and personal message from Him to me— words instructed the day after His passing, and they were: "Through love and devotion, everything is possible." To me, this message is absolutely beautiful, for it reminds me that no matter what crosses my path and no matter how complicated life seems, all i need to do is love God—it is simple, pure and so empowering.

∾

…my close friend called to inform me of Swamiji's Blessed Mahasamadhi reunion with His Beloved Divine! My spirit rejoices with him for this blessed event and my heart feels sad for us who remain. He was so very especially loving to this poor monk and always gave a generous sharing of his heart when we would meet (he called me his "secret lover" with a great smile).

We held a Vigil for him asking that we experience his presence in a new and more conscious way, and pray that all of his disciples feel the same!

—*A Zion Hermit-Monk, Arizona*

∾

Just as when He was physically here, His work is still mostly hidden from material eyes. Only now it feels that He is even more free to give as He wishes, completely unfettered and unbound by anything physical. Incognito could almost be the keyword of His incarnation this time, except that there was so much more. But what made it special this time was His great love of being incognito, as if the smallest of the small while being the All! i always loved that song, "Dressed in hues of the infinite; playing totally innocent…" Those who have eyes (and an open heart) will see. He remains ever the same.

∞

In a ride back to R̥ta Dharma Retreat from a lake nearby in Vermont, Master was telling us about the times that He had met death but was saved. There were two of water, and then this one: He was on a train between Pune and Mumbai in India, which was very packed, and near Him on the train was the owner of some sort of a manufacturing plant, a plant that had been emitting something that was dangerous to the boys' school He had founded. Master had brought His concerns to the owner and the owner hadn't heeded them. Then i guess Master took stronger action and made a complaint against this manufacturing plant or some sort of mill. And so one day Master was on this packed train and also that owner was on the train.

They were both standing near the door to get down and the door was open. The man was originally not standing close to Master but he had moved until he got next to Him. And, of course, this man had no good feelings for Master and Master looked at him and could see in his eyes what the man was going to do. It was the man's intention to actually push Master off of the moving train. The man's intention was to kill Him. Of course, it didn't happen, but i think Master said He looked at the man, knew the man's intention, and they were right there with the train door open. Master knew that the man was going to attempt to do this and i think He looked the man full in the eyes—then something happened; something intervened that kind of broke the opportunity for that man. Maa (Divine Mother) saved Him. i think somebody came between that man and Master and then the man's opportunity was gone. There was a moment when the man could have done it and no one would have seen it and then the man's opportunity was gone. Master told that story and i think another one. He talked about near death by water and by fire. Fire, maybe, was that man's burning hatred; it was evil. Somehow the thought came up and He said something like: "I won't go by that way," or "I won't leave my body by that way." i remember the thought was left hanging in the air that He never finished.

∾

He had many very long heated conversations with R------ [my husband]. They were so intense that at times i had to put my head down on the table while R------ yelled at the top of his lungs at the highest Being on the planet. Basically, Prabhushri was for oneness and equality of all races, religions and nations, and R------ was for the white race, Judeo-Christian religions, and American military. R------ was being mentally rolfed and all of this rabid, narrow, angry poison was coming out of him. To my horror and amazement, wave after wave of extreme political bias and diatribe was pulled out of him by Prabhushri. i was furious and planning to let R------ really have it on the return trip, but before we left, Prabhushri put a quick end to that plan by telling me that if i ever tried to make R------ ashamed or feel badly about speaking that way to Him, He (Prabhushri) would not come back to America(!!!) and that He loved R------ very much, like a brother. On the return trip, R------ commented that Prabhushri had pulled all of that out of him and he was amazed at what had happened. He had a very hard time "swallowing" the all-inclusive broad philosophy that Prabhushri was giving him.

   When Prabhushri was staying at our house, He asked how He could ever repay us for allowing Him to stay there. He really thought about it, and gazed off into space seeming to search for the answer, but more likely reading the future. About a year later, R------ was diagnosed with cancer of the esophagus, and had a hard time swallowing anything. As the disease progressed, the pain increased. Prabhushri cared tenderly as a mother for R------ , asking always first thing how he was, and sending articles from magazines and suggestions of things that may help. At this time He encouraged me to pray for R------ , as He was doing, and was very attentive to R------ 's diet and every detail of his illness. One day when the pain had gotten so bad that it was beyond the pain pills' reach, i tearfully asked Prabhushri to help him. He smiled, looking deeply pleased—and i felt the burden of relieving the pain pass to Him. R------ 's health continued to decline, as the cancer spread to his bones. During this time, Master was very ill as well and although He never wanted anyone to know about His illness, that was impossible. It was clear that He was suffering greatly, and was unable to come to the functions and programs He had previously come to. He had obviously taken R------ 's pain on Himself, because R------ , though in some pain, was astonishing the doctor with his lack of need of pain medication. Master was most tenderly attentive to every detail of R------ 's illness until his death on Guru Purnima, 1999. At that time, Master had lost much weight and had not been able to eat much to speak of for months. He was deeply saddened by the loss of R------ and gave the blessing of speaking well of him on the day he passed. Three days after R------ left, Master was able to eat regularly, to the great relief of all concerned, and His health picked up by leaps and bounds after that . . .

∞

In the movie *E.T.* the scene in which E.T. put his glowing finger on Elliot's forehead before he went back to his home planet, and said, "I'll be right here," was extremely moving to me. Seeing this made me weep inside, wishing that Prabhushri would do the same for me when He "left" our planet, although i never told anyone about this. During His last three days in Tucson (March 2000), while sitting at His Feet, He leaned over and put His finger on my forehead, and i closed my eyes and enjoyed every second of this! Only months later did i realize the utter sweetness of this gift—He had fulfilled my wish without my asking, most poignantly, since it was His last time here with us.

He let me know and comprehend what He was accomplishing

in the illness of His last days. He could have used His powers in an instant to be completely well, but He never asked for anything for Himself. He had decided to purify the earth by accepting all the darkness troubling humanity into Himself. The darkness hurled itself like missiles into His body, and as He drew each one in, He allowed it to make His body smaller and smaller. Even though this caused Him excruciating pain, He accepted all of it with Love and a sweet smile, because He wanted to free us more than He wanted to be well. He was using His Divine power of *laheema* (making Himself the smallest) to the maximum, as a certain type of star does when it implodes, resulting in a supernova blasting into extremely expanded brilliant, dazzling LIGHT. He had spoken about how the smallest indivisible particle is invincible, and how becoming the smallest "wins the game, whatever the game is . . ." And He made me understand that, by His making Himself the smallest in this way, He was making the forces of Light victorious.

∞

On His last Birthday on this earth, in early May 2001, Gurudeva was too ill to look at the many Birthday cards and letters that had arrived for Him. We had waited all day for a little betterment but it was one or two days later before we could even show them to Him. Even then He did not have any strength or interest to look at them. As i held up a few, one by one, to show to Him, one page He did shine His big beautiful eyes upon, amazingly. It was a quote from the Svetasvatara Upanishad, printed large on a piece of stationary with a background of white lightning against a blue-gray sky. A devotee had sent it and had written below the quote: "It is about You, and describes You very well."

> *I know that Great Person*
> *of the brightness of the sun*
> *beyond the darkness.*
> *Only by knowing Him*
> *does one go beyond death.*
> *There is no other way to go.*

Bibliography
Sources by Chapter

Although Gurudeva normally had all recordings of His personal life erased directly after they were recorded, between June 5-11, 1997, He gave what became a very unusual retreat at Sacred Mountain Ashram, later titled Grace of the Guru Retreat. *It was a rare blessing during those days that He spoke of His personal sadhana and experiences in the Himalayas and other parts of India. More than half of the Satsangs from this Retreat were not released. After Gurudeva's Mahasamadhi, recordings of these Satsangs were discovered at Jyoti Dham at Sacred Mountain Ashram. Some of these have been included in Chapters One, Three, Four, Eleven and Fifteen of this biography. Other unreleased Satsangs in this manuscript were recorded at seekers' and devotees' homes in 1961, 1974 and 1998. One of Gurudeva's rare compositions is included in Chapter Three:* A Tiny Form of the World Mother, *which He wrote in Hindi. Satsangs published by Truth Consciousness in audio format (compact disc and audiocassette) are listed below with their catalog number and retreat title, if part of a retreat. These Satsangs and over seven hundred others are available through the ashrams and at truthconsciousness.org.*

CHAPTER 1

The Dazzling Play of the Lord, from an unreleased Satsang given at Sacred Mountain Ashram on June 10, 1997, during the *Grace of the Guru Retreat*. *Night of Realization* from an informal Satsang given at a devotee's home in Tucson, Arizona, in March 1974.

Chapter 2

In July 2000, when Gurudeva's illness became serious, He started writing this "biography," as He called it. For about six to eight weeks, He wrote several hours daily until He had completed ninety-two pages by hand, which comprise this chapter.

Chapter 3

Renouncing College from an informal Satsang given at the home of a devotee family in Syracuse, New York, November 1998. *Refugee Camp of Bengal* and *Calcutta Experiences* from a Satsang given at Sacred Mountain Ashram on June 14, 1997. "A Tiny Form of the World Mother" was written by Prabhushri in Hindi and published in 1977 in *Pratibuddha* (Ananda Niketan Trust, Pune, India).

Chapter 4

Kutastha: The Great Silence from an unreleased Satsang given at Sacred Mountain Ashram on June 10, 1997. *Realization* from an informal Satsang given at a devotee's home in Tucson, Arizona in March 1974. *Initiation* from an informal Satsang given at a devotee's home in March 1974 in Tucson, Arizona. *Planned by God* was recorded in 1961 during a gathering at a home in San Francisco, California. Gurudeva was asked to speak about the purpose and dimension of His current and first visit to the United States.

Chapter 5

The Prophets: Pure Spirit Embodied from the published Satsang (K-94) given at Sacred Mountain Ashram on August 5, 1987, at the Twelfth Annual Spiritual Retreat entitled *The Oneness of Creation.*

Chapter 6

The Grace of Sri Krishna from the published Satsang (K-110) given at Sacred Mountain Ashram on the holy day of Sri Krishna Janmashtami (Birth of Sri Krishna), August 24, 1989.

CHAPTER 7

Lord Buddha: The Embodiment of Peace from the published Satsang entitled *The Mission of Lord Buddha* (K-130), given on the holy day of Buddha Purnima at Countryside Ashram in Rockford, Michigan, May 9, 1990.

CHAPTER 8

Jesus and the Quiet Revolution from the published Satsang (K-116), given on Christmas at Sacred Mountain Ashram, December 25, 1989.

CHAPTER 9

Sri Rama: The Upholder of Dharma from a published Satsang entitled *Law and Compassion of the Prophets* (K-157), given at Sacred Mountain Ashram on the holy day of Divali (Festival of Lights), October 30, 1996.

CHAPTER 10

God the Mother from the published Satsang (K-133) given at Desert Ashram on the holy day of Durga Puja (worship of Divine Mother), September 29, 1990.

CHAPTER 11

A Friend of the Birds from an unreleased Satsang given at Sacred Mountain Ashram on June 6, 1997.

CHAPTER 12

Divine Compassion of the Guru from the published Satsang (E-34) given at Desert Ashram on the auspicious occasion of Guru Purnima, July 12, 1995.

CHAPTER 13

God's Presence on Our Path from the published Satsang (M-86) given at Sacred Mountain Ashram on October 25, 1991, during the Fifteenth Annual Spiritual Retreat entitled *Realizing Cosmic Totality*.

CHAPTER 14
Giving God's Secrets from an informal Satsang given at a devotee's home in Tucson, Arizona, in 1974.

CHAPTER 15
Repaying the Guru, an unreleased Satsang given at Sacred Mountain Ashram on June 11, 1997, during the *Grace of the Guru Retreat.*

CHAPTER 16
Kalki Avatar: Prophet of This Age from a published Satsang entitled *Kalki Avatar, The Coming Prophet* (K-161), given at Sacred Mountain Ashram on June 8, 1997, during the *Grace of the Guru Retreat.*

Truth Consciousness
and Ashrams founded by
Swami Amar Jyoti

*F*ounded in 1974 by Swami Amar Jyoti, Truth Consciousness is a nonprofit spiritual organization that maintains ashrams and adjacent centers for *sadhaks* (seekers) based upon *Sanatana Dharma* (the eternal religion) and devoted to the unfolding of consciousness. They are universal and nondenominational, respecting all Prophets and faiths. The ashrams offer programs year-round and all sincere seekers are welcome. Satsang is held weekly on Sunday and Thursday, preceded by chanting and followed by meditation. *Sadhana* (spiritual practices) and karma yoga (selfless service) are an integral part of life for both ashramites and laypersons who wish to participate at the ashrams. The books and audio Satsangs of Swami Amar Jyoti as well as other publications by Truth Consciousness are available at the ashrams and through our website: truthconsciousness.org.

SACRED MOUNTAIN ASHRAM
10668 Gold Hill Road
Boulder, CO 80302-9716
Ph: 303-447-1637, Fx: 303-447-1920

DESERT ASHRAM
3403 West Sweetwater Drive
Tucson, AZ 85745-9301
Ph: 520-743-0384, Fx: 520-743-3394
Publications: 520-743-8821, truthconsciousness.org

JYOTI ASHRAM/ANANDA NIKETAN TRUST
68 Lulla Nagar, Pune 411 040 (Maharashtra) India
Ph: 20-6832632